W9-BGM-449

HARDWARE HACKING

Have Fun While Voiding Your Warranty

SYNGRESS®

HARDWARE HACKING

Have Fun While Voiding Your Warranty

Joe Grand Author of Stealing the Network
Ryan Russell Author of Stealing the Network and
Hack Proofing Your Network, Second Edition

And featuring Kevin D. Mitnick Technical Reviewer

Foreword by Andrew "bunnie" Huang

Lee Barken   Marcus R. Brown   Job de Haas   Deborah Kaplan
Bobby Kinstle   Tom Owad   Albert Yarusso

KEY	SERIAL NUMBER
001	HJIRTCV764
002	PO9873D5FG
003	829KM8NJH2
004	B7NMW3V9KM
005	CVPLQ6WQ23
006	VBP965T5T5
007	HJJJ863WD3
008	2987GVTWMK
009	629MP5SDJT
010	IMWQ295T6T

PUBLISHED BY
Syngress Publishing, Inc.
800 Hingham Street
Rockland, MA 02370

Hardware Hacking: Have Fun While Voiding Your Warranty

Printed in the United States of America
1 2 3 4 5 6 7 8 9 0
ISBN: 1-932266-83-6

Technical Editor: Joe Grand   Cover Designer: Michael Kavish
Technical Reviewer: Kevin D. Mitnick   Copy Editor: Darlene Bordwell
Acquisitions Editor: Catherine B. Nolan   Indexer: J. Edmund Rush
Page Layout and Art: Patricia Lupien   Editorial Assistant: Michael Rubin

Distributed by O'Reilly & Associates in the United States and Jaguar Book Group in Canada.

Acknowledgments

We would like to acknowledge the following people for their kindness and support in making this book possible.

To Jeff Moss and Ping Look of Black Hat for being great friends and supporters of Syngress.

A special thanks to Kevin Mitnick for sharing his invaluable expertise and knowledge, and to Darci Wood for her support of this book and the Syngress publishing program.

Syngress books are now distributed in the United States by O'Reilly & Associates, Inc. The enthusiasm and work ethic at ORA is incredible and we would like to thank everyone there for their time and effort in bringing Syngress books to market: Tim O'Reilly, Laura Baldwin, Mark Brokering, Mike Leonard, Donna Selenko, Bonnie Sheehan, Cindy Davis, Grant Kikkert, Opol Matsutaro, Lynn Schwartz, Steve Hazelwood, Mark Wilson, Rick Brown, Leslie Becker, Jill Lothrop, Tim Hinton, Kyle Hart, Sara Winge, C. J. Rayhill, Peter Pardo, Leslie Crandell, Valerie Dow, Regina Aggio, Pascal Honscher, Preston Paull, Susan Thompson, Bruce Stewart, Laura Schmier, Sue Willing, and Mark Jacobsen.

The incredibly hard working team at Elsevier Science, including Jonathan Bunkell, Duncan Enright, David Burton, Rosanna Ramacciotti, Robert Fairbrother, Miguel Sanchez, Klaus Beran, and Rosie Moss for making certain that our vision remains worldwide in scope.

David Buckland, Wendi Wong, Daniel Loh, Marie Chieng, Lucy Chong, Leslie Lim, Audrey Gan, and Joseph Chan of STP Distributors for the enthusiasm with which they receive our books.

Kwon Sung June at Acorn Publishing for his support.

Jackie Gross, Gayle Voycey, Alexia Penny, Anik Robitaille, Craig Siddall, Darlene Morrow, Iolanda Miller, Jane Mackay, and Marie Skelly at Jackie Gross & Associates for all their help and enthusiasm representing our product in Canada.

Lois Fraser, Connie McMenemy, Shannon Russell, and the rest of the great folks at Jaguar Book Group for their help with distribution of Syngress books in Canada.

David Scott, Tricia Wilden, Marilla Burgess, Annette Scott, Geoff Ebbs, Hedley Partis, Bec Lowe, and Mark Langley of Woodslane for distributing our books throughout Australia, New Zealand, Papua New Guinea, Fiji Tonga, Solomon Islands, and the Cook Islands.

Winston Lim of Global Publishing for his help and support with distribution of Syngress books in the Philippines.

To all the folks at Malloy who have made things easy for us and especially to Beth Drake and Joe Upton.

Technical Editor & Contributor

Photo by E.G. Weiss

Joe Grand; Grand Idea Studio, Inc. Joe Grand is the President and CEO of Grand Idea Studio, a product design and development firm that brings unique inventions to market through intellectual property licensing. Many of his creations, including consumer electronics, medical products, video games and toys, are sold worldwide.

A recognized name in computer security and electrical engineering, Joe's pioneering research on product design and analysis, mobile devices, and digital forensics is published in various industry journals. He is a co-author of *Hack Proofing Your Network, Second Edition* (Syngress Publishing, ISBN 1-928994-70-9) and *Stealing The Network: How to Own the Box* (Syngress, ISBN 1-931836-87-6).

Joe has testified before the United States Senate Governmental Affairs Committee on the state of government and homeland computer security, and is a former member of the legendary hacker think-tank, L0pht Heavy Industries. He has presented his work at numerous academic, industry, and private forums, including the United States Naval Post Graduate School Center for INFOSEC Studies and Research, the United States Air Force Office of Special Investigations, the USENIX Security Symposium, and the IBM Thomas J. Watson Research Center. Joe holds a BSCE from Boston University.

Joe is the author of Chapter 1 "Tools of the Warranty Voiding Trade," Chapter 2 "Electric Engineering Basics," Chapter 3 "Declawing Your CueCat," and Chapter 13 "Upgrading Memory on Palm Devices."

Contributors

Lee Barken (CISSP, CCNA, MCP, CPA) is the co-director of the Strategic Technologies and Research (STAR) Center at San Diego State University. He has worked as an IT consultant and network security specialist for Ernst & Young's Information Technology Risk Management (ITRM) practice and KPMG's Risk and Advisory Services (RAS) practice. Lee is the co-founder of the San Diego Wireless Users Group and writes and speaks on the topic of wireless LAN technology and security. He is the technical editor for *Mobile Business Advisor Magazine*, and the author of *How Secure Is Your Wireless Network? Safeguarding Your Wi-Fi LAN* (ISBN: 0-13-140206-4).

> *"Let's be grateful for those who give us happiness; they are the charming gardeners who make our soul bloom."* —*Marcel Proust*

With deepest appreciation for my charming gardeners, a special thank you to my love Stephanie, my mom and dad, Frieda and Israel, my brothers, Derren and Martin, my sister Randi and her husband Scott, my Uncle Harry and my Grandmother Sophie. Thank you for your support and love.

Lee is the author of Chapter 10 "Wireless 802.11 Hacks."

Marcus R. Brown is a software engineer at Budcat Creations. His work includes writing low-level drivers and system-level programming such as resource management, file loading, and audio streaming. He is currently working on an unannounced title for the PlayStation 2 and Xbox. Marcus lives in Las Vegas, Nevada.

Marcus is the author of Chapter 9 "Hacking the PlayStation 2."

Index   519

forces with Steve Jobs, and the two went on to found the Apple Computer that brought us the Apple II and the now ubiquitous Macintosh computer.

The gritty grass-roots hacking culture in the early days of electronics technology served as a kind of incubator for innovation that has resulted in many of the products we enjoy today. Hewlett and Packard, Jobs and Wozniak are just two examples of the influence of the hacker spirit on our society. The basic values of hacking—creating a good thing that is exactly what is needed at a particular time—are a good match with innovation. Furthermore, hackers' independently motivated nature means that thousands of ideas are tested and built by hackers in the absence of venture capital or the risk constraints of investors. Hackers play an important part in the growth of technology, so I am always pleased to see a greater interest and awareness of hacking in the general public.

Recently, hacking has taken on more of a software-oriented bent. This is due in part to the steady pace of hardware improvement guaranteed by Moore's Law. Hardware hacking is a time-consuming labor of love, and it is discouraging to know that almost any hack you can think of to double a computer's performance will be obsolete within 12 months. It is much more rewarding to work in the instant-gratification world of software and let the performance of your programs ride the Moore's Law wave.

Another factor working against hardware hackers is the barrier of entry that was created by the higher levels of integration that naturally followed as a result of Moore's Law. The hackability of the desktop PC met a turning point in the evolution of the IBM PC-XT to the IBM PC-AT. The IBM PC-XT motherboard was chiefly composed of chips that were essentially naked logic gates. This was very hacker-friendly, since most of the core functionality was exposed at a human-friendly scale. The IBM PC-AT, on the other hand, was one of the first desktop computers to use VLSI chips for the processor support logic. I remember my first look at the PC-AT motherboard: I was hoping to be able to read the board like a book, with all the logic gates' part numbers gleaming in their fresh white silkscreen against the matte epoxy bodies of chips. What I saw instead was a closed book; there were perhaps three or four curious, high pin-count chips with part numbers and a manufacturer's logo I had never seen before. These chips were proprietary, and any hope of a deeper level of understanding or hardware exploration seemed to be dashed.

I think perhaps a lot of prospective hardware hackers felt the same way around then, because since then hacking has taken on a distinct software-oriented slant. Some of the most famous hackers today are renowned for their software contributions. Richard Stallman and Linus Torvalds are perhaps household names among the technological elite due to their fantastic contributions to free software through GNU and Linux. The best part about software hacking is its very low barrier of entry. Any willing youth with access to a computer and an Internet connection can plug into any of the various free software efforts and make a contribution to the technology collective. All the tools required to generate high-quality code are virtually free, and aside from the time investment, it costs nothing to use them. On the other hand, hardware hacking has a very real entry cost associated with the activity; there is a bare minimum set of tools that are needed on a daily basis, and an unfortunately large and diverse assortment of expensive, specialized tools is required to accomplish specific jobs. Furthermore, producing a hardware hack typically requires real materials in addition to time and energy, thereby placing creative and/or bold (read: risky) hardware-hacking projects beyond the financial horizon of most young folk. Given that human nature is to follow the path of least resistance, it is no surprise that hacking today is primarily a software affair.

In a twist of fate, recent macro-economic and social trends have worked to reverse the trend and bring more people into hardware hacking. The detritus of the dot-com bubble created fertile soil for sprouting hardware hackers. An overall reduction in demand for components, design, and manufacturing services has resulted from the economic slowdown. High-quality, used test equipment is trickling down into the ranks of hackers, either snatched off the shelf of dead companies or snapped up for pennies on the dollar at auction. Scrap components are also finding their way into distribution, driving down component prices. Combined with an overall soft demand situation, individual hackers are able to command the same level of service and component choice as large corporations. Furthermore, fabrication and assembly services have been forced to drive their prices down, to the point where hardware hackers could purchase high-tech, custom-built multilayer boards for under $50 per board.

Hardware design tool vendors also experienced a corresponding price adjustment due to the economic slowdown. Perhaps the most significant recent technological change for hardware hackers is the introduction of professional-grade FPGA design tools for *free*. The motivating theory for this development is that FPGA manufacturers could "hook" more designers into a particular brand or architecture if an effective and powerful set of design tools were made freely available. Stiff competition and hungry manufacturers helped ensure that a very featureful set of tools found their way into the market at a very low barrier of entry.

The significance of easy and affordable FPGA development systems cannot be understated. FPGAs have the effect of transforming the traditional solder-and-wires world of hardware hacking into the much more accessible and more widely understood code-and-compile world. A single hardware hacker working alone or in a small group can realistically build a complex microprocessor using FPGAs. This kind of activity was unheard of before the advent of FPGAs. Also, the availability of "programming languages" for hardware that could be translated into FPGA configurations meant that software hackers could cross over into hardware hacking without much formal training in traditional hardware design and assembly.

I can relate a personal example of the positive impact of the economic slowdown on hobbyists and hackers. During the buildup to the dot-com bust, it was literally impossible to buy high-quality tantalum and ceramic capacitors of the type used in compact/mobile switching power supplies. Chronic shortages due to explosive demand for portable and mobile electronic technologies meant that hackers had to compete toe-to-toe with large OEMs for pricing and component availability. I remember back around 2000 looking for samples of the AVX TPS "low-ESR" capacitors for a demonstration project I was building. I swept through every distributor I knew of, and all of them were posting lead times of months, with minimum buy quantities in the thousands. Ultimately, I had to do a minor last-minute redesign of the circuit just before sending the board for fabrication to compensate for the lack of high-quality capacitance. In contrast, just last month I cranked out a design that used an AVX TPS capacitor, and multiple hacker-friendly (i.e., high in-stock availability, credit card payment terms, and low minimum buy restrictions) distributors posted thousands of parts in their inventories. It certainly was pleasant to be able to access, with great ease, the same quality of components that the "big boys" use.

Although the confluence of recent macro-economic events set the stage for hardware hacking to regain popularity, this alone is not enough.

Remember, hacking is a fundamentally grass-roots activity, and it does not happen on a large scale unless there is some kind of social drive to motivate people into action.

A small part of the renewed social awareness in hardware hacking may be due to the desire of young hackers to extend themselves and carve a new niche for themselves. The software hacking world is now more structured, and new hackers joining one of the major software hacking establishments feel more like cogs rather than inspired inventors. Change and new ideas are not always so welcome from so-called "n00bs," and some budding hackers may be turned off by the intense flame wars that are sometimes triggered by a newbie suggestion or mistake.

However, this kind of sociopathy is probably not the real drive behind the renaissance of hardware hacking. I feel that the larger impetus is the recent pertinence of reverse-engineering consumer hardware. Rather than looking to hardware hackers for new product innovation, the public is looking to hardware hackers for the extension and liberation of existing solutions. This trend is a result of the tension between corporate motivations and the public's desires. Corporations are motivated by profit; thus, accessories are expensive, feature sets are artificially limited to create price discrimination, and lately, hardware vendors are locking their products to particular brands of consumable goods via embedded security or ID chips. On the other hand, consumers desire featureful, inexpensive products that deliver exactly what the they need, with no hidden costs or accessories required.

The status quo going into the new millennium was a competitive hardware market. However, the introduction of hardware-locked goods, especially combined with the power of the DMCA, has created a series of mini-monopolies. Hardware locking enables manufacturers to create vertically controlled mini-monopolies that break the free market model. Given the increasing complexity of hardware, consumers have few advocates that can cogently combat such corporate advances. Some advocacy groups work through political and legislative means, but legal processes are slow relative to the rate at which hardware locking can damage a market.

A new law protecting consumers may take years to draft and pass; on the other hand, a determined corporation can radically change a vertical market segment within a single year. For example, a printer manufacturer can realistically deploy crypto-locks on all its ink-consuming products within the span of a single product family generation, typically under two years. This would mean that the market for third-party ink suppliers would dry up in the same amount of time. The companies that provide consumers with choice and prices that reflect a competitive market would be long out of business before legislators were even aware of the problem. By the time reactive legislation was passed, the economies of scale would have been tipped grossly in favor of the OEM ink supplier, and such reactive legislation could have little practical impact on the market.

Since hackers are by definition a grass-roots group, the hacker's interests in these issues are inherently aligned with those of the general public. As a result, hackers are becoming the natural stop-gap consumer advocates in hot-button technological issues. These hackers sometimes operate above ground, and they sometimes operate like vigilante groups, breaking the most obnoxious hardware-locking schemes and "liberating" hardware to the public. Some may not agree with my viewpoint, but I find it hard to believe that monopoly prices, narrow selection, and a lack of market competition can be construed as positive developments for consumers. I believe that the majority of hackers are at least partially motivated by a desire to contribute to some larger cause, and preserving the technological balance of power against corporate monopoly tactics may be a rallying point for hardware hackers.

The publicity surrounding the DMCA has served to increase the public's awareness of the potential shifting of power from free-market consumer economics to corporate-driven mini-monopolies. It has also sparked a renewed interest in hacking. This interest meets a newly fertile technology scene, enriched by the availability of affordable hardware-hacking tools and services enabled by the economic slowdown in technology. Hopefully, this renewed interest in hardware hacking will not only result in a better-informed general public that is better capable of defending itself in the technology marketplace, it will also result in a new round of innovative products and companies in the vein of HP and Apple Computer. I personally hope that you find this topic enjoyable, and I look forward to hearing more about your adventures and exploits in hardware hacking.

Happy hacking!

—Andrew "bunnie" Huang,
Author of *Hacking the Xbox: An Introduction to Reverse Engineering*
and hardware hacker

Introduction.

Hardware hacking. Mods. Tweaks. Though the terminology is new, the concepts are not: A gearhead in the 1950s adding a custom paint job and turbo-charged engine to his Chevy Fleetline, a '70s teen converting his ordinary bedroom into a "disco palace of love," complete with strobe lights and a high-fidelity eight-track system, or a techno-geek today customizing his computer case to add fluorescent lighting and slick artwork. Taking an ordinary piece of equipment and turning it into a personal work of art. Building on an existing idea to create something better. These types of self-expression can be found throughout recorded history.

When Syngress approached me to write this book, I knew they had hit the nail on the head. Where else could a geek like me become an artistic genius? Combining technology with creativity and a little bit of skill opened up the doors to a whole new world: hardware hacking.

But why do we do it? The reasons might be different for all of us, but the end result is usually the same. We end up with a unique thing that we can call our own—imagined in our minds and crafted through hours, days, or years of effort. *And* doing it on our own terms.

Hardware hacking today has hit the mainstream market like never before. Computer stores sell accessories to customize your desktop PC. Web sites are popping up like unemployed stock brokers to show off the latest hacks. Just about any piece of hardware can serve as a candidate to be hacked. Creativity and determination can get you much farther than most product developers could ever imagine. Hardware hacking is usually an individual effort, like creating a piece of art.

However, just like artists, hackers sometimes collaborate and form communities of folks working toward a similar goal.

The use of the term *hacker* is a double-edged sword and often carries a mythical feel. Contrary to the way major media outlets enjoy using the word to describe criminals breaking into computer systems, a hacker can simply be defined as somebody involved in the exploration of technology. And a *hack* in the technology world usually defines a new and novel creation or method of solving a problem, typically in an unorthodox fashion.

The philosophy of most hardware hackers is straightforward:

- Do something with a piece of hardware that has never been done before.

- Create something extraordinary.

- Harm nobody in the process.

Hardware hacking arguably dates back almost 200 years. Charles Babbage created his difference engine in the early 1800s—a mechanical form of hardware hacking. William Crookes discovered the electron in the mid-1800s—possibly the first form of electronics-related hardware hacking. Throughout the development of wireless telegraphy, vacuum tubes, radio, television, and transistors, there have been hardware hackers—Benjamin Franklin, Thomas Edison, and Alexander Graham Bell, to name a few. As the newest computers of the mid-20th century were developed, the ENIAC, UNIVAC, and IBM mainframes, people from those academic institutions fortunate enough to have the hardware came out in droves to experiment. With the development and release of the first microprocessor (Intel 4004) in November 1971, the general public finally got a taste of computing. The potential for hardware hacking has grown tremendously in the past decade as computers and technology have become more intertwined with the mainstream and everyday living.

Hardware hacks can be classified into four different categories, though sometimes a hack falls into more than one:

1. **Personalization and customization** Think "hot rodding for geeks," the most prevalent of hardware hacking. This includes things such as case modifications, custom skins and ring tones, and art projects like creating an aquarium out of a vintage computer.

2. **Adding functionality** Making the system or product do something it wasn't intended to do. This includes things such as converting the

iPod to run Linux, turning a stock iOpener into a full-fledged PC, or modifying the Atari 2600 to support stereo sound and composite video output.

3. **Capacity or performance increase**   Enhancing or otherwise upgrading a product. This includes things such as adding memory to your favorite personal digital assistant (PDA), modifying your wireless network card to support an external antenna, or overclocking your PC's motherboard.

4. **Defeating protection and security mechanisms**   This includes things such as removing the unique identifier from CueCat barcode scanners, finding Easter eggs and hidden menus in a TiVo or DVD player, or creating a custom cable to unlock the secrets of your cell phone. Theft-of-service hacks fall into this category, but this book doesn't cover them.

Creating your own hardware hacks and product modifications requires at least a basic knowledge of hacking techniques, reverse-engineering skills, and a background in electronics and coding. All the information you'll need is in the pages of this book. And if a topic isn't covered in intimate detail, we include references to materials that do. If you just want to do the hack without worrying about the underlying theory behind it, you can do that, too. The step-by-step sections throughout each chapter include pictures and "how to" instructions. The details are in separate sections that you can skip right over and get to the fun part—voiding your warranty!

This book has something for everyone from the beginner hobbyist with little to no electronics or coding experience to the self-proclaimed "gadget geek" and advanced technologist. It is one of the first books to bring hardware hacking to the mainstream. It is meant to be fun and will demystify many of the hacks you have seen and heard about. We, all the contributors to this project, hope you enjoy reading this book and that you find the hacks as exciting and satisfying as we have.

If your friends say "Damn, now *that's* cool," then you know you've done it right.

—Joe Grand, the hardware hacker formerly known as Kingpin
January 2004

Part I

Introduction to
Hardware Hacking

Chapter 1

Tools of the Warranty Voiding Trade

☑ **The Essential Tools**

☑ **Taking it to the Next Level**

☑ **Hardcore Hardware Hackers Only**

Introduction

You'll need the right arsenal of hardware hacking tools to get the job done right. For some hacks, you may just need a single screwdriver. For others, you may need a workshop complete with power tools and advanced electronic equipment. For the most part, it isn't necessary to have a world-class laboratory in order to conduct most levels of hardware hacking.

The tools and supplies listed in this chapter are just a baseline of any good hardware hacking cache. We don't list every possible tool, and specific types of hardware hacks will have their own set of tools that people like to use. A selection of pictures are included that show some of the more unique tools of the trade. With these lists, we're just trying to give you an idea to get a good start so you can jump in and get down to hacking.

We have separated the listings into three parts:

- The Essentials

- Taking it to the Next Level

- Hardcore Hardware Hackers Only

The work area where your hardware hacking takes place should be a clean, smooth, and well-lit area where you can easily organize and handle parts without losing them. An inexpensive sheet of white poster board makes an excellent construction surface, while providing protection for the underlying table or desk. If you live in a dry environment that is prone to static electricity, it is recommended that you purchase an anti-static mat from a local electronics store to prevent static discharge and protect the sensitive circuitry.

WARNING: PERSONAL INJURY

Safety is an important consideration. With many of the tools listed here, improper or careless use can lead to accidents and personal injury. Please take the time to read all necessary instruction manuals and safety documentation before starting your hack. Be sure to use a suitable stand for your soldering iron, keep your work area free of unnecessary clutter, wear protective gear at all times, and avoid tangling the wires of your various tools.

The Essential Tools

The following are a sampling of some basic tools for the beginner hardware hacker: someone who is curious about dabbling and experimenting with simple hacks. It always helps to have a good stock of various equipment, wires, tools, components, and other materials in your workshop so you do not have to run out to the store every time you need something.

- **Bright Overhead Lighting or Desk Lamp** Well-diffused overhead lighting is recommended – bright white fluorescent or incandescent bulbs serve this purpose. A smaller, high-intensity desk lamp will prove especially helpful for close-up work.

Figure 1.1 Protective Gear

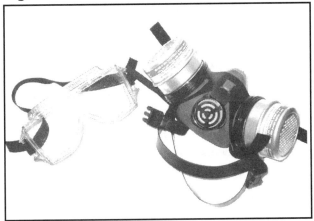

- **Protective Gear** A sampling of protective gear is shown in Figure 1.1. Mask/Respirator, Goggles, Rubber Gloves, Smock/Lab Coat, Ear Plugs. To be worn at all times. Use the respirator to prevent breathing in noxious fumes and fine dust from painting, cleaning, cutting, or soldering. The goggles protect your eyes from stray plastic or wood chips during drilling. Use the smock to prevent damage to clothing (e.g., burns and stains).

- **Screwdrivers** Phillips, Flat Head, Jeweler's. As many sizes and types as possible.

- **X -ACTO Hobby Knife** The modeling tool of choice for crafters, artists and hobbyists with over 50 different blade types. An essential general-purpose tool for hardware hacking.

Figure 1.2 Dremel Tool

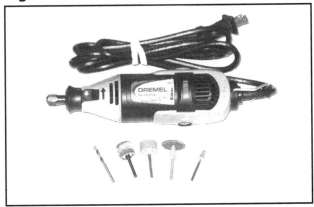

- **Dremel Tool** Extremely useful carving tool for detailed and delicate work. Helpful for case mods and opening housings. Some models support rotation speeds from single digit revolutions per second up to tens of thousands. Many various bit types (drills, sanding, carving, engraving), accessories, and attachments are available. Example: Dremel 395 Variable-Speed MultiPro, $74.99 (Figure 1.2).

Figure 1.3 Needle File Set

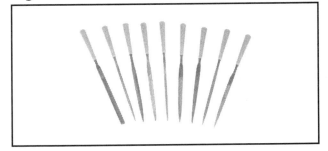

- **Needle File Set** Designed for precise filing. Ideal for deburring drilled holes and preparing modified surfaces. Most five-piece sets include a square, flat, triangle, round, and elliptical file. Example: Radio Shack Needle File Set #64-1985, $6.99 (Figure 1.3).

- **Sand Paper**   100, 220, 400, 600, and 1000 Grit.

- **Glues**   Wood glue, Super Glue, epoxy, hot glue, acrylic cement, the more types of adhesive that you have on hand, the better off you'll be. A sampling of glue is shown in Figure 1.4.

- **Tape**   Duct tape, masking tape, electrical tape, scotch/transparent tape.

Figure 1.4 Types of Glue

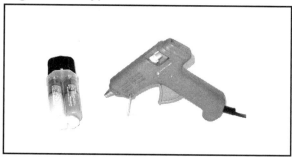

- **Cleaning Supplies**   A good workspace is a clean workspace, typical supplies are cotton swabs, alcohol pads, paper towels, and some type of sprayable cleaning solution.

- **Miscellaneous Mechanical Pieces**   These are the standard hardware that you should have around the house in any type of workshop and include nails, screws, stand-offs/spacers, washers, nuts, and bolts.

Taking it to the Next Level

These mid-range tools are for the more serious hardware hackers. With a few hacks under your belt, you might be getting more confident in your skills. Depending on your creativity and determination, you can use some of these tools to create your own hardware hacks and modifications.

- **Variable Speed Cordless Drill**   This is the essential multi-purpose tool. Especially useful for case mods. Example: Skil 18V Cordless Drill/Driver #2867 with 3/8" keyless chuck, and six torque settings, $69.99 (Figure 1.5).

Figure 1.5 Variable Speed Cordless Drill

- **Drill Bit Set**   What good is your variable speed cordless drill without a complete set of various sized drill bits?

Figure 1.6 Security Driver Bit Set

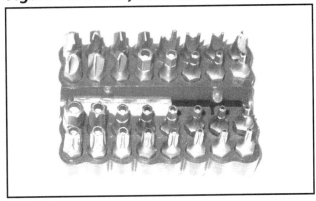

Figure 1.7 Nibbling Tool

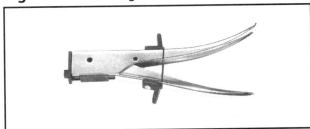

Figure 1.8 Soldering Station

■ **Security Driver Bit Set** Commonly used security/tamper resistant bits to open specially-shaped screwheads. Useful for opening certain types of product housings. To identify a particular bit type you might need to acquire for a hack, visit www.lara.com/reviews/screwtypes.htm. A sample of a driver bit set for security fasteners can be seen in Figure 1.6.

■ **Automatic Center Punch** Used to mark the target drill spot on a drilling surface.

■ **Nibbling Tool** This tool "nibbles" away at light-gauge sheet metal, copper, aluminum, or plastic with each squeeze of the handle. Good for housing modifications and custom shape creations. Example: Radio Shack Nibbling Tool #64-823, $9.99 (Figure 1.7).

■ **Wire Strippers** For cutting or stripping 10- to 22-AWG wire. Example: Radio Shack Precision Wire Stripper #64-1922, $7.99.

■ **Wire Clippers** Example: Radio Shack 4" Diagonal-Cutting Mini Pliers #64-2043, $4.99 or Radio Shack 5" Nippy Cutters #64-1833, $3.99.

■ **Needle Nose Pliers** Example: Radio Shack 6" Narrow Jaw Needle-Nose Pliers #64-1803, $5.99.

■ **Soldering Station** Soldering tools, ranging from a simple stick iron to a full-fledged rework station, come in many shapes and sizes. More advanced models include adjustable temperature control, automatic shut-off, and interchangeable tips for various component package types and soldering needs. Recommended is a fine-tip, 700 degree F, 50W soldering stick iron. Approximate price range $10.00 - $1,000.00 Example: Weller W60P Controlled-Output Soldering Iron, $67.95 (Figure 1.8).

- **Soldering Accessories** Essential soldering gear includes: solder, vacuum desoldering tool (a.k.a "solder sucker"), IC extraction tool, and ChipQuik SMD removal kit. Solder should be thin gauge (0.032" or 0.025" diameter) 60/40 Rosin core. The Desoldering Tool is a manual vacuum device that pulls up hot solder, useful for removing components from circuit boards (Radio Shack #64-2098, $6.99). The IC Extraction Tool helps lift integrated circuits from the board during removal/desoldering. The ChipQuik kit allows you to remove surface mount components quickly and easily. Some soldering accessories are shown in Figure 1.9.

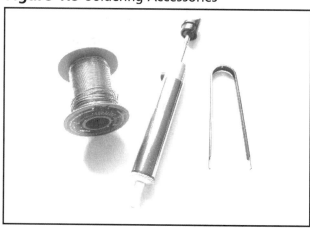

Figure 1.9 Soldering Accessories

- **Miscellaneous Cables** This category includes cabling and wiring such as test leads, alligator clips, spools of wire, and computer cables.

Hardcore Hardware Hackers Only

These tools are for the hardcore hardware hacker, the best of the best, seriously dedicated to his or her trade. More specific tools exist as well, but generally the tools in this section will get you as far as you need to go for a successful hardware hack of almost any type.

- **Jig Saw** Essential power tool for cutting and shaping. Example: Bosch 1587AVSK Top-Handle Jigsaw, $134.99.

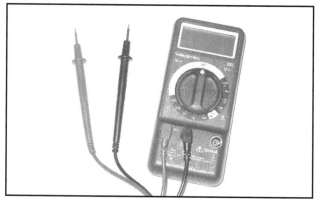

Figure 1.10 Digital Multimeter

- **Digital Multimeter (DMM)** Commonly referred to as the "swiss army knife" of electronics measurement tools (Figure 1.10). These are (usually) portable devices that provide a number of precision measurement functions, including AC/DC voltage, resistance, capacitance, current, and continuity. More advanced models also include frequency counters, graphical displays, and digital oscilloscope functionality. Reliable meters have high DC input resistance (also called *input impedance*) of at least 10Mohm. Approximate price range $20.00 - $500.00 Example: Fluke Model 111, $129.00.

Figure 1.11 Adjustable Power Supply

Figure 1.12 Device Programmer

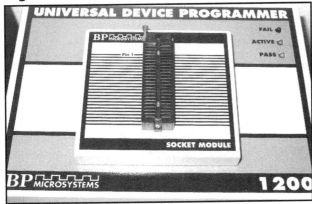

Figure 1.13 UV EPROM Eraser

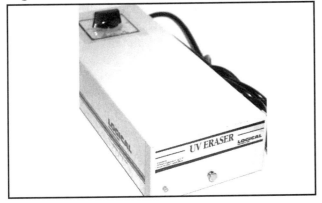

■ **Analog Multimeter** The older sibling to the DMM. These devices provide measurements of AC/DC voltage, resistance, current, and continuity on an analog meter display. Useful for showing slow variations or unusual wave shapes that a DMM may not be able to detect or recognize. Example: Radio Shack 8-Range Multimeter #22-218A, $14.99.

■ **Adjustable Power Supply** Useful for any electronics-related design or hacking. Adjustable, linear, current-limited DC supply (Figure 1.11). Current limiting often prevents parts from failing (burning up or exploding) when there is a short circuit. Approximate price range $100.00 - $1,000.00 Example: HP/Agilent Triple Output DC Power Supply E3630A, $588.00.

■ **Device Programmer** Used to read and write memories (RAM, ROM, EPROM, EEPROM, Flash), microcontrollers, and programmable logic devices (Figure 1.12). Extremely useful to extract program code and stored data. Approximate price range $10.00 (home-built) - $2,500.00 Example: EE Tools' ChipMax, $345.00.

■ **UV EPROM Eraser** This tool is used to erase UV-erasable EPROM devices in a matter of minutes using high-intensity ultraviolet light (Figure 1.13). Approximate price range $25.00 - $250.00. Example: Logical Devices Palm Erase, $59.95.

■ **PCB Etching Kit** These kits are used to create printed circuit boards for custom hardware hacks. This process is time consuming and uses hazardous chemicals. Radio Shack provides a kit that contains two 3" x 4.5" copper-clad circuit boards, resist-ink pen, etching and stripping solutions, etching tank, 1/16" drill bit, polishing pad, and complete instructions. PCB etching materials can also be purchased separately at any electronics distributor. Example: Radio Shack PC Board Kit #276-1576, $14.99.

Figure 1.14 Oscilloscope

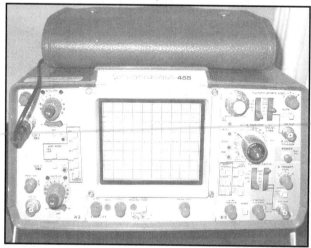

■ **Oscilloscope** Arguably the most important of advanced measurement tools. Provides a visual display of electrical signals and how they change over time (Figure 1.14). Available in analog, digital, and mixed-mode versions. Pre-owned analog oscilloscopes are typically the most economical and are available at many surplus electronics stores. Look for a bandwidth of greater than 50MHz. Approximate price range $100.00 (used) – $10,000.00. Example: Tektronix 475A 250MHz Analog, $250.00 or Tektronix TDS3034B 4-Channel 300MHz Color Digital Storage, $6,795.00.

■ **Basic Electronic Components** These include resistors, capacitors, diodes, transistors, LEDs, and switches. It is useful to have a "junk bin" of all sorts of electronics bits and pieces. At a minimum, you should have a basic assortment of the most common values of components. Example: Digi-Key 1/4 Watt Resistor Assortment #RS125-ND, $14.95 and Digi-Key Miniature Electrolytic Capacitor Assortment #P835-KIT-ND, $29.95.

Where to Obtain the Tools

This small list of available manufacturers and distributors is just to get you started. The hacks throughout this book list more specific outlets that are of interest to that particular type of hardware hack. Your local hardware store, art supply, hobby shop, or electronic surplus store may have also some useful equipment for you.

■ The Home Depot, The well-known nationwide hardware and home remodeling chain, 800-553-3199, www.homedepot.com

■ Lowe's, Another nationwide hardware and home improvement chain, 800-445-6937, www.lowes.com

■ Hobby Lobby, The nation's largest and most complete creative center, Over 60,000 items of arts and crafts supplies, www.hobbylobby.com

Chapter 2

Electrical Engineering Basics

☑ **Fundamentals**

☑ **Basic Device Theory**

☑ **Soldering Techniques**

☑ **Common Engineering Mistakes**

☑ **Web Links and Other Resources**

Note: Not all hacks in this book require electrical engineering.

Introduction

Understanding how hardware hacks work requires an introductory-level understanding of electronics. This chapter describes electronics fundamentals and the basic theory of the most common electronic components. We also look at how to read schematic diagrams, identify components, proper soldering techniques, and other engineering topics.

NEED TO KNOW...LIMITATIONS OF THIS CHAPTER

 Engineering, like hardware hacking, is a skill that requires time and determination if you want to be proficient in the field. There is a lot to discuss, but we have a limited amount of space. This chapter is not going to turn you into an electrical engineer or an electronics guru, but it will teach you enough about the basics of electronics and engineering that you can start to find your way around. For more detail on the subject, see the suggested reading list at the end of this chapter.

Fundamentals

It is important to understand the core fundamentals of electronics before you venture into the details of specific components. This section provides a background on numbering systems, notation, and basic theory used in all facets of engineering.

Bits, Bytes, and Nibbles

At the lowest level, electronic circuits and computers store information in binary format, which is a base-2 numbering system containing only 0 and 1, each known as a *bit* (derived from a combination of the words *binary*, which is defined as something having two parts or components, and *digit*). The common decimal numbering system that we use in everyday life is a base-10 system, which consists of the digits 0 through 9.

Electrically, a 1 bit is generally represented by a positive voltage (5V, for example), and 0 is generally represented by a zero voltage (or ground potential). However, many protocols and definitions map the binary values in different ways.

A group of 4 bits is a *nibble* (also known as a *nybble*), a group of 8 bits is a *byte*, and a group of 16 bits is typically defined as a *word* (though a *word* is sometimes defined differently, depending on the system architecture you are referring to). Figure 2.1 shows the interaction of bits, nibbles, bytes, and words. This visual diagram makes it easy to grasp the concept of how they all come together.

Figure 2.1 Breakdown of a 16-Bit Word into Bytes, Nibbles, and Bits

Word															
Byte 1 (High)								Byte 0 (Low)							
Nibble 3				Nibble 2				Nibble 1				Nibble 0			
Bit15	Bit14	Bit13	Bit12	Bit11	Bit10	Bit9	Bit8	Bit7	Bit6	Bit5	Bit4	Bit3	Bit2	Bit1	Bit0

The larger the group of bits, the more information that can be represented. A single bit can represent only two combinations (0 or 1). A nibble can represent 2^4 (or 16) possible combinations (0 to 15 in decimal), a byte can represent 2^8 (or 256) possible combinations (0 to 255 in decimal), and a word can represent 2^{16} (or 65,536) possible combinations (0 to 65,535 in decimal).

Hexadecimal format, also called *hex*, is commonly used in the digital computing world to represent groups of binary digits. It is a base-16 system in which 16 sequential numbers are used as base units before adding a new position for the next number (digits 0 through 9 and letters A through F). One hex digit can represent the arrangement of 4 bits (a nibble). Two hex digits can represent 8 bits (a byte). Table 2.1 shows equivalent number values in the decimal, hexadecimal, and binary number systems. Hex digits are sometimes prefixed with 0x or $ to avoid confusion with other numbering systems.

Table 2.1 Number System Equivalents: Decimal, Binary, and Hexadecimal

Decimal	Binary	Hex
0	0	0
1	1	1
2	10	2
3	11	3
4	100	4
5	101	5
6	110	6
7	111	7
8	1000	8
9	1001	9

Continued

Table 2.1 Number System Equivalents: Decimal, Binary, and Hexadecimal

Decimal	Binary	Hex
10	1010	A
11	1011	B
12	1100	C
13	1101	D
14	1110	E
15	1111	F
16	10000	10
17	10001	11
18	10010	12
19	10011	13
20	10100	14
21	10101	15
22	10110	16
23	10111	17
24	11000	18
25	11001	19
26	11010	1A
27	11011	1B
28	11100	1C
29	11101	1D
30	11110	1E
31	11111	1F
32	100000	20
...	...	...
63	111111	3F
...	...	...
127	1111111	7F
...	...	...
255	11111111	FF

American Standard Code for Information Interchange, or ASCII (pronounced *ask-key*), is the common code for storing characters in a computer system. The standard ASCII character set (see Table 2.2) uses 1 byte to correspond to each of 128 different letters, numbers, punctuation marks, and special characters. Many of the special characters are holdovers from the original specification created in 1968 and are no longer commonly used for their originally intended purpose. Only the decimal values 0 through 127 are assigned, which is half of the space available in a byte. An extended ASCII character set uses the full range of 256 characters available in a byte. The decimal values of 128 through 255 are assigned to represent other special characters that are used in foreign languages, graphics, and mathematics.

Table 2.2 The Standard ASCII Character Set

Hex	Symbol	Hex	Symbol	Hex	Symbol	Hex	Symbol
0x00	NUL (null)	0x20	SP (space)	0x40	@	0x60	`
0x01	SOH (start of heading)	0x21	!	0x41	A	0x61	a
0x02	STX (start of text)	0x22	"	0x42	B	0x62	b
0x03	ETX (end of text)	0x23	#	0x43	C	0x63	c
0x04	EOT (end of transmission)	0x24	$	0x44	D	0x64	d
0x05	ENQ (enquiry)	0x25	%	0x45	E	0x65	e
0x06	ACK (acknowledge)	0x26	&	0x46	F	0x66	f
0x07	BEL (bell)	0x27	' (apostrophe)	0x47	G	0x67	g
0x08	BS (backspace)	0x28	(	0x48	H	0x68	h
0x09	HT (horizontal tab)	0x29	)	0x49	I	0x69	i
0x0A	LF (line feed/new line)	0x2A	*	0x4A	J	0x6A	j
0x0B	VT (vertical tab)	0x2B	+	0x4B	K	0x6B	k
0x0C	FF (form feed)	0x2C	, (comma)	0x4C	L	0x6C	l
0x0D	CR (carriage return)	0x2D	-	0x4D	M	0x6D	m
0x0E	SO (shift out)	0x2E	. (period)	0x4E	N	0x6E	n
0x0F	SI (shift in)	0x2F	/	0x4F	O	0x6F	o
0x10	DLE (data link escape)	0x30	0	0x50	P	0x70	p
0x11	DC1 (device control 1)	0x31	1	0x51	Q	0x71	q
0x12	DC2 (device control 2)	0x32	2	0x52	R	0x72	r
0x13	DC3 (device control 3)	0x33	3	0x53	S	0x73	s
0x14	DC4 (device control 4)	0x34	4	0x54	T	0x74	t
0x15	NAK (negative acknowledge)	0x35	5	0x55	U	0x75	u
0x16	SYN (synchronous idle)	0x36	6	0x56	V	0x76	v
0x17	ETB (end of transmission block)	0x37	7	0x57	W	0x77	w
0x18	CAN (cancel)	0x38	8	0x58	X	0x78	x
0x19	EM (end of medium)	0x39	9	0x59	Y	0x79	y
0x1A	SUB (substitute)	0x3A	: (colon)	0x5A	Z	0x7A	z

Continued

Table 2.2 The Standard ASCII Character Set

Hex	Symbol	Hex	Symbol	Hex	Symbol	Hex	Symbol
0x1B	ESC (escape)	0x3B	;	0x5B	[	0x7B	{
0x1C	FS (file separator)	0x3C	<	0x5C	\	0x7C	|
0x1D	GS (group separator)	0x3D	=	0x5D	]	0x7D	}
0x1E	RS (record separator)	0x3E	>	0x5E	^	0x7E	~
0x1F	US (unit separator)	0x3F	?	0x5F	_ (underscore)	0x7F	Del (delete)

Reading Schematics

Before we get into the theory of individual electronic components, it is important to learn how circuit designs are drawn and described. A *schematic* is essentially an electrical road map. Reading basic schematics is a good skill to have, even if it is just to identify a particular component that needs to be removed during a hack. Reading schematics is much easier than it may appear, and with practice it will become second nature.

On a schematic, each component of the circuit is assigned its own symbol, unique to the type of device that it is. The United States and Europe sometimes use different symbols, and there are even multiple symbols to represent one type of part. A resistor has its own special symbol, as does a capacitor, a diode, or an integrated circuit. Think of schematic symbols as an alphabet for electronics. Table 2.3 shows a selection of basic components and their corresponding designators and schematic symbols. This is by no means a complete list, and, as mentioned, a particular component type may have additional symbols that aren't shown here.

A *part designator* is also assigned to each component and is used to distinguish between two parts of the same type and value. The designator is usually an alphanumeric character followed by a numerical value (R1, C4, or SW2, for example). The part designator and schematic symbol are used as a pair to define each discrete component of the circuit design.

Table 2.3 Designator and Schematic Symbols for Basic Electronic Components

Component	Designator	Symbol
Resistor	R	
Potentiometer (variable resistor)	R	
Capacitor (nonpolarized)	C	

Continued

Where…

- V = Voltage (V)
- I = Current (A)
- R = Resistance (in ohms, designated with the omega symbol, Ω)

Basic Device Theory

This section explores the basic device theory of the five most common electronic components: resistors, capacitors, diodes, transistors, and integrated circuits. Understanding the functionality of these parts is essential to any core electronics knowledge and will prove useful in designing or reverse-engineering products.

Resistors

Resistors are used to reduce the amount of current flowing through a point in a system. Resistors are defined by three values:

- Resistance (Ω)
- Heat dissipation (in watts, W)
- Manufacturing tolerance (%)

Figure 2.4 Various Resistor Types

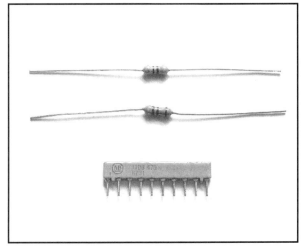

A sampling of various resistor types is shown in Figure 2.4. Resistors are not polarized, meaning that they can be inserted in either orientation with no change in electrical function.

The resistance value of a resistor is indicated by an industry-standard code of four or five colored bands (see Figure 2.5). The colors are printed directly onto the resistor. For example, any resistor with a black multiplier band falls between 10 and 99 ohms in value, brown designates a value between 100 and 999 ohms, red indicates a value from 1000 to 9999 ohms (also expressed as 1.0K to 9.9K), and so on. The manufacturing tolerance of the resistor, which is the allowable skew of a resistor value from its ideal rated value, is specified by another colored band.

A resistor's internal composition can consist of many different materials, but typically one of three are used: carbon, metal film, or wire-wound. The material is usually wrapped around a core, with the wrapping type and length corresponding to the resistor value. The carbon-filled resistor, used in most general-purpose applications such as current limiting and nonprecise circuits, allows a +/-5 percent tolerance on the resistor value. Metal film resistors are for more precise applications such as amplifiers, power supplies, and sensitive analog circuitry; they usually allow a +/-1 or 2 percent tolerance. Wire-wound resistors can also be very accurate.

When resistors are used in series in a circuit (see Figure 2.6), their resistance values are *additive*, meaning that you simply add the values of the resistors in series to obtain the total resistance. For example, if *R1* is 220 ohm and *R2* is 470 ohm, the overall resistance will be 690 ohm.

Parallel circuits always provide alternative pathways for current flow, although the voltage across the components in parallel is the same. When resistors are used in parallel (see Figure 2.7), a simple equation is used to calculate the overall resistance:

$$1 / R_{TOTAL} = (1 / R1) + (1 / R2) + ...$$

This same formula can be extended for any number of resistors used in parallel. For example, if *R1* is 220 ohm and *R2* is 470 ohm, the overall resistance will be 149.8 ohm.

For only two resistors in parallel, an alternate formula can be used:

$$R_{TOTAL} = (R1 \times R2) / (R1 + R2)$$

Figure 2.5 Resistor Color Code Chart

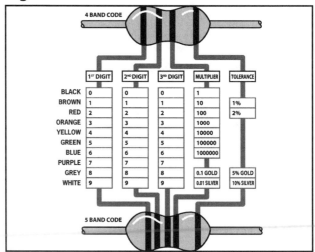

Figure 2.6 Resistors in Series

Figure 2.7 Resistors in Parallel

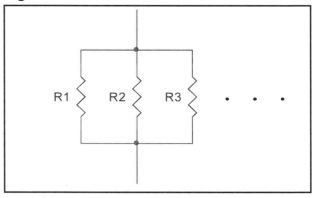

Carbon and metal film resistors typically come in wattage values of 1/16W, 1/8W, 1/4W, 1/2W and 1W. This corresponds to how much power they can safely dissipate. The most commonly used resistors are 1/4W and 1/2W. For large current applications, wire-wound resistors are typically used because they can support wattages greater than 1W. The wattage of the resistor usually corresponds to its physical size and surface area. For most consumer electronics, resistors greater than 1W are typically not used. To calculate the required wattage value for your application, use the following equation:

$P = V \times I$

Or...

$P = I^2 \times R$

Where...

- P = Power (W)
- V = Voltage across the resistor (V)
- I = Current flowing through the resistor (A)
- R = Resistance value (Ω)

Capacitors

A *capacitor's* primary function is to store electrical energy in the form of electrostatic charge. Capacitors are an essential component used in almost any circuit design. Consider a simple example of a water tower, which stores water (the charge): When the water system (or circuit) produces more water than a town or building needs, the excess is stored in the water tower (or capacitor). At times of high demand, when additional water is needed, the excess water (the charge) flows out of the water tower to keep the pressure up.

A capacitor is usually implemented for one of three uses:

- **To store a charge** Typically used for high-speed or high-power applications, such as a laser or a camera flash. The capacitor will be fully charged by the circuit in a fixed length of time, and then all its stored energy will be released and used almost instantaneously, just like the water tower example previously described.

- **To block DC voltage** If a DC voltage source is connected in series to a capacitor, the capacitor will instantaneously charge and no DC voltage will pass into the rest of the circuit. However, an AC signal flows through a capacitor unimpeded because the capacitor will charge and discharge as the AC fluctuates, making it appear that the alternating current is flowing.

- **To eliminate ripples** Useful for filtering, signal processing, and other analog designs. If a line carrying DC voltage has ripples or spikes in it, also known as "noise," a capacitor can smooth or "clean" the voltage to a more steady value by absorbing the peaks and filling in the valleys of the noisy DC signal.

Capacitors are constructed of two metal plates separated by a *dielectric*. The dielectric is any material that does not conduct electricity, and it varies for different types of capacitors. It prevents the plates from touching each other. Electrons are stored on one plate of the capacitor and they discharge through the other. Consider lightning in the sky as a real-world example of a capacitor: One plate is formed by the clouds, the other plate is formed by the earth's ground, and the dielectric is the air in between. The lightning is the charge releasing between the two plates.

Depending on their construction, capacitors are either *polarized*, meaning that they exhibit varying characteristics based on the direction they are used in a circuit, or *nonpolarized*, meaning that they can be inserted in either orientation with no change in electrical function. A sampling of various resistor types is shown in Figures 2.8 and 2.9.

Figure 2.8 Various Nonpolarized Capacitor Types (Ceramic Disc and Multilayer)

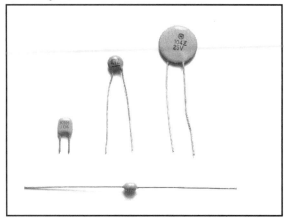

Figure 2.9 Various Polarized Capacitor Types (Electrolytic and Tantalum)

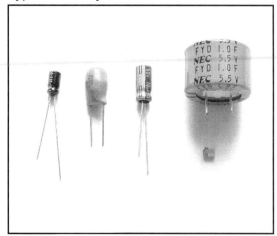

Capacitors have a unit of farad (F). A 1 farad capacitor can store 1 coulomb of charge at 1 volt (equal to 1 amp-second of electrons at 1 volt). A single farad is a very large amount. Most capacitors store a miniscule amount of charge and are usually denoted in uF (microfarads, 10_{-6} x F) or pF (pico-farads, 10_{-12} x F). The physical size of the capacitor is usually related to the dielectric material and the amount of charge that the capacitor can hold.

Unlike resistors, capacitors do not use a color code for value identification. Today, most mono-lithic and ceramic capacitors are marked with a three-number code called an *IEC marking* (see Figure 2.10). The first two digits of the code indicate a numerical value; the last digit indicates a multiplier. Electrolytic capacitors are always marked in uF. These devices are polarized and must be oriented correctly during installation. Polarized devices have a visible marking denoting the negative side of the device. (In the case of surface-mount capacitors, the marking is on the positive side.) There may be additional markings on the capacitor (sometimes just a single character); these usually denote the capacitor's voltage rating or manufacturer.

Figure 2.10 Examples of Some Capacitor IEC Markings

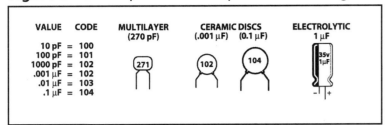

VALUE	CODE
10 pF	= 100
100 pF	= 101
1000 pF	= 102
.001 µF	= 102
.01 µF	= 103
.1 µF	= 104

The calculations to determine effective capacitance of capacitors in series and parallel are essentially the reverse of those used for resistors. When capacitors are used in series (see Figure 2.11), a simple equation is used to calculate the effective capacitance:

$$1 / C_{TOTAL} = (1 / C1) + (1 / C2) + ...$$

This same formula can be extended for any number of capacitors used in series. For example, if *C1* is 100uF and *C2* is 47uF, the overall capacitance will be 31.9uF.

For only two capacitors in series, an alternate formula can be used:

$$C_{TOTAL} = (C1 \times C2) / (C1 + C2)$$

When using capacitors in series, you store effectively less charge than you would by using either one alone in the circuit. The advantage to capacitors in series is that it increases the maximum working voltage of the devices.

When capacitors are used in parallel in a circuit (see Figure 2.12), their effective capacitance is additive, meaning that you simply add the values of the capacitors in parallel to obtain the total capacitance. For example, if *C1* is 100uF and *C2* is 47uF, the overall capacitance will be 147uF.

Capacitors are often used in combination with resistors in order to control their charge and discharge time. Resistance directly affects the time required to charge or discharge a capacitor (the larger the resistance, the longer the time).

Figure 2.13 shows a simple RC circuit. The capacitor will charge as shown by the curve in Figure 2.14. The amount of time for the capacitor to become fully charged in an RC circuit depends on the values of the capacitor and resistor in the circuit.

Figure 2.11 Capacitors in Series

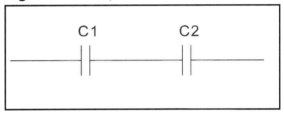

Figure 2.12 Capacitors in Parallel

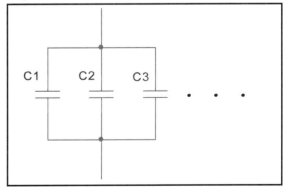

Figure 2.13 A Simple RC Circuit to Charge a Capacitor

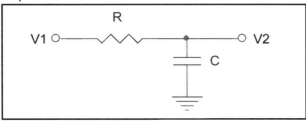

Figure 2.14 Capacitor-Charging Curve

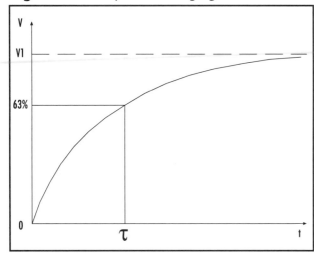

Figure 2.15 Various Diode Types Showing Direction of Current Flow

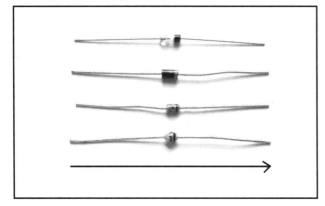

The variable τ (called the *time constant*) is used to define the time it takes for the capacitor to charge to 63.2 percent of its maximum capacity. The time constant can be calculated by the following formula:

$$\tau = R \times C$$

Where…

- τ = Time constant (seconds)
- C = Capacitance (*F*)
- R = Resistance (Ω)

A capacitor reaches 63.2 percent of its charge in one-fifth the time it takes to become fully charged. Capacitors in actual applications are usually not charged to their full capacity because it takes too long.

Diodes

In the most basic sense, *diodes* pass current in one direction while blocking it from the other. This allows for their use in rectifying AC into DC, filtering, limiting the range of a signal (known as a *diode clamp*), and as "steering diodes," in which diodes are used to allow voltage to be applied to only one part of the circuit.

Most diodes are made with semiconductor materials such as silicon, germanium, or selenium. Diodes are polarized, meaning that they exhibit varying characteristics depending on the direction they are used in a circuit. When current is flowing through the diode in the direction shown in Figure 2.15 (from anode, left, to cathode, right), the diode appears as a short circuit. When current tries to pass in the opposite direction, the diode exhibits a high resistance, preventing the current from flowing.

small footprint and low failure rates. The testing process (done during product manufacturing) is more expensive than other package types due to the fact that X-rays need to be used to verify that the solder has properly bonded to each of the ball leads.

With Chip-on-Board (COB) packaging, the silicon die of the IC is mounted directly to the PCB and protected by epoxy encapsulation (see Figure 2.24).

Figure 2.23 BGA Packaging

Figure 2.24 COB Packaging

Proper IC positioning is indicated by a dot or square marking (known as a *key*) located on one end of the device (see Figure 2.25). Some devices mark pin 1 with an angled corner (for square package types such as PLCC). On the circuit board, pin 1 is typically denoted by a square pad, whereas the rest of the IC's pads will be circular. Sometimes, a corresponding mark will be silkscreened or otherwise noted on the curcuit board. Pin numbers always start at the keyed end of the case and progress counter-clockwise around the device, unless noted differently in the specific product data sheet.

Figure 2.25 IC Package Showing Pin Numbers and Key Marking

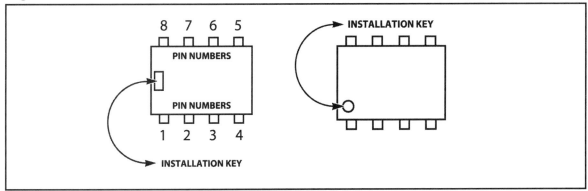

Soldering Techniques

Soldering is an art form that requires proper technique. With practice, you will become comfortable and experienced with it. The two key parts of soldering are good heat distribution and cleanliness of the soldering surface and component. In the most basic sense, soldering requires a soldering iron and solder. There are many shapes and sizes of tools to choose from; you can find more details in Chapter 1 "Tools of the Warranty Voiding Trade." This section uses hands-on examples to demonstrate proper soldering and desoldering techniques.

WARNING: PERSONAL INJURY

Improper handling of the soldering iron can lead to burns or other physical injuries. Wear safety goggles and other protective clothing when working with solder tools. With temperatures hovering around 700 degrees F, the tip of the soldering iron, molten solder, and flux can quickly sear through clothing and skin. Keep all soldering equipment away from flammable materials and objects. Be sure to turn off the iron when it is not in use and store it properly in its stand.

Hands-On Example:
Soldering a Resistor to a Circuit Board

This simple example shows the step-by-step process to solder a through-hole component to a printed circuit board (PCB). We use a piece of prototype PCB and a single resistor (see Figure 2.26). Before you install and solder a part, inspect the leads or pins for oxidation. If the metal surface is dull, sand with fine sandpaper until shiny. In addition, clean the oxidation and excess solder from the soldering iron tip to ensure maximum heat transfer.

Figure 2.26 Prototype PCB and Resistor Used in the Example

Bend and insert the component leads into the desired holes on the PCB. Flip the board to the other side. Slightly bend the lead you will be soldering to prevent the component from falling out when the board is turned upside down (see Figure 2.27).

Figure 2.27 Resistor Inserted into PCB

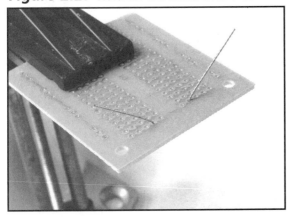

Figure 2.28 Heating the Desired Solder Connection

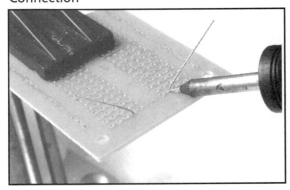

Figure 2.29 Applying Heat and Solder to the Connection

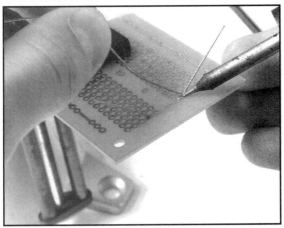

To begin the actual soldering process, allow the tip of your iron to contact both the component lead and the pad on the circuit board for about 1 second before feeding solder to the connection. This will allow the surface to become hot enough for solder to flow smoothly (see Figure 2.28).

Next, apply solder sparingly and hold the iron in place until solder has evenly coated the surface (see Figure 2.29). Ensure that the solder flows all around the two pieces (component lead and PCB pad) that you are fastening together. Do not put solder directly onto the hot iron tip before it has made contact with the lead or pad; doing so can cause a cold-solder joint (a common mistake that can prevent your hack from working properly). Soldering is a function of heat, and if the pieces are not heated uniformly, solder may not spread as desired. A cold-solder joint will loosen over time and can build up corrosion.

When it appears that the solder has flowed properly, remove the iron from the area and wait a few seconds for the solder to cool and harden. Do not attempt to move the component during this time. The solder joint should appear smooth and shiny, resembling the image in Figure 2.30. If your solder joint has a dull finish, reheat the connection and add more solder if necessary.

Once the solder joint is in place, snip the lead to your desired length (see Figure 2.31). Usually, you will simply cut the remaining portion of the lead that is not part of the actual solder joint (see Figure 2.32). This prevents any risk of short circuits between leftover component leads on the board.

Figure 2.30 Successful Solder Joint

Figure 2.31 Snipping Off the Remaining Component Lead

Every so often during any soldering process, use a wet sponge to lightly wipe the excess solder and burned flux from the tip of your soldering iron. This allows the tip to stay clean and heat properly. Proper maintenance of your soldering equipment will also increase its life span.

Figure 2.32 Completed Soldering Example

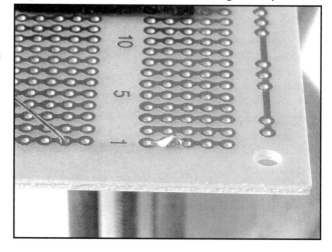

Desoldering Tips

Desoldering, or removing a soldered component from a circuit board, is typically more tricky than soldering, because you can easily damage the device, the circuit board, or surrounding components.

For standard through-hole components, first grasp the component with a pair of needle-nose pliers. Heat the pad beneath the lead you intend to extract and pull gently. The lead should come out. Repeat for the other lead. If solder fills in behind the lead as you extract it, use a spring-loaded solder sucker to remove the excess solder.

For through-hole ICs or multipin parts, use a solder sucker or desoldering braid to remove excess from the hole before attempting to extract the part. You can use a small flat-tip screwdriver or IC extraction tool to help loosen the device from the holes. Be careful to not overheat components, since they can become damaged and may fail during operation. If a component is damaged during extraction, simply replace it with a new part. For surface mount devices (SMDs) with more than a few pins, the easiest method to remove the part is by using the ChipQuik SMD Removal Kit, as shown in the following step-by-step example. Removal of SMD and BGA devices is normally accomplished with special hot-air rework stations. These stations provide a directed hot-air stream used with specific noz-

- **Installing parts backward** ICs have a notch or dot at one end indicating the correct direction of insertion. Electrolytic capacitors have a marking to denote the negative lead (on polarized surface mount capacitors, the positive lead has the marking). Through-hole capacitors also have a shorter-length negative lead than the positive lead. Transistors have a flat side or emitter tab to help you identify the correct mounting position and are often marked to identify each pin. Diodes have a banded end indicating the cathode side of the device.

- **Verify power** Ensure that the system is properly receiving power from the power supply. If the device uses batteries, check to make sure that they have a full charge and are installed properly. If your device doesn't have power, chances are it won't work.

Web Links and Other Resources

General Electrical Engineering Books

- Radio Shack offers a wide variety of electronic hobby and "how to" books, including an Engineer's Notebook series of books that provide an introduction to formulas, tables, basic circuits, schematic symbols, integrated circuits, and optoelectronics (light-emitting diodes and light sensors). Other books cover topics on measurement tools, amateur radio, and computer projects.

- *Nuts & Volts* (www.nutsvolts.com) and *Circuit Cellar* (www.circuitcellar.com) magazines are geared toward both electronics hobbyists and professionals. Both are produced monthly and contain articles, tutorials, and advertisements for all facets of electronics and engineering.

- Horowitz and Hill, *The Art of Electronics*, Cambridge University Press, 1989, ISBN 0-52-137095-7. Essential reading for basic electronics theory. It is often used as a course textbook in university programs.

- C. R. Robertson, *Fundamental Electrical & Electronic Principles*, Newnes, 2001, ISBN 0-75-065145-8. Covers the essential principles that form the foundations for electrical and electronic engineering courses.

- M. M. Mano, *Digital Logic and Computer Design,* Prentice-Hall, 1979, ISBN 0-13-214510-3. Digital logic design techniques, binary systems, Boolean algebra and logic gates, simplification of Boolean functions, and digital computer system design methods.

- K. R. Fowler, *Electronic Instrument Design*, Oxford University Press, 1996, ISBN 0-19-508371-7. Provides a complete view of the product development life cycle. Offers practical design solutions, engineering trade-offs, and numerous case studies.

Electrical Engineering Web Sites

- **ePanorama.net: www.epanorama.net** A clearing house of electronics information found on the Web. The content and links are frequently updated. Copious amounts of information for electronics professionals, students, and hobbyists.

- **The EE Compendium, The Home of Electronic Engineering and Embedded Systems Programming: http://ee.cleversoul.com** Contains useful information for professional electronics engineers, students, and hobbyists. Features many papers, tutorials, projects, book recommendations, and more.

- **Discover Circuits: www.discovercircuits.com** A resource for engineers, hobbyists, inventors, and consultants, Discover Circuits is a collection of over 7,000 electronic circuits and schematics cross-references into more than 500 categories for finding quick solutions to electronic design problems.

- **WebEE, The Electrical Engineering Homepage: www.web-ee.com** Large reference site of schematics, tutorials, component information, forums, and links.

- **Beyond Logic: www.beyondlogic.org** Tutorials, articles, product information, and links about Ethernet, USB/serial interfaces, and various other topics.

- **Electro Tech Online: www.electro-tech-online.com** A community of free electronic forums. Topics include general electronics, project design, microprocessors, robotics, and theory.

- **University of Washington EE Circuits Archive: www.ee.washington.edu/circuit_archive** A large of collection of circuits, data sheets, and electronic-related software.

- **Ohm's Law Calculators: www.eworld.contactbox.co.uk/calc/calcohm.htm**

Data Sheets and Component Information

When reverse-engineering a product for hardware-hacking purposes, identifying components and device functionality is typically an important step. Understanding what the components do may provide detail of a particular area that could be hacked. Nearly all vendors post their component data sheets on the Web for public access, so simple searches will yield a decent amount of information. The following resources will also help you if the vendors don't:

- **Data Sheet Locator: www.datasheetlocator.com** A free electronic engineering tool that enables you to locate product data sheets from hundreds of electronic component manufacturers worldwide.

- **IC Master: www.icmaster.com** The industry's leading source of integrated circuit information, offering product specifications, complete contact information, and Web site links.

- **Integrated Circuit Identification (IC-ID): www.elektronikforum.de/ic-id** Lists of manufacturer logos, names, and datecode information to help identifying unknown integrated circuits.
- **PartMiner: www.freetradezone.com** Excellent resource for finding technical information and product availability and for purchasing electronic components.

Major Electronic Component and Parts Distributors

- Digi-Key, 1-800-344-4539, www.digikey.com
- Mouser Electronics, 1-800-346-6873, www.mouser.com
- Newark Electronics, 1-800-263-9275, www.newark.com
- Jameco, 1-800-831-4242, www.jameco.com

Obsolete and Hard-to-Find Component Distributors

When trying to locate obscure, hard-to-find materials and components, don't give up easily. Sometimes it will take hours of phone calls and Web searching to find exactly what you need. Many companies that offer component location services have a minimum order (upward of $100 or $250), which can easily turn a hobbyist project into one collecting dust on a shelf. Some parts-hunting tips:

- Go to the manufacturer Web site and look for any distributors or sales representatives. For larger organizations, you probably won't be able to buy directly from the manufacturer. Call your local distributor or representative to see if they have access to stock. They will often sample at small quantities or have a few-piece minimum order.
- Be creative with Google searches. Try the base part name, manufacturer, and combinations thereof.
- Look for cross-reference databases or second-source manufacturers. Many chips have compatible parts that can be used directly in place.

The following companies specialize in locating obsolete and hard-to-find components. Their service is typically not inexpensive, but as a last resort to find the exact device you need, these folks will most likely find one for you somewhere in the world:

- USBid, www.usbid.com
- Graveyard Electronics, 1-800-833-6276, www.graveyardelectronics.com
- Impact Components, 1-800-424-6854, www.impactcomponents.com
- Online Technology Exchange, 1-800-606-8459, www.onlinetechx.com

any kind or ripping out the guts and making a CueCat-based flashlight. Although the company no longer exists, the CueCat has arguably become the most popular hacked and reverse-engineered hardware device to ever hit the mainstream market.

Model Variations

Three major varieties of the CueCat exist:

- PS/2 keyboard interface, four-screw model
- PS/2 keyboard interface, two-screw model
- USB interface, two-screw model

The overall functionality is essentially the same for each of the models. Each model also had sub-variations of component types and manufacturing processes. Because of the varying circuitry and architecture, the hacks we discuss are slightly different for each model.

NEED TO KNOW...

Each hack shown in this chapter has step-by-step instructions for the three model types. Be sure to follow only the instructions for your particular type, because the modifications vary from model to model.

Figure 3.1 The CueCat Optical Reader, Four-Screw PS/2 Interface with Original Materials

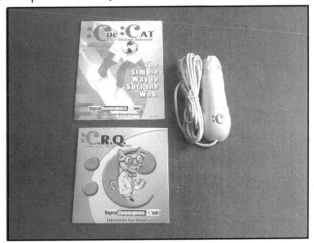

Figure 3.1 shows a product shot of the CueCat four-screw PS/2 version. The CueCat was distributed with a small user's manual and software CD. For all intents and purposes, you do not need the manual or CD, unless you are interested in these items for historical purposes. All we need for the hacks is the CueCat hardware itself.

Figure 3.2 shows a product shot of the CueCat USB version. This version was created toward the end of DigitalConvergence's life and did not gain wide distribution. The USB version is significantly harder to acquire than the more common PS/2 model.

Figure 3.3 is a comparison shot of all three CueCat variations. The bottom of each device clearly identifies the unit's interface type (either PS/2 or USB). A Radio Shack catalog number and optional revision sticker can also be seen. The units are shown in chronological order of their introduction, from top to bottom. The four-screw PS/2 version was the first to be manufactured and distributed. The two-screw PS/2 version came next and was the most widely distributed and most common version, followed by the scarce USB version. By comparing the internal circuitry of all three devices, we created this manufacturing time line, based on additions and enhancements to each subsequent device. You'll see the details of the varying circuitry in the hacks throughout this chapter.

Figure 3.2 The CueCat Optical Reader, USB Interface

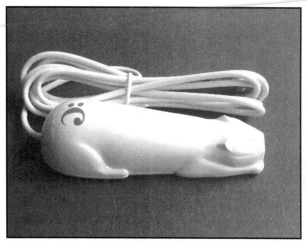

Figure 3.3 Bottom of the CueCat: Top, Four-Screw PS/2; Middle, Two-Screw PS/2; Bottom: USB

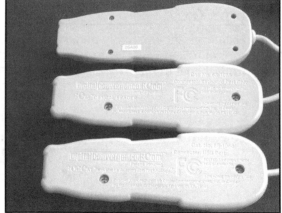

NEED TO KNOW... WHERE CAN I GET A CUECAT?

Although the CueCat isn't being manufactured anymore and its creator, DigitalConvergence, is out of business, the device is a great gadget and perfect for hardware hacking. Many tools are available all over the Web, and the CueCat can be modified into a general-purpose, computer-interfaced barcode reader. You can find CueCats at yard sales, on eBay, and at a few mail-order electronics distributors for only a few dollars each:

■ **eBay: www.ebay.com** New, used, and modified CueCats are often available on this popular auction site. Average prices range from $1.00 to $5.00 per unit, and you can even buy larger quantities of 10 or 100.

ACTO knife, carefully cut the trace connecting to pin 4 of the Serial EEPROM device (see Figure 3.16). Anywhere along the trace between the pin and the via on the left (the gold pad with the hole) is suitable. Be sure to cut completely through the trace. It is okay to dig a little "ditch" into the circuit board to ensure that the trace has been totally cut; just be careful to not go all the way through the board.

Figure 3.16 Cutting the Required Trace of the Serial EEPROM

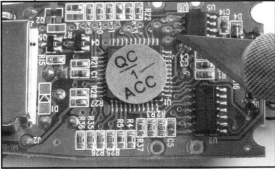

If your circuit board has the smaller five-pin SOT23 package Serial EEPROM, the trace to cut is still in the same location as described here.

WARNING: HARDWARE HARM

Using a knife to modify a circuit board can be a very tricky proposition. Be careful to apply only the necessary pressure to lift or cut the trace (which is just a thin layer of copper on top of the hard fiberglass material that makes up the circuit board). A single slip could damage components or other traces on the circuit board and cause irreversible damage to the device.

WARNING: PERSONAL INJURY

When using a knife to modify the circuit board, make sure your hands and fingers are safely out of the direction of the blade, and always wear proper eye protection. Be aware of stray solder or pieces of the cut trace that may loosen from the board.

With the trace successfully cut, your modified board should resemble the image in Figure 3.17. The hack is now complete.

Figure 3.17 Hack Complete: Successfully Cut Trace of the Serial EEPROM

An optional step is available to further ensure that the unique serial number cannot be transmitted by your CueCat device: Completely remove the Serial EEPROM from the circuit board with a soldering iron or very fine-tip clippers. If you choose to complete this step, your circuit board should now resemble the image in Figure 3.18.

WARNING: HARDWARE HARM

When removing this part, be careful not to scratch or damage any of the surrounding components or pull up any PCB traces. The easiest way to remove a surface-mount part is with an SMD rework station or using a flat-blade solder tip.

Figure 3.18 Optional Step: Circuit Board with Serial EEPROM Device Removed (Note the Additional SOT23 Footprint Within the Serial EEPROM Area)

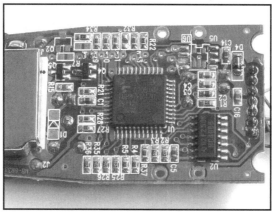

Removing the UID: Two-Screw PS/2 CueCat

Figure 3.19 shows the Serial EEPROM (denoted with an arrow) that we will be modifying. It is located on the front of the CueCat two-screw PS/2 circuit board.

Figure 3.19 Front of CueCat Two-Screw PS/2 Showing Serial EEPROM

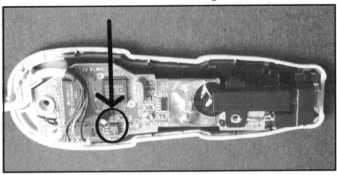

Our target trace to cut is connected to pin 1 of the Serial EEPROM. First, identify pin 1 on the device, which is the upper-left pin if your CueCat is oriented as shown in Figure 3.20. Using the X-ACTO knife, carefully cut the trace connecting to pin 1 of the Serial EEPROM device (see Figure 3.20). Anywhere along the trace between the pin and the via on the left (the gold pad with the hole) is suitable. Be sure to cut completely through the trace. It is okay to dig a little "ditch" into the circuit board to ensure that the trace has been totally cut; just be careful to not go all the way through the board.

WARNING: HARDWARE HARM

Using a knife to modify a circuit board can be a very tricky proposition. Be careful to apply only the necessary pressure to lift or cut the trace (which is just a thin layer of copper on top of the hard fiberglass material that makes up the circuit board). A single slip could damage components or other traces on the circuit board and cause irreversible damage to the device.

WARNING: PERSONAL INJURY

When using a knife to modify the circuit board, make sure your hands and fingers are safely out of the direction of the blade, and always wear proper eye protection. Be aware of stray solder mask or pieces of the cut trace that may loosen from the board.

Figure 3.20 Cutting the Required Trace of the Serial EEPROM

With the trace successfully cut, your modified board should resemble the image in Figure 3.21. The hack is now complete.

Figure 3.21 Hack Complete: Successfully Cut Trace of the Serial EEPROM

An optional step is available to further ensure that your CueCat device will never transmit the unique serial number. Simply remove the Serial EEPROM completely from the circuit board with a soldering iron or very fine-tip clippers. If you choose to complete this option, your circuit board should now resemble the image in Figure 3.22.

WARNING: HARDWARE HARM

When removing this part, be careful not to scratch or damage any of the surrounding components or pull up any PCB traces. The easiest way to remove a surface-mount part is with an SMD rework station or using a flat-blade solder tip.

Figure 3.22 Optional Step: Circuit Board with Serial EEPROM Device Removed

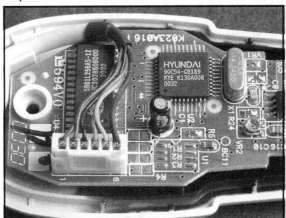

Removing the UID: USB CueCat

Figure 3.23 shows the Serial EEPROM (denoted with an arrow) that we will be modifying. It is located on the front of the CueCat USB circuit board.

Figure 3.23 Front of CueCat USB Showing Serial EEPROM

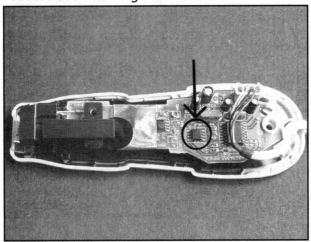

Our target trace to cut is connected to pin 4 of the Serial EEPROM. First, identify pin 4 on the device, which is the upper-right pin if your CueCat is oriented as shown in Figure 3.23. Using the X-ACTO knife carefully cut the trace connecting to pin 4 of the Serial EEPROM device (see Figure 3.24). Anywhere along the trace between the pin and the via on the right (the gold pad with the hole) is suitable. Be sure to cut completely through the trace. It is okay to dig a little "ditch" into the circuit board to ensure that the trace has been totally cut, just be careful to not go all the way through the board.

WARNING: HARDWARE HARM

Using a knife to modify a circuit board can be a very tricky proposition. Be careful to apply only the necessary pressure to lift or cut the trace (which is just a thin layer of copper on top of the hard fiberglass material that makes up the circuit board). A single slip could damage components or other traces on the circuit board and cause irreversible damage to the device.

WARNING: PERSONAL INJURY

When using a knife to modify the circuit board, make sure your hands and fingers are safely out of the direction of the blade, and always wear proper eye protection. Be aware of stray solder or pieces of the cut trace that may loosen from the board.

Figure 3.24 Cutting the Required Trace of the Serial EEPROM

With the trace successfully cut, your modified board should resemble the image in Figure 3.25. The hack is now complete.

Figure 3.25 Hack Complete: Successfully Cut Trace of the Serial EEPROM (Close Up)

An optional step is available to further ensure that your CueCat device will never transmit the unique serial number. Simply remove the Serial EEPROM completely from the circuit board with a soldering iron or very fine-tip clippers. Your circuit board should now resemble the image in Figure 3.26.

Figure 3.26 Optional Step: Circuit Board with Serial EEPROM Device Removed

Warning: Hardware Harm

Be careful when removing the part to not scratch or damage any of the surrounding components or pull up any PCB traces. The easiest way to remove a surface-mount part is with an SMD rework station or using a flat-blade solder tip.

Under the Hood: How the Hack Works

Before the hack, a typical unmodified CueCat response after scanning a sample Code 39 barcode (9105527106) looks as follows:

```
.C3nZC3nZC3n2ChPZEND1DxnY.ahb6.ENjZDNzXDhjZDq.
```

Each string returned by the CueCat contains three sections, all encoded with a proprietary encoding scheme devised by DigitalConvergence. The information includes a unique serial number, barcode type, and barcode data. For more information on the proprietary encoding scheme, see the "Technical Information" section toward the end of this chapter. The "Removing the Proprietary Barcode Encoding" hack in this chapter completely removes this obfuscation.

After we modify the CueCat to remove the unique identifier, the string corresponding to the identifier is now a nondescript pattern. Using the same Code 39 sample we examined previously, the modified four-screw PS/2 version returns the following string:

```
.BM5UBM5UBM5UBM5UBM5UBM5U.ahb6.ENjZDNzXDhjZDq.
```

The modified two-screw PS/2 and USB versions return another nondescript pattern with no relation to the original encoded serial number:

```
.VlY8VlY8VlY8VlY8VlY8VlY8.ahb6.ENjZDNzXDhjZDq.
```

Depending on the electrical characteristics of your version of CueCat, the pattern replacing the first part of the encoding barcode might vary from our examples. If CueCat no longer transmits the serial number portion, you can consider the hack complete.

The UID for each CueCat is stored in an industry-standard, nonvolatile Serial EEPROM device. Removing the Serial EEPROM device from the circuit board or cutting a particular trace coming from the Serial EEPROM will prevent data from being transmitted back to the CueCat microprocessor.

Serial EEPROMs are extremely common in the engineering industry and require minimal circuitry to read and write to. They are also notoriously insecure and as such often do not provide any type of security features. Thus, it is possible to attach a device programmer to the device, even while it is still attached to the circuit board, and read and write at will.

The primary Serial EEPROM used in the CueCat devices is an Antek Semiconductor 93LC46 or functional equivalent. The 93LC46 provides 1024 bits (128 bytes) of nonvolatile data storage. This is a small amount of memory, though it's well within reason to store the simple 18-byte serial number. The 93xx family of Serial EEPROMs use a three-wire interface to transfer data to and from the host:

- Serial Data Input (DI)
- Serial Data Output (DO)
- Serial Data Clock (SK or CLK)

An ORG pin is used to select the internal memory organization of the device. If the ORG pin is pulled HIGH, the memory is organized as 64 pages of 2 bytes (16 bits) each. If the ORG pin is pulled LOW, the internal memory of the EEPROM is organized as 128 pages of 1 byte (8 bits) each. For the four-screw PS/2 CueCat, the ORG pin is pulled HIGH. For the later two-screw PS/2 and USB CueCats, the ORG pin is pulled LOW. In either configuration, a total of 128 bytes of storage memory is available.

A clever design feature of the four-screw PS/2 CueCat is its support for a smaller five-pin SOT23 Serial EEPROM along with the larger eight-pin SOIC device. You can see the additional set of SOT23 pads within the larger SOIC footprint in Figure 3.18. The SOT23 version of the Serial EEPROM is a 24C01A part with rotated package pinout.

The 24xx family of Serial EEPROMs uses a two-wire I2C bus protocol to transfer data to and from the host:

- Serial Data (SDA)
- Serial Clock Input (SCL)

The SDA pin is bidirectional, providing both transmit and receive functionality. The SCL pin is used to clock data into the EEPROM device on a positive clock edge and out of the device on a negative clock edge. The memory in the 24C01A is internally organized as 16 pages of 8 bytes each, also corresponding to a total of 128 bytes (the same amount of memory as in the 93LC46).

Functionally, the two devices (the 24xx and the 93xx) will act the same, but technically they are different devices with different operating characteristics. This is why replacing an SOT23 device with an SOIC device on the CueCat, or vice versa, would not work. The firmware running on the CueCat needs to support the particular family of Serial EEPROM that is installed (e.g., the 93xx or 24xx, but not both).

Figure 3.27 shows the pinouts for both the 93LC46 and 24C01A Serial EEPROMs. In either case, the SDA line of the 24C01A and the DO line of the 93LC46 connect to pin 4 of the larger SOIC footprint on the circuit board, so regardless of which device is used, cutting the trace from pin 4 will prevent the unique serial number from being transmitted by the Serial EEPROM.

On the CueCat two-screw PS/2 version, the actual connection coming from pin 4 goes directly underneath the Serial EEPROM, making it impossible to cut unless the Serial EEPROM is completely removed (in which case, the hack would be complete). Instead, pin 1 of the Serial EEPROM is cut and achieves the same goal. Pin 1 corresponds to the Chip Select (CS) line, which enables or disables the Serial EEPROM depending on if that pin is LOW or HIGH. Since the microprocessor no longer has access to the CS line now that it has been cut, the Serial EEPROM cannot be enabled and will not transmit or receive data.

Figure 3.27 Serial EEPROM Pinout: Left, 93LC46 in Eight-Pin SOIC; Right, 24C01A in Five - Pin SOT23

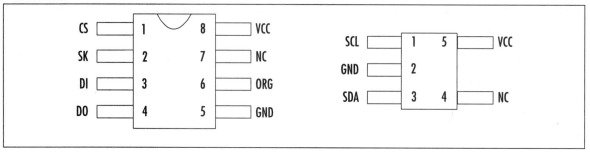

By comparing the contents of a number of CueCat Serial EEPROMs, it was easy to determine the location and method used to store the unique serial number.

The four-screw PS/2 version stores the unique serial number slightly differently than the two-screw PS/2 and USB versions. Each byte stored in the EEPROM is repeated to fill a 16-bit word. This seems to agree with the fact that the Serial EEPROM on the four-screw PS/2 version pulls the ORG pin HIGH to enable an internal memory configuration of 64 pages of 16 bits each. Since there is extra space in the memory device, the bytes might have been repeated for error checking or other purposes. Each byte corresponds to two digits of the CueCat serial number. For example, if the byte is 14 in hexadecimal, that will equal the two digits 1 and 4 in the serial number.

The following memory map is for a four-screw PS/2 version with a serial number of 000000000114555002:

```
00000000:   0000 0000 0000 0000 0101 1414 5555 5050   .............UUPP
00000010:   0202 FFFF AAFF AAFF AAFF AAFF AAFF AAFF   ................
00000020:   AAAA AAAA AAAA AAAA AAAA AAAA AAAA AAAA   ................
00000030:   AAAA AAAA AAAA AAAA AAAA AAAA AAAA AAAA   ................
00000040:   AAAA AAAA AAAA AAAA AAAA AAAA AAAA AAAA   ................
00000050:   AAAA AAAA AAAA AAAA AAAA AAAA AAAA AAAA   ................
00000060:   AAAA AAAA AAAA AAAA AAAA AAAA AAAA AAAA   ................
00000070:   AAAA AAAA AAAA AAAA AAAA AAAA AAAA AAAA   ................
```

The Serial EEPROMs in the two-screw PS/2 and USB versions both pull the ORG pin LOW, which enables an internal memory configuration of 128 pages of 8 bits (1 byte) each. This makes it easier to identify the serial number within the memory map. Furthermore, the serial number is stored in plain ASCII, big endian format (the lower addressed byte of each word has higher significance). In order to read the actual serial number properly, the first and second bytes of each word should be swapped.

The following memory map is for a two-screw PS/2 version with a serial number of 000000004767401401:

```
00000000:   FFFF 3030 3030 3030 3030 3734 3736 3034    ..00000000747604
00000010:   3431 3130 FFFF FFFF FFFF FFFF FFFF FFFF    4110............
00000020:   FFFF FFFF FFFF FFFF FFFF FFFF FFFF FFFF    ................
00000030:   FFFF FFFF FFFF FFFF FFFF FFFF FFFF FFFF    ................
00000040:   FFFF FFFF FFFF FFFF FFFF FFFF FFFF FFFF    ................
00000050:   FFFF FFFF FFFF FFFF FFFF FFFF FFFF FFFF    ................
00000060:   FFFF FFFF FFFF FFFF FFFF FFFF FFFF FFFF    ................
00000070:   FFFF FFFF FFFF FFFF FFFF FFFF FFFF FFFF    ................
```

The next memory map is for a USB version with a serial number of 000000005390946601:

```
00000000:   FFFF 3030 3030 3030 3030 3335 3039 3439    ..00000000350949
00000010:   3636 3130 FFFF FFFF FFFF FFFF FFFF FFFF    6610............
00000020:   FFFF FFFF FFFF FFFF FFFF FFFF FFFF FFFF    ................
00000030:   FFFF FFFF FFFF FFFF FFFF FFFF FFFF FFFF    ................
00000040:   FFFF FFFF FFFF FFFF FFFF FFFF FFFF FFFF    ................
00000050:   FFFF FFFF FFFF FFFF FFFF FFFF FFFF FFFF    ................
00000060:   FFFF FFFF FFFF FFFF FFFF FFFF FFFF FFFF    ................
00000070:   FFFF FFFF FFFF FFFF FFFF FFFF FFFF FFFF    ................
```

Removing the Proprietary Barcode Encoding

Performing this hack will allow you to read standard barcodes with the CueCat and obtain plain ASCII output as opposed to the proprietary CueCat format (which was nothing more than a weak obfuscation scheme; see the "Technical Information" section at the end of this chapter for more information). The output is sent to your computer via the PS/2 or USB interface treated as typed text (normal decoded keyboard characters). Once the device is plugged into your PC, the barcode text will be output wherever the cursor is positioned. The text output could then be passed into any number of data cataloging programs, spreadsheets, or other user-specific application.

This modification is especially useful now that DigitalConvergence is essentially defunct and the CueCat is just another commodity gadget. Creating a computer-interfaced barcode scanner in only a few minutes of hacking is time well spent.

Preparing for the Hack

The hack to convert the proprietary barcode encoding into a plaintext output is very simple. You need the following tools for this hack:

- An X-ACTO hobby knife
- A flat-head screwdriver, jeweler's size
- A soldering iron for the four-screw PS/2 model

■   A 4- to 5-inch piece of jumper wire For the four-screw PS/2 model, solid or twisted braid, 22AWG or thinner

For the two-screw PS/2 and USB versions, the hack consists simply of lifting the proper pin of one of the chips (the microprocessor) on the circuit board. This can usually be done by just heating the desired pin with the soldering iron while gently prying the pin off the pad with the X-ACTO knife or the flat-tip screwdriver. The four-screw PS/2 version requires a jumper wire to be added to the circuit board instead.

Removing the Encoding from the Four-Screw PS/2 CueCat

Hacking this early version of the CueCat is slightly more complicated than the subsequent versions released by DigitalConvergence, because it requires you to solder a jumper wire between two points on the circuit board.

On the front of the device, located on the left side, a large square pad is denoted with a white + sign and has a red wire already connected to it (Connection 1 in Figure 3.28). First, solder one side of the jumper wire to this point. Make sure that the red wire remains soldered to the pad when you are done with your addition.

Figure 3.28 Front of Four-Screw PS/2 Showing Connection Points

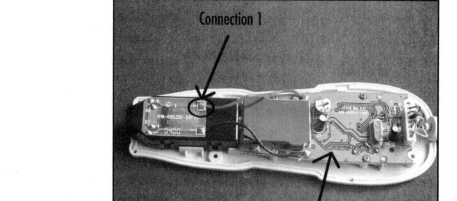

On the bottom-right section of the circuit board is a row of solder pads (also called *testpoints*). Depending on the revision number of your CueCat (which can be found silk-screened in white on top of the circuit board, as shown in Figure 3.31), the other end of the jumper wire will connect to one of these testpoints. The desired test point is always the pad that is connected to resistor R29 (identified in Figure 3.29).

Figure 3.29 Back of Four-Screw PS/2 Showing R29 and Testpoint

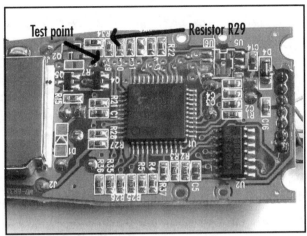

The test point makes an easy location to which to solder the jumper wire. Table 3.1 shows the location of the testpoint for the different known PCB revision numbers. If your revision is not listed in Table 3.1, simply visually trace the connection from R29 to the testpoint or use a multimeter to check continuity between the two points.

Table 3.1 Testpoint Location for Various CueCat Four-Screw PS/2 Revisions

CueCat Board Revision	Testpoint Location (Pad # from Left When Device Is Oriented as in Figure 3.31)
FM+H Rev. 0.3	2
TO+E Rev. 2.1	2
TM+H Rev. 0.3	2
HO+E Rev. 0.3	4
HW+H Rev. 2.1	4
HM+H Rev. 1.1	4

In this example, our CueCat is revision TO+E Rev. 2.1, so the jumper wire will be connected to the second pad from the left (Connection 2 in Figure 3.28).

Once the jumper has been added, your modified CueCat should resemble the image in Figure 3.30. Figure 3.31 shows a close-up of the row of test points.

Figure 3.30 Hack Complete: Jumper Wire Added

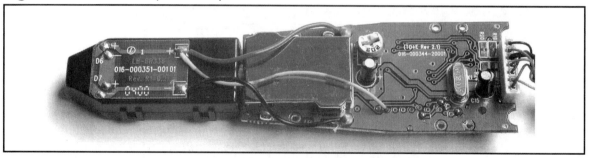

Figure 3.31 Hack Complete: Jumper Wire Added (Close-Up)

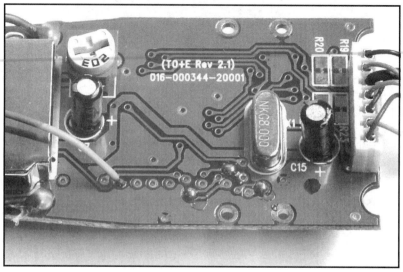

Removing the Encoding
from the Two-Screw PS/2 CueCat

For this hack, a single pin on the microprocessor that controls the CueCat simply needs to be lifted or cut, which will enable the decoded barcode output. The Hyundai Microelectronics (now Hynix Semiconductor) GMS90C54–GB189 microprocessor is labeled U2 on the circuit board and is a 44-pin MQFP package. Pin 10, the target pin that needs to be lifted, is designated with a silk-screened white line and shown with an arrow in Figure 3.32.

Figure 3.32 Front of CueCat Two-Screw PS/2 Showing Microprocessor Pin

Some versions of the CueCat two–screw PS/2 version may use a SyncMos SM2958 microprocessor in place of the more common GMS90C54. The SyncMos part is a direct clone of the GMS90C54, and the described hack functions exactly the same.

Simply use a soldering iron to heat the pin and lift it up with a small jeweler's screwdriver or the edge of an X-ACTO knife (see Figure 3.33). If desired, the pin could be clipped off and completely removed.

WARNING: HARDWARE HARM

While lifting the desired pin off the circuit board, be careful not to heat up the device too much or cause any surrounding pins to be lifted up, bent, or shorted together with solder. The pins are very close together, and you might want to use a magnifying glass to inspect your work.

Once pin 10 has been lifted, the hack is complete. Your modified CueCat should resemble the image in Figure 3.34.

Figure 3.33 Heating and Lifting the Pin of the Microprocessor

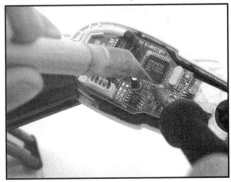

Figure 3.34 Hack Complete: Pin 10 of Microprocessor Lifted (Close-Up)

www.syngress.com

Removing the Encoding from the USB CueCat

For this hack, a single pin on the microprocessor that controls the CueCat simply needs to be lifted or cut, which will enable the decoded barcode output. The Hyundai Microelectronics (now Hynix Semiconductor) HMS91C7316 microprocessor is labeled U2 on the circuit board. Pin 5 is the target pin that needs to be lifted (denoted with an arrow in Figure 3.35).

Figure 3.35 Front of CueCat USB Showing Microprocessor Pin

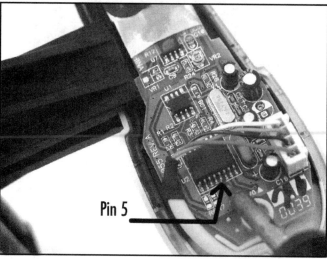

Pin 5

Simply use a soldering iron to heat the pin and lift it up with a small jeweler's screwdriver or the edge of an X-ACTO knife (see Figure 3.36). If desired, the pin could be clipped off and completely removed.

WARNING: HARDWARE HARM

While lifting the desired pin off the circuit board, be careful to not heat up the device too much or cause any surrounding pins to be lifted up or shorted together with solder. The pins are very close together, and you might want to use a magnifying glass to inspect your work.

Once pin 5 has been lifted, the hack is complete. Your modified CueCat should resemble the image in Figure 3.37.

Figure 3.36 Heating and Lifting the Pin of the Microprocessor

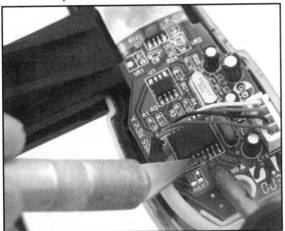

Figure 3.37 Hack Complete: Pin 5 of Microprocessor Lifted (Close-Up)

Under the Hood: How the Hack Works

Once the CueCat has been successfully "neutered" to read all standard barcodes, the raw ASCII data of the barcode will be transmitted via the PS/2 or USB port to the PC and displayed as regular keyboard input. The barcode type is no longer transmitted. Table 3.2 shows the various barcode types that can be read and are supported by the CueCat (listing provided by http://mailcom.com/BarcodeTest).

Before the hack, a typical unmodified CueCat response after scanning a sample Code 39 barcode (9105527106) looks as follows:

```
.C3nZC3nZC3n2ChPZEND1DxnY.ahb6.ENjZDNzXDhjZDq.
```

Or, if the CueCat has been modified to remove the unique serial number as described in the "Removing the Unique Identifier" section of this chapter, the sample Code 39 barcode would appear as something like this:

```
.BM5UBM5UBM5UBM5UBM5UBM5U.ahb6.ENjZDNzXDhjZDq.
```

After modifying the CueCat to remove the proprietary encoding, the same Code 39 sample will display simply as a string of raw ASCII barcode data:

```
9105527106
```

Table 3.2 Barcode Types Supported by CueCat

Barcode Category	CueCat Identifier	Barcode Type
Alphanumeric	128	Code 128
	E28	UCC/EAN 128 (Code 128 starting with the FUNC1 character)

Continued

Table 3.2 Barcode Types Supported by CueCat

Barcode Category	CueCat Identifier	Barcode Type
	C39	Code 39
Numerical	ITF	Interleaved 2 of 5
	CBR	Codabar
	PLS	Plessey
	MSI	Modified Plessey
Product codes (fixed length)	UPA (UA)	UPC-A
	UPE (UE)	UPC-E
	E13 (E3)	EAN-13
	E08 (E8)	EAN-08
	J13 (J3)	JAN-13 (same as EAN-13 when the first two digits are 49)
	J08 (J8)	JAN-08
	IBN (IB)	ISBN (same as EAN-13 when the first three digits are 978)
	ISN (IS)	ISSN (same as EAN-13 when the first three digits are 977)
	xx2 (see Note 1)	Code of the specified type with two additional digits
	xx5 (see Note 1)	Code of the specified type with five additional digits
	CCx (see Note 2)	CueCat Proprietary ":Cue," Code 128 without the Start symbol

Note 1: xx is any of the two-character abbreviated types in the table.

Note 2: x is any ASCII character from ! to ~.

The various models and revisions of CueCat handle some of the barcode types differently. Certain versions of modified CueCats display some additional, nonstandard information when reading Code 128 barcode. An entire extra line of data is transmitted and appears to be diagnostic information. This line can simply be ignored because the next line of data transmitted by the CueCat is the actual decoded Code 128 information.

Essentially, this hack works because the particular pin lifted on the microprocessor is a standard I/O pin that serves as a "switch" between transmitting encoded and raw data output. Most CueCat hackers believe that this feature was used during development or testing of the CueCat to ensure that barcodes were being read correctly before being encoded with DigitalConvergence's proprietary scheme. The support for this "switch" is embedded in the CueCat's firmware running on the microprocessor, and it was only a matter of time before a hardware hacker accidentally discovered it.

Technical Information

Although the hardware designs of the CueCat revisions varied slightly, the functional operation of the unit was the same. Figure 3.38 is a system block diagram for the CueCat's major functions. (The concept illustrated here is from *EDN*, "Not Every Cat Lands on Its Feet," September 4, 2003.)

Figure 3.38 CueCat System Block Diagram, PS/2 Model

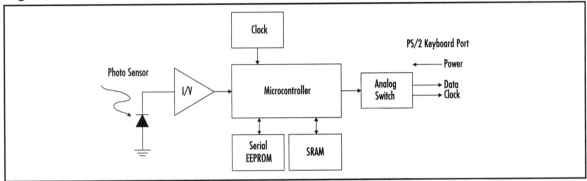

At a high level, the operation of the CueCat is as follows:

1. LEDs from inside the CueCat are enabled to illuminate the scanning surface.

2. As the CueCat is moved over the barcode on the printed page, the reflections from the black and white "bars" of the barcode are detected by the photosensor, resulting in a varying current. The photosensor is protected by a metal shield to reduce AC-induced noise into the circuit.

3. The output from the photosensor is passed through a high-gain amplifier and filter to clean up the signal.

4. The microprocessor then samples the signal at a high clock rate and processes the information into actual barcode data.

5. The unique serial number of each device is read from the Serial EEPROM.

6. The unit then encodes the unique serial number and barcode data into a proprietary format (see the "CueCat Encoding Scheme" section that follows for more information), which is now ready to be transmitted to the host PC.

For the PS/2 version, an analog switch serves as a multiplexer to effectively seize control of the PS/2 bus and disable any actual keyboard input to the PC while the CueCat is sending its data. The USB model operates in essentially the same manner, except the analog switch in the final stage is replaced with a USB interface.

The CueCat Encoding Scheme

The proprietary encoding scheme CueCat uses is nothing more than base-64 encoding with an additional XOR against a constant (the ASCII character *C*) to first obfuscate the data. Base-64 (formally defined as part of RFC 1521, www.faqs.org/rfcs/rfc1521.html) is used to simply convert a general byte array (such as raw binary data) into a printable byte array of ASCII characters.

After Stephen Satchell performed detailed cryptanalysis of the CueCat encoding scheme in September 2000, it was hypothesized that the encoding scheme was not used to hide or protect the transmitted data (as many people thought) but that it simplified the process of placing the data into a URL with a minimum of post-processing on the server side. The added step of the XOR operation could not be determined, however, and might have been a thinly veiled attempt by DigitalConvergence to make its data appear more proprietary than it actually was.

The encoded string transmitted by the CueCat consists of three parts, with a period (.) serving as a delimiter:

- Unique serial number

- Barcode type

- Barcode data

A typical unmodified CueCat response after scanning a sample Code 39 barcode (9105527106) looks as follows:

```
.C3nZC3nZC3n2ChPZEND1DxnY.ahb6.ENjZDNzXDhjZDq.
```

So, in this example, the three encoded parts are:

- Unique serial number = C3nZC3nZC3n2ChPZEND1DxnY

- Barcode type = ahb6

- Barcode data = ENjZDNzXDhjZDq

The base-64 encoding table used is an alternate of the regular scheme, placing the lowercase alphabet before the uppercase:

```
abcdefghijklmnop
qrstuvwxyzABCDEF
GHIJKLMNOPQRSTUV
WXYZ0123456789+/
```

After running our three encoded parts through a base-64 decoder, we are left with intermediate results of *sssssssssvpzszwuusr* for the serial number, *pz* for the barcode type, and *zrsvvqtrsu* for the barcode data. Passing the components through an XOR against the ASCII character *C* (43 in hexadecimal) gives us the final decoded information:

- Unique serial number = 000000005390946601

- Barcode type = C39
- Barcode data = 9105527106

After the CueCat scheme was discovered, open-source software and drivers began popping up for every language, operating system, and interface imaginable, including but not limited to C, C++, PHP, Java, JavaScript, Python, Perl, PAM, Microsoft Windows, Macintosh, Linux, and other UNIX variants. These tools would decode the proprietary CueCat encoding scheme and display the decoded information without using the software provided by DigitalConvergence. See the "Open-Source CueCat Software and Drivers" in the "CueCat Litter Box: Web Links and Other Resources" section for links. The most compact and efficient decoder is a Perl script by Larry Wall, Perl creator and guru, shown here:

```
#!/usr/bin/perl -n
printf "Serial: %s   Type: %s   Code: %s\n",
    map {
        tr/a-zA-Z0-9+-/ -_/;
        $_ = unpack 'u', chr(32 + length()*3/4) . $_;
        s/\0+$//;
        $_ ^= ""C" x length;
    } /\.([^.]+)/g;
```

More Physical Model Variations

As mentioned throughout this chapter, there are three major designs of the CueCat, each with its own set of revisions. Although there are too many distinct revisions to discuss in this chapter, we have covered the most common set. This section shows some additional physical differences among the major versions: the four-screw PS/2, the two-screw PS/2, and the USB. Most of the noted differences are from the original four-screw PS/2 design and the subsequent two-screw PS/2 and USB designs (which appear to be very similar, if not exact, in physical housing design).

Figure 3.39 Length Comparison of CueCat Housings: Top, Four-Screw PS/2; Bottom, Two-Screw PS/2

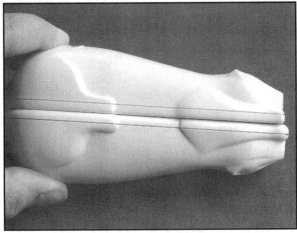

Figure 3.39 shows a side-view comparison of the CueCat housings from the four-screw and two-screw PS/2 versions. The length of the four-screw housing is slightly shorter than the two-screw version. The length was increased slightly for later versions of the CueCat, possibly because of a change in manufacturing technologies or to support additional circuitry or a new photo sensor design.

Figure 3.40 shows another variance between the original four-screw PS/2 version and subsequent versions. The scanning "orifice" (or "mouth") of the device where the LED and photosensor are positioned (the primary components of a barcode scanner that "read" the barcode) is a large square shape for the four-screw version and a narrow rectangular shape for the others.

Figure 3.40 Front of CueCat Showing Scanning "Orifice" Variations: Left, Four-Screw PS/2; Center, Two-Screw PS/2; Right, USB

Figure 3.41 Back of CueCat Showing Connector Cable Variations: Left, Four-Screw PS/2; Right, Two-Screw PS/2

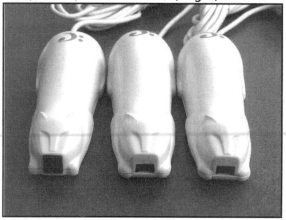
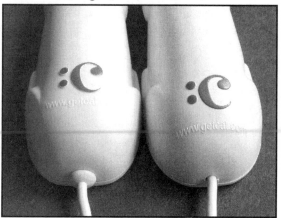

Finally, we examine the back (or "tail") of the CueCats. As shown in Figure 3.41, the only major variation is the existence of a stress-relief grommet on the four-screw device. (We previously showed an internal view of the cable and circuitry in Figure 3.6.) This appears to have been removed in all later versions of CueCat hardware, since cable stress-relief features were built right into the plastic enclosure (as shown in Figures 3.11 and 3.14).

More History of Political and Legal Issues

Between August and September 2000, lawyers representing DigitalConvergence began a witch hunt and crackdown on all Web sites that discussed and/or detailed any modifications to the CueCat hardware or software. As a result, not only were the hardware hacking and experimentation with the CueCat not deterred, but dozens of mirror Web sites popped up to make sure the information up to that date would not completely disappear. Although over time many of the mirror sites and personal Web pages of those who experimented with the CueCat were taken down, a handful of sites still remain with enough information for any reader to spend a weekend modifying his or her CueCat. Figure 3.42 is a sample of one of the many "notice of infringement" letters (essentially just a form letter) sent to potential violators by New York-based law firm Kenyon & Kenyon.

Figure 3.42 A Notice of Infringement Sent from DigitalConvergence's Legal Counsel to a Potential Violator of CueCat Intellectual Property

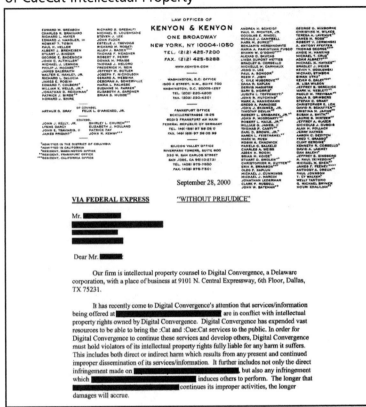

The core of the debate is that DigitalConvergence claimed that the intellectual property rights of the CueCat were being violated by people opening up and modifying the CueCat hardware. Furthermore, DigitalConvergence claimed that the end-user license agreement (EULA) included with the CueCat hardware and software stated that the CueCat hardware was only on loan to the end user and that the end user did not own the hardware. This claim was challenged by the fact that many users were sent the CueCat as unsolicited mail, which then classifies the product as a gift that the recipient then legally owned. Restrictions on the use of the company's C.R.Q. software that came with the CueCat were also detailed in the license agreement, though most hardware hackers didn't even bother to open up the software in the first place. The EULA was incrementally updated and posted to DigitalConvergence's Web site, apparently in an attempt to close any loopholes in the document that allowed any reverse-engineering activities that many people were doing.

The privacy statement, shown in Figure 3.43 from a screenshot taken during the C.R.Q. software installation process, was a concern for many users, since one major facet of the CueCat technology was to capture end-user demographics and track Web site usage. Although the privacy statement claimed that "We believe that all consumers who become members and use our products deserve to know that their personal information is protected under all circumstances," many end users did not truly believe this claim.

Figure 3.43 C.R.Q. Installation Software Screenshot: Privacy Statement

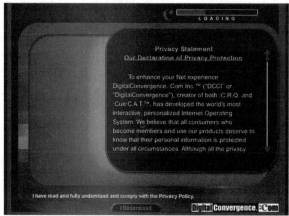

DigitalDemographics, a sister site to DigitalConvergence, located at a non-existant www.digi-taldemographics.com, was not shy in hiding the true intentions of CueCat data gathering. At one time, its Web site stated: "DigitalDemographics' parallel mission is to gather demographic and psycho-graphic information from our :CRQ users, subscribers, and :CueCat device users." It went on to list the various data types that were collected and analyzed:

■   Demographic profiles

■   Historical cue data

■   Responsiveness to relevant information on the tabs

■   Responsiveness to relevant information on the On:CRQ Web site

■   Polling data

■   Panelist data (from volunteers who participate in special interest panels)

■   Specific program cue and scratch data

■   Survey data from opt-in respondents and volunteer panelists

■   Direct responsiveness to offers

■   Cross-media response profiles

■   Multiple response profiles from same segment/media

■   Industry-specific demographic profiling

Not surprisingly, after DigitalConvergence came under scrutiny for its disregard of personal pri-vacy, the DigitalDemographics site was taken down and redirected to the main CueCat site.

At least one known public attack on DigitalConvergence's servers leaked personal information about a number of the company's customers. On September 15, 2000, DigitalConvergence updated its Web site with the following news: "DigitalConvergence Corporation experienced a security breach that may have exposed certain members' names and email addresses. The company was alerted of breach efforts by Peter Thomas at Securitywatch.com. The company has secured the site and is conducting a thorough security examination." DigitalConvergence tried to reduce the impact of the attack by releasing a press release on a Friday evening, hoping that the news would be forgotten over the weekend. Fortunately, media outlets picked up the story on Monday morning. It turns out that a plain-text file containing user information was left accessible on a public-facing Web server, open to all the world. The "security breach" was nothing more than sloppiness by the administrators of the DigitalConvergence Web servers. To attempt to pacify affected users of the breach, DigitalConvergence was offering free $10 Radio Shack gift certificates for a short period of time.

Figure 3.44 shows a rather humorous ending to this story as the C.R.Q. installation software attempts to "phone home" to the now-departed DigitalConvergence Web server.

Figure 3.44 C.R.Q. Installation Software Trying to Connect to the Now-Defunct DigitalConvergence Server

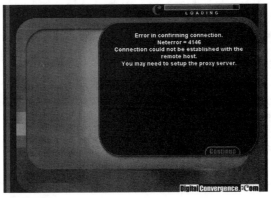

CueCat Litter Box:
Web Links and Other Resources

The following list is a selection of the most informational and complete CueCat Web sites still available. At the peak of the CueCat controversy (circa 2000), hundreds of Web sites existed with hardware hacking, reverse-engineering, and software decoding techniques. Many of those sites have since been removed due to threatening legal actions of the law firm representing DigitalConvergence. A Google search of the term *CueCat* should give you enough news articles, personal rants, and technical information to last quite a while.

- **Dissecting the CueCat: http://air-soldier.com/~cuecat** The premier Web site for all things CueCat. Reverse engineering, technical details, political issues, and additional links.

- **CueCat: www.flyingbuttmonkeys.com/foocat** News, information, and software for the free software community.

- **How to Neuter a Cat: www.cexx.org/cuecat.htm**.

- **Azalea Software CueCat Portmortem: www.azalea.com/QTools/CueCatPostmortem.pdf** Commentary on the CueCat technology.

- **CueCat Principles of Operation: www.fluent-access.com/wtpapers/cuecat/index.html** A collection of essays.

- **"The CueCat: Balancing Function and Privacy Can Be a Challenge," Lauren Weinstein, September 2, 2000: www.vortex.com/privacy/priv.09.19**.

- **"Perl and :CueCat Help You Roll Your Own Data Capture," Brent Michalski, Dr. Dobb's Online: www.ddj.com/documents/s=1498/ddj0101pl**.

Open-Source CueCat Software and Drivers

- **http://freshmeat.net/search/?q=cuecat** A collection of open-source projects.

- **http://blort.org/cuecat** Another collection of open-source projects.

- **Linux CueCat driver and CueAct barcode utility: http://webperso.easyconnect.fr/om.the/web/cuecat** Allows you to execute specific commands when a barcode is swiped with a CueCat reader.

- **Azalea Software QTools: www.azalea.com/QTools/qtools-1.0.2.zip** Create CueCat-compatible barcodes.

- **www.cuecatastrophe.com** Independent CueCat driver for Windows 2000 and XP.

- **CueJack: www.cuejack.com** A software application that lets you scan a product with a CueCat scanner, then displays a Web page with "alternative information" about the product's company.

DigitalConvergence Patents for CueCat Technologies

- **US6384744** Method and system for data transmission from an optical reader, www.delphion.com/details?pn=US06384744__.

- **US6526449** Method and apparatus for controlling a computer from a remote location, www.delphion.com/details?pn=US06526449__.

- **US6377986** Routing string indicative of a location of a database on a web associated with a product in commerce, www.delphion.com/details?pn=US06377986__.

Chapter 4

Case Modification: Building a Custom Terabyte FireWire Hard Drive

Hacks in this Chapter:

- Creating a 1.2TB FireWire RAID

- Custom Case Modification for the FireWire RAID

Introduction

With digital media becoming ever more popular, demands on storage space are increasing at a phenomenal rate. MP3s, digital video, and DVDs all consume vast amounts of space on computer hard disks. Integration of computers and home theater has only made the problem worse. With the idea of building a central media server that can serve audio and video content to any room in my home, I set out to build the ultimate FireWire drive. Of course, the ultimate FireWire drive requires the ultimate case mod to enclose it. Both are described in the following pages for your hacking pleasure.

Case Mod Primer

When most people think of "hardware hacking," case mods come to mind. Fans of custom computer case modifications have become a huge community in the past few years. In fact, the community, once a small underground group of artistically inclined hackers, has become so large that there are numerous mail-order outlets in which to buy case mod supplies! This chapter is one of two (see Chapter 5, Macintosh, for the other) in this book that focuses on case mods.

Case modding is the ultimate in personalization and expression. Just as many people consider tattoos or piercing to be "body art", case mods can most definitely be considered "computer art." There are different categories of mods you can do. We list the more common ones here:

- **Painting** Adding a custom paint job to your creation
- **Case Windows** Creating "windows" in the case using Plexiglas and edge molding.
- **Case and Drive Lighting** Custom light creations using LEDs and cold cathode lights.
- **Power Supply** Modifications of the power supply unit to add a shutdown timer, change fans, or add some artistic features.
- **Cable Management** Adding decorative braided sleeves or rerouting cables in some custom or unique fashion.
- **Airflow Management** Modifying the case and internal components to allow for increased (or decreased) airflow through the system by using various sized fans, fan grills, and fan filters.
- **Case Silencing** Reducing noise of the system by using noise reduction padding or fan speed controllers

There are hundreds, if not thousands, of Web sites dedicated to case modifications and which serve as showcases and galleries for hardware hackers to show off their latest creations. Some Web resources are listed here:

- **Mini-motherboards** mini-itx.com, www.mini-itx.com
- **The Ultimate Computer Case Mod Web site** www.thebestcasescenario.com
- **PimpRig: Smack Ya Rig Up!** www.pimprig.com
- **Lucent Rigs** www.lucentrigs.com

Creating a 1.2TB FireWire RAID

The concept for this project started out with me wondering how much hard drive space I would need to hold all my music and video files. Because I could not anticipate my future needs, it became a contest of how much storage I could stuff into one box. With 200GB drives being the largest I could afford, and with the case that I planned to use holding only four drives, this put my drive at 800GB. Although this amount of storage is vast and impressive, it was dangerously close to the coveted 1 terabyte barrier—the Holy Grail of computer nerds. I wasn't the first to create such a large array, but I was possibly the first home user to do so. One TB is considered a major milestone for computer owners, just as the sound barrier was for aviators before Chuck Yeager exceeded it.

The answer to my dilemma came in the form of backplanes that held three 3.5-inch drives in the space of two 5.25-inch drive bays. With six drives, the total capacity was catapulted to 1.2 TB. The subsequent Slashdotting on September 24, 2003 (http://slashdot.org/article.pl?sid=03/09/24/1755201&mode=thread&tid=137&tid=198) and the 3.5 million hits on my Web page that followed it carved my name into the online hall of Übernerds.

Preparing for the Hack

This hack requires a substantial commitment of funding. High-capacity hard drives are currently pretty expensive, but even without the drives, the case and remaining electronics for the hack in this chapter run over $600. Also, prepare to spend a significant amount of time fabricating and hacking components to get them to fit in the case. Soldering skills are optional, and lack of fear is a must. Table 4.1 shows the components required for the project. The necessary tools are listed in Table 4.2.

 Even though these lists of parts and tools seem rather specific, all are quite common and generic in nature and can be easily found online. The industrial parts and tools are also commonly found at any hardware store.

Table 4.1 Required Components for the Custom Terabyte Hack

Component	Notes
Generic four-bay SCSI case with power supply	Available at many computer stores
Six identical IDE hard drives	As large capacity as you can afford
Three dual-drive FireWire-to-IDE bridges	
Two three-bay IDE backplanes	
FireWire hub	To fit in the SCSI-1 mount on the case

Continued

Table 4.1 Required Components for the Custom Terabyte Hack

Component	Notes
Three FireWire cables, six-pin	6-inch length
Two fans, 80 x 80 x 15mm	PanaFlow FBA08T12L
Two fans, 80 x 80 x 25.5mm	PanaFlow FBA08A12L1A
Four 80mm wire fan grilles	
Three Molex Y power adapters	
Three 12-inch round IDE cables	Master and slave
12 3/4-inch standoffs	Plastic or metal
12 1-inch screws	#4/40
E6000 industrial glue	Available at TAP Plastics, www.tapplastics.com
Heat-shrink tubing	3/32 inch

Table 4.2 Required Tools for the Custom Terabyte Hack

Tool	Notes
Phillips head screwdriver	
Wire cutters	
Sheet-metal shears	
Half round bastard file	Coarse file for metal
Soldering iron and solder	
Tap and drill set	#4/40
Drill press	
Heat gun	

Performing the Hack

Do the following:

1. Begin by removing the covers from your generic case. Often this is as simple as removing four to six screws in the back and lifting off the sheet metal cover. The opened case will resemble the image in Figure 4.1. The first thing we need to change on this case is replacing the original noisy fans with nice quiet fans with fluid bearings, like the PanaFlow series from Panasonic.

Figure 4.1 Empty Beige SCSI Case

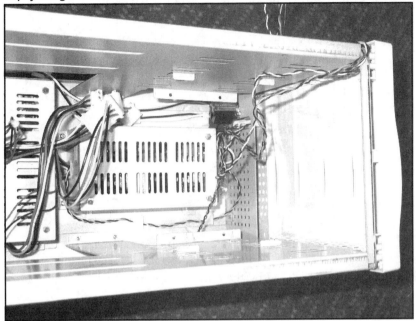

NEED TO KNOW... CHOOSING PROPER FANS

In a push-pull fan configuration such as this, where fans are forcing air both into and out of the enclosure, fan sizing becomes important to ensure that air moves through case openings without forced induction. If we use higher volume fans in the exhaust than in the intake, the air pressure inside the case will become slightly lower than the surrounding atmospheric pressure, and more air will be sucked into normal openings in the case. Without this planning, the power supplies in this case would overheat.

2. The cheap fans that came installed in my original drive case were very noisy. In addition, the stamped sheet metal grilles (see Figure 4.2) created lots of turbulent noise. To fix this, I simply used the sheet metal shears to remove the grilles by cutting the spokes of the grilles on the outermost ring. Eight snips and some quality time with a half round bastard file and they were but a fading memory.

Figure 4.2 Cheap Fan Grilles in the Original Drive Case

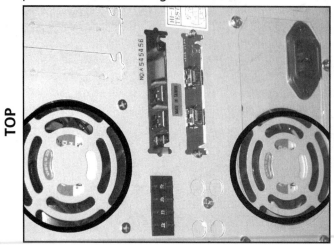

3. The original fans were replaced by the 80mm × 25mm PanaFlow fans with wire grilles. The lower fan's screws are covered by another sheet of metal, so I had to glue the grille to it with some E6000 industrial adhesive (see Figure 4.3). As you can see, because the lower fan was glued in place, the mounting tabs that are present on the upper fan needed to be removed. I accomplished this task by scoring the break point of each mounting tab with a file and simply bending the metal until it broke.

Figure 4.3 New Fan Grilles

NOTE

RAID 0 is used extensively for storage of video files during editing and in many home computers. It gives a speed boost and has only one logical volume to deal with. Given the enormous cost of real RAID controllers and the incredible reliability of modern drives, RAID 0 is great for many uses *provided* that the user understands the risks involved. RAID 5 is the type people use when data integrity is more important than speed or capacity. The cost of a RAID 5 controller puts it out of the grasp of home users.

For around $2,000, a hardware RAID controller can be added to the drive enclosure to perform RAID 5. The usable space on the array will shrink by 20 percent, but the array will continue to function even if one drive fails. In RAID 5, data is split into chunks where the data would be written to five of the six drives and a calculated CRC value written to the sixth drive. Each time a new chunk is written, a different drive is used to store the CRC value. RAID 5 currently requires an excessive amount of processing power for the host computer to perform the calculations at an acceptable speed, which is why it requires using an external RAID controller.

For visual readers, Figure 4.12 shows a block diagram of how the devices should all be connected, illustrating the progression from the FireWire hub to the IDE bridge boards and then to the drives.

Figure 4.12 Functional Block Diagram

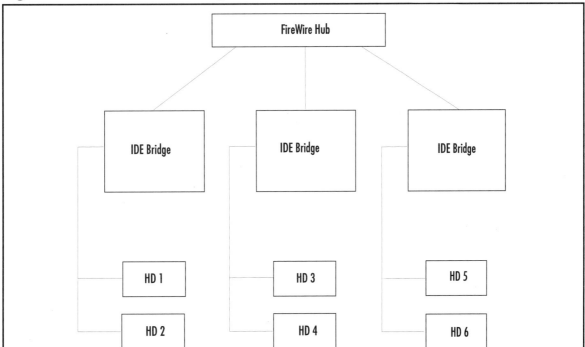

Custom Case Modification for the FireWire RAID

A terabyte drive deserves a cool case. Generic beige boxes, although inexpensive, lack the flair and commanding presence that a project of this nature demands. In this hack I set out to take something uninteresting (the plain beige box) and create a personal work of art that would showcase my accomplishment and not only make the project a conversation piece because of its internals but for its external appearance as well.

Preparing for the Hack

Before embarking on the journey of a case modification, you should spend serious time considering the aesthetic and artistic aspects of the finished product. Try to imagine how it will look on completion. Consider different colors, designs, and lighting placements before buying any supplies. Don't be afraid to be daring with your designs, but don't let the design elements clash with each other in a way that could be distracting or even worse … garish (unless, of course, that is your intent).

Since the acts of painting, drilling, and cutting are very messy, it is imperative that you prepare your workspace by, at a minimum, setting down newspapers. However, we recommend using a drop cloth for more thorough protection. It is also recommended (but not required) that you invest in a small handheld vacuum cleaner to clean up metal or plastic filings that have a tendency to accumulate during case modifications. The last thing you want is the interior of your case to be contaminated with these filings!

The parts required for this particular case modification are presented in Table 4.3. The tools you'll need are listed in Table 4.4.

Table 4.3 Required Components for the Custom Case Modification

Component	Notes
16 oz. of paint that adheres to your materials	Thousands of kinds of paint are available for metal in every delivery method imaginable. Due to the artistic nature of this mod, we leave it up to you to select a paint that suits the effect you are trying to achieve. The paint I used did not stick to metal very well and is now chipping off
Two 12-inch cold cathode lights	Color of your choice
Two 6-inch cold cathode lights	Color of your choice
Four cold cathode inverters	Matched for the tubes
Small 18–26 AWG wire	Preferably red and black wires. The length of the wires will vary with each implementation, depending on your needs
Small heat-shrink tubing	
Plexiglas round, 0.1-inch thick	Available at TAP Plastics, www.tapplastics.com

Continued

Table 4.3 Required Components for the Custom Case Modification

Component	Notes
Plexiglas sheet, 0.1-inch thick	Available at TAP Plastics, www.tapplastics.com
E6000 industrial adhesive	Available at TAP Plastics, www.tapplastics.com
Five T1-size LEDs	Various colors of your choice. LED size may also vary depending on the case you are using, so verify your size requirements before purchasing
Spray contact adhesive	
Double-sided foam tape	

Table 4.4 Required Tools for the Custom Case Modification

Tool	Notes
Phillips head screwdriver	
Dremel rotary tool	
Small carbide cutting bit for Dremel rotary tool	Available at most hardware stores, carbide bits are for metal; however, your exact needs will vary depending on the design you want to cut
Wire cutters	
Soldering iron and solder	
Half round bastard file	Coarse metal file
Fine metal files	Various shapes and sizes
Sandpaper	Various grit

Performing the Hack

Start by removing the outer case panels and bezels to be painted. Even the power button should come out. Most case bezels are held on by two or three screws and two to six plastic hooks just inside the case. The power button is usually held by four plastic hooks into the front bezel.

1. Before the case painting can start, we need to cut a custom case window. For this case modification I decided that since this was a FireWire case, it should have a FireWire logo on top as its window. Obtaining the artwork for the logo was easy; scalable EPS art is available for free download from Apple Computer's Web site. Then it was just a matter of scaling it to the right size and printing it. This created a stencil for my case window.

2. Next, glue the stencil onto the surface of the metal so it will serve as a template when you begin cutting. You can see the stencil glued to the top of the case in Figure 4.13.

WARNING: PERSONAL INJURY

Always wear eye protection and other safety gear when using power tools. Beware of hot tools and surfaces.

3. Let the cutting begin! Drill pilot holes into the metal to allow room for the carbide cutting bit to fit (see Figure 4.13). Never attempt to use a carbide cutting bit as a drill, because it may slip off its course and damage the surface.

Figure 4.13 Template With Pilot Holes and Initial Cuts

4. Once the pilot holes are drilled, carefully start cutting using the Dremel tool and carbide cutting bit. This is a very slow and laborious process. Cutting too fast will overheat the bit and may damage it. Smaller bits cut faster but are harder to control. A jigsaw tool works well for removing large areas of metal quickly. However, it is critically important not to cut beyond the edges of your template. Once the metal is cut away, it's gone forever (unless you are very skilled at repair and touchup). Figure 4.14 shows the cutting process. The final rough-cut product should look something like Figure 4.15.

Figure 4.14 Cutting Along the Template

Figure 4.15 Rough Cut of the Template Using the Dremel and Carbide Cutting Bit

5. A cutting bit and power tools cannot give you the fine detail that you need to make your case window look respectable, because they are too hard to control precisely. Now, grab your coarse file and start filing. A half round bastard file is great for doing both flat and round surfaces. Even with a coarse file, it might take several hours to make the holes smooth. When the edges are the correct size and shape, switch to a finer, smaller file and make every edge clean and smooth (see Figure 4.16). You should be able to run your fingers over every edge without fear of cuts or snags.

Figure 4.16 Rough Cut After Filing

6. Remove the paper template and sand every surface. Start with coarse sandpaper and work down to finer grits. If you are cutting plastic, it will only need a quick pass with fine-grit paper, since plastic is generally a very soft material. Metal, especially painted metal, should be sanded down as close to the bare metal as practical or the new paint might not adhere properly.

7. Sanding is an important step because the surface smoothness directly impacts the quality of the finish after painting. If the surface is rough, the final product will also look rough. The smoother, the better. After sanding, wipe every surface with rubbing alcohol, then a dry towel. This will remove the dust and particles from your soon-to-be painted surfaces. An alcohol sweep also removes any remaining mold release agent from cast-plastic parts.

Warning: Personal Injury

Always paint in a well-ventilated, dust-free area. Paint fumes are flammable and hazardous to your health. Read and obey all directions and warnings included with your paint products.

Warning: Hardware Harm

If you're using spray paint, be sure to cover or protect any nearby items that you do not want to get sprayed. If used improperly, spray paint can cover an entire room with a fine mist of pigment.

Always verify material compatibilities when you select paints. Some plastic paints will not stick to metal, and many metal paints will melt plastic. You might want to test your specific paint on a nonvisible or small section of the case before painting the entire surface.

8. After putting down a large area of newspaper (at least 5 feet by 5 feet), begin spraying the case, bezel, and any other parts that require painting. If your metal paint requires a primer, apply it before applying the actual coat of paint. Patience is very important at this step. The best-quality finishes are made with numerous fine coats of paint. Hold the spray can approximately 10 inches away from your surface, and paint across in wide, sweeping strokes. The first few coats will not completely cover the surface. That's okay. Allow each coat 5 minutes to dry before applying the next coat. When applied thinly, the coats of paint will dry fairly quickly.

Another good technique for consistent paint delivery is nozzle control. During the sweep, depress the nozzle to spray before reaching the surface, and hold it down past the end of the surface. Although this technique wastes a little bit of paint, it gives you far better deposition consistency because spray cans tend to shoot blobs out at the start and sputter when the nozzle is released. When the final coat is applied, set the parts aside and let them dry for at least 24 hours. Polymerizing paints should dry for at least seven days without any handling. Figure 4.17 shows a completed paint job of the case's front panel and power button.

Figure 4.17 Painted Front Panel and Power Button

9. To maintain the proper airflow as it was intended for your case, any holes that you cut for windows must be covered by a transparent material such as polycarbonate or glass. For my FireWire logo, I went to my local TAP Plastics and purchased a 5 × 7-inch sheet of 1/16-inch clear Lexan and glued it into the inside of the case with E6000 industrial adhesive, as shown in Figure 4.18. Make sure that your plastic does not interfere with internal structural components of the case. Most plastics come with a protective film layer on each surface. To keep your plastic clean and scratch free, leave the film in place until you are ready to glue it in.

Figure 4.18 Plastic Sheet Covering the Inside of the Cutout

10. The FireWire logo has a floating circle in the middle. For that reason, I purchased a 1.25-inch round that was 0.1 inches thick. Figure 4.19 shows the plastic sheet with the protective film and the round sitting on top of it.

Figure 4.19 The Window Elements

11. When the window fits to your satisfaction, glue it down and place a heavy object on it. With the additional weight, the glue will harden thinner and stronger, leaving you with a more durable and visually appealing bond. While the glue is drying, we can begin to work on the lighting.

12. This case has numerous other holes in the front and rear that we can take advantage of for cool lighting effects. For the maximum lighting effect, I purchased four cold cathode fluorescent lighting (CCFL) tubes. CCFL lights are much brighter than electro-luminescent (EL) lighting, and they are even visible in a photo taken using a camera flash!

    I installed two 6-inch tubes straddling the window (see Figure 4.20) and two 12-inch tricolor CCFL tubes along the bottom of the case (see Figures 4.21 and 4.22). By selecting tubes of different colors, you can create visually interesting lighting and blending effects. For example, a red light near a blue light will appear to have a purple region between them. Primary color spectral highlights will appear randomly among reflective surfaces as well. Use double-sided foam tape to hold the CCFL lamps in place.

Figure 4.20 Lamp Placements, Top

Figure 4.21 Lamp Placements, Left Side

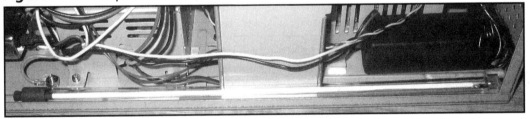

Figure 4.22 Lamp Placements, Right Side

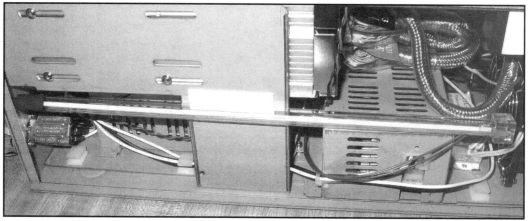

13. All CCFL tubes require high-voltage inverters to illuminate. This high voltage is created using a special CCFL inverter, which usually requires a standard 12VDC input. Lucky for us, 12V is common on all PC power supply cables. Solder the inverter power leads to the yellow +12 volt and black ground wires coming out of the case power supply and put heat-shrink tubing over the joints to protect and insulate them.

WARNING: HARDWARE HARM

Never apply power to an inverter without a lamp attached to its output. Doing so can damage the inverter.

WARNING: PERSONAL INJURY

Inverters generate extremely high voltages that are very dangerous and can be deadly. The CCFL inverters generate between 3,000 and 15,000 volts. Never wear ESD protection while handling inverters or lamps. A fatal electrocution hazard may exist if a conductive path across the heart is established.

14. Simply mount the inverter(s) with double-sided foam tape to a suitable location inside the case and connect the power. Figure 4.23 shows a dual-output inverter tucked between a fan and a power supply.

Figure 4.23 High-Voltage Inverter

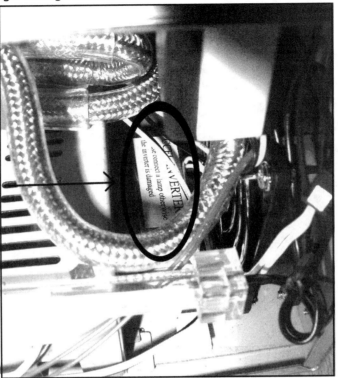

15. The final lighting mod involves replacing the original yellow and green LEDs on the front of the case with something a little more interesting, colorful, and unique. This case uses T1–sized (3mm) LEDs to show hard drive activity and power. The IDE backplanes have their own set of LEDs, which I decided not to replace for this hack. I used an ultrabright green LED for power and patriotic red, white, and blue LEDs for the activity outputs of the three FireWire bridgeboards. This case uses friction-fit LED sockets, so no soldering was required. However, there are multiple examples of soldered LED replacement hacks throughout this book, so fear not if your project entails something a bit more complicated. LEDs are polarity sensitive and will not function if installed backward. The disconnected LEDs on the front panel are shown in Figure 4.24 The new LEDs are shown in Figure 4.25.

Figure 4.24 New LEDs Replace the Originals on the Front Panel

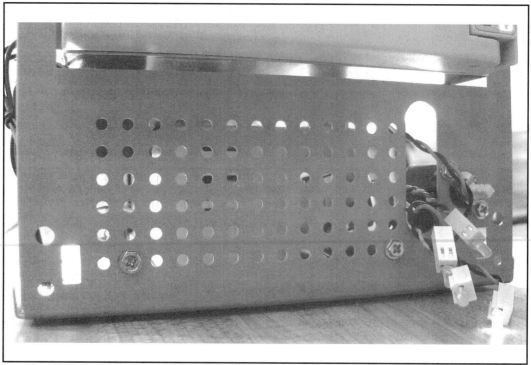

Figure 4.25 LEDs when Lit

16. Hopefully by now all your paints and glues are fully dry. Go ahead and put the painted front bezel and power button back onto the enclosure. Snap the locking tabs down firmly, and replace the bezel retaining screws. Did you peel off the protective film from the window yet? Next, carefully slide the case back on and tighten the back panel screws. A fabric washer placed underneath each screw will prevent the screws from gouging the paint. With the unit fully assembled, move it to its new home on a solid, level surface. Expect the fully assembled unit to be very heavy. Mine weighs around 40 pounds.

Under the Hood: How the Hack Works

Throughout this chapter, we covered various elements of case modifications, including case window creation, painting, custom lighting, and LED replacement. Until you put the finished product together, it is sometimes difficult to guess how it will turn out. Figure 4.26 shows a picture of the final hack.

Figure 4.26 Breathtaking View of the Final Hack

With 12 watts of cold cathode lighting coming from four different angles, multicolored light escapes from every crevice, seam, joint, and gap on this box. Creating a work of art involves attention to detail and completeness in design. Leave no surface unmodified and no cavity void of lighting. Don't worry about tiny flaws; most people will never notice them. This hack works because the coloring and lighting are so fantastic and the fans so quiet that viewers can only sit back in awe, silenced by its splendor. Figures 4.27 though 4.30 show various other views of the completed hack.

Figure 4.27 Another View

Figure 4.28 Another View

Figure 4.29 Another View

Figure 4.30 FireWire Logo

Additional Resources

The following is a list of vendors for hardware hacking materials and parts:

- Digi-Key Corporation: www.digikey.com
- Tap Plastics: www.tapplastics.com
- Panasonic Fans: www.panasonic.com/industrial/appliance/appliance_fans_panaflo_axial.htm
- FireWire Depot: www.fwdepot.com
- Case Mod Supplies: www.xoxide.com
- Directron.com: www.directron.com/mods.html

Case Modifications

If you're looking for ideas, inspiration, or other case modders, these sites are a great place to begin:

- Mini-motherboards: www.mini-itx.com

- The Ultimate Computer Case Mod Web site: www.thebestcasescenario.com

- Case mods, PimpRig: Smack Ya Rig Up!, www.pimprig.com

- Case mods, Lucent Rigs: www.lucentrigs.com

- Case mods, Pyramac, BlueIce G4, Mac Mods, riscx.com: www.riscx.com/pyramac

Chapter 5

Macintosh

Hacks in this Chapter:

- Building the Compubrick SE
- Building a UFO Mouse
- Power Macintosh G4 Cube Hacks

Compubrick SE

As computer hardware became a commodity in the mid-1980s, the importance of focusing on software became increasingly apparent to many at Apple, as did the need for an open platform. Apple's John Fitch devised the Jonathan architecture, consisting of a simple backplane that would accept book-like modules. Using this design, modules for running a variety of operating systems could be developed and placed on the same backplane. This would allow users to easily experiment with new operating systems—a feature Fitch believed would work very much to Apple's advantage. However, John Sculley, CEO of Apple, feared just the opposite would occur, and the project was canceled.

Jonathan could have changed the way we think about computers, each user starting out with a bare-bones system and then adding and upgrading individual components as needed. Jonathan's modular design lends itself very well to building blocks. Need a new hard drive? Snap off the old one and snap a new one into place. Each computer component is a giant building block, allowing the user to mix and match any combination of components and snap them together in whatever form factor is most convenient. The Compubrick SE is a proof-of-concept artist's rendering of this methodology.

Fanaticism meets fanaticism with the Compubrick SE, combining the thrill of hardware hacking with the joy of building. We start with a Macintosh SE, strip it down to its individual parts, then build it back up again in cases of multicolored plastic Mega Bloks. Each component becomes its own block, attached to the system however the builder chooses.

NOTE

More information on the Jonathan concept is available in *AppleDesign* by Paul Kunkel, published by Graphics Inc., 1997.

 ## Preparing for the Hack

Before we begin the Compubrick SE hack, you will need to gather all required materials and tools. Figure 5.1 shows most of the items.

Figure 5.1 Getting Ready for the Compubrick SE Hack

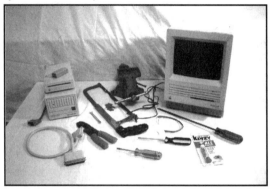

Table 5.1 is a list of components that you will need to build a Compubrick SE.

Table 5.1 Required Components for the Compubrick SE

Component	Notes
Macintosh SE	
800K external drive	Model number M0131
Mega Bloks, about 2,500	A few of Mega Bloks' 600-piece bins will work. Be careful when estimating the number you'll need; many of the smaller pieces won't be usable in this project.
Erector set	
Internal-to-external SCSI cable	Found in external hard drives
SCSI terminator	
18-22AWG wire, 26 feet	

Table 5.2 presents a list of tools that you will also need to build a Compubrick SE.

Table 5.2 Required Tools for the Compubrick SE

Tool	Notes
Super Glue	
T15 x 6 in. screwdriver	Sears Craftsman part #47431
Straight screwdriver	
Philips screwdriver	
Wire stripper/crimper	Found in external hard drives
Wire snips or hobby knife	
Vise	
Hacksaw	

A Craftsman T15 x 6 in. screwdriver is available at Sears for under $5. A longer shaft is convenient but not necessary. Mega Bloks and Erector sets can be found at any toy store. Try salvaging an internal-to-external SCSI cable from an old external hard drive. Computer swap meets will often have used hard drives, disk drives, and the Mac SE for pennies on the dollar. If you're not inclined to go searching, you can easily purchase all these components online for a few dollars plus the cost of shipping. Here are a few sources to consider:

- eBay: www.ebay.com
- USENET Groups: groups.google.com
- Applefritter Forums: www.applefritter.com

Performing the Hack

The disassembly and reassembly of the Compubrick is a multistep process. To make this process easier to understand, we have broken the hack into different modules, as follows:

- Taking Apart the Mac
- Speaker
- Keyboard and Mouse
- Disk Drive
- Hard Drive
- Motherboard
- Cathode Ray Tube (CRT)

Taking Apart the Mac

Steve Jobs saw the Macintosh as an appliance not meant to be taken apart. As such, the compact Macs are very difficult to open. In order to disassemble the Mac, complete the following steps:

1. Locate the four T15 Torx screws that need to be removed. Two are on the back, just above the line of ports. The other two are inside the handle, for which the long screwdriver shaft is necessary. You can see the removal process for the screws inside the handle in Figures 5.2 and 5.3.

Figure 5.2 Locations of Screws

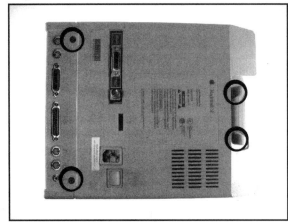

Figure 5.3 Unscrewing the Screws

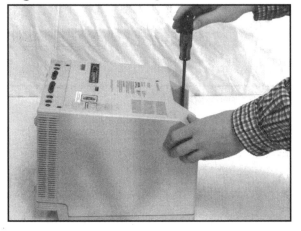

2. Once you have removed the screws, pry open the case by gently tugging at each corner of the case until the two pieces separate (see Figure 5.4).

Figure 5.4 Prying the Case Apart

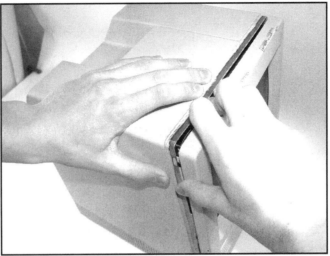

3.   Once the case is open, discharge the CRT. This is a dangerous and critical step.

WARNING: PERSONAL INJURY

The CRT inside a compact Macintosh can potentially hold a charge of up to 13,000 volts, which can give you quite a shock. Take extreme caution to discharge the CRT properly. An example of discharge procedure can be found at www.jagshouse.com/CRT.html. Never perform a CRT discharge alone—always have a friend present in case of emergency.

4.   Next, remove the analog cable from the motherboard. Figure 5.5 shows a photo of the inside of the Mac with the analog cable in place. The cable is a snug fit; be careful not to bump the CRT's neck when the cable gives way, because it could easily snap off and destroy the monitor!

Figure 5.5 Inside the Mac SE with the Analog Cable in Place

5.   Now slide the motherboard upward about an inch and pop it out (see Figure 5.6).

Figure 5.6 Removing the Motherboard

With the case opened, we can now begin to dismantle the chassis:

1.   Remove the two screws (shown in Figure 5.7) that hold the hard drive and floppy enclosure in place. The drive unit will now easily lift out of the case and can be set aside.

Figure 5.7 Hard Drive Screws

2.   Next, detach the frame from the front cover. The frame has five screws holding it in place; four of these screws are pictured in Figure 5.8.

Figure 5.8 Frame Screws: Four of the Five

3. To be able to remove the fifth screw that attaches the front cover, we have to first detach the power supply, which is mounted to the analog board with six screws on its right side.

NEED TO KNOW...

The analog board is the circuit board mounted vertically beside the power supply. It provides power to the CRT and motherboard.

4. Push the power supply out of the way, as shown in Figure 5.9, to reach the last screw.

Figure 5.9 Removing the Fifth Frame Screw

5. With the frame now disconnected, lift it out of the case and set it aside (see Figure 5.10).

Figure 5.10 Frame Removed from the Case

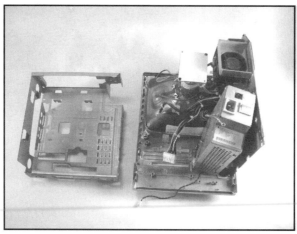

6. Next, remove the power supply after disconnecting it from the analog board. Disconnect the short cable that connects the CRT to the analog board (see Figure 5.11). This allows you to spread out the remaining parts as shown in Figure 5.12.

Figure 5.11 Disconnect the Power Supply   **Figure 5.12** The Analog Board

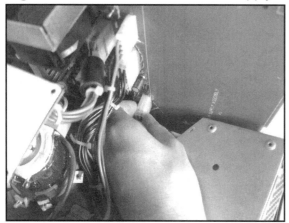 

7. Finally, disconnect the CRT from the front plate by removing the four screws, one in each corner of the CRT. This is done so that you can remove the speaker from the front case. The speaker is held in place by two flimsy plastic tabs, as shown in Figure 5.13. Just break these off using the wire snips or a hobby knife.

Figure 5.13 Moving the Speaker

Need to Know... Building Techniques

The Compubrick design is based primarily upon the use of 2x4 bricks, making flat regions a bit tricky because the block segments are so short. These regions are built using two layers of bricks, with the second layer offset from the first, as shown in Figures 5.14 and 5.15. This technique is known as *layering*.

Figure 5.14 Mega Blok Layering Example, Underside

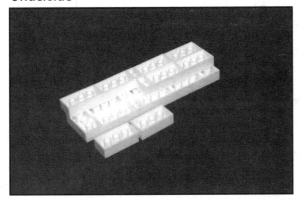

Figure 5.15 Mega Blok Layering Example, Top

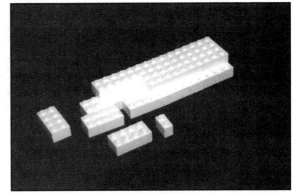

Assembling the bricks in this manner is adequate for use on small surfaces such as the top or bottom of the hard drive or disk drive. For the larger areas, however, this technique results in a connection that is too flimsy. In this case, it is necessary to reinforce the assembly with Super Glue. Figure 5.16, the top of the CRT case, is an example of an area so large that it requires gluing for strength. Place a dab of glue on the edges of a few studs on the brick, then quickly snap the piece above it into place. Avoid placing glue on the sides of the bricks. It will seep out when you press them together.

Figure 5.16 Mega Blok Layering Example, Top of the CRT Case

Encasing the Speaker

The first task of assembling the Compubrick is constructing the speaker encasement. This is a relatively simple step. You need to encase the speaker with blocks, using cylindrical 1x1s for the speaker grill. Any color or size brick that you prefer to use is acceptable; however, the case should be relatively the same size as the example shown in Figure 5.17.

Figure 5.17 Partially Assembled Speaker

A completed version of the speaker encased in blocks is shown in Figure 5.18.

Figure 5.18 Completed Speaker

Covering the Mouse and the Keyboard

The blocks on the keyboard and mouse serve only aesthetic purposes, in keeping with the theme of covering a Macintosh SE with Mega Bloks. The Compubrick mouse is completed by gluing blocks to the surface and has no function other than a visual one. The ADB Mouse I that shipped with the Mac SE has a flat surface, making the gluing fairly simple. The Mega Blok–covered ADB Mouse I is shown in Figure 5.19.

Figure 5.19 Completed ADB Mouse I

NEED TO KNOW...

If you attempt to use a newer ADB Mouse II (see Figure 5.20), you may run into problems because the mouse does not have flat surfaces. Getting square blocks to mount correctly on a curved surface is a challenge, and you may have to experiment with a few configurations before adhering the blocks to the surface.

Figure 5.20 ADB Mouse II

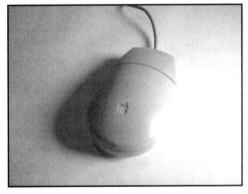

The choice of keyboards is unimportant; any keyboard will do. For this example, an Apple Extended Keyboard II was used.

1. Dismantle the keyboard by removing both the top and bottom pieces of the case. The top and bottom of the keyboard case is usually connected by a variety of simple screws that can be accessed from the bottom of the keyboard. In the case of the Extended Keyboard II, there is only one screw (see Figure 5.21). Remove it, then pry the keyboard apart.

2. Now remove the keyboard mechanism from the case (see Figure 5.22). To do this, first release the keyboard from underneath the snaps, then pop out the ADB connectors. Finally, slide the keyboard upward out of the tabs. Once you have separated the top and bottom portions of the keyboard case, discard the top piece.

Figure 5.21 Bottom of Keyboard

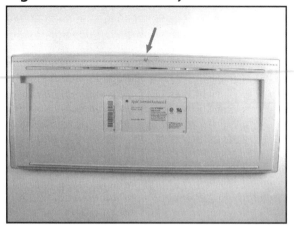

Figure 5.22 Removing the Keyboard Mechanism

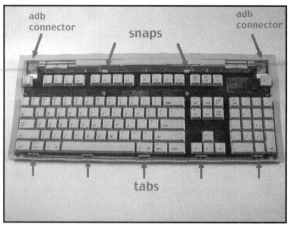

3. Next, take the bottom half of the keyboard and, using the hacksaw, saw off any tabs that protrude from the case (Figure 5.23). This is done so you have as smooth a surface as possible on which to place the bricks.

Figure 5.23 Sawing Off the Tabs

4. Now place the keyboard back into the lower case and build your frame around it, filling in the spaces between rows of keys with blocks (see Figure 5.24). When you have a frame that you're happy with, remove it, apply glue to the keyboard, and press the frame into place. The finished keyboard will resemble Figure 5.25.

Figure 5.24 Partially Assembled Keyboard

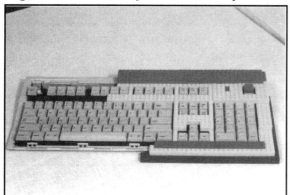

Figure 5.25 Completed Keyboard

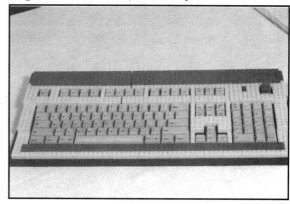

Encasing the Disk Drive

To encase the disk drive with the Mega Bloks, you will first have to remove the disk drive from its plastic case, but keep the metal chassis and cable intact.

1. There are four screws on the bottom of the case (see Figure 5.26). Remove these, and remove the bottom piece of plastic.

Figure 5.26 Bottom of the Floppy Drive

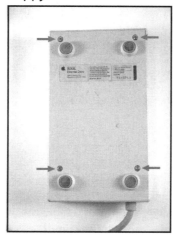

2. To remove the drive's chassis from the remaining plastic, remove the two screws shown in Figure 5.27 and lift out the metal enclosure. These uncased elements are shown in Figure 5.28.

Figure 5.27 Inside the Floppy Drive

Figure 5.28 Disk Drive Mechanism

3. Now that the disk drive is uncovered, you can begin by building the base using the previously described layering technique. Then add two rows of blocks for the sides, leaving a hole for the cable. The assembled base is shown in Figure 5.29.

Figure 5.29 Partially Assembled Disk Drive

4. The third row should have a slot in the front to allow a disk to be inserted (see Figure 5.30). On the right-hand side, we used an angular block so that the eject mechanism could still be reached (but only with a paperclip—this being a Macintosh, after all!). A fourth row finishes the sides, and the top is built using the layering technique, for a more aesthetically pleasing crown (see Figure 5.31).

Figure 5.30 Eject Mechanism

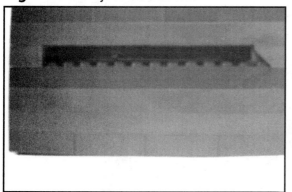

Figure 5.31 Completed Disk Drive

Encasing the Hard Drive

The goal of this step is to remove the SCSI internal hard drive from your Mac SE and create an external, modular SCSI drive. To do this:

1. Take the hard drive out of your Mac SE (or use any other SCSI hard drive) and the internal-to-external SCSI cable you salvaged from the external hard drive.

2. Connect them together, and then connect the SCSI cable and terminator. Now build the base and the top using layering, and build up the sides around the drive and cables, as shown in Figure 5.32.

Figure 5.32 Partially Assembled Hard Drive

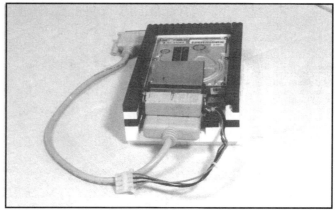

3. If you used a cable and terminator as shown in Figure 5.32, you'll find that the two stacked components are just barely too high to allow the top to fit on. The difference is slight enough that shaving a layer of plastic off the SCSI terminator will allow everything to fit properly, so stick the terminator in a vice and grab a hacksaw (see Figure 5.33).

Figure 5.33 Hacksawing the SCSI Terminator

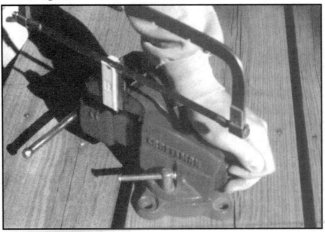

Figures 5.34 and 5.35 show the finished product: a nice square unit with the cables neatly protruding from the back.

Figure 5.34 Completed Hard Drive, Front

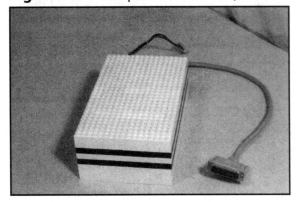

Figure 5.35 Completed Hard Drive, Back

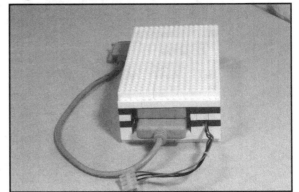

Encasing the Motherboard

The Mac SE motherboard is exactly 28 2x4 bricks wide, which will sit perfectly upon a baseplate (see Figure 5.36). However, doing so makes it nearly impossible to securely snap the motherboard on top of another component, but it gives us a lower-profile motherboard.

Figure 5.36 Baseplate

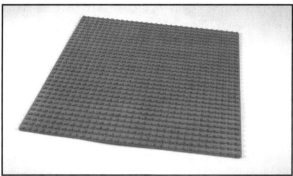

If you lack a baseplate or want the ability to snap the motherboard on top of another component, layering and gluing 2x4 bricks will also work well here. For this example, we used a baseplate for the bottom. The layering scheme, with gluing, is used for the top (see Figure 5.38). The back is left open, but cutting the shielding down to the right height (see Figure 5.37) will give it a nice, finished look, as shown in Figure 5.38. Figure 5.40 shows the top, with the hole left for the analog cable. I used black bricks for part of the underside because I was short on green.

Figure 5.37 Cutting the Shielding

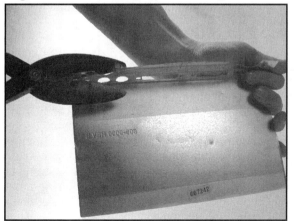

Figure 5.38 Underside of the Motherboard's Cover

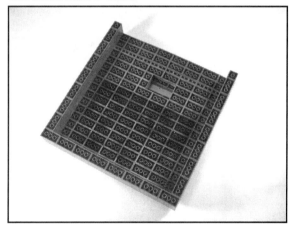

Figure 5.39 Partially Assembled Motherboard

Figure 5.40 shows us the completed motherboard case. Note the hole left for the analog cable, denoted by the arrow.

Figure 5.40 The Finished Motherboard Enclosure

Encasing the CRT

Mounting the CRT to the analog board is tricky because we're no longer using the original plastic encasements. We will first use Erector set beams to build a frame across the top and bottom and down the side of the CRT, then connect it to the analog board using the holes already available (see Figure 5.41). Use whatever Erector set pieces you have available to build a frame that extends from the back, affixing to the analog board using the holes already present. Then extend beams from the CRT to the brackets in the back (see Figure 5.42) Connect the grounding wires (circled in Figure 5.43) anywhere on the frame. Figures 5.43 and 5.44 show the back of the completed CRT and analog board structure.

Figure 5.41 CRT and Analog Board Structure, Front View

Figure 5.42 Affixing Erector Set Pieces

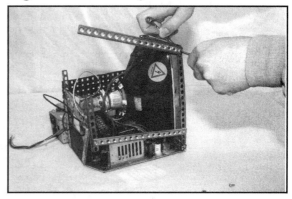

Figure 5.43 Completed CRT Structure, Top View

Figure 5.44 Completed CRT Structure, Bottom View

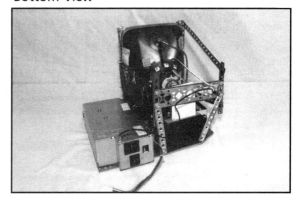

Since the cable that runs from the analog board to the motherboard must reach outside of your CRT case, it must be extended. To do this:

1. Cut the cable in half (see Figure 5.45) and use your stripper to bare the edges (see Figure 5.46).

2. Then crimp both ends to a new series of wires (see Figure 5.47), each about two feet long.

Figure 5.45 Cutting the Wire

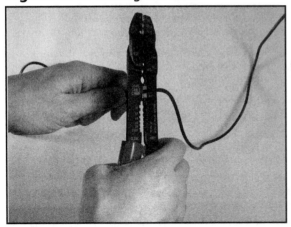

Figure 5.46 Stripping the Wire

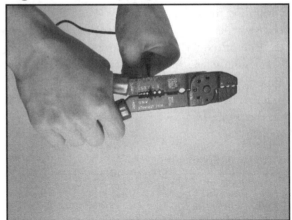

Figure 5.47 Crimping the Wire

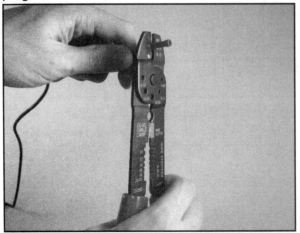

3. Begin the Mega Bloks construction by building a base large enough for the CRT, analog board, and power supply (Figure 5.48). Build support beams for the CRT and glue them into place. You can see these black beams in Figure 5.48, holding up the CRT. The beams are then built up the sides.

Figure 5.48 CRT on a Mega Bloks Base

4. As you build, leave a hole in the front around the contrast knob. You'll also need to leave a hole in the back for the cable. The cable is already wired into place, so when you reach the height at which you want it, just build around it. Likewise, build around the power supply and the fan, so they are even with the back.

5. Build the top using the layering technique (Figure 5.49) and gently snap it into place. Figure 5.50 shows an almost complete CRT encasement.

Figure 5.49 Top of the CRT, Built with Layering

Figure 5.50 CRT Nearing Completion

How the Hack Works

Now that we're finished preparing the individual components, we can snap them together and arrange them in whatever manner you desire. Using a few extra blocks to widen the top of the

Compubrick, we can place the floppy drive and hard drive side by side, as shown in Figure 5.51, or we can spread everything out, like Figure 5.52.

Figure 5.51 Compubrick SE, Partially Stacked Setup

Figure 5.52 Compubrick SE, Wide Setup

If we want a compact, minimalist system, the hard drive and speaker can be removed and the motherboard stacked on top of the CRT. The analog cable that comes out of the top of the motherboard prevents us from putting the disk drive directly on top, but a set of legs (in white) for the floppy drive quickly fixes that problem (see Figure 5.53).

Figure 5.53 Compubrick SE, Minimal Setup

Building a UFO Mouse

"Today we brought romance and innovation back into the industry," Steve Jobs proclaimed as he introduced the iMac on May 6, 1998. It was the dawn of a new era for Apple. Gone was SCSI, gone was ADB, and *gone was beige*. Heralded as the most innovative computer since the original Macintosh, the iMac was as revolutionary in its industrial design as it was in its architecture. Curved sheets of translucent

"Bondi Blue" plastics replaced the old beige metal cases with rigid corners. Apple's new design was an instant hit, and soon the entire industry was following suit, rounding their corners and making their plastics translucent. Few matched the elegance of the iMac, with its close attention to detail.

Even the iMac's mouse sported a unique new design (see Figure 5.54). Perfectly round, the iMac mouse was denounced for its ergonomics but lauded for its style. At the iMac's introduction, the translucent mouse was set upon a lighted pedestal, causing it to glow and leading to rumors the mouse itself was lit. The rumors were false but, for the aspiring hacker, inspirational.

The goal of this hack is to modify a standard Apple USB Mouse to add an LED, giving the mouse a glowing appearance.

Figure 5.54 Apple USB Mouse

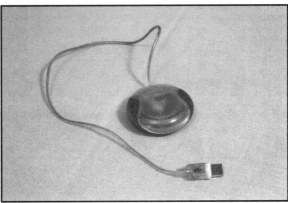

 ## Preparing for the Hack

The UFO mouse is a simple hack to perform and requires relatively few parts or tools. A picture of the materials is shown in Figure 5.55. The components that you will need outlined in Table 5.3.

Figure 5.55 Getting Ready for the UFO Mouse Hack

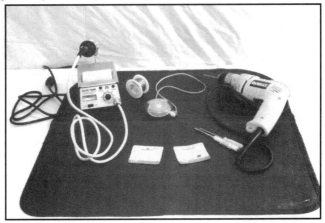

Table 5.3 Required Components for the UFO Mouse Hack

Component	Notes
Apple USB mouse	Also known as the "puck mouse"
Blue LED	Radio Shack Part #276-311, 5V, T1 3/4 size

The tools that are required for this hack are described in Table 5.4.

Table 5.4 Required Tools for the UFO Mouse Hack

Tool	Notes
Soldering iron and solder	
Drill and 7/32-inch drill bit	
Small flat-head screwdriver	
Small Philips screwdriver	
Small jeweler's screwdriver	

As an alternative to the blue LED, Radio Shack also sells a blinking red LED, part #276-036, that runs off 5V and will work in the mouse. If you want something a bit wilder (and potentially headache inducing), consider this LED in lieu of the blue one.

Performing the Hack

Building an illuminated puck mouse consists of four steps:

1. Opening the mouse
2. Drilling the hole
3. Soldering the LED
4. Reassembling the mouse

Opening the Mouse

1. You'll see a translucent blue plastic covering on both the right and left sides of the mouse. To open the mouse, you'll have to remove this covering. The plastic coverings are each attached to the body of the mouse with three tabs. The locations of the tabs are shown in Figure 5.56.

Figure 5.56 Tab Locations on the Plastic Covering

2. With a small flat screwdriver, gently pry the two tabs on the mouse's underside loose and then wiggle the third one free (see Figure 5.57).

Figure 5.57 Removing the Plastic Coverings

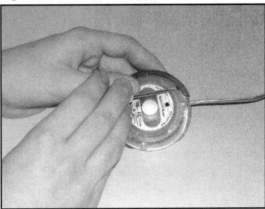

3. With the plastic coverings removed, locate the two screws on the bottom of the mouse that were previously hidden (Figure 5.58). Using a small jeweler's screwdriver, remove these two screws and then pry upward on the back end of the plastic casing to remove the top cover.

Figure 5.58 Unscrewing the Mouse

Drilling the Hole

To achieve a more diffused glow that really illuminates your puck mouse, you need to drill a hole into the ball chamber and point the LED into it.

1. Remove the circuit board from the mouse and place it as far away as the cable will allow (see Figure 5.59).

Figure 5.59 The Circuit Board Removed from the Case

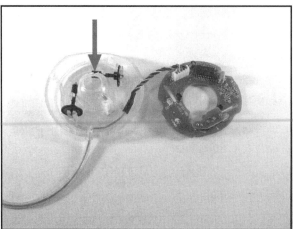

2. Using the 7/32-inch drill bit, drill a hole into the backside of the mouse housing (the side opposite the button), as indicated by the arrow in Figure 5.59. The hole should be just low enough so that the rim around the top of the chamber will not be broken. The proper positioning of the drill is shown in Figure 5.60.

Figure 5.60 Drilling the Hole

Soldering the LED

Now that the hole is prepared in the plastic mouse housing, it's time to attach the LED to the mouse.

NEED TO KNOW... **LED POLARITY**

An LED typically has two leads projecting from its base (see Figure 5.61). The longer lead is the positive lead (also known as the *anode*). The shorter lead is the negative lead (also known as the *cathode*). The cathode is also denoted by a flat edge on the plastic LED housing. The anode will connect to a positive voltage (5V in this case) and the cathode will connect to ground.

Figure 5.61 LED Diagram

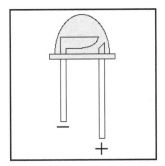

1. Turn the mouse so that the cable is facing away from you (Figure 5.62). Opposite the cable, you should notice that there are five pins outlined in white.

Figure 5.62 Close-Up of the Pins

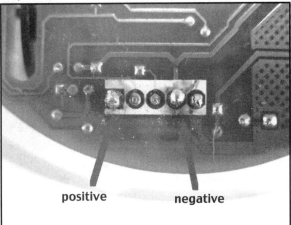

positive   negative

2. Snip the leads on the LED so that they are the appropriate length to reach from these pins into the hole that you drilled.

3. Now solder the positive lead of the LED to the leftmost pin (Figure 5.63). If you turn the circuit board over, you'll see that the wire going into this pin is red.

4. Next, solder the negative lead (the flat side of the LED) to the second pin from the right. If you turn the circuit board over, you'll see that the wire going into this pin is black.

WARNING: HARDWARE HARM

When soldering the LED to the circuit board, be careful not to heat up the device too much or cause any surrounding pins to be lifted up or shorted together with solder. The pins are very close together, and you might want to use a magnifying glass to inspect your work.

Figure 5.63 Soldering the LED

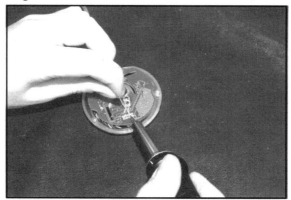

Reassembling the Mouse

Now put your mouse back together:

1. Carefully adjust the head of the LED to stick into the hole you drilled in the plastic housing. Be careful not to snap the LED off the circuit board. Make sure the circuit board is firmly connected to the base. Two spokes stick up from the base, one in the upper right and one in the lower left. Make sure these spokes go through the appropriate holes in the circuit board, rather than allowing the board to rest on top of them. When properly aligned, the board will fit snugly on the posts (see Figure 5.64).

Figure 5.64 Properly Aligned Mouse

2. Finally, take the plastic cover and place the tabs on its front into the corresponding slots on the base. Then snap the backside of the two pieces together (see Figure 5.65).

Figure 5.65 Closing the Mouse

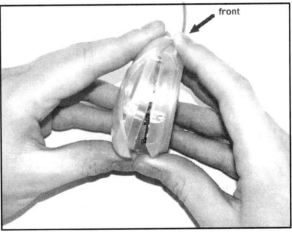

3. Return the two screws and snap the plastic sides into place. The hack is now complete!

Figure 5.66 shows a picture of the completed UFO mouse in all its glowing glory.

Figure 5.66 Completed UFO Mouse

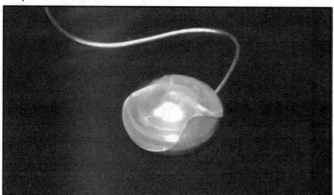

How the Hack Works

This hack is extremely simple—all we need to do is add an LED onto the circuit board of the USB mouse. The LED receives its power directly from the USB port, which provides a 5VDC supply. The LED is connected to the power supply using the two pads provided for us on the circuit board. Since we are using an LED with a forward voltage of 5V, we do not see a need to include a current-limiting resistor. Note that if any other LED is used, you may have to add a current-limiting resistor between the 5V supply line from the mouse and the positive lead of the LED—otherwise, you could damage the LED when it received power. See the "Electrical Engineering Basics" chapter and other LED hacks in this book for more details.

Adding Colored Skins to the Power Macintosh G4 Cube

One of the most popular consumer-based Macintosh systems from Apple Computer Inc. was the Power Mac G4 Cube (also known simply as the Cube), announced at MacWorld New York 2001. This machine's compact size and high CPU power made it an instant hit with users in every market who wanted a full-powered desktop computer in a tastefully artistic and compact enclosure. The G4 Cube was built to accept many of the same components as a full-size desktop computer, such as 3.5-inch hard disks, standard PC100 memory, and processor expansion cards.

Of course, the big downfall to all modern computer designs is the rapidly changing pace of technology. Eventually a machine, no matter how cool and sexy it is, is overtaken by the next new interesting design. Although the G4 Cube's lifespan far exceeds that of most personal computers, it is true that this wonderful machine is leaning toward obsolescence. However, a growing community of die-hard Cube fans, including myself, will go to great lengths to keep their machines useful.

This hack allows you to change the external appearance of your G4 Cube from the original, boring gray to any design you choose. You can make your Cube any color you want. Since the Cube comes in a gray metal box suspended inside a clear plastic box, any design that can be put to paper can be inlaid inside the cube.

This construction also has the advantage of protecting your artwork from external abrasions due to handling. However, the clear plastic case is far from scratch proof, so handle with care.

Preparing for the Hack

To prepare for this hack, you need to choose the artwork for your case design. Literally thousands of public domain textures are available online for free download, or you could create your own custom design in any number of art programs, such as Adobe Illustrator. A "wrappable" texture design flows from the edge of one sheet of paper perfectly to the second sheet, creating an appearance of the design being on one single, long sheet of paper. Instructions on how to create your own wrappable artwork for your cube are available at www.resexcellence.com/hack_html_00/12-15-00.shtml.

WARNING: HARDWARE HARM

If you decide to print out your own texture, be aware that the pigments printed by thermal printers (e.g., laser or dye sublimation) can adhere to the plastic shell of the Cube when the machine heats up. This will cause inconsistencies in the appearance of the texture, and if the shell is removed later, the texture will be destroyed. Excess pigment left inside the clear shell can be removed with rubbing alcohol and a soft cotton cloth.

The parts required for this hack are shown in Table 5.5.

Table 5.5 Required Components for the Colored Skins Hack

Component	Notes
Custom texture design	Paper design 7.25 inches square, 5 sheets of 8.5 x 11-inch paper
Glossy clear tape	Scotch Transparent Tape 600, 1/2-inch width
Felt-tip marker	As close to texture color as possible

The tools required for this hack are listed in Table 5.6.

Table 5.6 Required Tools for the Colored Skins Hack

Tool	Notes
Small Phillips screwdriver	
Scissors	
Torx screwdriver, size T-10	Available at most hardware stores
X-ACTO knife	
Cloth gloves	Optional—to prevent leaving fingerprints on the plastic casing

Performing the Hack

1. The first step in the hack is to open your G4 Cube by removing the screws that hold the acrylic cube in place. Remove the Cube core (the actual CPU that sits inside the clear case) and set it aside someplace safe.

2. Inside the shell you will find two Phillips head screws and four T-10 Torx screws (see Figure 5.67). Remove all six screws.

Figure 5.67 Screw Locations Inside the G4 Cube

3. Next, you must remove the black screen grate that covers the vent slots on top, also shown in Figure 5.67. The easiest way to do this is to unhook the screen and then lift up the shell. The grill should drop away. Once the grill is gone, you can remove the metal shell from inside the plastic shell. Be careful not to touch the inside of the plastic shell unless you're wearing cloth gloves or you'll leave fingerprints in it.

WARNING: PERSONAL INJURY

The hobby knife used for preparing your custom skin is extremely sharp. Extra care should be taken to always cut in a direction away from your body.

4. The next step in the hack is to prepare the texture sheets to be inserted into the Cube case. The hardest part of this exercise is the top sheet. Fortunately, Apple was kind enough to provide a "template." For our purposes, the template is a plastic sheet with all the slots and holes traced in it. This sheet lies between the metal shell and the acrylic case. Simply lay the Apple template on top of your printed texture and use it as a guide to carefully cut out the openings with an X-ACTO knife (see Figure 5.68). The smaller holes should be traced with a pencil or fine-point marker before cutting.

Figure 5.68 Using the Included Template

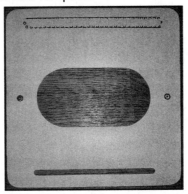

5. Run a felt marker that matches the color scheme of your wrappable skin all around the top and bottom edges of the metal box. This will help conceal your seams once you apply your texture sheets to the Cube core.

6. Tape two pages of the artwork to the Cube core, as shown in Figure 5.69. You will have to pull these sheets rather tightly to avoid any wrinkling of the paper when you slide the clear case back over the core.

Figure 5.69 Applying the Texture Sheets

7. Apply the two remaining panels for the top and the rear of the Cube core, lining up the edges with the front of the Cube. Secure these sheets using a piece of clear tape at least 8 inches long. Make sure that the ends of the tape are cut with scissors, rather than torn with your fingers, to ensure a smooth edge. Make sure to trim any excess tape once you have tightly wrapped the Cube design. Using this method, your seams will be placed on the corners and thus make the seams much less visible. Figure 5.70 shows a close-up of the finished seam.

Figure 5.70 Taping the Seams

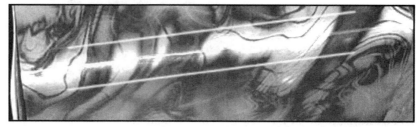

8. After every sheet is secure, carefully return the wrapped core Cube back into the acrylic shell. You might want to run a clean cloth around the inside of the shell to remove any fingerprints or debris.

Once the Cube is fully assembled, your hack is complete! Figure 5.70 shows my personal G4 Cube with a custom skin.

Figure 5.71 G4 Cube with a Custom Skin

Under the Hood: How the Hack Works

All we are doing for this hack is slipping colored paper between the clear plastic outer shell and the gray metal box of the G4 Cube. The thick plastic causes some interesting visual effects with certain abstract designs, so experiment with various colors and shapes. The protection of the clear shell will keep your art looking great for years to come. Just be sure to keep your custom Cube away from direct sunlight.

Other Hacks and Resources

This chapter includes only the beginning of the things that you can do to your Mac. The following are lists of some of our favorites!

Desktop Hacks

- **Compubrick 160: www.applefritter.com/compubrick/compubrick160** The original Mega Blocks Macintosh.

- **DLZ-3: www.applefritter.com/hacks/dlz3** Devin Durham's Mac in a 1940's Zenith Radio case. Note the beautiful CD-ROM drive.

- **030 MacAquarium: www.applefritter.com/hacks/68Kfish** Jeff Knox turned his SE/30 into an aquarium—and it still runs!

- **Duo Digital Frame: www.applefritter.com/hacks/duodigitalframe** This elegant hack by James Roos places a Powerbook screen inside a picture frame.

- **Ze PowerSuitcase: www.applefritter.com/hacks/zepowersuitcase** Bernard Bélanger built his Macintosh into a suitcase.

- **Red Rocket: www.applefritter.com/hacks/redrocket** This rugged case was built from scratch by Mark Fisher to house his Power Mac 7300.

- **21" iMac: www.applefritter.com/hacks/21imac** Don Hardy rebuilt the original iMac, with its 15-inch display, into a 21-inch Nokia monitor.

Laptop Hacks

- **Tron Book: www.applefritter.com/hacks/tronbook** icruise stripped the paint off his iBook with alcohol, then painted the case a translucent blue.

- **ZebraBook: www.applefritter.com/hacks/zebrabook** In this simple hack, Mark Herbert replaced half of his Powerbook's black keys with white keys from an iBook, creating an elegant "zebra" effect.

- **Monster Ti: www.applefritter.com/hacks/monster_ti** Ted Warren painted his Powerbook G4 black, then added flames.

- **TiDrag: www.applefritter.com/hacks/tidrag** Artist Marek Jusiega used aerograph painting techniques to create this masterpiece on the back of a Powerbook G4.

Electrical and Optical Hacks

- **IlluminatedMac: www.applefritter.com/hacks/illuminatedmac** Matt Riley used electro-luminescent string to make this iMac glow.

- **Metamorphosis: www.applefritter.com/hacks/metamorphosis** Mad Dog soldered two additional PCI slots into his Umax J700 Macintosh clone.

- **Blue Ice G4: www.applefritter.com/hacks/blueiceg4** Kent Salas used neon and cold cathode tubes to make this G4 glow an icy blue.

- **BlueCube: www.applefritter.com/hacks/bluecube** Richard Chang added cold cathode tubes to his Power Mac Cube.

Case Mods

- **Mercury: www.applefritter.com/hacks/mercury** Myles Robinson used automotive paint to make this Mac Classic look stunning. Wax regularly.

- **Hal: www.applefritter.com/hacks/hal** This Mac Classic by Shane Hale features a case window and an eerie paint job.

- **MacRock: www.applefritter.com/hacks/macrock** Mike @ pigpen digital used "Stone Creation" paint to give his Mac a rugged look.

- **Candy Apple: www.applefritter.com/hacks/candy_apple** Alison Friedman used Clear Candy Apple Red Spray to paint this stunning Power Mac 7300.

Software

- **ResExcellence: www.resexcellence.com** Mac OS customizations.

- **The Iconfactory: www.iconfactory.com** A collection of beautifully rendered icons.

- **Kaleidoscope: www.kaleidoscope.net** This software allows complete customization of the Macintosh interface.

Discussion

- **Applefritter Forums:** www.applefritter.com
- **MacAddict Forums:** www.macaddict.com/phpBB2

Chapter 6

Home Theater PCs

Hacks in this Chapter:

- Before you Begin: Research and Plan

- The Components of an HTPC Project

- Building a Windows HTPC

- Building a Linux HTPC

- Further Hacking and Advanced Topics

Introduction

An oversimplified definition of a *home theater PC* (HTPC) is a customized computer that connects to your entertainment system and is used to play video and audio information. A more complete definition could include discussions about specific functions, such as DVD playback, video capture, CD ripping, and many others. We cover these functions in this chapter, but for now let's just say that there are as many different types of HTPCs as there are HTPC builders. Examples of commercial, pre-built HTPCs include TiVo, ReplayTV, and networked DVD players. So if you don't see exactly what you're looking for among the examples in this chapter, fear not. A little ingenuity and a lot of research can show you the way.

This chapter covers a slightly different kind of hacking than many of the other chapters in this book. Other hacks in this book cover ways to make a piece of hardware less restrictive than originally intended or to modify a product to make it do something it wasn't intended to do. To be sure, some HTPC hacks have those aspects, depending on what you are doing. However, if you turn into a full-blown HTPC enthusiast, chances are excellent that you will *not* be saving money over what you would buy off-the-shelf to perform similar functions. If you'd like to go the inexpensive route, there are ways to do so, but that's less often what HTPC builders are after.

Generally, most HTPC projects feature two central themes:

- Control
- Aesthetics

The HTPC hackers who are after control are typically concerned with flexibility. Maybe they want more hard disk space than can be bought in a stock unit. Maybe they are concerned that they won't be able to play newer video files when the formats are updated. Whatever the concern is, HTPC control hackers have a goal of creating an HTPC that incorporates the desired functions they want and that those functions work the way they want them to.

The aesthetics aspect is also very interesting. Most of you reading this book will be familiar to some degree with *case modding*, the art of carving up your computer case to make it more personalized and appealing. Aesthetic HTPC building is related but different. Usually, the idea with an HTPC is to *not* make it look like a computer. Many of the HTPC cases on the market are designed to look like high-end AV equipment. You might be hard pressed to spot a well-done HTPC in a rack of other AV gear. Often the cases are horizontal (think back to the old "mini-desktop"-style cases), are silver or black, have hidden drives, and in some cases, have just a power button for visible front controls.

Given the massive number of combinations of features, hardware devices, operating systems, and control devices, it is impossible to comprehensively cover HTPCs in one chapter. Couple the enormous breadth of knowledge available with the evolution speed of HTPC-related topics, and it becomes apparent that trying to cover *everything* is hopeless. Rather, in this chapter we cover terminology and technology as it exists today and where it *might* be going tomorrow and demonstrate some arrangements with a few concrete examples.

This chapter is primarily written for HTPC novices. However, to fully make use of this chapter, readers should have some experience building their own PCs. An HTPC project isn't the most forgiving for learning how to assemble your first custom PC.

Before You Begin: Research and Plan

One of the more difficult aspects of HTPC projects is the fact that you need to understand the jargon from numerous industries. HTPCs unite the industries of PCs, video, audio, and sometimes even satellite, cable, and radio. For example, one of the most commonly discussed topics is connecting a PC to a TV.

HTPCs can range from simple to complex, inexpensive to exorbitant in price; therefore, it's important that you plan your projects very carefully. The last 20 percent of your project may be fine-tuning your interface and fighting with drivers, but if you spend 80 percent of your resources and time up front researching, reading, and verifying interoperability before you ever buy anything, you will save yourself a lot of time, trouble, and investment.

NEED TO KNOW... CONVENTIONS AND DISCLAIMERS

I live in the United States. Like most Americans, I suffer from a U.S.-centric view of things. This includes prices (which are listed in this chapter in U.S. dollars), standards, services, and laws. I talk about NTSC in this chapter. Other parts of the world use PAL or SECAM. These standards are comparable to NTSC, if slightly better. NTSC is the North American TV broadcast standard, and is defined in a bit more detail shortly. Phase Alternating Line (PAL) is the standard used in much of Europe. SECAM (whose acronym only makes sense in French) is the standard used in much of Africa, and the parts of Europe not using PAL. However, when I later say that NTSC offers poor quality for graphics display, the same applies to PAL and SECAM, even though they offer a slight increase in picture quality.

When I talk about cable and satellite, I'm referring to how they exist in the United States. I talk about a lack of high-definition TV (HDTV) programming, and I understand that in other parts of the world HDTV is more readily available. Please adjust any information given to suit your locale.

The legal area is one in particular that varies greatly from place to place; it's not a technology or standard that we can simply convert. For example, in parts of this chapter I talk about ripping DVDs. Depending on where you live, this activity might get you in some trouble. This is true even in (or especially in) the United States. Just because I might *show* you how to do something doesn't necessarily mean that it's *legal* for you to do it. In the United States, we have the Digital Millennium Copyright Act (DMCA), which prohibits some of these activities. Other countries have similar laws. If you have any doubt whatsoever about the legality of topics discussed in your area, please consult your attorney before proceeding.

For a successful HTPC project, planning is essential. The very last thing you want is to find out after you've purchased everything you need that some expensive component such as a high-end video card or television set won't work with the rest of your system. Such a mistake can set you back hundreds or even thousands of dollars. You can avoid the vast majority of these mistakes by researching the components on the Internet. There's always a slim chance that you'll be the first to get "into" a particular area, if you like living on the bleeding edge, but most of the time, someone else has tried and failed, or they've succeeded, and they can tell you what they think of the setup. If you are the type that likes being the first to try hacking the hardware, pay special attention to the return policy of the store where you buy your gear.

NOTE

 Interested in reading about what other HTPC hackers are doing? What they're working on? What their problems are? I recommend you review the archives of the AVS Forums HTPC forum. This is probably the best online community for HTPC information. You can access it at www.avsforum.com/avs-vb/forumdisplay.php?forumid=11.

The first thing you should do is create a list of the functions that you want your HTPC to perform. Here's a partial list of functions that you might include on your list:

- Video capture
- Video playing
- DVD playing
- DVD ripping
- CD playing
- CD ripping
- TV time shifting/pausing
- High-end audio playback
- Surround-sound decoding
- Videogames
- Web surfing/general computing

This list is not intended to be comprehensive. Anything you can do with a computer, you can do with an HTPC. After all, it *is* a PC—just one assembled with a particular purpose in mind: to drive your TV and home stereo system (or equivalents).

Several of the items on the list are obviously very related. For example, you're really not going to have the ability to do DVD ripping without also being able to play DVDs, too, if you choose to do so.

How Much Could It Cost?

Allow us to take a moment to revisit the issue of cost and reiterate that HTPCs are often not about saving money. For the sake of discussion, say that you merely want to play DVDs. To do so with an HTPC, you need a PC, a DVD drive, an operating system, a decent video card and CPU, and some way to accept input from a remote control. In your head, calculate how much you think all that will cost you. New, used, doesn't really matter. Now, think to yourself how long the PC will take to boot up and be ready to play a DVD. Picture what happens to the files on the hard drive when the PC gets powered off without a proper shutdown.

Now, compare this figure and the complications with cost and ease of a factory-built DVD player. An inexpensive DVD player can be obtained for less than $50 and will be ready to play DVDs a few seconds after you turn it on. It (hopefully) will easily connect to your TV. You can power it off manually if your remote is lost or destroyed, or a generic replacement can typically be purchased for approximately $7. Also, if you don't do a good job of picking your HTPC components, a factory-built DVD player's output will probably look *better* on the screen than your HTPC, and it probably won't be as noisy.

Abandon all hope of flawless, economical home theatre, ye who enter here! If, however, you derive satisfaction from doing it yourself, and costs be damned, then read on …

Did Someone Already Build It?

Let's assume that your list of features includes the following:

- DVD playing
- CD playing
- CD ripping
- Surround-sound decoding
- Videogames

Guess what? That's an Xbox. With no modification, a $170 Xbox (plus $40 in accessories) will play DVDs with Dolby 5.1 sound, play CDs (and copy the music onto the built-in hard drive for you), and allow you to play videogames—no hacking or modding required.

Obviously, the Xbox may not be what you wanted, even if the list of functions exactly matches what you need. For one, it may just look wrong. Maybe you don't want a black and green plastic case with the rest of your AV equipment. Maybe an Xbox has too much functionality. For example, my wife *doesn't* want the videogame function, something to do with the kids having more than enough things to waste their time on. Fortunately, it's pretty easy to disable the game functionality on an Xbox if you like, with the simple addition of a modchip with an open-source BIOS replacement.

The point here is: has someone already built the features you want into an existing, (relatively) inexpensive piece of consumer hardware? If so, you have to weigh your needs against the benefits and the cost of purchasing a ready-made item. Maybe the Xbox isn't particularly physically attractive, but is the aesthetic factor worth spending an additional $800 on parts and HTPC components that would look much nicer near the TV? On the other hand, maybe the Xbox does what you need right now, but it has no expansion slots. Maybe you can shoehorn the TV capture function in by modding the box to run your own software and attaching a USB TV capture device to one of the front controller ports, but are you concerned that at some point you'll just run out of power on the Xbox? Of course you are! Therefore, you must have the $1,000 custom HTPC. Read on …

The Components of an HTPC Project

The bulk of the work for planning an HTPC project involves making a detailed list of components that will go into it. In some ways, this is similar to building a custom PC from parts purchased at the local computer shop or by mail order. However, in other ways it's a bit backwards from what you are used to, depending on the factors you consider most important. It's possible to build a variety of configurations, some of which will separate some of the functions to a central server and allow you to access them over a network. Until we get into that discussion in detail, I'll refer to the box attached directly to the TV as the *set-top box* and the central server as a *media server*.

At the very least, for a standard HTPC, you will require the following parts:

- A case
- A motherboard
- A CPU
- Memory
- An optical drive
- A boot device
- A hard drive
- A network card
- A video card
- A sound card
- A keyboard
- A mouse

As always, these lists are merely suggestions. Some components may need to be added, others may need to be left off, depending on the functions you've picked. For example, for playing or ripping physical DVDs, you'll obviously require a DVD drive. If you're not performing those activities, maybe an optical drive is not required at all, or maybe you may just require a temporary CD-ROM drive to install the OS software.

That's where the similarities end. Contrary to what you're probably used to, you could find that you have to begin your entire design with the case. Or you might have to start with the video card and ensure that everything else works with that. You may find that your choice of operating system severely restricts the hardware you can consider, much more so than usual. You might have to plan for a setup that can boot quickly or tolerate being powered off (or maybe hibernated) at will. How about the keyboard and mouse? Chances are, you're not planning to have your HTPC at a desk. In fact, most of the time, you'll want to use a remote control for playback purposes, but if you plan to use your HTPC to surf the Web, you'll require a keyboard and a mouse. That almost always means you'll need some kind of wireless keyboard and mouse (or mouse substitute) setup.

Here are some brief constraints to keep in mind before we get to the parts details:

- If you're planning to use a special enclosure for your HTPC, you may have to pick that first and work from there. Sometimes, size really *does* matter.

- If you'll be working with a lot of video input and output, that will often determine the types of video cards, OSs, motherboards, and cases that you can consider.

- If you require optical drives, your case will have to accommodate those. For example, if you are planning a compact setup, you may have to look for slimmer laptop DVD drives, which are more expensive.

- Will you use any functions that require a keyboard and mouse? Look for wireless. If not, can you do everything you need from the remote? Do you need to consider a remote with a mouse function?

- If you're going to capture video, you'll want to get tons of disk space.

- Don't forget about noise! You don't want to be able to hear the HTPC fans and drives over the movie, or when you're trying to sleep.

Beyond whether your parts will work together, your biggest external constraint is the kinds of inputs and outputs of your non-HTPC devices (such as your television and audio receiver). We'll talk about the different signal and connector standards throughout the chapter.

Chances are, you'll want to be able to drive the rest of your AV equipment in the optimum manner from your HTPC, at least within your budget. For example, if you have an audio receiver that can take fiber optic inputs, you might want to make sure you have audio hardware on the HTPC that has fiber optic outputs. More important (for most people), you'll want to be able to drive your television at the absolute best quality mode possible. This is especially important if you plan to display anything on the television besides video, such as text or icons.

The Display

Regular (non-HD) television sets are highly unsuitable for displaying small text and icons. This is due to the fact that they incorporate relatively low-resolution displays. For example, the National Television Standards Committee (NTSC) standard, which has been employed in North America for the past 50 years, is theoretically about 640 × 480 resolution. Have you tried running your computer monitor at 640 × 480, lately? You'll see what I mean. But it's worse than that, because the "pixels" on a standard television are about twice as fuzzy in the horizontal direction as compared to a standard VGA monitor. For all intents and purposes, this means that you're able to display about half as many characters across the TV screen as you would be able to display on a low-res VGA monitor, in order to cleanly tell them apart. This is an oversimplification, however; you should forget about plugging your desktop PC into the TV in your den and being able to surf the Web the way you typically do. If you are an older reader, you'll recall that at the introduction of 8-bit computers you could only view between 22 and 40 columns of text on your TV.

This does not mean that you *have* to invest in a new HDTV. Your existing TV will display video as well as it ever did. If that's what you are after, then no problem. Still pictures will look a bit fuzzy. And you *can* do text—you just have to account for what is going to be readable. So, if you want an interface that shows movie or song titles, you can do it—you just have to plan for fewer lines of titles per screen than what you're used to on your desktop monitor. To illustrate this idea, consider that most cable or satellite systems have some kind of program-listing channel or functions. Take a look at yours, and count how many lines of text are showing on any given screen. Figures 6.1 and 6.2 are examples of the Program Guide from Comcast, a digital cable company.

Ignoring the fact that a large portion of the screen has been used for advertising, look at the amount of text that is visible on the screens. In each screen, approximately one-third is used for text, so triple that number, vertically. Additionally, about one-fifth of the screen is utilized horizontally to show the channel numbers. In Figure 6.1, you're seeing about three lines of text using that kind of separator line, so you could guesstimate a full screen is nine or 10 lines high.

Figure 6.1 Screen Capture of the TV Guide Channel

For a more compact example, look at Figure 6.2. The bottom portion of the screen shows several lines of text packed together, paragraph style. That's four lines in about one-fifth the height of the screen, so you could again guesstimate that the screen is about 20 lines high using this style. The middle line is about 46 characters wide, in a proportionally spaced font. If it were the full width of the screen, it would extend to about 57 characters.

■ If you need to install a couple of cards, the case has to accommodate those. Even if you've got a motherboard with slots, keep in mind that not all horizontal cases have room for cards to stand up in the slots, or even the spaces in the back where the back of the card goes. Some cases mount the cards horizontally, too, and you have to have a riser of some sort that your cards plug into. This may accommodate only one or two cards.

To give you an idea, look at some examples of the Hush Technologies Silent Mini-ITX PC extreme cases (http://mini-itx.com/store/hush.asp) from Mini-itx.com, shown in Figures 6.3 and 6.4. From the outside, the case is simplicity itself and looks like a piece of high-end audio gear.

Figure 6.3 An Exterior View of the Silent Mini-ITX PC Case (Photo Courtesy of Mini-itx.com)

Figure 6.4 An Interior View of the Silent Mini-ITX PC Case (Photo Courtesy of Mini-itx.com)

This PC is based on the VIA Epia M10000 motherboard. As you can see, everything fits together rather tightly. It uses a slim laptop-style CD or DVD drive and can fit a 3.5-inch hard drive and one PCI card. The card goes in the upper left corner of Figure 6.4 and plugs into a riser, which plugs into the motherboard. The motherboard even has TV-out, so this could be someone's ideal HTPC, as long as they can live with the somewhat limited amount of CPU power.

The Hard Drives

If you're going to do anything besides play optical disks (and if *that's* all you want, you'd probably be better served by a quality DVD player), you're going to need some mass storage *somewhere* in your HTPC setup. I say "somewhere" because it is entirely possible to have the bulk of your storage located in a server; separate from the box that actually drives your video and audio. Keep in mind that the set-top box may still require enough storage to boot up the OS. This storage could be something solid-state, such as a Flash ROM device. Alternately, if you like, you can boot Linux entirely off the network. The option of having no hard drive in the set-top box may be particularly attractive if you're trying to go for small, reliable, and silent.

The remainder of the HTPC network setup is explored later in the chapter. For the moment, let's limit the discussion to drives physically installed in the set-top box. As a quick reminder, here is a partial list of functions that require mass storage:

- Video capture
- CD/DVD ripping
- TV time shifting/pausing
- Media file storage
- Videogames
- General desktop use

If you plan to save any TV shows that you've captured or create a media library of MP3s or video clips that you've downloaded or ripped, you will require a hard drive. Furthermore, you're going to need a *large* one, or possibly even more than one. How much space do you need? It depends entirely on the resolution and video codec you use, of course. Consider a couple of examples:

- NTSC quality using MPEG2 uses approximately 1 gigabyte per hour.
- DVD quality in its native format (also MPEG2) uses around 5 or 6 gigabytes for a typical two-hour movie.

NOTE

Using the latter example, you'll fit about 15 DVD movies on an 80-gigabyte drive.

This brings us to a couple of performance characteristics of hard drives that are critical for HTPC applications:

- Speed
- Noise

Your drive must be fast enough to keep up with the data streaming in and out, and it must be quiet enough so that it doesn't disturb you while you're trying to watch TV or maybe sleep in the same room. For TV recording, the HTPC will most likely have to be operating 24 hours a day, 7 days a week, 365 days a year.

A popular choice is the Sound Blaster Audigy 2 family, which supports pretty much all of the important PC sound standards, and is an excellent choice for gamers. Another is the M-Audio Revolution 7.1. For sound mixing applications, the M-Audio Audiophile 2496 has a good reputation. The M-Audio cards seem to be somewhat better supported under Linux, if that's a consideration for you.

The Controller

In most cases it is desirable to have some sort of remote control device with which to control your HTPC. When performing maintenance tasks, you will also probably want to have real keyboard and mouse capability, but the bulk of the time you will want to use a remote control. There are a fair number of remotes on the market, although you won't find them in your local stores—you'll have to order them. Most of the suitable remotes look like an elongated rectangle, similar to the remote controls that accompany any AV equipment. You will probably want your remote to have a mouse function, a numeric pad (for channel changing), channel and volume rockers, and a number of free programmable buttons to launch applications and such.

You don't necessarily have to get a remote specifically designed for HTPCs. You can get an infrared (IR) receiver and use any existing IR remote. However, these types of setups usually don't include a sufficient number of buttons, and you will probably miss having a mouse function. If you do decide to pursue the IR receiver route, make sure you get one that can "speak" consumer IR (CIR), which is the term for what most household remotes emit. Computers also do IrDA, which is a form of network communications over IR. The majority of IrDA equipment is *not* compatible with CIR.

The Software

Are we ready to open a can of worms? Let's discuss the operating system and application software you might want to use for the various HTPC functions. The first place to start is with the operating system. The two most viable operating systems with which most people could conceivably build an HTPC are:

- Microsoft Windows
- Linux

Did I leave out your favorite OS? If you'd like to proceed using another OS, please don't let us stop you. Most OSs can be manipulated to control your HTPC—they just require some work.

The main difficulty with other OSs is obtaining the right drivers. You need drivers for sound, graphics output, video capture, and DVD drives, among others. Most versions of UNIX can support graphics output to a degree, largely due to the Xfree86 project. DVD drives are often well supported. The major difficulties seem to arise with sound support and video capture. When considering hardware, be sure to spend extra time researching support for your choice of hardware, which is dependent on your choice of OS. I intend to provide information useful for both Windows and Linux. Each has its strengths and weaknesses. You have no doubt picked the OS you'd like to use, so read on for what it can do.

As an aside, Mac seems to have built-in support for many of these features, but the hardware options are perhaps a bit slimmer. In any case, I'll skip the Mac here in favor of the roll-your-own approach. We will say that Apple was "there" first by releasing the MacTV in 1993. Refer to Chapter 5 for some interesting Macintosh hacks, compliments of the team at Applefritter (www.applefritter.com).

NEED TO KNOW... THE HARD TRUTH ABOUT HTPC OSs

What it boils down to is that in terms of drivers, online help, places to ask questions, discussion forums, application software, and so on, Windows and Linux are the most popular OSs for HTPC purposes. Furthermore, most new hardware is better supported under Windows than Linux. You don't have to like it, but it's a market reality. There are many more Windows systems in the world, so for now it makes financial sense for most hardware vendors to offer primary software support for Windows and possibly secondary support for other OSs like Linux. By "better supported" I mean by the original hardware vendor. I am in no way disclaiming that some hardware may work better under Linux with the open-source drivers the community has come up with, or that the Linux community does a better job of supporting hardware which has been abandoned by the vendor. I like and use Linux myself and would be thrilled if all hardware vendors treated Linux as a first-class citizen in terms of drivers. I commend the ones that do.

I'm here to help enable and encourage Linux use for HTPCs. But I'm also a realist, and I am willing to admit that in some cases it may be easier for a user who is familiar with Windows to make a Windows HTPC support arbitrary hardware and get up and running more quickly. Personally, I find Linux a bit easier to customize to a given function, such as an HTPC (or a router or firewall) than Windows. Plus, who wants to buy another Windows license for the house if they don't have to?

The next step after picking your OS is to get it loaded. There are a number of versions of Windows to choose from. Currently the supported versions of Windows are:

- Windows Me
- Windows 2000
- Windows XP
- Windows Server 2003

"Currently supported" means that these versions are sold new and Microsoft still produces patches and updates for them. Of course, you can use an older version of Windows if you like, but you may find that it will eventually lag behind as Microsoft stops producing new updates for it. Hardware vendors tend to stop updating drivers for older versions of Windows as well.

We recommend going with Windows XP if we're buying new. We have found XP to be more stable than Me. Windows 2000 is architecturally similar to XP, but it contains less support for multimedia. Windows Server 2003 severely lacks multimedia drivers; therefore, we would not consider using it for HTPC purposes. Additionally, Windows Server 2003 is strictly a server platform, so it is significantly more expensive.

If you have chosen to use Windows XP, the question still remains as to which version you should use:

- Windows XP Home
- Windows XP Professional

Windows XP Professional costs approximately $100 more than the Home version of Windows XP; however, XP Professional provides a few features that might be of use to you. These include Remote Desktop (which allows you to remotely control the desktop with the Terminal Services client). This could be handy if you run the HTPC headless and the TV-out is not a primary display. There are also differences in file sharing and domain membership between XP Professional and XP Home. You also get the remote control feature for free with a program like VNC, but if you have a home domain for some reason, you can't join XP Home into a domain.

NOTE

A great side-by-side comparison of the XP Home and XP Professional versions is available online at www.microsoft.com/windowsxp/pro/howtobuy/choosing2.asp. For additional information on VNC, check out these two Web sites:

- www.realvnc.com
- www.tightvnc.com

You may be aware of the existence of a new version of Windows XP: Media Center Edition 2004 (www.microsoft.com/windowsxp/mediacenter). Right now this version is only available with the purchase of specific models of new PCs. Therefore you have to buy an entire Media Center PC model from a brand-name manufacturer. This might change at some point in the future, but at present it is not a feasible option for HTPC hackers.

For a Linux distribution, you will want to be sure to select a distro with above-average multimedia support. Some common Linux distros used by HTPCers are:

- **Red Hat** www.redhat.com
- **Debian** www.debian.org
- **Mandrake** www.mandrakesoft.com
- **Gentoo** www.gentoo.org
- **Suse** www.suse.com

If you already have a favorite Linux distro, go ahead and use that. One of the nice things about Linux is that, as a fundamental idea of the software, it is highly customizable. In this chapter you will have the opportunity to see a system that is running Red Hat. At the moment, Red Hat is in a state of flux as the distribution model moves toward a more community-supported distro, currently named Fedora. Red Hat Linux 9.0 should still be viable for the immediate future until Fedora is finalized.

Red Hat is a decent choice for beginners as well, since a lot of information about it is available online and the file distribution mechanism it uses (RPM) is fairly user-friendly for people who like to avoid compiling their own software when they can.

I won't cover how to actually install the operating systems here. The HTPC aspects shouldn't come into play immediately when installing the base OS. If you're planning an all-in-one set-top box (all components together in the same unit), this process will be much like installing the OS on any other PC. Some more exotic options might include booting entirely from the network or from a Flash card. Chances are that you'll have a much easier time doing that with Linux, since it is a well-documented option. It takes a little experimentation to get it working right, but it can be done. This is useful if you're planning a silent PC or a media server architecture.

Not to be outdone, Microsoft has released a version of Windows XP called Windows XP Embedded, which the company claims can also boot over a network or from a Flash card or read-only media. I haven't had an opportunity to try XP Embedded myself. However, you can obtain additional information on this topic at www.microsoft.com/windows/embedded/xp.

One of the reasons to be concerned with the variety of OS boot options is for the purpose of making your HTPC tolerant of being powered off without doing a proper shutdown. Think about power outages or small children who like to push buttons. These setups can often help speed boot time, too, if you don't plan to have it on all the time.

Once the base OS is installed, the next step is to get the drivers working. We show a couple of concrete examples later in the chapter, but for the moment we'll proceed with a high-level discussion. For Windows, the job is relatively easy, as long as you're not suffering from any hardware conflicts. Visit the Web site for each hardware vendor and download the latest driver. Of course, this has to be done after setting up your machine for Internet access. It never hurts to put your patches on *before* you connect to the Internet, if you can arrange it (such as retrieving them from an existing machine on your network). On the Linux side, you'll want to obtain the patches from your vendor, as well. In particular, look for any updates to the kernel and modprobe, sound drivers (ALSA, in particular), video drivers, your X software, and the desktop software (Gnome, KDE, and so forth).

If you've got your drivers in place, you ought to be able to test all the functions you want to do. Try playing a DVD, see if you've got surround sound, capture some video, watch TV in a window, rip a CD. See how the display looks on screen; does it look like you're getting the full resolution you expect?

Of course, some of these functions might be difficult to perform yet, because you might need to install some additional software. We'll cover some of the specific software in each of the upcoming sections.

Eventually, you will decide on exactly the right combination of hardware and OS, and you'll begin the process of assembling and configuring your HTPC. For illustration purposes, I'll describe two of my HTPCs, and the reasons behind my decisions for the various components, including the process of assembling them and installing and using the software. One of the HTPCs is Windows-based, and the other is Linux-based. The Windows computer serves as a desktop/server as well as an HTPC, and the Linux box is dedicated to the HTPC function.

Building a Windows HTPC

In this section we cover building and configuring a Windows-based HTPC. We'll be using a high-end video card and adding lots of storage. When I started this project, my functionality list appeared similar to the following checklist:

- General desktop use
- Capture TV
- Play videogames
- Play/Rip discs (CD and DVD)
- Act as a home media server

Preparing for the Hack

The components used in this hack are as follows:

- ASUS A7V8X motherboard
- AMD Athlon XP 2700+ CPU
- 512MB DDR333 RAM
- Generic midtower ATX case
- Antec True480 power supply
- Maxtor 5T060H6 60GB hard drive
- Western Digital WD2000JB 200GB hard drive
- CyberDrive CW078D CD-R/RW (40X CD burner)
- Toshiba SD-M1712 DVD-ROM (16X DVD)
- ATI All-in-Wonder 9700 Pro
- ATI Remote Wonder

The Windows box also includes some other standard items, such as a diskette drive, a keyboard, a mouse, a printer, and a scanner, which aren't particularly HTPC relevant. This PC is my main desktop machine at home, to which I've added HTPC functionality. Referring back to the previous functionality list, you'll see that there is no requirement to incorporate a television display, since my monitor will be adequate. Furthermore, since this particular PC is in my office, I found no reason for it to incorporate an exotic case, and I decided to utilize a run-of-the-mill tower case. With the addition of the All-in-Wonder (AIW), this PC can now perform all the desired HTPC functions.

This HTPC is a standard PC except that it has a bit more hard drive space than usual and can perform TV capture. The second hard drive was purchased for the specific purpose of storing media files and large games. At $350, the AIW was a significant price increase over a typical TV capture card. This purchase was influenced by my desire for a new 3D accelerator card to use in upcoming shoot-em-up games like Half Life 2 and Doom 3.

The AIW is also one of the faster general video cards out there (video cards generally cost between $200 and $400), so it was worth it to me at that price to also have the AV functionality. The particular retail bundle I bought also included a remote control (covered shortly) and various AV connectors. Some bundles for this family of cards do not necessarily include all the extras. Pricewatch.com quotes this particular accelerator card at $285 (as of this writing). There is a faster model, the AIW 9800 Pro, which is quoted at $365 for the "retail box." The next model down, the AIW 9600 Pro (which was introduced as a value model, after the AIW 9700 Pro was released) is going for about $215 for the "retail box." The AV features of all the recent AIW cards are more or less identical, except that now the AIW 9600 Pro is the first AIW card to include an FM tuner for radio capture. If you're interested in the relative 3D performance differences, check your favorite hardware benchmarking site. If all you want is video capture, don't spend all that money. You can get a good video capture card for under $100, easily. For example, I paid significantly less than that for the capture card in the Linux HTPC; see the "Building a Linux HTPC" section in this chapter for details.

Because of the generic hardware, there's not much to look at. However, Figure 6.5 shows the guts of the HTPC after installing the components.

Figure 6.5 Interior of the Windows HTCP System

It's a bit of a mess inside, but that's fine for this application, since the case is normally closed. There's quite a tangle of cables in the back, too, which also doesn't normally show since they're tucked into a shelf area behind the computer. You can see the rear of the case and the tangle of cables in Figure 6.6.

Figure 6.6 Rear Shot of the Closed Case with Wires

The AIW card has a DVI-to-VGA adapter plugged into it, with the VGA monitor cable plugged into that, and the AIW AV connector and CATV F-connector attached. You can also see the Remote Wonder receiver dangling from the top of the case, which attaches to a USB port in the back. The AIW AV connector is necessary because it feeds the audio out from the AIW card into the line-in connector on the motherboard. The audio signal is fed in this way for most TV capture cards.

Figure 6.7 ATI All-In-Wonder 9700 Pro

Figure 6.7 shows the ATI All-In-Wonder 9700 Pro used in this HTPC. Of special note are the large heatsink and fan as well as the auxiliary power connector in the upper-right corner. This particular power connector is the type you would usually use to power a 3.5-inch diskette drive. It has become extremely common for the latest video cards to require an additional power connection, since they can't draw enough power from the AGP slot. This could be a consideration if you're working with a limited power supply for a very SFF PC or if you're out of power connectors (though a Y-splitter works just fine). Some of the highest-performing 3D cards on the market at present have a massive heatsink and fan and may be wide enough to block adjacent slots. Those kinds of cards are often not suitable for HTPC projects because of power requirements, size, and noise (the big fans make a lot of noise). For this card, I can't hear its fan over the CPU and power supply fans. The big silver square in the upper-left corner is indicative of radio frequency (RF) shielding. You'll almost always see something similar where there's a TV tuner involved or a device (referred to as an *RF modulator*) designed to output on a TV "channel," as opposed to composite or S-Video.

Figure 6.8 AIW 9700 Pro rear connectors

Figure 6.8 shows the back of the card. The VID IN connection appears similar to an S-Video connector, but you'll notice that the number of pins is different. This jack connects to an external box that has inputs for composite, S-Video, and left and right audio. You would use those to grab video from a VCR, a camcorder, and so forth. The CATV jack is a standard cable TV F-connector. You can screw your coax cable right into the back of the card. The VID OUT connection is another custom connector. The retail package comes with a couple of different splitter cables. One of them has composite, S-Video, S/PDIF, and audio-out connectors. The other has component (YPbPr), S/PDIF, and audio-out connectors. You'll always be using one of the connectors, since you need the audio-out to get the TV tuner audio channel into your system. This goes into your line-in connector on your sound card. If you don't set it up that way, you won't have any sound with your picture.

Finally, the ATI Remote Wonder (Figure 6.9) comes with the retail box AIW cards. The receiver connects to the USB port of the PC and receives commands over RF.

Figure 6.8 ATI Remote Wonder

Performing the Hack: Software

For this HTPC, we use Windows XP Professional as the operating system. If you're building a similar system using an AIW card, get the OS installed and working with the card, load whatever video driver version came with the card or let Windows use a default driver for the time being. Use Windows Update to install all the patches, including XP SP1. Install Windows Media Player 9 (WMP) and DirectX 9.0b (or whatever the latest versions are) before continuing with any of the additional ATI software.

Next, download the latest version of the software from ATI (www.ati.com). As I was writing this, these were the latest versions:

- Catalyst drivers 6.14.10.x (wxp-w2k-catalyst-7-95-031028m-011774c.exe)

- DVD Decoder (atiCDwiz-v2-1.exe)

- DAO/MDAC (mmc-8-1-0-0-dao-mdac.exe)

- Multimedia Center 8.7 (mmc-8-7-0-0.exe)

- Remote Wonder 2.1 (remote-wonder-2-1-english.exe)

- Hydravision (hydravision-3-21-2108.exe)—optional

Install the files in the order shown. You may have to reboot several times during the process. A couple of notes:

- The Catalyst driver bundle includes the video card driver, the control panel, and the WDM (capture) drivers. You can also download them separately. In any case, be prepared for some large downloads—a couple of the files are 25MB each.

- The "DVD Decoder" is actually a program that checks to see if you have your original ATI CD and then downloads the DVD Decoder program and runs it. So, don't lose your CD that came with your card.

- The DVD drivers that ATI supplies are nice, since WMP can't play DVDs without an add-on such as this. Microsoft doesn't seem willing to pay the DVD player license fees so they rely on the vendors to provide drivers. WMP also cannot rip audio to MP3 without a similar add-on. If you ever try, it will inform you of that fact and send you to a Web page that discusses this topic. They list a few vendors that will sell you a DVD decoder for $14.95, an MP3 encoder for $9.95, or both for $19.95. If you want to play DVDs in WMP, ATI just saved you a few bucks.

- The DAO/MDAC program is basically a database that the Multimedia Center (MMC) uses. We'll get to MMC in a moment. The Remote Wonder program, as you might imagine, is a driver for the remote.

- Hydravision is an ATI tool for managing multiple "monitors." Note that on an AIW card, the TV-out is a separate display, so if you plan to have a monitor and TV-out simultaneously, you may want to install Hydravision.

Congratulations! Aside from finishing the configuration of the ATI programs, you now have pretty much everything installed to meet the basic HTPC requirements. The MMC will record TV; allow live TV to be paused; play DVDs, CDs, general audio and video files; and has an attractive TV-suitable front end. WMP will rip CDs for you, but it can only do it to Windows Media Audio (WMA) files without the MP3 add-on. Windows itself is adept at game playing (once you install a game, of course), and WMP will do a music "jukebox" function quite well. Obviously, the Remote Wonder remote control is well integrated into this system.

Let's take a look at some of the MMC functions. There are three main ways to access the MMC features:

- Through Eazylook
- Through the launcher
- Using Guide Plus+

Eazylook

Eazylook is what you get when you use the remote control. Across the top of the remote are several buttons: TV, DVD, Web, Library, and Screen grab. When you're in regular desktop mode, pressing TV, DVD, or Library will launch Eazylook (Figure 6.10).

Figure 6.10 The Eazylook Welcome Screen

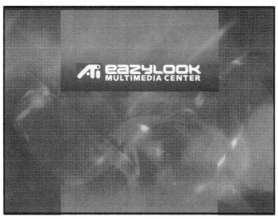

The various text elements are sized appropriately for television display. For example, Figure 6.11 displays what the small library of shows I have captured to my local PC looks like on-screen.

Figure 6.11 Eazylook Text on Screen Text Layout

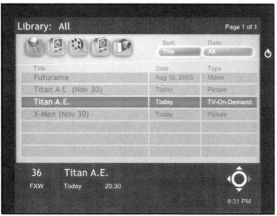

The DVD and TV functions show the appropriate video and overlay the status information as needed. The menus that pop up over the video are partially transparent, and the overall look is fairly nice. All the functions you need while watching TV are available from the remote.

Using the Launcher

ATI also provides a program called Launchpad, which allows you access to all the major functions. It can function as a menu or a floating toolbar (Figures 6.12 and 6.13).

Figure 6.12 ATI Launchpad

Figure 6.13 Launchpad (floating)

Alternatively, if you prefer to not give up the screen real estate, by default ATI leaves an app running in the Taskbar (Figure 6.14). If you right-click it, you can access the programs that way.

And, of course, you can get at them via the Start button, in the ATI Multimedia Center program group. When launched this way, they look like normal Windows desktop apps as shown in Figure 6.15.

Figure 6.14 ATI Taskbar Program

Using Guide Plus+

Finally, there's Guide Plus+, which is a program guide and scheduling application. The Welcome screen for Guide+ as shown in Figure 6.16.

Figure 6.15 The ATI MMC DVD Player Program

You can right-click any of the listings (shown in Figure 6.16) and schedule a program to be recorded. If the program is playing now, you can click it, and your device will start showing that channel. You can even schedule it to "watch" so it comes on in the future, if that is useful to you. There is also a search function, so you can look for all the showings of your favorite show and schedule those to record. You have a choice of several recording qualities, with the requisite size/quality tradeoffs. These days, Guide Plus+ provides functionality closest to an off-the-shelf TiVo.

Figure 6.16 Guide Plus+ Main Screen

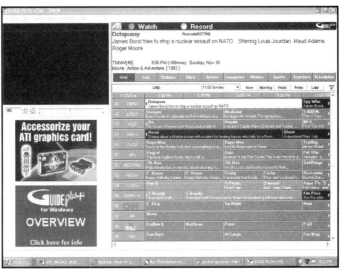

We won't cover WMP usage here, since most of you are probably already familiar with it and it is quite easy to use. If you buy an MP3 encoder module for it, it will make MP3s for you, as well. Instead, we will briefly cover two free software packages: CDex and FairUse.

CDex

CDex is my favorite all-around Windows CD ripper (Figure 6.17). CDex is capable of digital ripping. It can also rip to a variety of other file formats, including uncompressed WAV, MP3, Ogg Vorbis, and others. It integrates with the CDDB to get track titles for you, and it works the way you would expect. You can download CDex from the following location: http://cdexos.sourceforge.net.

Figure 6.17 The CDex Main Interface Page

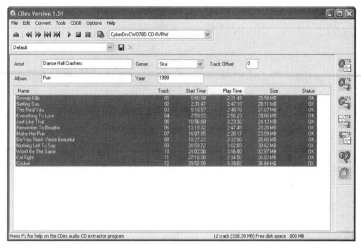

When you install CDex, you simply set your preferences (directory to rip to, compression type, rate, and so forth) and pop in a disc. CDex will find the album on the CDDB (unless you've got something pretty obscure) and fill in the track names. Then you simply start it up, and it goes to work ripping CDs at lightning speeds.

FairUse

FairUse (FU) is billed as DVD backup software (Figure 6.18). FU is free of charge and comparable in functionality to CDex—it works just as well. You can download FairUse from the following location: http://fairuse.sourceforge.net.

Figure 6.18 The FairUse Wizard Welcome Screen

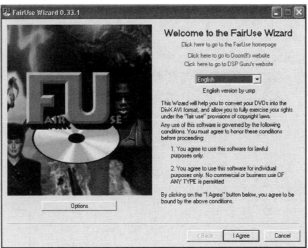

There are several steps to ripping a DVD with FU. After clicking the **I Agree** button on the Welcome screen, you'll be asked to pick a project name and location, as shown in Figure 6.19.

Figure 6.19 The New Project Name and Location Screen

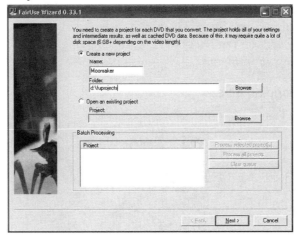

Click **Next**, and FU will ask you to confirm the drive letter of your DVD drive. Pick the appropriate one. After it scans the disc for a moment, it will display the "chains" on the DVD, as shown in Figure 6.20.

Figure 6.20 Chain Display of the FU Wizard

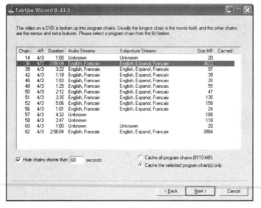

The chains are simply the various bits of video contained on the disc. You'll have to figure out which ones are which by trial and error. This particular disc (the James Bond film *Moonraker*) contains both standard and wide-screen versions of the film, which are the two two-hour chains. Here we'll demonstrate chain 57, which happens to be the theatrical trailer included on the disc. Select the appropriate chain(s), and click **Next**. After FU scans the selected chain for a period of time, you're presented with a screen where you can select (with some cropping) the frames you want. An example of the cropping screen is shown in Figure 6.21.

Figure 6.21 The FU Cropping Screen

You can set the bounding box around the picture, so you're not spending time and space working on the black areas (though they should compress nicely). The **Auto set** feature seems to do a decent job detecting the appropriate area most of the time. You can set a specific frame range if you don't want the whole thing. The slider underneath the picture window lets you look at various frames, so you've got a visual way to pick. The next screen (not shown) lets you choose between a variety of video modes. Most of the time, you'll want to stick with what Auto Detect picks.

Next, you are able to choose from different compression types and resolutions, as shown in Figure 6.22.

Figure 6.22 Selecting a Compression Type

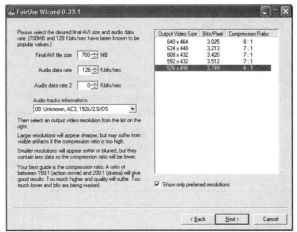

Pick the size you want, and click **Next**. On the following screen, select the encoding types (Figure 6.23). In this example, we've selected **Auto Add** under XviD and picked the only choice given under **Audio Encoding**.

Figure 6.23 Selecting the Encoding Method

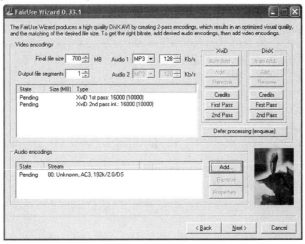

The next screen is where all the magic happens. On my Athlon XP 2700+, it takes several minutes to encode the 4.5-minute clip.

WARNING: HARDWARE HARM

Video encoding is one of the most CPU-intensive things you are likely to do on your computer. Funny story: When I was preparing this section of the chapter, this step kept crashing on me. My computer rebooted a couple of times and once powered down spontaneously. When I opened the case to take the pictures earlier in the chapter, I had to dislodge a whole herd of dust bunnies before taking the pictures. I did so with a can of air. That meant there was a lot of free dust in the case. After I closed it back up and starting doing some test DVD rips, the CPU fan was going and managed to lodge a fair bit of the free dust into the CPU heatsink, thus clogging it up. When I was troubleshooting the shutdown, I happened to check the monitor in the BIOS, and it said the CPU was 70 degrees Celsius (approximately 158 degrees Fahrenheit)! I realized what was happening, opened the case back up, and used the can of air to unclog the heatsink. After that, the CPU was running at a normal 48 degrees Celsius or so. Still, now that I was on the alert, I watched the temperature monitor while I was ripping. The CPU temperature climbed to about 54 degrees Celsius, one degree at a time, due to the intensive work required by the ripping software. After the rip was done, the temperature settled back down to 48 degrees Celsius. Heat kills!

After the rip is done, it's ready to add to your media library. Then, you can safely store the original DVD away where children or your pets can't destroy it.

The ATI Remote Wonder is well suited to Windows use. It can act as a two-button mouse and has pretty much all the buttons you would want for an HTPC remote. The buttons can perform somewhat different functions depending on the application that is in focus, and it provides six general-purpose programmable buttons (*A* through *F*). The remote functions with just plain Windows as well, with the buttons producing Windows messages, which is how Windows informs applications of keyboard and mouse events. Several of the buttons produce WM_APPCOMMAND messages, so if the application you use understands those (as WMP does), it will work for that, too. If that's not enough, an SDK is available from ATI that will allow you to make custom plug-ins for the Remote Wonder software for any application you like. ATI gives you plug-ins for PowerPoint and Winamp, and you can download plug-ins for TheaterTek and DivX Player.

NOTE

For additional information on the ATI Remote Wonder, refer to the following sites:

- www.ati.com/products/remotewonder/index.html
- www.ati.com/products/remotewonder2/index.html

Windows Summary

Overall, I'm very satisfied with the functionality of the Windows HTPC I've described. The hardware is first-class. I could always stand a little more CPU, RAM, drive space, and the like, but they're certainly adequate as-is. One thing I wished I had planned for better is IDE ports. This particular motherboard has the standard primary and secondary port, of which I'm using the master and slave on each. For performance, it's nice to have just one drive per channel when possible. My main complaint about this setup is cost. If I wanted to replicate something like this for each TV in the house, buying a $200 Windows license per box would be somewhat painful.

Building a Linux HTPC

The Linux HTPC was designed with set-top use in mind. The chosen case is small, attractive, and quiet. I went light on the disk space, since I'm planning to have a lot of the storage on a server elsewhere in the house (the Windows HTPC previously described, for the time being). I've installed a DVD drive, so it can be used for walk-up DVD playing as well as ripping.

Preparing for the Hack

The following parts were used to create this particular HTPC running Red Hat Linux 9.0:

- Shuttle SB51G
- Intel 2.4 GHz Pentium IV
- 256MB DDR266 RAM
- Shuttle CV21 TV-out/DVI card
- Shuttle PN31 remote control
- Silver Artec 16X DVD-ROM
- Western Digital WD400BB 40GB hard drive
- AITech WaveWatcher TV-PCI TV tuner/video capture card

Performing the Hack: Hardware

You'll notice that the list for the Linux HTPC is much shorter and contains fewer components than the Windows machine. This is due to the fact that I selected the Shuttle SB51G. The Shuttle SB51G is part of the Shuttle XPC family (www.shuttle.com), which is a well-known SFF format that includes the case, motherboard, and power supply. You supply the CPU, RAM, drives, and up to one AGP and one PCI card, depending on the model you select. The particular model tells you what kind of motherboard, chipset, and video it supports. Figure 6.24 shows what the Shuttle SB51G case looks like from the front.

Figure 6.24 The Shuttle SB51G Box

You can see from the size of the DVD drive in comparison to the rest of the case how truly compact this case is. The dimensions are 7.9"W × 7.3"H × 11.8"D. In other words, the footprint is approximately the same as an 8.5" × 11" piece of paper with the height about the same as a stack of books.

For this case, I was more concerned with aesthetics than with the HTPC in my office. I went out of my way to find a silver DVD-ROM drive. Incidentally, if you're looking for silver optical and diskette drives, Directron.com is one of the few places I found that carries a selection of them (www.directron.com). Also, if you are interested in further customization, it is possible to purchase a variety of multicolored kits for the Shuttle XPC to suit your needs.

These boxes make excellent HTPCs for a couple of reasons:

- They look nice
- They're quiet
- They're small enough to fit in your TV/VCR cabinet
- They're full of features

One thing you might miss are additional expansion slots, since they've only got a single PCI and a single AGP slot available (though that should be enough for your HTPC). Figure 6.25 shows the back of the case, which includes:

- Two serial ports
- Ethernet jack
- Built-in VGA
- Fiber audio-out
- Two Firewire ports

- Two USB ports
- Keyboard and mouse ports
- Built-in audio (multipurpose, depending on settings)

All of these listed features are in addition to the front of the case, which contains another set of audio connectors, two more USB ports, and another Firewire port.

Figure 6.25 The Rear of the Shuttle SB51G

Shuttle keeps coming out with new models, so you can generally get one with the latest chipset and processor for both AMD and Intel. The only real limitation is expansion. There's room available for a full-size optical drive, a 3.5-inch diskette drive, and a 3.5-inch hard drive. You can install a second hard drive if you want to forego the diskette drive. As you might imagine, the inside is rather tightly packed, as shown in Figure 6.26.

Figure 6.26 The Interior of the Shuttle Case

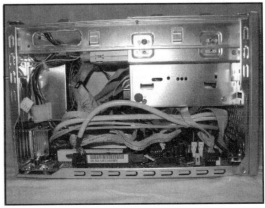

Still, Shuttle has made it relatively easy to get your parts in and out. As you can see in Figure 6.27, unscrewing two screws and disconnecting the various cables from the drives allows you to easily remove the entire drive cage.

Figure 6.27 Removing Parts from the Shuttle Case

Inside the case are your standard two IDE controllers, a diskette controller, two RAM slots, power connectors, various headers for USB ports, and so on. The Shuttles typically have two fans—one in the power supply and a main case/CPU fan. One of the reasons the Shuttles are quiet is that they have an innovative heatpipe cooling system with a variable-speed fan, as shown in Figure 6.28.

NOTE

An excellent review of this heatpipe cooling system is available on the Web at www.overclockers.com/articles651.

Figure 6.28 The Shuttle Heatpipe Cooling System

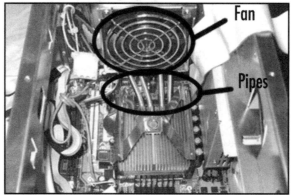

NOTE

For more information on the Video 4 Linux resources, check out the following Web site: www.exploits.org/v4l.

NEED TO KNOW... A NOTE ABOUT CHANNEL FREQUENCIES

I've indicated that my capture card was supported out of the box. Well, it was, but I didn't know it! The first time I tried working with the card, I followed the advice in various documentation and mailing lists posts. They said to use the xawtv application to test your card. So I did, and I was getting nothing but a mostly blue/green screen. All the help I could find indicated that this meant my tuner wasn't configured properly. I grabbed the latest bttv version and compiled and installed it myself, double-checked the kernel loadable modules (KLMs) that support the various v4l and bttv drivers, and tried a variety of different settings—all to no avail. Finally, just an as experiment, I grabbed an old VCR I had lying around. I attached the VCR to the composite-in port on the card, set xawtv to Composite, and got a picture, no problem. That indicated that at least part of the setup was working. Having an external tuner is a great troubleshooting tool, and you probably won't find a cheaper one than an old VCR. When I was trying to use xawtv, another error message I got consistently was:

```
tuner: TV freq (268435455.93) out of range (44-958)
```

I also couldn't find where in the xawtv options that I could change channels. The documentation seemed to imply that when the tuner was working, I'd be able to do so.

I had already installed MPlayer, which I had used to verify CD and DVD playback. I highly recommend MPlayer for a variety of uses, and often other software you'll want to use will use MPlayer behind the scenes, so you may need it anyway. I found out that MPlayer can do capture as well, and I figured I would try that, just because. So I executed this command:

```
mplayer -tv driver=v4l:norm=ntsc:channel=3:chanlist=us-cable
    :width=352:height=240 tv://
```

And, lo! I had TV, with sounds and everything. Okay, so I figured that xawtv was just broken somehow, which seemed strange, since it was from the same programmer who did the bttv drivers. After some poking around, I eventually tried xawtv again, and now it was working, too! Turns out that xawtv needs to be provided with a list of channel frequencies before it will do anything with channels, and my card was set to some nonexistent channel. The usual way to solve this is to use the scantv utility, which Red Hat does not supply with xawtv, even though it normally comes with it. Once you have scantv, do:

```
scantv -o ~/.xawtv
```

This will fill in the settings file with all the channels it can find, and *then* xawtv lets you pick.

Install MPlayer and CODECs

At this point, if all your drivers and software are working properly with your hardware, then you've got enough to actually watch TV and record it. The ALSA and v4l drivers take care of the hardware, and MPlayer can tune, display, and capture TV feeds. Of course, MPlayer by itself doesn't do all the features we would like, which is why we need to install MythTV.

Installing MythTV

MythTV (www.mythtv.org) aspires to be a full-featured HTPC system, including features for HTPC networking. It has ambitious goals, but even at only version 0.12, it does pretty well. My main complaint is that it's a pretty heavyweight set of packages and takes a fair bit of work to install. As with just about any open-source package, you've got the choice to install from source or from a binary package.

   We won't show the process for compiling from source here. The MythTV site has an excellent and lengthy set of instructions on how to do so.

   If you want to try installing from binaries, a site named ATrpms (http://atrpms.physik.fu-berlin.de) has binaries for Red Hat distributions, with an emphasis on multimedia and a few other package types. This is in addition to the binaries that Red Hat supplies, since Red Hat doesn't maintain MythTV binaries for you. However, be aware that ATrpms uses *apt-get* for dependencies, and it will replace/upgrade quite a few packages for you, generally breaking the Red Hat versioning scheme for those packages. In my case, I ended up with a fully working system, but I am now running their kernel, drivers, media packages, and a number of other items. MythTV uses MySQL as a database and there is a *mythbackend* daemon you'll need to run when you're using it. A Myth Transcode Daemon (*mtd*) needs to be running to rip DVDs. Finally, there's *mythfrontend*, which is the foreground app shown in the following screenshots. The backend stuff can all be run on a separate server box, which allows you to have a separate or multiple frontend boxes.

   The MythTV front end is shown in Figure 6.33.

Figure 6.33 Front End of MythTV

The white arrow in the lower-right corner of Figure 6.33 indicates that more choices can be found by scrolling down. Not shown in this picture are News Feeds, DVD, and Setup.

Myth performs all the functions you would expect, including videogames, as it can act as a front end for the popular Multiple Arcade Machine Emulator (MAME) engine. You customize the Weather section for your area so you can get the weather at a glance (Figure 6.34).

Figure 6.34 MythTV Weather Screen

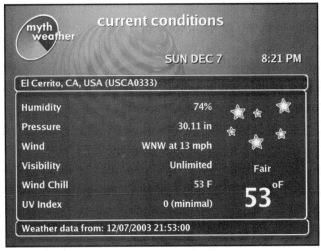

Myth also automates some of the more difficult functions, like CD ripping and DVD ripping. The DVD ripping is particularly easy (Figure 6.35).

Figure 6.35 MythTV DVD Screen

Figure 6.36 MythTV DVD Ripping Screen

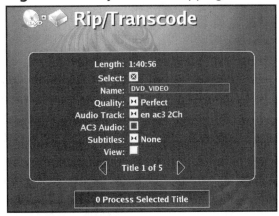

From the DVD menu, pick **Rip DVD** (Figure 6.36).

On the next screen, pick the section of video you want to rip. In this screen, there are five sections. The first one is the main movie, which we can identify by its length. The other options shown here aren't necessarily functional yet, such as the quality selection. The default Perfect quality results in a direct translation of the MPEG2 from the DVD. The movie ripped in this example came out to just over 4 gigabytes.

Give the video clip a name, and press the 0 (zero) key to start the process (Figure 6.37).

Figure 6.37 MythTV DVD Rip In Progress

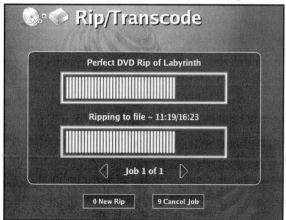

Figure 6.38 MythTV Video Library Item

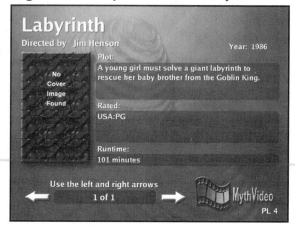

Once ripped, the movie will be added to the Video list (Figure 6.38).

The naming was done in an earlier step (not shown) where it accessed the Internet Movie Database (IMDB) and presented me with a list of movie names similar to *Labyrinth*.

Of course, Myth does your standard TV functions (Figure 6.39), including an initial pass at a "favorites" system for TV shows. You can watch "live" TV (with pause and rewind functionality) or schedule recordings. A Perl program, XMLTV, is used to feed Myth a program guide for your area. XMLTV can be found at www.xmltv.sourceforge.net.

Figure 6.39 MythTV TV Screen

NEED TO KNOW... LINUX USB WOES

Of all the things that might have given me trouble on the Linux project, I didn't expect the remote control to be the worst. I learned a lot more about how USB works under Linux than I ever wanted to. The short version of the story is that I ended up compiling my own kernel and patching one of the USB drivers in order to get the Shuttle remote fully functional. It's unclear whether the USB support for this device just wasn't all there in the earlier kernel (2.4.20), but the remote wasn't even recognized properly until I compiled and booted 2.4.23. Then, the mouse didn't work properly.

After some searching and mailing, I was given a working patch to hid-core.c by Norbert Federa. Many thanks to Norbert, Peter Bergmann, and the Linux-usb-uses mailing list for all the help.

Hopefully, by the time you read this, it will be incorporated in an easily downloaded kernel binary for you. The patch follows:

```
--- hid-core_orig.c   Mon Dec  8 23:11:58 2003
+++ hid-core.c    Mon Dec  8 23:14:33 2003
@@ -272,6 +272,11 @@

    field->unit_exponent = parser->global.unit_exponent;

    field->unit = parser->global.unit;


+    if(field->logical_minimum == field->logical_maximum) {

+        field->logical_minimum = -1;

+        field->logical_maximum = 1;

+    }

+

    return 0;

}
```

Linux Summary

The Shuttle makes an excellent HTPC platform, though the software configuration required a bit more effort than I would have liked. The weakest link in this particular HTPC is the cheap video capture card. The card produces electrical interference that causes static and a wavy picture on the display. Since I only paid about $16 for it, that's not at all a surprise. I chose that card mostly as an experiment and to illustrate a point (that Linux has good legacy support).

Here are Web sites related to Linux HTPC that you may find useful:

- **Fedora Linux distribution** http://fedora.redhat.com
- **Remote controls** www.shuttle.com/hq/support/download/dwn2.asp?model=PN31
- **Video 4 Linux resources** www.exploits.org/v4l

- **bttv drivers** http://bytesex.org/bttv

- **Mplayer** www.mplayerhq.hu

- **Atrpms** RPMs for most of the Linux software discussed http://atrpms.physik.fu-berlin.de

- **MythTV** www.mythtv.org

- **Linux USB users mailing list** http://lists.sourceforge.net/lists/listinfo/linux-usb-users

Further Hacking and Advanced Topics

The two HTPCs shown in this chapter together represent Phase 1 of my planned home media network. The Windows HTPC is an experimental media server and the Linux HTPC is an experimental set-top box. My ultimate plan is to have a dedicated media server in the garage with a terabyte of storage and multiple capture cards. I plan to make the set-top boxes extremely simple. The Windows HTPC is my prototype server, as it has the storage space, and capture and rip capabilities. Obviously, it's not presently dedicated solely to this purpose as I use the machine for other computing tasks, as well.

One way to achieve this goal is to push as many of the functions as possible to the back end and make the front end very lightweight. For example, say your front end has a modest CPU and can only do MPEG2 videos. You could have the back end transcode everything (maybe in real time) to MPEG2 for the light front end.

There are front end products on the market that are supposed to do just that. Some of them are called "media receivers" or "networked DVD players." For example, the MediaMVP Model 1000 by Hauppauge. It only does composite out to the TV and it takes MPEG1 and MPEG2 streams over Ethernet. I haven't even had a chance to take it out of the box yet, so I can give no specific feedback, but it was only $88 new. It requires Windows XP but it claims to be "Linux based," which I take to mean that it's running some kind of Linux kernel inside the device itself. There is great potential for these types of devices to be hacked in the future.

There are many HTPC topics we didn't have space to cover in this chapter. For example, all the TV capture examples here are NTSC captures. We didn't touch on HDTV broadcast at all. Capturing HD signals is a whole different ballgame. However, we hope that you've been inspired to create an HTPC of your own!

Chapter 7

Hack Your Atari 2600 and 7800

Hacks in this Chapter:

- Atari 2600 Left-Handed Joystick
- Use an NES Control Pad with Your 2600
- Atari 2600 Stereo Audio Output
- Atari 7800 Blue LED Modification
- Atari 7800 Game Compatibility Hack to Play Certain 2600 Games
- Atari 7800 Voltage Regulator Replacement
- Atari 7800 Power Supply Plug Retrofit
- Other Hacks

Introduction

When Atari introduced the Video Computer System (VCS) back in 1977, nobody, not even Atari, knew it would ultimately become a wild success and be the catalyst that would spawn the multibillion-dollar gaming industry we know today. The VCS (see Figure 7.1), later renamed the 2600, was part of the first generation of videogame systems that weren't hardwired to play a certain set of games. Instead, they could be reprogrammed time and time again by the user, who purchased new game cartridges. This flexibility helped propel the VCS to the top of the sales charts, where it sat as king for many years until the videogame market crashed in 1984.

Figure 7.1 A First-Generation Atari Video Computer System

The Atari VCS initially shipped with a pair of joystick controllers, a pair of paddle controllers, and the two-player game Combat. Atari released additional controllers for the system, such as the driving controllers (used by only a single game—Indy 500), keypad controllers, and even a Trak-Ball controller. The initial library of 2600 titles was small (nine games were offered), but the 2600 catalog would eventually encompass hundreds of titles produced by a wide range of companies.

One important first for the young videogame industry was the creation of Activision in 1980, formed by several Atari employees who were dissatisfied with how they were being treated at Atari. Activision was the first third-party company to produce videogames for the Atari 2600, a move that Atari unsuccessfully tried to quash in the courts. Activision's high-quality games were well received by the public, and Activision grossed $70 million in its first year.

The Atari 2600 lived a long life, if somewhat bumpy in later years. In 1986 Atari released the 2600 Jr., a repackaged 2600 in a smaller case, a $50 price tag, and a fresh marketing campaign. Atari would continue to push the 2600 in the United States until 1989, at which time production was finally ceased on this model. With a run lasting over 10 years and millions of consoles sold, the Atari 2600 is one of the most successful game consoles of all time, with a place in history as the machine that started the home videogame craze.

The Atari 7800 ProSystem

Under pressure from competitors that were eroding Atari's market share by producing competing consoles as well as clones of the 2600, Atari hastily released the Atari 5200 SuperSystem in 1982. The Atari 5200 was a repackaged Atari 400 computer and did not represent development of a new game system from scratch. That would not happen until the introduction of the Atari 7800 (see Figure 7.2) five years later. Atari's original plans were to release the Atari 7800 in 1984, but those plans were shelved when the company was purchased by the Tramiel family, who wanted to concentrate on the computer side of Atari's business. If you're looking for Atari 5200 hacks, the next chapter contains several for the 5200 as well as the related Atari 8-bit computers.

Figure 7.2 The Atari 7800 ProSystem

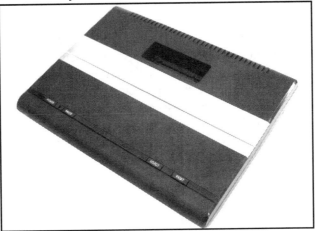

The 7800 was finally released in 1987 as a response to Nintendo's successful Nintendo Entertainment System (NES). Ironically, Nintendo had once approached Atari about selling the NES in the United States, but Atari spurned the offer. Had the 7800 been released in 1984 as originally planned, it likely would have done quite well. But the 7800 quickly succumbed to the NES juggernaut and was unsuccessful at keeping the Atari name in the minds of videogame fans.

The Atari 7800 is more closely related to the 2600 than it is to the 5200, which is why we have grouped the 2600 and 7800 systems together in this chapter. For starters, the Atari 7800 is backward compatible with 2600 games—the only system Atari would ever produce with built-in backward compatibility. The cartridges for the two systems are the same size, with the only discernable difference being two additional "fingers" on the cartridge connector for 7800 games. Both systems feature 9-pin controller ports, and 2600-compatible controllers work just fine with the 7800. In fact, 2600 controllers can be used with 7800 games, except for those that require two independent fire buttons. The 7800 also uses the same hardware as the 2600 to produce sound, which unfortunately hinders the 7800 in the audio department. One game, Ballblazer, actually contains a custom Atari "POKEY" chip inside the cartridge, which is the same sound chip built into the Atari 8-bit computers and the 5200. Thus, Ballblazer is the best-sounding game in the entire 7800 library.

The 7800 suffered a fairly short lifespan, partly because of the fierce competition from Nintendo and the Sega Master System and partly because retailers were growing wary of Atari's increasing inability to deliver on its promises. Only three games shipped at the system's launch, with Atari announcing many games that were never delivered. The system received poor distribution and weak support from third-party companies, with only three additional developers (Activision, Absolute Entertainment, and Froggo) producing games for the system.

Although the 7800 didn't leave much of a mark on the videogame industry, it is a popular system with Atari fans. Nearly 60 games were released for the 7800, many of them quite enjoyable. It's an easy system to build up a complete collection of games for, since none of the 7800 titles is exceedingly rare. And because of the system's backward compatibility with the 2600, you get the benefit of using one system to play both 7800 and 2600 games.

Hacks in This Chapter

Although these systems are now over 20 years old, they have a large fan base keeping them alive and thriving in the 21st century. The classic gaming system with the most fans is easily the Atari 2600, with hundreds, if not thousands, of Web sites devoted to the game system that formed the basis of the videogame industry today. A large community of programmers and hobbyists creates new games for these systems, most notably the 2600, with access to resources the original programmers could only dream of. Thanks to the Internet, fans of less popular and even very obscure systems can also get together to discuss their favorite games, share information, and most important, have fun!

Part of that fun is hacking these systems to do things they were never intended to do. The hacks in this chapter for the 2600 and 7800 only scratch the surface of what can be done. In this chapter, we cover how to:

- Fix your 2600 joystick for left-handed gamers
- Use an NES Control Pad with your 2600
- Add stereo output to your 2600
- Spice up your 7800 with a blue LED
- Apply a 2600 compatibility fix to the 7800
- Repair your 7800's broken voltage regulator
- Install a standard power jack in your 7800

If the hacks detailed here whet your appetite, we've put together a list of additional hacks that you can pursue by following the links at the end of this chapter. Let's get started!

Atari 2600 Left-Handed Joystick Modification

The Atari CX-40 joystick that shipped with the Atari 2600 is probably the single most recognized controller in videogame history. However, in the late 1970s, ergonomic controller design was not a concern of hardware designers, and in the case of the venerable CX-40, left-handed players were ignored. The CX-40 was designed to be held with your left hand, leaving your right hand to operate the joystick, pictured in Figure 7.3. The single joystick button is then triggered with your left thumb. Unfortunately, this arrangement is counterintuitive for people who are left-handed.

Figure 7.3 The Atari CX-40 Joystick

The goal of this hack is to transform a CX-40 joystick into one that can more easily be enjoyed by left-handed players. We will do this by modifying the joystick so that it can be rotated 90 degrees clockwise. This will place the fire button in the upper-right corner, where it can be operated by your right thumb, leaving your left hand to manipulate the joystick.

Preparing for the Hack

This is a fairly simple hack, which requires only:

- An Atari CX-40 joystick
- A Philips head screwdriver
- An optional pair of needlenose pliers

You should select a joystick that is in good operating condition. If your joystick is not working well before the hack, it's not likely to serve you well afterward. Also, this hack is easily reversed if you decide you don't like the rotated nature of the joystick.

Performing the Hack

Do the following:

1. Flip the joystick over and use a Philips head screwdriver to remove the four screws, as shown in Figure 7.4.

Figure 7.4 Removing the Four Screws

2. With the joystick still upside down, carefully remove the base. There is a small spring beneath the orange fire button—be careful not to lose it! Pull the top half of the joystick away; this part will contain a clear plastic post (which gives the joystick its rigidity), the orange fire button, and the spring inside the button (see Figure 7.5). Put these aside for now.

Figure 7.5 Taking the Joystick Apart

Performing the Hack

Do the following:

1. Use a jeweler's Philips head screwdriver to remove the six screws from the bottom of the NES control pad, as shown in Figure 7.11.

Figure 7.11 Bottom of NES Control Pad

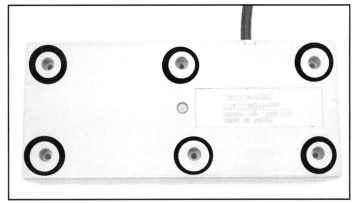

2. Once you have removed the screws, lift up the back half of the control pad. You'll see a simple circuit board, to which five wires and single IC are attached, as shown in Figure 7.12.

Figure 7.12 Inside the NES Control Pad

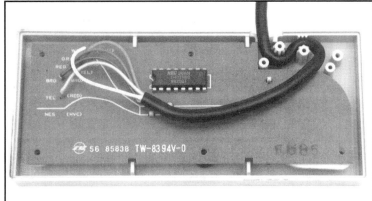

3. Remove the circuit board from the case, making sure to leave the rubber button mechanisms resting in the top half of the case. Unsolder the five wires as well as the chip from the board. Be careful not to damage the solder pads for the chip on the opposite side of the board, because this is where we'll be attaching the wires from the Atari 2600 joystick cable. When you are finished, the board should resemble Figure 7.13.

Figure 7.13 Bare NES Control Pad Board

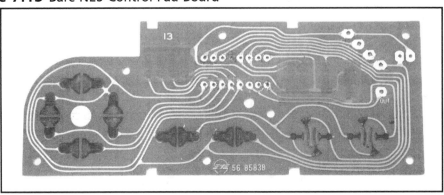

4. Now it's time to disassemble the Atari 2600 joystick. Using a standard Philips head screwdriver, remove the four screws on the bottom of the joystick. Pull apart the two halves of the joystick, revealing a circuit board in the bottom half, to which six wires are attached, as depicted in Figure 7.14. Remove the board from the bottom of the case and then pull each of the six connectors from the board, as highlighted.

    The only portion of the Atari 2600 joystick we'll be using is the cable. This includes the DB9 connector that plugs into the 2600 as well as the stripped wires on the other end of the cable. You can save the remainder of the joystick for spare parts.

Figure 7.14 The Atari 2600 Joystick Circuit Board

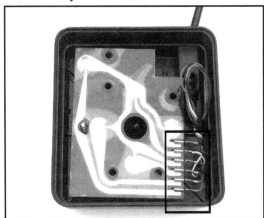

5. With the wires disconnected from the board, you can now remove the cable from the joystick base. We will not need any additional parts from the 2600 joystick. Figure 7.15 shows the joystick cable removed from the joystick.

Figure 7.15 Joystick Cable Removed

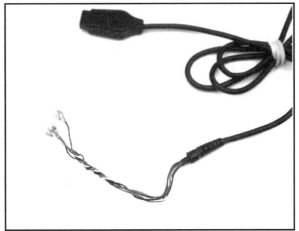

6. Using a pair of wire cutters, cut the metal connectors from the end of each wire. Now use wire strippers to remove a short length of insulation from each wire (see Figure 7.16).

Figure 7.16 Prepped Wires

7. Before we solder these wires to the NES board, we must first cut some traces on the board. With the traces of the circuit board facing you, we will number the pins 1–8 on the bottom row where the IC was located. Using a sharp razor or Dremel tool, cut the trace immediately above the solder pads for holes 2, 3, 4, and 5, as shown in Figure 7.17.

WARNING: HARDWARE HARM

Make sure when cutting the traces that you do not damage the solder pads, because we will be soldering the wires from the Atari 2600 to these pads. Also make sure you cut the traces above the pads and not below or you will render the circuit board unusable.

Figure 7.17 Cutting Traces

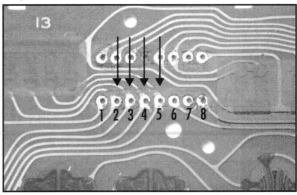

8. Now you need to cut one more trace. To the right of the holes for the IC are four vertical black strips. You need to cut the trace immediately below the fourth black strip, as shown in Figure 7.18. Be careful to cut only the vertical trace, not the horizontal trace running below the row of black stripes.

Figure 7.18 One More Trace to Cut

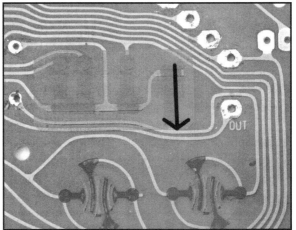

9. Now it's time to solder the Atari 2600 joystick cable to the NES control pad circuit board. The individual wires need to be soldered to the holes numbered in Figure 7.15, as described in Table 7.2. You might want to tin the tip of each wire with solder before inserting them through the holes and soldering them into place.

Table 7.2 NES Control Pad Wiring

Hole	Atari Joystick Wire Color
1	Black
2	Brown
3	Green
4	Blue
5	White
8	Orange

10. When you're finished, the wires should look as they do in Figure 7.19, as seen from the opposite side of the board.

Figure 7.19 Wiring Complete

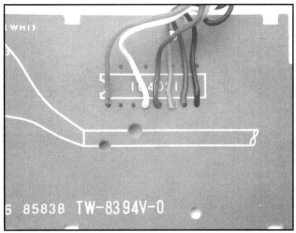

11. Now place the board trace side down into the bottom half of the controller and thread the cable as shown in Figure 7.20. Be sure that the rubber cups for each button are sitting properly in the bottom half of the controller. If you decided instead to cut the 2600 joystick cable before the stress relief connector, your wiring will look a bit different (and closer to the original NES control pad cable).

Figure 7.20 Reassembly of the Modified NES Control Pad

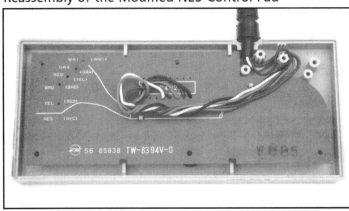

12. Now place the back half of the NES control pad cover in place and affix the cover with the six screws removed earlier (see Figure 7.21). You can test your new controller by plugging it into an Atari 2600 (or another system that accepts 2600 controllers) and enjoying your favorite games!

Figure 7.21 Hack Complete!

Atari 2600 Stereo Audio Output

When Atari introduced the 2600, many home videogame consoles (which consisted mostly of Pong machines at the time) had a built-in speaker for audio output. It appears that Atari was originally going to take this same route with the 2600, since the original six-switch model contains two receptacles for mounting small speakers inside the case. However, and thankfully, Atari decided to instead send the audio output to the television via the standard radio frequency (RF) output, so no Atari

2600 models ever shipped with internal speakers. Figures 7.22 and 7.23 show how these speakers were to be mounted in the case.

Figure 7.22 The Top Half of the Original Atari 2600 Case Showing Two Circular "Speaker Grills"

Figure 7.23 Receptacles Inside the Case for Speakers

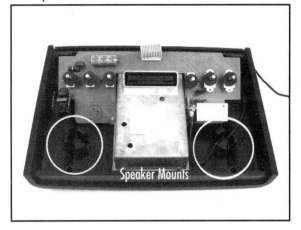

Speakers? Yes, the Atari 2600 hardware supports left and right audio outputs. Unfortunately, the outputs from the Television Interface Adapter (TIA) chip are tied together on the circuit board, leaving users with a single, mono audio output. It is unknown why Atari abandoned stereo output, but it is relatively easy to tap into the individual audio outputs from the TIA and add two RCA ports to your 2600. RCA ports are the standard jacks for making audio connections between audio/video components and are usually white and red, to denote left and right stereo output, respectively.

Several Atari games actually benefit from stereo output—most notably early two-player games such as Combat, Indy 500, Air-Sea Battle, and others. With these games, Player 1's sound effects are heard in the left sound channel, and Player 2's sound effects in the right channel. There's even a new homebrew game for the 2600, Skeleton+, which takes advantage of stereo output to aid the player in locating a skeleton roaming around a 3D maze.

This particular hack will upgrade the audio output for the Atari 2600 from mono to stereo, but you'll still need to get video output by connecting the RF signal to your television. This means you'll need to use a stereo receiver or similar method to take the stereo output of the 2600 and direct it through speakers, unless your television allows you to change the audio input to a different selection (and some will). This hack will remove the audio output from the RF signal, so you will not hear any audio unless you use the newly added stereo jacks.

NOTE

If you're up for more of a challenge, you can modify your 2600 to give it composite and/or S-video output as well as stereo audio output. This will result in a superior picture, but composite and S-video modifications can be tricky. A video hack for the 2600 is beyond the scope of this book, but you can examine the Atari 2600 FAQ (www.atariage.com/2600/faq) for more information.

 # Preparing for the Hack

The first thing you'll need is the Atari 2600 system that you want to modify. We will modify a four-switch Atari 2600, since these are the most common. Modifying other versions of the 2600 is similar, since they all use the same TIA chip. Most Atari 2600 consoles also use the same basic physical housing, except for the Atari 2600 Jr., which features a much smaller footprint.

Parts you'll need for this hack are:

- Two 2.0K 1-percent tolerance resistors
- Two 0.1uF capacitors
- Two RCA phono jacks
- 18" AWG wire

Tools required to perform this hack are as follows:

- Phillips head screwdriver, standard size
- Wire cutters and strippers
- Needlenose pliers
- Soldering iron
- A drill or Dremel tool with a 1/4" drill bit

If you have a glue gun, you can use it to secure the audio cables to the 2600 board for a cleaner appearance (and to keep the cables out of harm's way).

Performing the Hack

Do the following:

1. To begin, remove the screws from the bottom of the 2600 using a standard Philips screwdriver. Four screws secure the case together. Note that the two bottom screws are longer, so you'll want to be sure to insert these into the correct holes when you are reassembling the unit (see Figure 7.24).

Figure 7.24 The Underside of a Four-Switch Atari 2600

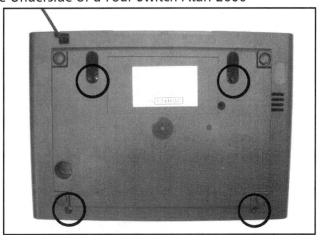

2. Once you have removed the screws, pull the two halves of the case apart, unplug the RF cable from the board, and remove the circuit board from the case. Your system will now resemble the illustration shown in Figure 7.25.

Figure 7.25 Atari 2600 Circuit Board with the RF Shield Attached

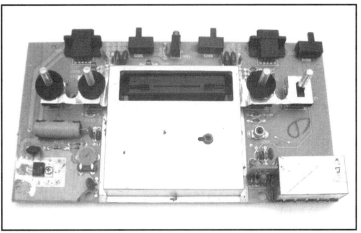

3. Now you will need to remove the metal RF shield. To do this, use a pair of needlenose pliers to twist the small metal tabs along the edges of the RF shield so that the tabs line up with the holes in the shield. You should then be able to pull the two halves of the shield apart. Put the shield aside for now. Once the RF shield is removed, the board should resemble Figure 7.26. The TIA chip is at the bottom of the board, as highlighted in the picture.

Figure 7.26 Atari 2600 Circuit Board with RF Shield Removed

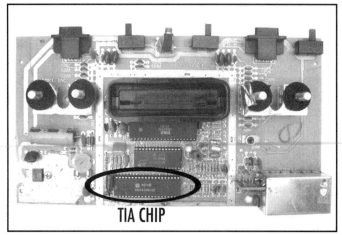

TIA CHIP

4. If your TIA chip is socketed as shown in Figure 7.26, your job will be easier, since it is a simple matter to remove the chip and bend the two pins we'll need to access. Otherwise you will need to carefully cut the two pins, which is somewhat more tricky. What we're after are pins 12 and 13, which represent the two audio channels of the 2600. If you look at the opposite side of the board, you'll see that these pins are tied together. An alternative to soldering directly to the pins is to cut the trace between pins 12 and 13 on the opposite side of the board and then solder to the connections on the bottom side of the board instead. However, there is less clearance with the RF shield on the bottom of the board, so care must be taken to insulate any work performed on the backside of the board.

    If the TIA chip is socketed, remove it and bend pins 12 and 13 upward, as shown in Figure 7.27. Then reinsert the chip into the socket, taking care to note the proper orientation of the chip. If the chip is soldered to the board, you can use a Dremel tool to cut the pins as close to the board as possible and then bend them upward.

Figure 7.27 TIA Chip with Pins 12 and 13 Bent Upward

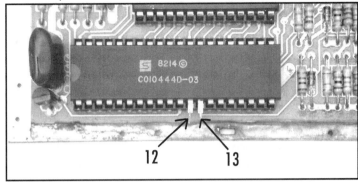

5. Now warm up your soldering iron and solder the two 2.0K ohm resistors from pins 12 and 13 to the 5V solder pad shown in Figure 7.28.

Figure 7.28 Resistors Soldered to the TIA

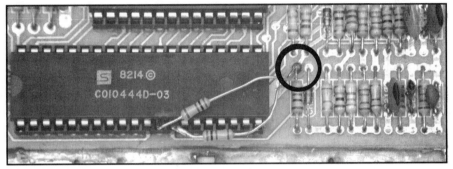

6. Now prepare the two wires that you will be soldering to the audio jacks on the back of the 2600 case. Cut two lengths of 18-gauge wire, each about a foot long. These wires will run from the TIA chip to the back of the case. Solder a 0.1uF capacitor to each of these cables. You might want to cut a 1-inch or so length of 1/32-inch heat-shrink tubing and slide it over each of these cables—these will help shield the connections you make to the TIA chip. If you don't have heat-shrink tubing, you can also use electrical tape to insulate the connections, but it's important that they are shielded in some fashion to prevent shorts from occurring when the RF shield is replaced. Now take the opposite end of each capacitor and solder one each to the joints formed by pins 12 and 13 and the two resistors you previously soldered, as shown in Figure 7.29.

Figure 7.29 Capacitors Soldered to the TIA

7. We now have to prepare the 2600 case to mount the two RCA jacks. The easiest place to mount the jacks is along the back side of the top half of the case. This is the same side that the RF cable resides on. Using a drill or Dremel tool with a 1/4" drill bit, drill the two holes (see Figure 7.30).

WARNING: HARDWARE HARM

Do not place the holes too close to the side of the case, or too low, or they will be difficult to access from either inside the case or the outside (when the top half of the 2600 case sits on the bottom half, there is a lip that overlaps). Also, space the holes sufficiently wide apart so that the two jacks are not too close to one another.

Figure 7.30 Cutting Holes in the 2600 Case

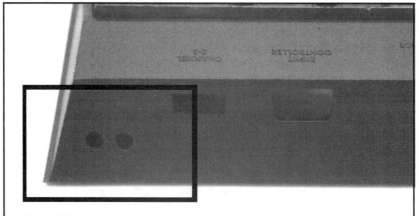

8. Once the holes are drilled, you can attach the two RCA jacks. They should comprise three pieces: the jack itself, a small washer, and a nut. For each jack, remove the washer and nut, and push the threaded side of the jack through from the outside of the case. Then slide the washer over the jack and screw the nut into place. When attached, they should resemble Figure 7.31.

Figure 7.31 RCA Jacks Attached

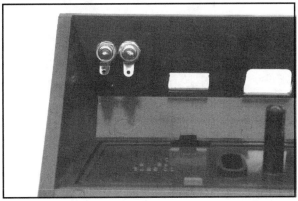

9. With the jacks attached, you can now solder the last few connections. The tab on the outside ring of each jack needs to be soldered to ground. Join these two tabs together with a piece of wire (preferably black so it is easy to denote as a ground connection), and then using a longer length of wire, solder one of the tabs to an available ground on the circuit board. If you flip the board over, you'll see that the most convenient solder point is connected to the Channel 3/4 switch. Solder the wire to this location, as shown in Figure 7.32.

Figure 7.32 Solder RCA Phono Jacks to Ground

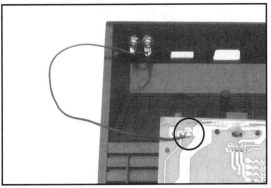

10. The only two remaining connections are for the wires you soldered to the TIA chip. Solder one wire each to the center post of each RCA jack, as shown in Figure 7.33.

Figure 7.33 Solder Wires from TIA to Center Posts of RCA Jacks

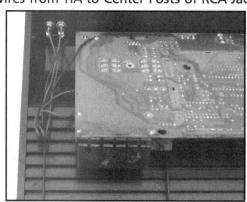

11. You're done! Your completed hack should look similar to Figure 7.34. You can use a glue gun to securely attach the wires to the circuit board, to make sure that they don't get in the way of the cartridge port or switches.

Figure 7.34 Completed Stereo Hack

Reassemble the 2600 by replacing the RF shield, plugging the RF cable into the board, placing the board back in the case, and screwing the case back together. (Remember, the long screws are for the bottom holes.) Once the device is assembled (see Figure 7.35), hook your 2600 up to your television and stereo system and fire up a game of Combat. You should distinctly hear Player 1's tank in one speaker and Player 2's tank in the other. Try some other games as well—you might be surprised at the stereo effects you find!

If you'd like to try your hand at Skeleton+, a modern homebrew game programmed to take advantage of stereo output, you can purchase the game in cartridge form at AtariAge (www.atariage.com/store). You can also download the binary from AtariAge so that you can try it in your favorite Atari 2600 emulator before buying—the author has made it freely available for anyone to download.

Figure 7.35 Stereo Jacks on Outside of Case

Under the Hood: How the Hack Works

The specialized TIA chip in the Atari 2600 supports two audio channels, which are output separately on different pins exiting the chip. As soon as these pins connect to the circuit board, they are tied together, resulting in a monaural output from your television. Because the signals for these two channels exit the TIA separately, we can tap into them and direct the signals elsewhere, as we have done with this hack.

Many games are stereo in nature, due only to the fact that the Atari 2600 has two audio channels. Many of Atari's earlier games used one channel for Player 1's sound effects and the second channel for Player 2's sound effects. This results in a very noticeable and useful stereo effect. A recent homebrew game for the 2600, Skeleton+, intentionally uses the stereo effect to help direct the player to his foe in a 3D maze. However, with some games, the stereo effect might be less desirable, as is the case with Pitfall II, where the (excellent) music plays in one channel and the sound effects in the other.

A useful addition to this hack is to add a switch that allows you to toggle between stereo output and mono output. This would allow you to enjoy games like Pitfall II, without having to deal with potentially annoying stereo sound effects.

Atari 7800 Blue LED Modification

The Atari 7800 features a red LED that is illuminated when the system power is on. This hack explains how you can replace this stock LED with a blue LED to add a unique touch to your Atari 7800 system.

Preparing for the Hack

For this hack you'll need two components (shown in Figure 7.36):

- A 3.7V, 20mA, 2600mcd blue LED, Radio Shack part #276-316
- A 470 ohm, 1/4 watt, 5-percent resistor, Radio Shack part #271-1317

Figure 7.36 Required Parts

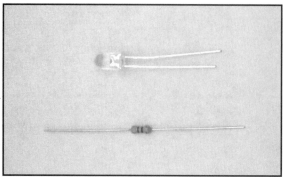

We'll use a blue LED with forward voltage of 3.7V and a brightness of 2600mcd, coupled with a 470 ohm current limiting resistor. You can experiment with different values of resistance if you'd like a brighter or dimmer LED. The resistor installed in the 7800 is 120 ohms, which, if paired with the 3.7V LED, results in significantly higher light output.

The tools required for this hack are as follows:

- Phillips head screwdriver, standard size
- Soldering iron
- Solder sucker or solder braid
- Wire cutters

Performing the Hack

Do the following:

1. We first need to open the 7800. Flip the case upside down and remove the five screws holding the case together, as shown in Figure 7.37. The bottom-center screw may be covered by a small, round sticker, in which case you'll have to remove the sticker first.

Figure 7.37 Remove Screws as Shown

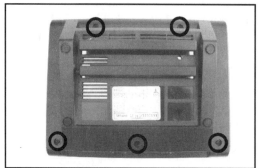

2. Turn the case back over and then remove the top half of the case. The board will be sitting inside; remove it from the case. It is not necessary to remove the RF shield from the board to perform this hack, but we removed it to make the board easier to work on. To remove the RF shield, use a pair of needlenose pliers to straighten all the metal tabs holding the shield in place, and simply pull the shield up off the board, as shown in Figure 7.38.

Figure 7.38 Remove RF Shielding

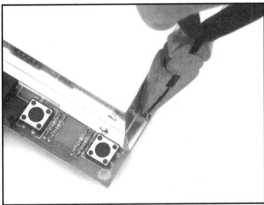

3. We're going to be working with the lower-left portion of the Atari 7800 circuit board where the LED is located, as highlighted in Figure 7.39.

Figure 7.39 The Atari 7800 LED

4. The next order of business is to remove the existing LED and the accompanying resistor, as highlighted in Figure 7.39. Flip the board over and unsolder the four connections shown in Figure 7.40. To remove the LED from the board, you will need to squeeze the two plastic tabs holding the plastic housing for the LED to the board.

WARNING: HARDWARE HARM

Be careful when removing the LED from the board—you don't want to pull up the solder pads from the front side of the board, to which you don't have access due to the LED's plastic spacer. Try to remove as much solder as possible from the joints on the bottom of the board, and then carefully pull the LED up from the board while heating the connections.

Figure 7.40 Unsolder and Remove

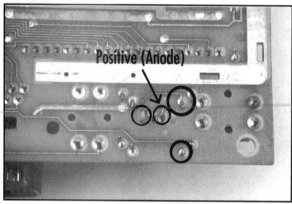

5. Once you have unsoldered the resistor and LED, remove the red LED from the white plastic spacer. Place the blue LED into the spacer and then solder it to the board. The long lead of the LED is positive and must be soldered to the connection closest to the resistor you removed. The positive lead is highlighted on the back of the board in Figure 7.40. Next, solder the 470 ohm resistor in the space formally occupied by the original resistor you removed. When you're done, the LED and resistor should resemble Figure 7.41.

Figure 7.41 New LED and Resistor

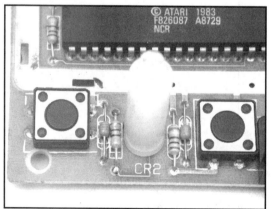

6. If you are careful and don't have anything underneath the 7800 that could short any connections on the bottom side of the board, you can plug in the power supply and press the power button (lower-left corner, as denoted in Figure 7.42) to see how the new LED looks. However, for a more accurate gauge of how the LED looks, you should view the LED inside the assembled case, since the hole for the LED on the 7800 is fairly small.

Figure 7.42 Power Applied

7. You can now reassemble your 7800 by placing the board back in the bottom half of the case, fitting the top half of the case back in place, and then screwing the case back together using the five screws you removed earlier (see Figure 7.43). Enjoy the new look of your Atari 7800!

Figure 7.43 Blue LED Happiness on the Atari 7800

Under the Hood: How the Hack Works

So how did we decide to use a 470 ohm resistor and an LED with a forward voltage of 3.7 volts? We use Ohm's Law, which allows us to calculate a reasonable value for the resistor based on what we know about the available voltage and the specifications of the LED. In this case, we have 5 volts available as supplied to us by the 7800. The existing resistor in the 7800 is 150 ohms. The specifications of the blue LED we'd like to use are:

- Forward voltage (V_F): 3.7V
- Forward current (I_F): 20mA

The resistor is placed in series with the LED to act as a current limiter and to let only the desired current pass to the LED. This is done to protect the LED from exceeding its maximum current specification. By adjusting the value of the resistor, we adjust the amount of current going to the LED, which in turn changes the brightness of LED illumination. Armed with this information, we can calculate our desired resistor value using Ohm's Law, which states:

Voltage = Current x Resistance, or V = I x R

To calculate resistance, we use the formula as follows:

Resistance = Voltage / Current, or R = V / I

Plugging in the values for the voltage and current expected by the LED, we get:

R = (5V – 3.7V) / 0.02A = 65 ohm

So, in this case, if we were to use a 65 ohm resistor, this would power the LED at its 20mA forward current (essentially the full brightness of the LED), and given the LED's high efficiency (2600mcd), it would be very bright indeed. We want to see the LED, but we don't want it so bright that our eyes are drawn to it while we're trying to focus on the games we're playing. Therefore, we want more resistance before the LED, which will limit more current going to the LED and cause the LED to be dimmer in appearance.

With an application such as this, you often need to experiment to find a brightness that is appropriate. Applying Ohm's Law allows us to determine the minimum resistance required so we don't overpower the LED, which could cause it to burn out. A 470 ohm value seems to result in a reasonable level of brightness that is easily visible when the 7800 case is put back together, but not overbearing. Again using Ohm's Law, we can determine how much current this results going to the LED:

Current = Voltage / Resistance, or I = V / R

I = (5V – 3.7V) / 470 ohms = 0.0027A = 2.7mA

Using this formula, we can see that we are driving the LED at 2.7mA, which is only a fraction of the current the LED is rated at, significantly reducing its brightness. Feel free to experiment with different values of resistance to increase or decrease the LED's light output.

Atari 7800 Game Compatibility Hack to Play Certain 2600 Games

The Atari 7800, Atari's third-generation cartridge-based game console, will play Atari 2600 games without needing an additional adapter, unlike Atari's second-generation system, the 5200, which requires the VCS Cartridge Adapter to play 2600 games. However, some cartridges will not work on many 7800 consoles, including Activision games that use the FE bank-switching method (Space

Shuttle, Robot Tank, and Decathlon), as well as the Supercharger and Cuttle Cart, two RAM-based devices that allow games to be loaded into their memory.

Atari added a circuit to later versions of the Atari 7800 to fix a compatibility problem with the 2600 game Dark Chambers but in the process broke compatibility with other previously mentioned titles. This hack will show you how to modify your 7800 to fix the compatibility problems and let you play more 2600 games. However, executing the hack will prevent the 2600 version of Dark Chambers from playing (though the 7800 version will still work fine).

NEED TO KNOW... WHAT IS BANK SWITCHING?

When Atari designed the 2600, they gave it a 12-bit-wide external address space and an 8-bit-wide data bus, limiting 2600 games to a maximum size of 4KB without any special circuitry. At the time the 2600 was designed, Atari's hardware engineers felt that 4K would be more than enough for any 2600 game.

To get around the cartridge size limitation, Atari introduced bank switching with the release of the game Asteroids. Bank switching is a method used to overcome a memory size limitation (such as 4KB for the Atari 2600) and allows a larger-size memory device to be used with a cartridge, thus providing more data storage for the system. Bank switching requires specially designed logic circuitry on the cartridge to handle the specific schemes. In the case of Asteroids, Atari used what is now known as the F8 bank-switching scheme (for 8K), although they would later create games that use F6 (for 16K games) and F4 (for 32K games). Third-party companies such as Activision would develop their own bank-switching schemes independently, leading to a wide variety of bank-switching methods, including the FE method Activision uses that causes problems on many Atari 7800 consoles.

Bank switching generally works by defining "hot spots" the game program uses to switch between memory sections (or *banks*) of the game ROM. In the case of Atari's F8 method, this is used to switch between two 4K banks of memory. Having two 4KB banks gives the system a possible 8KB of accessible data space. If the game accesses address 1FF8, the first 4KB bank is used. If the game accesses address 1FF9, the second 4KB bank is used. This is the simplest bank-switching method and the most commonly implemented.

For a thorough explanation of the majority of known bank-switching methods, refer to www.tripoint.org/kevtris/files/sizes.txt, written by Kevin Horton.

Preparing for the Hack

This is a quick and easy hack. The required tools as follows:

- Phillips head screwdriver, standard size

- Wire cutters and stripper

- Needlenose pliers

- Soldering iron (optional) if you want to remove the component instead of just clipping it out

■   Solder sucker or solder braid (optional) if you want to remove the component instead of just clipping it out

Performing the Hack

Do the following:

1.   The first thing we need to do is open the 7800. Flip the case upside down and remove the five screws holding the case together. The bottom-center screw might be covered by a small sticker. A picture of the bottom of the 7800 case with the screw locations highlighted can be found in Figure 7.37 earlier in this chapter. Remove the top of the case, and then extract the board from the case. Using a pair of needlenose pliers, straighten all the metal tabs holding the RF shielding in place, as shown in Figure 7.44. Don't forget the two that are between the top of the cartridge port and the metal heat sink at the top of the board.

Figure 7.44 Removing the RF Shield

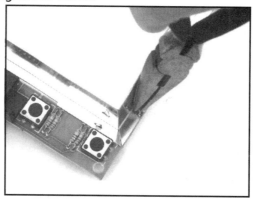

2.   Once you have the RF shield removed, you need to verify that this compatibility fix applies to your particular 7800. The area we are interested in is depicted in Figure 7.45.

Figure 7.45 Atari 7800 Board

3. There are two things to look for to make sure you can perform the 7800 compatibility hack on your system. First, verify that there are four ICs in a row along the right side of the board (see Figure 7.46). If only three ICs are present, then this mod does not apply. Second, verify that R66 is installed on the board. R66 is the rightmost resistor above the 74LS174 chip. There should be seven resistors and two capacitors lined up in this row. If not, this modification does not apply to your 7800.

Figure 7.46 Verify That Your 7800 Has These Components

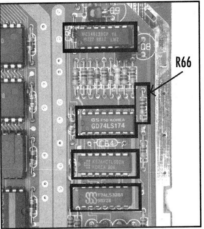

4. If your board qualifies, all you need to do is clip the capacitor at location C64 from the board, as highlighted in Figure 7.47. Note that the capacitor has already been removed in Figures 7.46 and 7.47. You can also unsolder the capacitor instead of clipping it out, if you choose. If you're feeling ambitious, you can install a switch to enable and disable this capacitor, for on-demand compatibility with the 2600 version of Dark Chambers.

Figure 7.47 Remove the Capacitor at Location C64

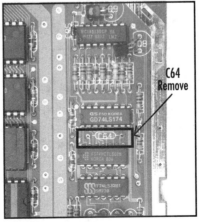

5. Now you can reassemble your 7800. First, replace the RF shield, making sure you retwist the metal tabs that keep the two halves of the RF shield together. Then place the board in the bottom half of the 7800 shell, attach the top half of the case, and screw the case back together with the five screws you removed earlier.

You can now test some of the games known to have problems with the Atari 7800, including Activison's Decathlon, Robot Tank, and Space Shuttle. In addition, the Supercharger and Cuttle Cart cartridges should also work without problems.

Under the Hood: How the Hack Works

This hack works by disabling a circuit that Atari apparently installed in order to fix a compatibility issue with Atari's 2600 version of Dark Chambers. This timing circuit involves the 74LS02 (a Quad 2-Input NOR gate), the logic chip directly below the C64 capacitor you clipped or removed. Some Atari 7800 systems are missing this chip as well as C64 and R66. Figure 7.48 highlights a 7800 board that never had these parts installed.

Figure 7.48 A 7800 Board Without the Compatibility Circuit

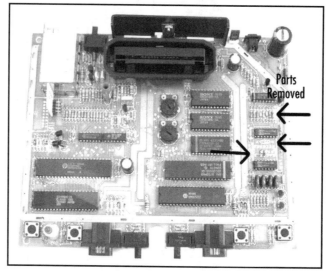

Atari 7800 Voltage Regulator Replacement

A common problem for the Atari 7800 is for the 5V voltage regulator to fail. This will render your 7800 inoperable because the system will not receive power. It's even possible for the regulator to completely snap off the board due to the weight of the attached heat sink. On many 7800s the heat sink is not soldered into place, allowing it to wobble back and forth, which causes stress and wear on the pins. This simple hack simply involves opening the 7800, removing the existing voltage regulator, and soldering a new one in place.

Preparing for the Hack

If your 7800 is not powering up, it could be for several different reasons, one of which could be a voltage regulator failure. If your voltage regulator seems to be functioning properly, then there is no need to replace it and you'll need to troubleshoot your system further to diagnose the problem.

If you do need to replace the voltage regulator, you'll need a replacement 7805 5V, 1A linear voltage regulator (Radio Shack part #276-1770), as depicted in Figure 7.49. This is a common part that you should be able to find at most electronics stores. You'll also want some heat sink compound (Radio Shack part #276-1372A) to place between the heat sink and regulator, which assists in heat transfer from the regulator to the heat sink.

Figure 7.49 7805 Voltage Regulator

The required tools for this hack are as follows:

- Multimeter
- Phillips head screwdriver, standard size
- Wire cutters and stripper
- Needlenose pliers
- Soldering iron
- Solder sucker or solder braid

Performing the Hack

Do the following:

1. First we need to open the 7800. Flip the case upside down and remove the five screws holding the case together. The bottom-center screw might be covered by a small sticker. A picture of the bottom of the 7800 case with the screw locations highlighted can be found in the Figure 7.37 earlier in this chapter. Remove the top of the case and then extract the

board. Using a pair of needlenose pliers, straighten all the metal tabs holding the RF shielding in place. Don't forget the two that are between the top of the cartridge port and the metal heat sink at the top of the board. The voltage regulator is located at the top of the board, immediately above the cartridge port, as shown in Figure 7.50.

Figure 7.50 Atari 7800 Voltage Regulator and Heat Sink

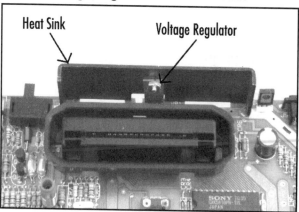

2. You'll first want to test the voltage regulator to see if power is even reaching it and then check to see what the output voltage is. To do this, plug the 7800 power supply into the board, and then apply power to the system by pressing the power button located in the lower-left corner of the board. Then carefully flip the board over and use a multimeter to measure the voltage on the input and output pins of the regulator. Figure 7.51 highlights the relevant pins on the reverse side of the 7800 board. You should measure approximately 12V on the input side and 5V on the output. If you do not measure a voltage on the input to the regulator, the regulator might be loose or broken on the board (or your problem lies elsewhere). If you measure a voltage on the input side but do not measure a voltage on the output side (or if your output voltage is not hovering around 5V), this hack is for you!

Figure 7.51 Voltage Regulator Connections

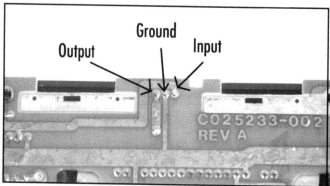

3. To continue with the hack, turn the power off to the 7800 and unplug the power adapter from the board. To remove the voltage regulator, unsolder the three connections for the voltage regulator on the backside of the board. If the heat sink is also soldered in place, unsolder that from the board as well. Figure 7.52 shows which connections you want to unsolder.

Figure 7.52 Unsolder the Heat Sink and Voltage Regulator

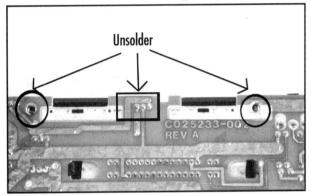

4. Flip the board back over so that the component side is visible, and lift the voltage regulator and heat sink as one piece from the board. Unscrew the voltage regulator from the heat sink. Discard the regulator but keep the screw, nut, and washer. Apply a small amount of thermal transfer compound to the backside of the new voltage regulator. Attach the new regulator to the heat sink using the screw, nut, and washer you saved, as shown in Figure 7.53. The washer and nut should be used on the side of the heat sink opposite the voltage regulator.

Figure 7.53 New Voltage Regulator Attached to Heat Sink

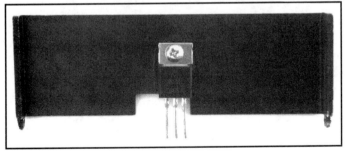

5. Carefully place the leads for the voltage regulator through the three holes in the circuit board, as well as the mounts for the heat sink through the larger holes intended for them. Flip the board over and solder the voltage regulator in place. You should also solder the heat sink in place so it is more secure, but you will need to use a higher-temperature soldering

iron, since the heatsink will quickly draw away heat as you attempt to solder it. Trim the leads of the voltage regulator.

6. You can do a quick test to see if your repair worked by plugging the power supply into the board and then turning the power on (see Figure 7.54). Before you do this, make sure there are no loose screws, wires, or other conductive materials underneath the circuit board. If the only problem with your 7800 board was the voltage regulator, it should turn right on!

Figure 7.54 Testing the Repair

7. Reassemble the 7800, first by replacing the RF shield, then placing the board in the bottom half of the 7800 shell, attaching the top half, and then screwing the case back together with the five screws you removed earlier.

Under the Hood: How the Hack Works

If you've opened many electronic devices (such as the Atari 7800 described in this hack), you've probably come across a voltage regulator fairly often. A voltage regulator takes an input voltage on one pin and regulates it to a fixed voltage, which is output on another pin. A third pin is used as a connection to ground. The Atari 7800 requires a 5V source to power the system, so Atari chose a common 7805 linear voltage regulator.

The connection diagram for the 7805 voltage regulator used in the 7800 is shown in Figure 7.55 and Table 7.3.

Figure 7.55 7805 Voltage Regulator Mechanical Outline

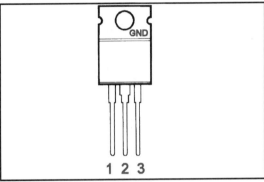

Table 7.3 7805 Voltage Regulator Pinout

Pin	Function
1	Input voltage (7V-20V)
2	Ground
3	Output voltage (5V)

When looking at a voltage regulator of the same type as found in the 7800, hold it so that the flat portion of the regulator that is connected to the heat sink faces you. The left pin is the input voltage, the middle pin (as well as the mounting point for the heat sink) is ground, and the right pin is the output voltage.

In order to function properly, linear voltage regulators must be fed a higher voltage than is expected on output. The 7805 requires a minimum input voltage of about 7V in order to produce a reliable 5V output. Linear regulators are notoriously inefficient, and most of the unused energy is lost as heat, which is why voltage regulators often have a heat sink attached. Without the heat sink, the voltage regulator might possibly overheat and malfunction.

Atari 7800 Power Supply Plug Retrofit

The Atari 7800 uses a proprietary power connector instead of a standard power connector typically used on electronic devices (as well as all of Atari's other game consoles). Due to this proprietary connector, it can often be difficult to find a replacement power supply to power your system, since the system has not been on the market in over a decade. The plug attached to the power cord is shown in Figure 7.56, and the connector it plugs into is shown in Figure 7.57. We'll never know the logic behind Atari's decision to use this odd connector (were they worried about losing sales of replacement power supplies to third-party companies?), but at least we can easily rectify the situation. This hack will show you how to add a standard power jack to your Atari 7800 so you can use an off-the-shelf power adapter. We'll leave the existing 7800 power jack in place so you can continue to use it if you choose.

Figure 7.56 Atari 7800 Power Connector

Figure 7.57 Atari 7800 Power Receptacle

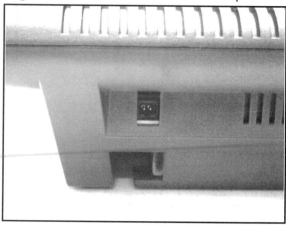

Preparing for the Hack

For this hack you'll need:

- A panel-mount 1/8-inch phone jack, Radio Shack part #274-248
- Two lengths of 18AWG insulated copper wire to connect the phone jack to the 7800 power connections, each about a foot long, preferably red and black

You'll also want a 5V, 1A power supply with a 1/8-inch connector, center positive, to use with your new power jack once it's assembled. You can also use a 2600 power supply, which is more common though only supplies 500mA of power. This is sufficient to power the 7800, but some cartridges, such as the Cuttle Cart, may not operate properly with the 2600 adapter. The tools required for this hack are as follows:

- Phillips head screwdriver, standard size
- Wire cutters and stripper
- Soldering iron
- Small adjustable wrench or needlenose pliers
- Heat gun
- Drill or Dremel tool

Performing the Hack

Do the following:

1. The first thing we need to do is to open the 7800. Flip the case upside down and remove the five screws holding the case together. The bottom-center screw might be covered by a small sticker. A picture of the bottom of the 7800 case with the screw locations highlighted can be found in Figure 7.37 in this chapter. Remove the top of the case. The board will be sitting inside; remove it from the case. Using a pair of needlenose pliers, straighten all the metal tabs holding the RF shielding in place. Don't forget the two that are between the top of the cartridge port and the metal heat sink at the top of the board. Once the RF shielding is removed, the 7800 circuit board should resemble Figure 7.58.

Figure 7.58 Atari 7800 Circuit Board

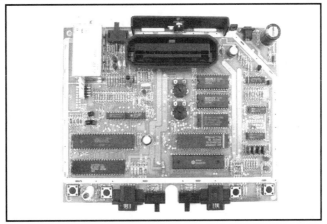

2. The existing power supply connector is on the upper-right corner of the board, adjacent to a large capacitor, as shown in Figure 7.59. We'll be leaving the existing connector in place, but an alternative to this hack is to remove the existing power connector and place a new connector directly on the board. We'll mount the new connector in the bottom shell of the case, about a half-inch down from the top edge of the shell.

Figure 7.59 Existing Power Connector

3. Remove the nut and washer from the 1/8-inch phono jack. These will be used to secure the jack to the case, so put them aside for now. Cut two 4-inch lengths of the 18AWG wire. You can use longer lengths of wire to give you more flexibility. These wires will connect power and ground from the 7800 board to the phono jack. If you can, use black wire for the ground connection and red wire for the positive connection, as shown in Figure 7.60. Strip a short piece of insulation from the ends of each wire.

Figure 7.60 Wired Phono Jack

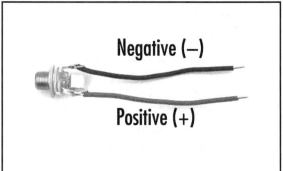

Negative (–)

Positive (+)

4. Solder one wire to the center post of the phono jack (which will be positive) and the other to the ground terminal. There may be more than two terminals, so if you're unsure what's positive and negative, use a continuity tester to verify that you are attaching the wires to the correct locations.

5. Now it's time to solder these connections to the 7800 board. It's easiest to solder these connections to the backside of the board, so that's what we'll do here. Flip the board over and locate the corner where the existing power connector is attached. We will solder to the two large solder pads directly to the right of the connector (as shown in Figure 7.61). Solder the positive wire to the right solder pad, and the ground wire to the left solder pad.

WARNING: HARDWARE HARM

Ensure that the wires are connected to the proper locations on the phono jack and the 7800 circuit board. Failure to do so may cause damage to your 7800, power supply, or circuit breakers in your home when you apply power.

Figure 7.61 Solder Wires to Board

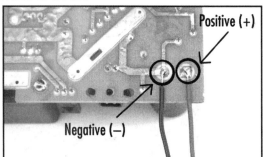

Positive (+)

Negative (–)

6. The next step is to mount the phono jack onto the back of the 7800 housing. Using a Dremel tool or drill, drill a hole in the bottom half of the 7800 case, as indicated in Figure 7.62. The size of the opening you need to drill should be specified on the packaging for the connector. If it's not, you can eyeball the size, taking care not to drill a hole that is too large. It's better to err on the small size and work your way up if need be. You may opt to place the connector elsewhere, but make sure the connector and wires will not interfere with placement of the circuit board in the case.

Figure 7.62 Drilling a New Hole in the 7800 Case

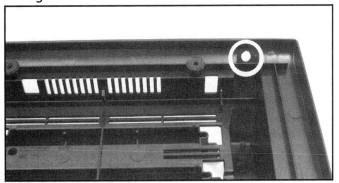

7. Replace the RF shield back onto the 7800 circuit board, place the board back into the bottom of the 7800 case, and place the phono plug connector through the hole you just created. Thread the washer and nut onto the opposite side of the jack, tightening them so that the connector is securely attached to the 7800 case, as shown in Figure 7.63.

Figure 7.63 Attaching the New Power Connector to the Case

8. Finish reassembly of the 7800 by attaching the top half of the case and then screwing the case back together with the five screws you removed at the beginning of this hack. When reassembled, your system should resemble Figure 7.64.

Figure 7.64 Outside View

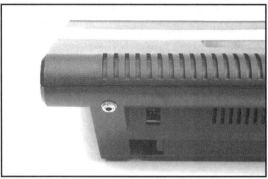

Now it's time to test your work! Hook the 7800 to a video source, insert a 2600 or 7800 game, and plug in an appropriate power supply to the new jack you just added. Turn the system on, and enjoy!

Other Hacks

The hacks presented in this chapter are only the beginning of what you can do with your old gaming systems. We've listed some of the more complex and advanced hacks here; detailed instructions for many of these are available on the Internet. Whenever possible we've pointed you toward resources for additional information.

2600 Composite/S-Video Modifications

The quality of the standard RF output on an Atari 2600 can be lacking, especially if you're using a TV/Game switchbox that further reduces the video signal. The first and easiest thing you can do to improve your video signal is to replace the TV/Game switchbox with a coaxial (F-Type) to Female RCA adapter, which you can find at Radio Shack (part #278-276, pictured in Figure 7.65). This allows you to directly connect the RF signal into the cable jack on your television, bypassing the switchbox and generally resulting in a much cleaner picture.

If this isn't sufficient, you can try your hand at one of the various composite and S-video mods for the Atari 2600. These mods have varying results, but generally they should give you a better picture than the built-in RF signal. Several such mods are detailed in the Atari 2600 FAQ (www.atariage.com/2600/faq/index.html#composite).

Figure 7.65 Coaxial (F-Type) to Female RCA Adapter

Nathan Strum has put together a Web page with comparisons of several composite and S-Video mods, as well as screenshots showing the differences between them and the 2600's built-in RF output. You can find the page at www.cheeptech.com/2600mods/2600mods.shtml.

Atari 7800 Composite and S-Video Output

Although the standard RF output on the Atari 7800 seems to be a bit better than that of the 2600, it can be improved further by performing a composite and/or S-Video mod. Jay Tilton (http://home.earthlink.net/~resqsoft/7800_mod.htm) and Mark Graybill (www.geocities.com/atari7800mod/7800_vidmod_construction.html) have both created video modifications for the 7800.

Sega Genesis to Atari 7800 Controller Modification

Whether through accident or design, Atari did a reasonably good job with the ergonomics of the original joystick and paddle controllers for the Atari 2600. Unfortunately, Atari's follow-on game systems, the 5200 and 7800, suffer from very uncomfortable controller designs. Although the Atari 7800 controller is more bearable than the troublesome 5200 controller, many still find its design uncomfortable to use for extended durations. With the 7800, Atari returned to an industry-standard DB-9 connector for the controller jacks, maintaining backward compatibility with 2600 controllers (since the 7800 itself is backward compatible with 2600 games). However, games that require the two distinct fire buttons of the 7800 controller cannot be enjoyed with standard 2600 controllers, which only have a single fire button.

One side benefit of this backward compatibility is that Sega Genesis and Sega Master System controllers, both of which use a DB-9 connector, can be modified for use with the 7800 to support both fire buttons. Instructions on how to do so can be found in the Atari 2600 FAQ (www.atariage.com/2600/faq/index.html#sega).

If you'd prefer to build an adapter instead of modifying existing Sega controllers, John Soper has posted schematics and instructions on how to build three different circuits (www94.pair.com/jsoper/7800_gen_adap.html).

NES Control Pad to Atari 7800 Controller Modification

Along the same lines as the Sega Genesis modification previously mentioned, an NES control pad can also be modified to work with the Atari 7800 and support both fire buttons. This hack differs from the Atari 2600 NES control pad hack described earlier in this chapter. Complete instructions can be found at www.atariage.com/2600/archives/nes_atari.html.

Atari 7800 DevOS Modification and Cable Creation

The BIOS built into the Atari 7800 can be replaced with a Development Operating System (called the DevOS), which was created by Eckhard Stolberg, an avid classic gamer and master programmer. The DevOS allows the Atari 7800 to be used to dump 7800 and 2600 cartridges to a PC via a parallel cable. With the DevOS installed, your 7800 will display a menu that allows you to transfer data from the 7800 to the PC, load data into a special RAM cartridge, or play whatever cartridge is inserted into the 7800. Complete information on how to perform this hack and build the necessary cable (and even a RAM cartridge) can be found at Eckhard Stolberg's VCS Workshop Page (http://home.arcor.de/estolberg/tools/index.html).

Atari Resources on the Web

Atari game console and home computer enthusiasts will find a great number of resources on the Web. Whether you're looking for information about your favorite games, how to hack your system to give it capabilities never intended by the designers, or forums where you can discuss Atari systems with other fans, you're sure to find it online somewhere. The following is a list of some of our favorite Atari-related sites:

- **AtariAge: www.atariage.com** Evolved from The Atari 2600 Nexus in 2001, AtariAge contains a wide variety of information about Atari game systems, featuring thousands of scans of 2600, 5200, 7800, Jaguar, and Lynx games, manuals, and boxes. In addition, you'll find the latest Atari-related news, updates on new homebrew games in development, an online store featuring classic gaming hardware and software, and an active community discussing Atari systems in online forums.

- **Atari History Museum: www.atarimuseum.com** The Atari History Museum is a comprehensive Web site covering the entire range of Atari's history, from its early days of Pong to the days when the Atari Jaguar was state of the art. You'll find a huge wealth of historical information and pictures about Atari game consoles, computers, arcade games, and much more. The Atari History Museum got its start on the Web in 1997 and has been adding to and expanding its collection ever since. Its curator, Curt Vendel, originally ran a bulletin board system in the 1980s dedicated to Atari history and information.

- **AtariArchives.org: www.atariarchives.org** AtariArchives.org is an impressive collection of books, information, and software for Atari and other classic computers. The highlights include an APX software and information archive, the Cleveland Free-Net Atari SIG Archive, and the full text of many classic computing books. AtariArchives.org is an invaluable and high-quality reference for any fans of classic computing.

- **AtariProtos.com: www.AtariProtos.com** AtariProtos.com is devoted to unearthing the secrets of Atari prototypes and features a growing repository of comprehensive prototype reviews for the 2600 and 5200. Each prototype is vigorously played and studied until enough is learned that a thorough review can be written. Even minor details between different versions of the game are highlighted and are often accompanied by many screenshots. AtariProtos.com is a great site for people who are curious about the oft confusing world of prototypes.

- **The Atari Times: www.ataritimes.com** The Atari Times is a frequently updated site dedicated to Atari game systems and computers, with a large number of comprehensive reviews, features, interviews, and other informative content.

- **B&C ComputerVisions: www.myatari.com** B&C ComputerVisions has been serving the Atari videogaming and Atari computing communities for nearly 20 years. B&C stocks over 5,000 Atari-related products and accepts and ships orders for Atari computers, videogames, and parts worldwide. They also service most Atari products, except for monitors, power supplies, and coin-operated Atari games.

- **Best Electronics: www.best-electronics-ca.com** Best Electronics carries a large range of replacement parts and accessories for Atari game systems and computers, serving Atari users for 20 years. Featuring one of the largest inventories of Atari parts, Best Electronics has a printed catalog of more than 200 pages with over 4,000 Atari products, parts, and accessories.

- **Classic Computer Magazine Archive: www.atarimagazines.com** The Classic Computer Magazine Archive (formerly known as The Digital Antic Project) contains the full texts of several classic computing magazines such as *Antic, STart,* and *Hi-Res*. In addition, the full texts of a large number of *Creative Computing* magazine issues are online, as are both issues of *Creative Computing Video & Arcade Games*.

- ***MyAtari Magazine*: www.myatari.net** *MyAtari Magazine* is a free monthly online magazine for Atari users, featuring in-depth articles, reviews, and tutorials.

Chapter 8

Hack Your Atari 5200 and 8-Bit Computer

Hacks in this Chapter:

- Adding a Blue Power LED to Your Atari 5200

- Creating an Atari 5200 Paddle

- Free Yourself from the 5200 Four-Port Switchbox

- Build Atari 8-Bit S-Video and Composite Cables

Introduction

In 1979, two years after the introduction of the Atari Video Computer System (later known as the 2600), Atari released its first line of personal computers. Based on the Motorola 6502 8-bit microprocessor, the Atari 8-bit computers were well-engineered, easy to use, and modular in design. At the time of their release, they featured powerful graphics and sound hardware not available on other personal computers, simple connection of peripherals via the Serial Input/Output (SIO) connector, four controller ports, and a sophisticated (for the time) operating system (OS).

The first two computers in the Atari 8-bit computer line were the Atari 400 and the 800. The 800 (Figure 8.1) was Atari's flagship model, featuring a full typewriter-style keyboard, two cartridge ports, internal expansion through the use of add-in card modules, and a monitor port. The Atari 400 was Atari's entry-level system housing a membrane keyboard, one cartridge port, only 8K of memory (16K would later become standard), and no monitor port.

Figure 8.1 The Atari 800 Personal Computer

In 1982, Atari updated its aging 400/800 line with the introduction of the Atari 1200XL. This new machine featured a sleek, low-profile case, 64K of built-in memory, and an improved OS with several new enhancements. Unfortunately sales of the 1200XL were extremely poor due to the fact that the revised operating system caused incompatibilities with many programs and the 1200XL did not support internal expansion. This makes the 1200XL one of the least common Atari 8-bit computers you'll encounter today.

After the poor showing of the 1200XL, Atari went back to the drawing board and in 1983 released two new XL computers, the 600XL and the 800XL. These new machines addressed the problems inherent in the 1200XL, while retaining the same physical style. The 600XL was Atari's new low-end machine, featuring 16K and a full-typewriter style keyboard, expandable to 64K with the external 1064 module. The 800XL replaced the 800, equipped with 64K of memory and a standard monitor port. One important new feature of both machines was the addition of the Parallel Bus Interface (PBI) port, giving peripherals high-bandwidth access to the machine's internal architecture. Unfortunately, Atari shelved plans to release the 1090XL Expansion Module, which would have allowed the use of external cards (such as a CP/M module) with the XL computers, and very few peripherals were ever released that take advantage of the PBI.

Atari released their third generation of 8-bit computers not long after the company was purchased by the Tramiel family. Styled in appearance after Atari's new 16-bit ST computer line, the XE (XL Enhanced) computers came in two flavors, the 65XE and the 130XE. The 65XE featured 64K of memory; the 130XE included 128K of memory and a new version of the PBI that combined the PBI and cartridge port into one interface called the Enhanced Cartridge Interface (ECI). Atari would later repackage the XE line of computers as the XE Game System in 1987, which came with a detachable keyboard, joystick, light gun, and the built-in game Missile Command.

The Atari 5200 SuperSystem

In 1982, Atari revealed the Atari 5200 SuperSystem to the gaming public. Based on the Atari 400 8-bit computer, the 5200 was Atari's answer to the competition it was receiving in the videogame market from companies such as Coleco with its ColecoVision. Atari had been working on a sequel to the 2600 called the 3200, but development was halted when it was determined that the system was too difficult to program. Atari, knowing its 8-bit line of computers already had an excellent game library, decided instead to transform its 8-bit computer into a powerful game system.

In most respects, the 5200 was very similar to the Atari 400 computer, but it featured a sleek, wedge-shaped case with only a single power button on the unit itself. The most noticeable change from the Atari 8-bit line was the inclusion of two analog joysticks. These new controllers allowed for a full 360 degrees of movement, but unfortunately they were not self-centering and proved awkward to use with many games. In addition, the controllers were highly prone to failure and became the primary bane of the system. In addition to the analog control stick, the 5200 controllers also featured two independent fire buttons, a numeric keypad, and Start, Reset, and Pause buttons built into the controller (Figure 8.2).

Figure 8.2 The Atari 5200 SuperSystem

Another poor design decision with the original 5200 system was the inclusion of an RF switchbox through which the system's power was routed. Although this is a clever design that allows the system to automatically switch the TV input to the 5200 when power is applied and eliminates the need to connect an additional cable to the 5200, the fact that the design was proprietary meant that if your RF switchbox died, you needed an expensive replacement from Atari. With the introduction of the 2-port Atari 5200, Atari changed the system's design so that the power pack plugs directly into the 5200, allowing the use of a standard RF switchbox.

Hacks in This Chapter

The Atari 8-bit computers and Atari 5200 SuperSystem have been around for over 20 years now, and in that time many hacks have been developed to enhance these systems. In addition, a large "home-brew" community is developing new software for the systems, keeping the spirit alive for Atari fans. In this chapter we describe how to perform the following Atari 8-bit and 5200 hacks:

- Adding a Blue Power LED to Your Atari 5200

- Creating an Atari 5200 Paddle

- Free Yourself from the 5200 4-Port Switchbox

- Build Atari 8-Bit S-Video and Composite Cables

Several additional hacks are described briefly at the end of this chapter, including pointers to where you can learn more about them.

Atari 5200 Blue LED Modification

The Atari 5200 uses a momentary pushbutton switch to toggle power on and off. Since this switch doesn't give a visual indication of whether the unit has power, Atari added a red LED that is illuminated when the unit is on (Figure 8.3). Blue LEDs weren't available when the Atari 5200 was designed over 20 years ago, but they are now commonplace and easily obtained. This hack details how you can install a stylish blue LED into your 5200, giving it a personal touch.

Figure 8.3 Stock 5200 Power with a Red LED

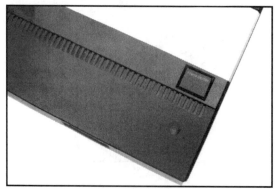

Preparing for the Hack

For this hack you'll need two additional pieces of equipment:

- 3.7V, 20mA, 2600mcd blue LED Radio Shack part number #276-316
- 470 ohm, 1/4 watt, 5% resistor Radio Shack part #271-1317

These parts can be seen in Figure 8.4. We'll use a blue LED with a forward voltage of 3.7V and a brightness of 2600mcd, coupled with a 470 ohm current limiting resistor. You can experiment with different values of resistance if you'd like a brighter or dimmer LED. The stock resistor installed in the 5200 is 150 ohms, which, if paired with the 3.7V LED, results in significantly higher light output. We'll therefore be replacing the stock resistor.

Figure 8.4 Required Parts for the 5200 Blue LED Hack

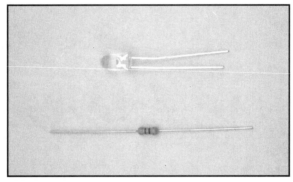

The only tools required for this hack are as follows:

- A Philips head screwdriver to open the 7800 case
- A soldering iron
- A solder sucker or solder braid
- A pair of wire cutters

Performing the Hack

Follow these steps:

1. The first order of business is to turn the Atari 5200 upside down and remove the seven screws holding the case together. The locations of the screws are shown in Figure 8.5.

WARNING: HARDWARE HARM

The two screws at the top are shorter than the rest, so you'll need to be careful to insert the longer screws into the correct holes when reassembling the 5200. Failure to do so can result in damage to the case, especially if you insert a long screw into a hole meant for one of the shorter screws.

Figure 8.5 Screw Locations of the Atari 5200

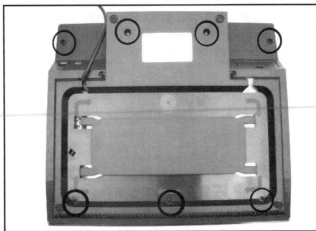

2. After removing the screws, turn the 5200 back over and slowly remove the top of the case, exposing the PCB inside.

    ■ If the RF cable is plugged into the board as shown in Figure 8.6, unplug it first.

Figure 8.6 Unplug the RF Cable, If Applicable

■ If the cable is instead soldered to the board (as shown in Figure 8.7), you may want to thread it through the hole on the bottom of the case to make the board easier to work on. Figure 8.51 further in the chapter shows how the cable is fed through the hole from inside the case. In Figure 8.5 the hole can be seen in the upper-left portion of the image (where the cable exits the case).

Figure 8.7 RF Cable Soldered to Board

Now remove the board from the case.

WARNING: HARDWARE HARM

Near the bottom of the board are two small plastic posts that are stuck through the PCB to help hold it in place. Be careful not to snap these off when you remove the board. You can use a flathead screwdriver to carefully pry the board up between the bottom edge of the board and the case to make it easier to remove. Figure 8.8 highlights where the two plastic posts are on the board.

Figure 8.8 Plastic Posts on 5200 Board

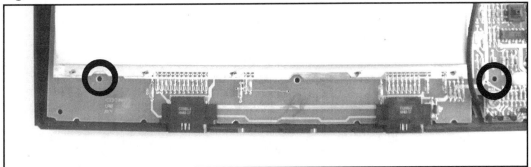

3. We're going to be working with the lower–left portion of the board where the LED is located, which fortunately does not require removal of the metal RF shield. First, unsolder the existing LED and the accompanying resistor, as denoted in Figure 8.9. To remove the LED from the board, you will need to squeeze the two plastic tabs holding the plastic housing for the LED to the board.

WARNING: HARDWARE HARM

Be careful when removing the LED from the board; you don't want to pull up the solder pads from the front side of the board, which you don't have access to due to the LED's plastic spacer. Try and remove as much solder as possible from the joints on the bottom of the board, and then carefully pull the LED up from the board while you heat the connections.

4. Flip the board over and unsolder the four connections shown in Figures 8.9 and 8.10.

Figure 8.9 Resistor and LED

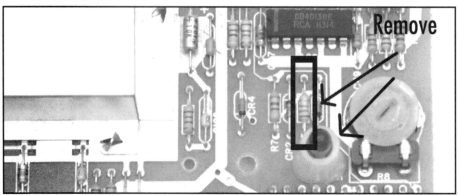

Figure 8.10 Unsolder These Four Connections and Remove the Resistor and LED

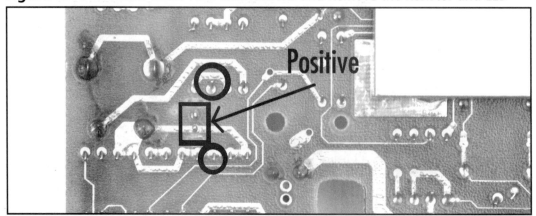

Once you have unsoldered the resistor and LED, remove them from the board. Remove the LED from the white plastic spacer. Place the blue LED into the housing and then solder it to the board. The long lead of the LED is positive and must be soldered to the upper connection, as shown in Figure 8.10. Next, solder the 470 ohm resistor in the space formally occupied by the original resistor you removed. When you're done, the LED and resistor should resemble Figure 8.11.

Figure 8.11 New LED and Resistor

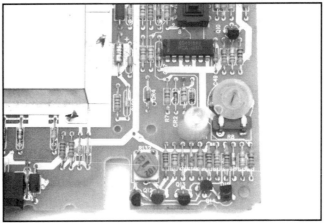

If you are careful and don't have anything underneath the 5200 that could short connections on the bottom of the board, you can now plug in the power supply and press the power button (the black button above the LED) to see how the new LED looks (Figure 8.12). However, you won't have an accurate feel for how the LED looks until you put the 5200 back together and see it shining through the dark plastic of the case.

Figure 8.12 Power Applied

You can now reassemble your 5200 (Figure 8.13). First, place the board back in the bottom half of the case, remembering that there are two small posts that need to stick through the board near the bottom. Next, plug the RF cable back into the board (if applicable). Now you can place the top half of the case back in place and then screw the case back together using the seven screws you removed earlier, keeping in mind that the two short screws are for the two holes at the top. Plug your 5200 back in, insert a cartridge, and power it up! Enjoy the new look of your Atari 5200!

Figure 8.13 Blue LED Happiness on the Atari 5200

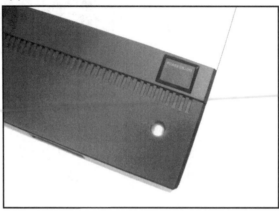

Under the Hood: How the Hack Works

The "Atari 7800 Blue LED Modification" section in Chapter 7 features a discussion of how the LED and resistor values were chosen for this hack. The Atari 5200 uses a 150 ohm resistor to limit the current flow through the LED, compared to the 120 ohm resistor found in the 7800.

Creating an Atari 5200 Paddle

Unlike the Atari 2600 for which Atari included a pair of paddle controllers (Figure 8.14), the Atari 5200 shipped only with analog joystick controllers (Figure 8.15). Fortunately for hardware hackers, the Atari 5200 controller can be merged with an Atari 2600 paddle, allowing you to enjoy a few select games that work very well with it. These games are:

- Gorf
- Kaboom!
- Moon Patrol
- Super Breakout

Additionally, a new homebrew game for the 5200, Castle Crisis, has been developed which also takes advantage of 5200 paddle controllers. Other games will also work with the paddle controller, notably any that require only horizontal movement. However, the preceding list highlights those games that work best with it. Once you see the final result of this hack, you'll be amazed at how the 5200 controller appears to have been designed with the 2600 paddle controller in mind—the two are a near-perfect match!

Figure 8.14 An Atari 2600 Paddle Controller

Figure 8.15 An Atari 5200 Controller

Preparing for the Hack

The most important things you'll need for this hack are a 5200 controller and a 2600 paddle controller, both of which you will use to hack apart and create the new 5200 Paddle Controller. You'll want to ensure that you find a 5200 controller that has good working fire buttons and a keypad—the condition of the joystick itself is unimportant since we'll be replacing it with the rotary mechanism from the 2600 paddle controller. As for the 2600 paddle controller, try to find one that is free from the jitter that often plagues old 2600 paddle controllers, because this jitter will translate to the 5200 controller, making your new controller less enjoyable to use (however, this jitter can be fixed by spraying contact cleaner directly into the potentiometer inside the paddle). The following is a list of the parts required for this hack:

- Atari 5200 controller
- Atari 2600 paddle controller
- 3/8" hex nuts (Optional)

As an optional part of this hack, you can also weigh down the paddle controller using 3/8-inch hex nuts to give it a higher-quality, heavy feeling that you might find in an arcade rotary controller. If you do this part of the mod, you'll need to use a glue gun (hot wax can be used as a substitute) to secure the nuts into the base of the spinner.

Other items you'll need include Super Glue to attach two plastic plates together inside the 5200 controller, as well as a Philips head screwdriver to disassemble the controllers and reassemble the 5200 controller when finished. You'll also need a pair of wire cutters or another cutting tool to slice open a plastic joint inside the 5200 controller and a pair of needle-nose pliers or a small wrench. You may also need a soldering iron if the connectors from the 5200 controller won't fit onto the potentiometer you remove from the 2600. The following is a list of the tools that the paddle controller hack requires:

- Phillips head screwdriver, standard size
- Needle-nose pliers
- Wire cutters
- Super Glue
- Soldering iron (optional)
- Hot-glue gun (optional)

Performing the Hack: Disassembling the Paddle Controller

The first task that needs to be completed is to disassemble the Atari 2600 paddle controller. Pull the dial off the paddle controller. It should pop off easily; just make sure you pull straight upward, as shown in Figure 8.16.

Figure 8.16 Removing the Paddle Dial

Using a pair of needle-nose pliers or similar tool, carefully unscrew the nut that was under the dial, as shown in Figure 8.17.

Figure 8.17 Removing the Paddle Nut

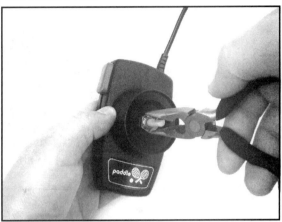

Flip the paddle controller over and remove the two screws with a Philips head screwdriver. Separate the two halves of the controller.

Pull out the paddle mechanism (the potentiometer, also known as a "pot", as denoted in Figure 8.18) and disconnect the two wires plugged into it. If the wires are soldered to the potentiometer, you'll need to first desolder them. You'll want to do this cleanly because we'll be attaching two wires from the 5200 controller when we transplant the potentiometer.

Figure 8.18 Paddle Disassembled

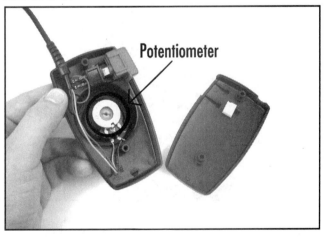

Now that you have the paddle controller disassembled, you'll want to put aside the potentiometer, nut, and plastic dial (Figure 8.19).

Figure 8.19 Paddle Parts to Save for Transplanting

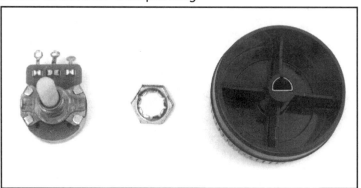

Performing the Hack:
Building the 5200 Paddle Controller

With the paddle disassembly out of the way, we can now concentrate on the 5200 controller itself. First, remove the three screws from the bottom of the 5200 controller, as shown in Figure 8.20.

Figure 8.20 Remove the Three Screws from the Back of the 5200 Controller

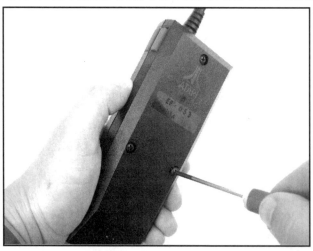

Before you pull the controller apart, you first need to pop the bezel off the top of the controller, which houses the Start, Pause, and Reset buttons. Using a thin flathead jeweler's screwdriver, carefully pry between the bottom of the bezel and the 5200 controller to slowly raise it up, as shown in Figure 8.21. It should eventually pop out, along with the rubber buttons underneath. Place all the removed pieces aside for now.

Figure 8.21 Removing the Upper Bezel

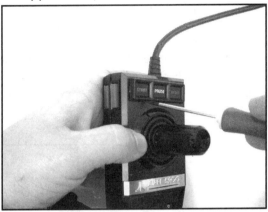

Under the rubber buttons are traces mounted on a piece of thin, flexible plastic. This is part of a much larger sheet that contains the traces for all the buttons in the controller, which you can see in Figure 8.22. Carefully slide this out from a slot on the left side of the controller.

WARNING: HARDWARE HARM

The 5200 controller contains a single, folded Mylar sheet with all the traces for the keypad buttons, fire buttons, and Start, Reset, and Pause buttons. Care must be taken not to scratch or damage this flexible circuit or you may render your 5200 controller unusable.

Figure 8.22 Bottom Half of 5200 Controller

You can now pull the two halves of the controller apart. There are two posts at the bottom of the controller, and you will need to lift the top half straight up in order to get the controller apart. Place the top half of the controller with the joystick mechanism aside for now. The bottom of the controller contains two potentiometers—one that controls the horizontal motion and one that controls the vertical motion. Both of these pots need to be removed, but they are glued to the base of the controller. The easiest way to remove them is to pry a thin, flathead screwdriver under the base of the mechanism and twist the screwdriver, as shown in Figure 8.23. As the glue separates, you should hear it peeling.

Figure 8.23 Removing Pots

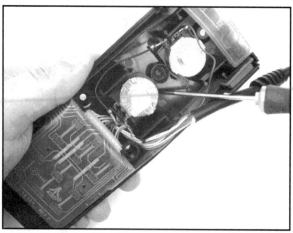

Once you have popped out the potentiometers from the base of the controller, you can disconnect the wires from the upper potentiometer and cut the wires where they exit the cable bundle entering the 5200 controller, since we won't be needing them (Figure 8.24).

Figure 8.24 Removing Wires from the Upper 5200 Pot

Concentrating on the bottom potentiometer, remove the middle connector and plug it into to the middle connector of the potentiometer you removed from the 2600 paddle controller. Remove the other wire from the same 5200 pot and, while holding the 2600 pot with the plastic post face down and the connectors pointed towards you, attach this wire to the right-most connector (Figure 8.25). You may be able to slide the connectors on, but if they don't fit you'll have to solder them into place.

Figure 8.25 Wiring the 2600 Pot in Place of the Lower 5200 Pot

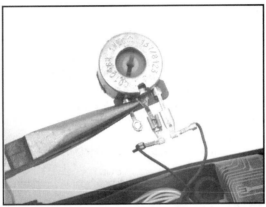

We're done with the base—now we need to spend time on the upper half of the controller which contains the joystick mechanism. We need to remove the joystick that is still attached to this half. A small, white, rectangular ball joint keeps the joystick from coming out. We need to cut this housing along one edge so the joystick can then be pulled straight out. To do this, use a pair of wire cutters, a sharp knife, or a Dremel tool to cut through one side of the white plastic housing, as shown in Figure 8.26. Take care not to damage the two sliding plates (one is black, the other white) underneath this housing, because we need those to complete the hack.

Figure 8.26 Freeing the Joystick

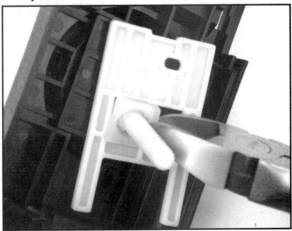

Once you have successfully cut and removed the ball joint, you can pull the joystick out from the other side. Leave the rubber boot in place for now.

Place the top half of the controller housing upside down on a flat surface. Remove the top, white plastic plate and slide the bottom plate so that the hole in the middle is aligned with the hole of the rubber boot. Using Super Glue, glue the edges of this plate in place.

After waiting a bit for the glue to dry, place the white plate in its tray and then align it so its window is centered with the hole of the rubber boot. Super Glue it into place. The two plates should resemble Figure 8.27 when you are done.

NOTE

Take care to properly align these plates, because you will be placing the post of the 2600 paddle controller through these two openings. If they are not properly aligned, the paddle dial will be off-center in relation to the round edge on the exterior of the 5200 controller.

Figure 8.27 Glue the Plastic Sliding Plates into Place

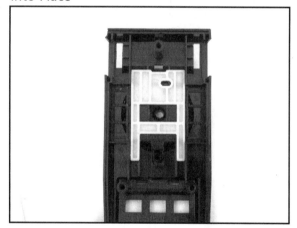

Figure 8.28 Removing the Rubber Joystick Boot

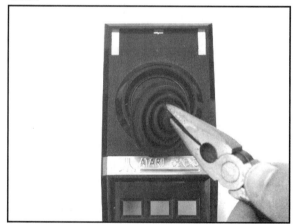

Wait for the glue to dry, then flip the top half of the controller over so it is right-side up. Using a pair of pliers, remove the rubber boot, as shown in Figure 8.28.

Take the 2600 paddle mechanism and place the post of the potentiometer through the plates so it protrudes through the top half of the 5200 controller. Align the connectors of the potentiometer with the bottom of the controller. Use the hex nut you saved from disassembling the 2600 paddle controller and thread it onto the 2600 potentiometer. Tighten the nut, making sure that the paddle mechanism is properly aligned on the back side of the controller housing. The tightened 2600 paddle mechanism should appear as it does in Figures 8.29 and 8.30.

Figure 8.29 Assembling the 2600 Potentiometer

Figure 8.30 Inside the 5200 Paddle Controller

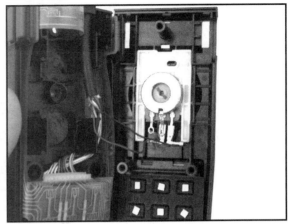

You can now reassemble the controller. The easiest way to do this is to hold the top half of the controller upside down, place the rubber keypad buttons into the keypad holes, and then slide the thin Mylar film used for the Start, Pause, and Reset buttons through the slot at the top of the controller, as shown in Figure 8.31.

Figure 8.31 Assembling the Controller

Carefully fit the two halves of the controller together, making sure not to pinch the Mylar film at the top of the controller. Once the two halves are snug, you can then snap the Start, Pause, and Reset buttons and their bezel into the top of the controller. Finally, place the paddle dial on top of the potentiometer shaft. Before replacing the three screws that hold the controller together, you should test the controller with an Atari 5200 game (Gorf, Kaboom!, Moon Patrol, or Breakout) to make sure it works.

Congratulations! You now have a 5200 Paddle Controller that looks as if it came straight from the Atari factory (Figure 8.32). If you want to improve the controller even further, then read on …

Figure 8.32 Assembly Completed! The Atari 5200 Paddle Controller

Performing the (Optional) Hack: Weighted Dial

If you want to go the extra mile, you can give a more realistic arcade feel to your new 5200 paddle controller by weighing down the dial. To do this, you'll need eight 3/8-inch hex nuts. You'll also need either a hot glue gun or some wax that you can melt. For this example we use a hot-glue gun.

Start by popping off the plastic rotary dial from the top of the 5200 paddle controller. Flip the dial upside down and stack two hex nuts into each compartment of the dial, for a total of eight nuts total, as shown in Figure 8.33.

Figure 8.33 Weighing Down the Dial with Hex Nuts

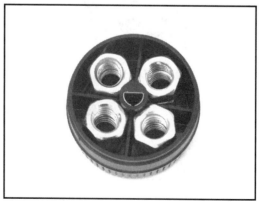

NOTE

Instead of using two 3/8″ hex nuts in each compartment, you can substitute six pennies standing vertically.

Using the hot-glue gun, fill the dial with a sufficient amount of glue to keep the nuts in place (Figure 8.34). Fill the center of the nuts and then the gaps around the sides of the nuts between the edges of each compartment. Try not to get glue on the top outer edge of the dial or in the center hole where the dial attaches to the potentiometer.

Figure 8.34 Gluing the Nuts in Place

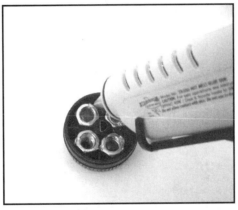

After the glue has had time to set, reattach the dial to the controller. You now have a weighted 5200 paddle controller that feels as though it belongs in an arcade!

Under the Hood: How the Hack Works

Although the Atari 8-bit computers (on which the Atari 5200 is based) use standard, digital controllers with four directions, Atari decided to "innovate" with the 5200 and design unique, analog controllers. These controllers allow 360 degrees of movement and variable movement in any direction by using two potentiometers.

A *potentiometer* is a variable resistor whose output is determined by the position of a "sweeper" that moves along a resistive strip. The resistance for each potentiometer in the 5200 controller ranges from 0 ohms to 500k ohms, with 250k ohms when the potentiometer is in the center position. As the sweeper moves, the resistance changes in a linear fashion, which is then read by the 5200 which calculates discrete values that the game software can read. One potentiometer is used for horizontal position and another is used for vertical position. Fortunately for us, the potentiometers in the 5200 controller and the 2600 paddle controller can easily be swapped as they are the same physical size.

Since we're only interested in horizontal movement, our modified 5200 controller only needs a single potentiometer. This hack is made easier in that the 5200 controller housing seems to have been designed with the potential for an official 5200 paddle controller, so retrofitting the 2600 paddle is a piece of cake.

What appears to be an actual Atari 5200 paddle controller (a CX-52P, versus the CX-52 for the standard 5200 controller) has been found, but it's unknown if this was indeed an official Atari prototype or a controller that someone modified in similar fashion to the hack described in this chapter.

Free Yourself from the 5200 Four-Port Switchbox

When Atari designed the Atari 5200, they decided to create a unique TV/game switchbox that would not only supply the audio/video signal to the television but also provide power to the 4-port 5200. The Atari 5200 power supply is plugged directly into the switchbox instead of the 5200, which reduces cable clutter. Additionally, when power is applied to the 5200, the switchbox automatically switches the video/audio signal from the antenna input of the TV to the 5200, saving the owner from having to get up and manually slide a switch, as was required on most TV/game switchboxes (see Figure 8.35) when the 5200 was released.

Figure 8.35 Old style TV/Game Switchbox

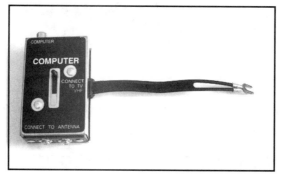

Figure 8.36 shows the switchbox that shipped with the 5200. The connector at the upper-right corner plugs into the 5200, feeding power to the 5200 and the RF signal back to the television. The connector at the bottom (near the sliding switch) is where the power is connected.

Figure 8.36 The Atari 5200 Four-Port Switchbox

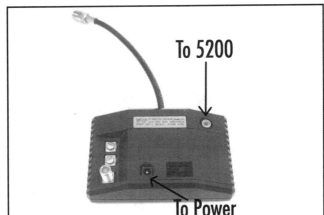

Although Atari's intentions were noble, this proprietary switchbox precluded the use of a standard switchbox since it was the only way to supply power to the 5200. This wasn't a problem when Atari was still producing the 5200, because replacement switchboxes were easy to come by, though more expensive than a standard switchbox. But, the most common problem today is finding a switchbox to go along with your 4-port 5200. Atari recognized the problems of this switchbox and ultimately changed it to a simpler design when they later introduced the two-port Atari 5200.

The hack in this section removes the four-port Atari 5200's dependence on this special switchbox, allowing you to use a normal TV/game switchbox. As part of this hack, we'll add a connector to the back of your 5200 where the 5200 power supply can be plugged directly in to the unit.

Preparing for the Hack

To perform this hack you'll need the parts shown in Figure 8.37. To mount the power connector to the 5200 case, you'll need two 7/16-inch metal washers to facilitate fitting the connector in the large rectangular hole at the back of the 5200 case. If you prefer, you can simply drill a 7/16-inch hole in the back of the 5200 case, rendering the washers unnecessary and resulting in a slightly cleaner appearance. Some 3/16- and 3/32-inch heat-shrink tubing will also be used to shield the connections on the power cable we'll be building.

- Size N power jack, 2.5" inner diameter, 5.5" outer diameter Radio Shack Part #274-1576

- Metal washers (2), 7/16" inner diameter

- 47uF electrolytic capacitor, 35V or higher Radio Shack Part #272-1027

- 1N5391G rectifier diode — this part is difficult to obtain but the NTE5800 is a close match and is what we will use to perform the hack (www.nteinc.com). You can also substitute a 1N4001 diode if you cannot find the others.

- 0.1uF ceramic capacitor, 50V Radio Shack Part #272-109

- 18AWG wire, two pieces, each about a foot long, preferably red and black

- 3/16" heat-shrink tubing

- 3/32" heat-shrink tubing

- Electrical tape

Figure 8.37 Required Parts for the 5200 4-Port Switchbox Hack

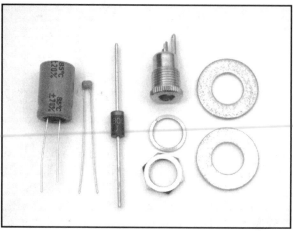

For the power connector, a panel-mount connector works well because it can be mounted into an existing hole in the back of the case. This existing hole was actually used in the 2-port 5200 to expose its built-in power connector. You can also mount a power connector directly to the board, once again taking advantage of this built-in hole, but that requires additional work including drilling a hole in the 5200 PCB, so is not explored here.

Tools required for this hack include a regular Philips head screwdriver, wire cutters and strippers, soldering iron, and a small adjustable wrench or needle-nose pliers. A heat gun will also be required to shrink the heat-shrink tubing. The list of tools is as follows:

- Phillips head screwdriver, standard size, to open 5200 case

- Wire cutters and stripper

- Soldering iron

- Small adjustable wrench or needle-nose pliers

- Heat gun

Performing the Hack

Place the 5200 upside down on a flat surface, and remove the seven screws from the bottom. The locations of the screws are shown in Figure 8.38.

WARNING: HARDWARE HARM

The two screws at the top are shorter than the rest, so you'll need to be careful to insert the longer screws into the correct holes when reassembling the 5200. Failure to do so can result in damage to the case, especially if you insert a long screw into a hole meant for one of the shorter screws.

Figure 8.38 Screw Locations of the Atari 5200

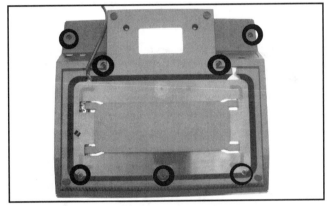

Once you have the screws removed, you can slowly pull the case apart. Remove the 5200 PCB from the case and put the case aside for now. Figure 8.39 highlights the area of the PCB we'll be working on, in the upper-right corner.

Figure 8.39 The 5200 Four-Port PCB

Now that you have the 5200 board removed from the case, it's time to warm up the soldering iron. We need to remove two components from the board: L8, a 2.7uH inductor located immediately to the left of the RF box, and C45, a large 4700uF electrolytic capacitor located just above the RF socket. Both components are denoted in Figure 8.40.

WARNING: HARDWARE HARM

Care must be taken in removing the capacitor from the 5200. Because of the capacitor's large size and location on the board, you will only have access to the solder joints on the bottom side of the board. Remove as much solder as you can from the bottom of these joints, and slowly work out each of the capacitor's leads by heating the joint and pulling up on the capacitor. Failure to do this carefully may result in traces being lifted from the front side of the circuit board when you pull up the capacitor, thus damaging your system.

Figure 8.40 Removing Two Components

With these components removed, it's time to build a cable that will connect the 5200 PCB with the power connector that we'll be attaching to the case. Start by cutting two lengths of 18-gauge wire, each about a foot long. The wires can be a bit shorter, but since the cable will be attached to the case, but a longer length makes it easier to work on the board should you ever need to remove it. If possible, use red and black wires (red for positive, black for ground).

Take the red wire and strip a short piece of insulation from each end. Solder the anode end (the side without the stripe) of the 1N5391G diode to one side of the wire. After you've soldered the diode to the wire, use a piece of small-diameter heat-shrink tubing to cover the exposed connection, as shown in Figure 8.41.

Figure 8.41 Attaching the 1N5391G Diode to the Red Wire

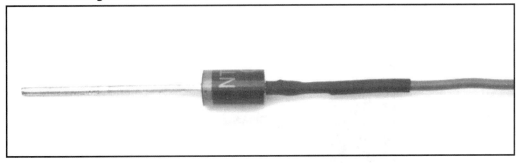

Now take the opposite end of the red wire and solder it, along with one leg of the 0.1uF capacitor, to the center post of the power connector (Figure 8.42). Before making the solder connection, slide a piece of 3/32-inch heat-shrink tubing over the wire and capacitor lead.

Figure 8.42 Soldering the Red Wire and Capacitor to the Connector's Center Post

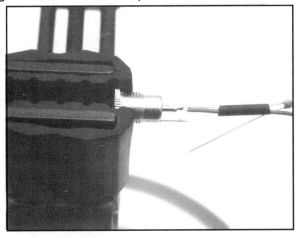

Take the black wire, strip a short length of insulation from each end, and solder it, along with the other lead of the 0.1uF capacitor, to the outside post of the power connector (Figure 8.43). Again, slide a piece of heat-shrink tubing over the wire and capacitor lead to help shield the connections once everything is soldered together.

Figure 8.43 Soldering the Black Wire and Capacitor to the Connector's Outer Post

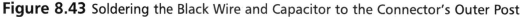

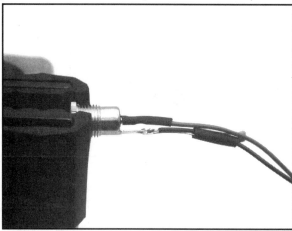

Slide the heat-shrink tubing over the terminals on the power connector and use a heat gun to shrink them down. Next, wrap electrical tape around any remaining exposed leads (such as from the capacitor) to prevent any shorts.

WARNING: HARDWARE HARM

It's important that any exposed wire and component leads be properly shielded so they do not come in contact with other components or wires. Because we are working on the 5200 power input, electrical shorts can cause damage to the 5200 power supply or the system board, rendering your 5200 inoperable.

After that, cut and slide a piece of 3/16" heat-shrink tubing down from the opposite end of the cable over the end of the cable with the connector, covering everything from the power connector terminals to the capacitor. Use the heat gun to shrink this tubing, as shown in Figure 8.44.

Figure 8.44 Building the Power Cable

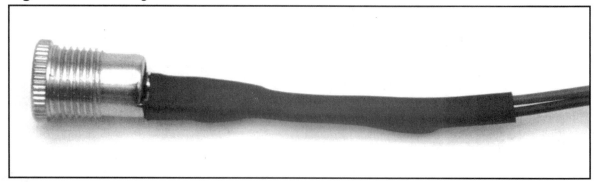

With the cable complete, we now need to attach the power connector to the bottom half of the 5200 case. We'll use the large, square hole between the edge of the case and the hole for the channel select switch (which is marked with a square and circle on the case). Figure 8.45 shows which hole we'll be using.

Figure 8.45 Power Connector Hole

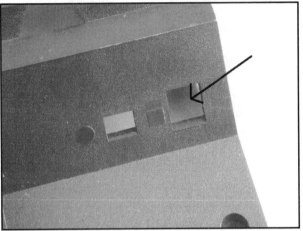

Slide one of the 7/16-inch washers over the cable and against the lip of the power connector. Then feed the cable through the hole in the 5200 case from the outside, as shown in Figure 8.46.

Figure 8.46 Power Connector: External View

Once the washer is flush with the wall of the 5200 housing, push the other 7/16-inch washer over the cable until it is resting against the interior wall of the case. Then, take the nut that came with the power adapter and screw it onto the adapter's threads. Use a pair of pliers or an adjustable wrench to tighten it. The connector should now resemble Figure 8.47.

Figure 8.47 Power Connector: Internal View

Now we can solder the other end of the newly added power cable to the Atari 5200 PCB. Solder the cathode end (the side with the stripe) of the 1N5391G diode to the right solder pad of C45 (the location where you previously removed the 4700uF capacitor). After securing the diode to the board, bend it down as shown in Figure 8.48, as you'll need to leave space to add the 47uF electrolytic capacitor next to it. Solder the black wire to the right negative solder pad from C45, also shown in Figure 8.48.

Figure 8.48 Soldering the Power Cable to the 5200 PCB

Now, solder the 47uF electrolytic capacitor to the board using the adjacent set of solder pads for C45 (Figure 8.49). Take care to note polarity of the capacitor. The long lead is positive and must be placed through the solder pad adjacent to the diode. The shorter lead is negative (denoted with a black stripe on the capacitor). Ensure that the capacitor has a good solder connection to the PCB.

Figure 8.49 Adding the Capacitor to the 5200 PCB

The hack is now complete and should resemble the image in Figure 8.50.

Figure 8.50 Completed Power Supply Hack: Internal View

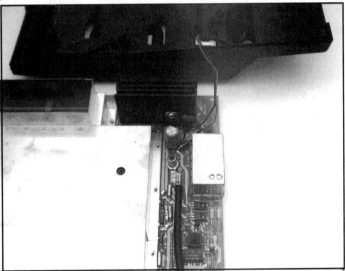

You can now reassemble the 5200. Start by threading the 5200 RF cable through the hole in the back of the case and pushing the cable into the stress-release clip in the bottom of the case, as shown in Figure 8.51.

Figure 8.51 Reassembling the 5200

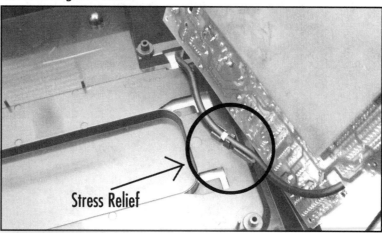

With the RF cable threaded properly into the case, you can now place the 5200 PCB in the bottom half of the case. Figure 8.52 shows how the hack appears after the board has been properly fitted in the case.

Figure 8.52 Almost Done!

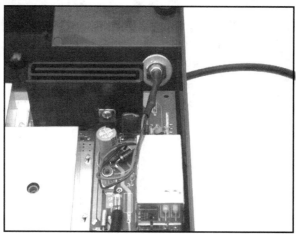

Complete the reassembly of the 5200 by replacing the top cover and then attaching and tightening the seven screws. Test your new 5200 modification by plugging the 5200 power supply into the power connector you just installed. You can now use a regular TV/game switchbox with your 5200, or use a coaxial (F-type)-to-female RCA adapter, which gives you an even better picture by bypassing the switchbox entirely. Figure 8.53 shows an external view of the 5200 case with the power supply plugged into the connector you just installed.

Figure 8.53 Give Me Power!

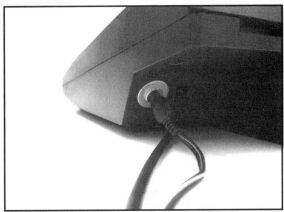

Under the Hood: How the Hack Works

This hack effectively mimics Atari's modification of the two-port 5200 revision, where they removed the reliance on the proprietary switchbox and installed a power connector into the 5200. Look at Figure 8.54 and you'll see that Atari changed several power components from the four-port design, adding a power connector, diode, using a smaller capacitor, and removing the 2.7uH inductor. You can look back at Figure 8.40 to compare this with the power section of the four-port board.

Figure 8.54 Power Supply Circuitry of the 2-Port Atari 5200 Showing Changes from the 4-Port Version

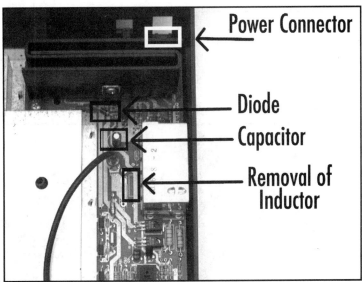

Build Atari 8-Bit S-Video and Composite Cables

Many models of the Atari 8-bit computer line contain a monitor port that allows you to connect the computer to a monitor or television using a composite video signal. Although this is a great improvement over the more commonly used RF output that combines video and audio frequencies into one signal that must then be split apart (often poorly) by a television. The composite video signal can be improved further with S-Video, which divides the video signal into two separate components, chroma and luminance, providing an even sharper video image. Several Atari 8-bit computers containing a monitor port can drive televisions that support S-Video inputs. Figure 8.55 shows the monitor and RF ports on an Atari 130XE computer.

Figure 8.55 Atari 130XE Monitor, RF, and Power Jacks

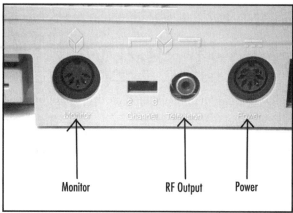

Figure 8.56 shows the various connectors used for composite, S-Video, and the Atari 8-bit monitor port. Composite video generally uses a male RCA connector; S-Video has its own unique, four-pin mini-DIN connector; and the 8-bit monitor port uses a larger, five-pin DIN port.

Figure 8.56 Composite, S-Video, and Atari 8-Bit Monitor Connectors (Left to Right)

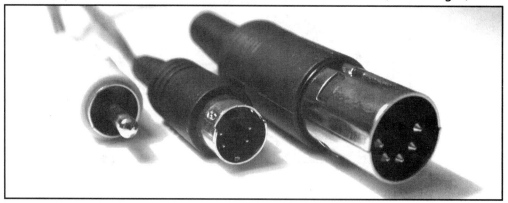

Getting composite and S-Video output from an Atari 8-bit computer involves building a custom cable that plugs into the Atari 8-bit's monitor port on one end and into a television's input jack on the other. This is a simple and worthwhile hack for fans of Atari 8-bit computers who are using one of these machines with a monitor or television with an available S-Video input.

All 8-bit computers with a monitor port support composite output. A smaller subset of these machines includes the necessary chroma signal required to output an S-Video signal:

- Atari 800
- Atari 65XE
- Atari 130XE

NOTE

Although the 800XL, 1200XL, and the European version of the 600XL all have a monitor port, they do not have the separate chroma video signal necessary to build an S-Video cable. It is possible to modify these systems to restore the chroma signal to the monitor jack, but generally it's just easier to use one of the systems listed here.

Details of the various video signal types can be found in the "Technical Information" section at the end of this chapter.

Preparing for the Hack

If you have a television that supports S-Video, it is best to build a cable that supports S-Video so you end up with the best signal quality. If you want the best of both worlds, you can build a cable that supports both S-Video and composite, which is what we will do in this hack. Figure 8.57 shows typical audio/video jacks on a consumer electronics device, with the S-Video jack highlighted in the picture. You can easily determine if your television supports S-Video by looking for an S-Video jack on the back of your television.

Figure 8.57 Typical Audio / Video Jacks

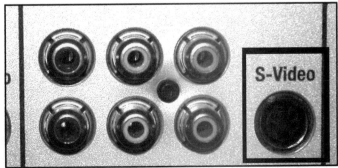

To perform this hack, you'll need a cable with audio, composite video, and S-Video connectors on one end (the other end is not important, as we'll be cutting it off) as shown in Figure 8.58. You can purchase this type of cable inexpensively from just about anywhere that sells videogames. The cable we use in this example was purchased for $9.99 at Fry's Electronics. You'll also need a five-pin male DIN connector, as shown in Figure 8.59. This connector will plug into the Atari 8-bit's monitor port. The list of parts for this hack are as follows:

- Five-pin male DIN connector, Fry's Electronics part# DIN-5-M
- S-Video/composite/audio cable
- 3/16" diameter heat-shrink tubing, approximately 1" in length
- 4 pieces of 3/32" diameter heat-shrink tubing, approximately 1/4" in length

Figure 8.58 Combination S-Video/Composite/Audio Cable

Figure 8.59 A Five-Pin Male DIN Connector

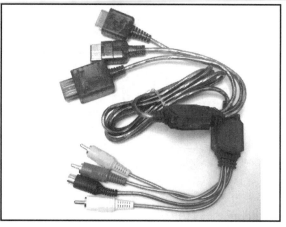
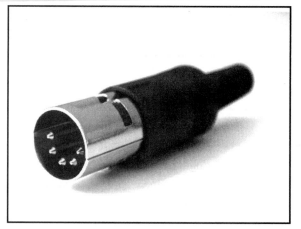

The tools required for this hack are as follows:

- Wire cutters
- Wire strippers
- Soldering iron
- Solder
- Multimeter/Continuity tester

Performing the Hack

The first step in the hack is to cut the connectors off the end of the audio/video cable that we won't be using (Figure 8.60). In this case, cut the cable before the junction where the connectors for the Playstation, Dreamcast, and Nintendo 64 branch out.

Figure 8.60 Pruning the Cable

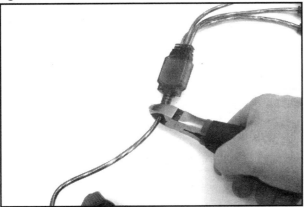

Disassemble the five-pin DIN connector into its component parts. There should be a plastic sleeve; two metal halves that form the bulk of the connector, and a plastic disk that contains the pins (Figure 8.61).

Figure 8.61 Five-Pin DIN Connector Components

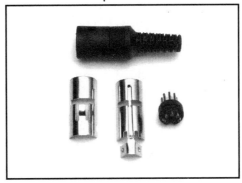

Slide the plastic sleeve of the DIN connector, narrow end first, down the end of the cable you just cut. Next, cut a 1" length of 3/16" heat-shrink tubing and slide it down the same end of the cable, as shown in Figure 8.62.

Figure 8.62 Preparing the Cable

Using a wire stripper, carefully remove about 1" of insulation from the end of the cable. This will reveal several individual wires. Separate the individual wires and strip about 1/4" of insulation from the end of each wire, as shown in Figure 8.63. One or more wires will likely have uninsulated and unbraided ground wires wrapped around them. You'll want to keep these separate from the other wires.

Figure 8.63 Stripping the Wire

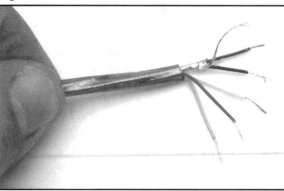

Using a continuity tester, you will need to identify each of the wires with the various connectors that plug into the television, as this will vary depending on the type of cable you purchase. The connectors on the end of the cable are for composite video, audio left, audio right, chroma, and luminance. While touching one end of a probe to one of the wires you stripped, touch the other probe to the center post of each connector (or the individual pins of the S-Video connector) until you have identified each wire, as shown in Figure 8.64. Write down the colors of each wire and their respective connector, as you will be referring to this list in the upcoming steps.

Figure 8.64 Identifying Wire Connections on the Cable

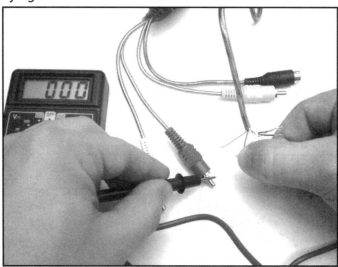

Using the list you created, you are now ready to solder the wires to the five-pin DIN. Figure 8.65 shows how the monitor connector on the Atari 8-bit is wired, when looking at the front of the cable.

Figure 8.65 Atari 8-Bit Monitor Connector Pinout

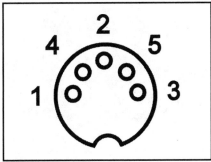

Pin	Function
1	Luma
2	Ground
3	Audio
4	Composite video
5	Chroma

NOTE

The Atari 8-bit computers support only monaural audio output. The cable you purchased supports stereo audio outputs (left and right). You will want to tie the two audio outputs together, soldering them both to pin 3 on the DIN connector. This will send the mono audio output from the Atari 8-bit to both the left and right speakers.

Before you solder each wire, cut a short 1/4" length of heat-shrink tubing and push it over the wire out of the way. After you solder each wire, push the heat-shrink tubing over the connection and use a heat gun to shrink the tubing until it is tight around the connection (Figure 8.66). Make sure to tie any ground wires together and solder them to pin 2.

Figure 8.66 Soldering the Five-Pin DIN

Once you have finished soldering the individual wires to the DIN connector, slide the larger piece of heat-shrink tubing back over the individual wires and use a heat gun to shrink the tubing, as shown in Figure 8.67.

Figure 8.67 Adding Heat Shrink Tubing to the Cable

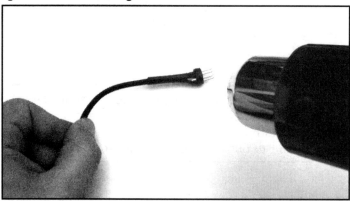

Attach the two metal halves of the DIN connector over the pin housing. Each half of the DIN connector will fit in a groove, and the metal halves are keyed so they will only fit over the proper half of the plastic pin housing. Figure 8.68 highlights one of the grooves with the plastic pin housing already in place.

Figure 8.68 Assembling the Connector

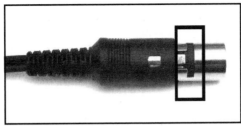

Then, slide the plastic DIN connector sleeve over the two metal halves. Push the sleeve over the metal tab until you have pushed the hole in the plastic sleeve past the tab. This will keep the sleeve in place so it will not slide backwards. The assembled monitor connector should resemble the image in Figure 8.69.

Figure 8.69 Assembled Monitor Connector

Your cable is now complete! Plug the monitor connector into your Atari 8-bit computer (Figure 8.70) and then plug the S-Video or composite connector, as well as the audio connectors, into your television. Power the system up and you should now see a much sharper and more vibrant picture than you previously experienced with your computer's RF output.

Figure 8.70 We're Done! The Final Atari 8-Bit S-Video and Composite Cable

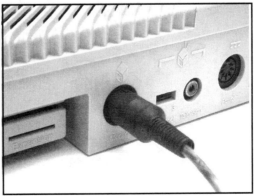

Cable Hack Alternatives

Here are some alternatives to building the hybrid composite/S-Video that we described in this section:

- If you don't need S-Video, you can create a more simple composite video/audio cable that allows you to connect your 8-bit computer to a composite video source. Only the composite video and audio pins need to be connected, each soldered to an individual male RCA connector.

- Apple Desktop Bus (ADB) cables use the same type of connector as S-Video cables, so if you have any of these lying around, you can use them to build an S-Video cable. ADB is used to connect a keyboard and mouse to older model Macintosh and Apple IIgs computers. These cables are generally short and coiled, so this may not be a useful unless the television or monitor you use with your 8-bit is fairly close to you (such as on a desk near the computer).

- If you have a Commodore 1702 monitor, you can go one step further and build a cable with three male RCA connectors, two for video and one for audio. The Commodore 1702 has composite video and audio jacks on the front, but it also has another set of inputs on the back with separate chroma and luminance inputs (Figure 8.71). This is equivalent to having an S-Video input, with two RCA connectors instead of the S-Video connector that is common on modern televisions.

  Commodore 1702 monitors are popular with Atari 8-bit and vintage computer enthusiasts because of their excellent picture quality, support for S-Video via the chroma and luminance connectors, convenient carrying handles on the sides, a flat top that allows for items to be placed on top of the monitor, and their reliable nature.

Figure 8.71 Commodore 1702 Rear Input Jacks

Under the Hood: How the Hack Works

This hack works by building a cable that takes advantage of signals already exposed at the monitor port of the 800, 65XE, and 130XE computers. Composite Atari 8-bit monitor cables were fairly easy to come by back when Atari was producing the Atari 8-bit computers, but you're much less likely to encounter them today, so if you want composite or S-Video output from your 8-bit, you'll often need to resort to building your own cable. It's unfortunate that Atari did not include the S-Video chroma signal on all Atari 8-bit machines with a monitor port, but at least two of the most common 8-bit machines (800 and 130XE) have them.

Technical Information

There are four common standards for transmitting a video signal to a television:

- **Component Video** This is a relatively new method employed by the latest televisions, DVD players, and game systems to transmit high-quality video signals. It comprises of three signals: one containing black and white picture information, or LUMA (Y), and two signals Cr and Cb, that contain matrixed color information to extract the Red and Blue picture information from the Y signal. The Green picture information is what remains once the Red and Blue information is extracted. This is the preferred choice for hooking up consumer-grade video components. Component video connectors are generally RCA jacks, often labeled *Y, Cr,* and *Cb.*

- **S-Video** S-Video output is split into two signals: one containing the black and white picture information, LUMA (Y), and another signal, CHROMA (C), that contains all the color information. S-Video connectors are now standard on most televisions, DVD players, digital video recorders, and other consumer video equipment. An S-Video connector is a small, four-pin mini-DIN. S-Video is sometimes labeled *Y-C.*

- **Composite Video** Composite video output contains a single signal of all brightness, color, and timing information. Due to this combination of signals, it is impossible for the video to be reconstructed without noticeable artifacts. Composite video generally consists of a single RCA jack, usually yellow to differentiate it from audio jacks (which are generally red and white).

- **RF (Radio Frequency)** In addition to containing the video signal, RF also introduces audio into the signal and is the lowest-quality method of signal distribution to a television. RF is most commonly used to broadcast television signals via over-the-air transmission (picked up with an antenna) or via cable television. RF is capable of carrying a wide range of video and audio signals on different frequencies on a single wire and is prone to interference from many sources. RF jacks on televisions and other equipment usually employ a coaxial F-type adapter. Older televisions may not even have a coaxial jack, instead using two screws to which a switchbox or antenna is attached to..

Although Component Video is beginning to be used more, S-Video is still much more common. RF should be avoided whenever possible due to the poor signal quality, although it is difficult to do so when working with old videogame systems and vintage computers built in the 1970s and '80s. Because of the inherent problems with RF signals, hacking old systems to add composite or S-Video output is fairly common and well worth the effort.

It is interesting to note that although the Atari 8-bit computers had support for S-Video as far back as 1979 with the Atari 800, it wasn't until the release of the Atari Jaguar in 1994 that an Atari game console had official S-Video support (through purchase of an Atari-branded cable).

Other Hacks

The hacks presented within this chapter are only the beginning of what you can do with your old gaming systems and computers. We've listed some more complex and advanced hacks here; and detailed instructions for many of these are available on the Internet. Whenever possible we've pointed you towards resources for additional information.

Atari 5200 Four-Port VCS Cartridge Adapter Fix

In order to make the Atari 5200 model more attractive to consumers, Atari eventually developed a VCS cartridge adapter to allow 2600 games to be used with the 5200. This adapter plugs into the 5200 cartridge port and contains a slot to accept 2600 cartridges, two controller ports, and the various switches found on a regular 2600 console. All two-port models of the Atari 5200 accept this adapter without problems. However, the original 4-port Atari 5200 model is incompatible with the VCS adapter, except in rare cases (see the following note). Atari quickly released a technical bulletin and component kit to allow dealers to correct the problem with incompatible units.

NOTE

Not all Atari 5200 four-port models suffer from the incompatibility problem with the VCS cartridge adapter. If the serial number for your Atari 5200 contains an asterisk (*), then the VCS cartridge adapter will work in your 5200 without modifications. It's unclear how many such models exist, but it seems only a small portion of four-port 5200 models fall into this category.

You can find scans of the original Atari Service Bulletin so you can perform this hack on your four-port 5200 at www.atariage.com/5200/archives/VCSFix.

Atari 5200 Composite/S-Video Modification

Like most videogame systems at the time, the Atari 5200 only supported an RF connection to the television. Better quality output can be had by way of a composite or S-Video mod to your 5200, allowing you to use the composite video and S-Video jacks on your television. Section 4.13 of the Atari 5200 FAQ (www.atariage.com/5200/faq.html?SystemID=5200) contains information on how to do the modification.

Atari 8-Bit SIO2PC Cable

The Atari 8-bit computers, via its SIO (Serial I/O) port, can be interfaced with a PC to simulate various peripherals, such as disk drives and printers. You can boot your Atari 8-bit directly from files located on your PC and you can print to your PC printer from your Atari 8-bit! The Atari computer will never know that you've secretly switched real peripherals with a simple cable that plugs into your PC's serial port. This is one of the most useful mods you can perform on your 8-bit computer.

A thorough SIO2PC FAQ can be found at www.tcainternet.com/wa5bdu/siofaq.htm, which should answer all your questions about the SIO2PC and also provides links to schematics and software.

Another useful program to have is Atari810, a disk drive emulator that can be used with an SIO2PC cable: http://retrobits.net/atari810.html. You can also build a ready-to-use SIO2PC cable from AtariAge (www.atariage.com/store/product_info.php?products_id=141).

Atari Resources on the Web

A large number of Web sites are dedicated to Atari game systems and computers. There is a large list at the end of the Hack Your Atari 2600 and 7800 chapter to get you started. We listed several of our favorite sites at the end of Chapter 7 to get you started.

Chapter 9

Hacking the PlayStation 2

Hacks in this Chapter:

- Getting Inside the PS2

- Installing a Serial Port

- Booting Code from the Memory Card

- Other Hacks: More Independent Hard Drives

Introduction

With over 60 million consoles sold worldwide as of August 2003, Sony's PlayStation 2 (PS2) has the largest user base of the current generation of gaming consoles. Surprisingly, the PS2 has the least amount of hardware hacks and homebrew software projects, compared to Microsoft's Xbox or Sega's now defunct Dreamcast. There is an active community of PS2 homebrew software developers, but its size doesn't compare to the number of Xbox or Dreamcast homebrew hackers. Outside of "modchip" manufacturers, very few hardware hackers are dedicated to exposing the PS2's internals.

One of the reasons that not a lot of hardware hacking is done on the PS2 is that a large number of the talented individuals who decide to reverse-engineer the PS2's hardware are modchip manufacturers. These manufacturers guard the information they find as trade secrets, rarely revealing information to the public (usually providing just enough detail to allow a user to install the modchip). Another reason is that even though the PS2 contains a few standard connections such as USB and IEEE1394, internally the PS2 is vastly different from other "standard" architectures such as the PC architecture that the Xbox is based on. A lot more work is involved in locating and snooping the data buses and determining the signals output by the custom chips found on the PS2's mainboard.

Commercial Hardware Hacking: Modchips

For all consoles, software piracy is a thriving business. Although console manufacturers implement security features that make it difficult or impossible for the average gamer to copy games, hardware hackers employ seasoned techniques to make short work of defeating hardware security methods. Such techniques include snooping the system's data bus with a logic analyzer and dumping an image of the BIOS to look for software workarounds. Once just simple shims to allow a user to play unauthorized copies of games, modchips are now complex devices that allow much more.

When a viable set of exploits and workarounds is found to bypass a particular security feature, the modchip is born. Modchips are small printed circuit boards (PCBs) with wires that attach to various components on the console's main board. A modchip is usually controlled by a Microchip PIC or standard programmable logic (such as a programmable logic device [PLD]), but modern modchips for the PS2 and other systems include an FPGA and Flash ROM so that they can be updated with bug fixes and new features. Normally, a modchip sends a signal to the console's security system to fool the system into thinking the user has inserted a valid game disc. Modchips can also bypass other systems, including code in the BIOS, or the default video mode (PAL or NTSC) output by the console's graphics hardware.

On the PS2, modchips are primarily used to bypass the hardware authentication performed on PS1 and PS2 game discs. They also are used to patch the BIOS to disable Macrovision for recording DVD content to a VCR, to enable region-free DVD playback, and to override the video mode used by games in other regions (for example, playing PAL games on an NTSC system). The original PS2 modchips were crude, simple devices that could only bypass PS1 game disc authentication and facilitate a "swap trick" for PS2 game discs only if the user had bought a separate and unsupported boot disc. These boot discs (written and sold by unlicensed third-party vendors) contain code to stop the PS2's DVD drive from spinning. Once the drive has spun down, the user forces the drive open, using a special case modification (called a *fliptop*) or sometimes using a plastic knife or a credit card–sized device. The user then puts in the copied PS2 game and closes the drive, and the PS2's hardware authentication will be defeated, having failed to detect the forced opening and closing of the drive.

The main disadvantage of physical swapping is that using an object to force open the PS2's DVD drive can shorten the life of the drive. Modern modchips have done away with the destructive swap method by authenticating a copied PS2 game disc directly in hardware. Some of these modchips include an FPGA and Flash memory so that users can apply bug fixes and add new features by simply booting a disc. They also include a special loader that executes a program stored on the PS2 memory card when the PS2 is powered on. This program is usually another loader, but with a graphical user interface (GUI) for running other programs and utilities for installing programs to the memory card or a hard drive from a CD. Figure 9.1 shows the LisaZero PAL-only modchip, which uses a QuickLogic PLD that contains fixed boot code.

Figure 9.1 The LisaZero "No-Swap" Modchip

The engineers and hackers behind commercial modchips invest a lot of time and money reverse-engineering the hardware and testing their findings. The low-level information that they discover is rarely (if ever) shared with the public, since by doing so they would lose their edge over competing manufacturers. Other modchip makers can still offer the same or similar features by reverse engineering a competing modchip or using the same techniques to document the hardware. Although some of the information they discover is only useful to someone who wants to bypass PS2 hardware security, most of the information would benefit anyone who wanted to develop their own hardware or software for the PS2. This information includes the pinouts and signals of the PS2's processors and buses, expansion port, and BIOS.

Not having this information available to everyone stifles the PS2 hardware-hacking and home-brew development communities. As presented later in this chapter, some of the hidden hardware information enables the PS2 developer to gain better control over the system and access to powerful debugging methods. My main motivation for releasing the Independence exploit (see the "Booting

Code from the Memory Card" section) was to allow anyone interested in writing PS2 software to do so without having to physically modify their console.

NEED TO KNOW...

Some sections of this chapter contain source code examples. Unless specified otherwise, all examples were written for use with PS2Lib, an Open Source library for the PS2. You can obtain PS2Lib from http://ps2dev.sourceforge.net/ps2lib.html.

A couple of comments on the conventions used in the code:

- PS2Lib's *tamtypes.h* header defines the basic types used on the PS2. A *u* followed by a number indicates an unsigned type with the specified number of bits, and an *s* followed by a number indicates a signed type. For example, *s8* indicates an 8-bit signed integer and *u32* indicates a 32-bit unsigned integer.

- *tamtypes.h* also defines macros for convenient access to hardware registers. These macros are similar to the *inb()* and *outb()* style macros found in low-level PC programming. The *_lw()* macro is a synonym for the MIPS *lw* instruction, which returns a 32-bit value read from the given address (the address is specified as an unsigned 32-bit integer). Likewise, the *_sw()* macro stores a 32-bit value to the given address. Each of these macros represents the corresponding MIPS instruction, so there are *_lb()/_sb()*, *_lh()/_sh()*, and *_ld()/_sd()* macros for reading and writing 8-bit, 16-bit, and 64-bit values, respectively.

Getting Inside the PS2

The following is a guide to identifying your PS2's mainboard revision and steps to disassemble the PS2.

Mainboard Revisions

At this writing, there are 11 known major revisions of the PS2 mainboard and about a dozen BIOS revisions. Mainboard revisions are usually denoted with *V* (for version), followed by the major revision number—for example, V7. The revision number is commonly referred to as just the PS2 version number. Numbering starts at V0, which is the version of the original PS2 launched in Japan. There is no notation for minor revisions.

There are a number of reasons that Sony would want to revise the PS2 internally:

- To fix hardware and software bugs

- To move separate peripherals onto a single chip to lower manufacturing costs

- To implement new security measures to keep attackers out

The problem with major mainboard revisions is that the physical layout of the board and its components changes from one revision to the next. This means that the instructions for locating a particular component or testpoint will be different on a V1 than on a V7. Some revisions have a close enough layout so that the same instructions will apply to both, as is the case for V5s and V6s. The hacks demonstrated in this chapter have been performed on a V4 PS2. If you own another revision, you will need to adapt the instructions to your mainboard. Where possible, I will note instances where the boards differ across revisions.

Identifying Your Mainboard

To find out your PS2 version number, do the following:

- Flip over the PS2 and count the number of square screw covers on both the bottom and near the expansion (or PCMCIA) slot.

- Look at the sticker on the rear of the PS2. First, write down the text that follows "Model Number." Next, record the first two digits of the serial number and finally, the two-digit date code (Figure 9.2).

Figure 9.2 Model and Serial Numbers and Date Code

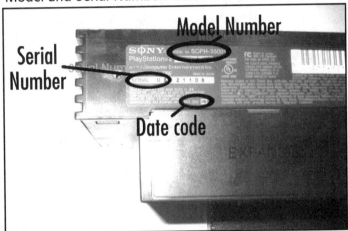

- Check for any physical variations that would set your PS2 apart. For example, only V0 (Japanese) machines have a PCMCIA slot; the rest have an expansion bay for the internal HDD. V9 and higher are missing the IEEE1394 port (next to the USB ports) and may have a small infrared receiver between the Reset and Eject buttons.

- If your model number is SCPH-10000 or SCPH-15000, or if you have a rear PCMCIA slot instead of an expansion bay, you have a V0 PS2.

- If you have 10 screws on the bottom of your PS2, it's a V1, V2, or V3. Refer to Table 9.1 to determine the exact version.

- If you have eight screws on the bottom of your PS2, you have a V4 or higher. V4s include model numbers SCPH-30000 through SCPH-30006 and SCPH-35001 through SCPH-35006. If you have an electrical hazard warning underneath the PS2, it's a V4. If you remove your expansion bay cover and notice a metal shield on the inside of the cover, you most likely have a V4.

■ V5 or V6 PS2s (there aren't a lot of differences between these internally) use model numbers SCPH-30000R through SCPH-30006 R (note the space) or SCPH-30000 through SCPH-30004. To distinguish a V5 or V6 from a V4, remove the expansion bay cover and look for a small screw at the top of the expansion bay, closest to its left side. If this screw is there, you have a V5 or V6. Also check the inside of the expansion bay cover. If it's plastic, chances are you have a V5 or V6.

■ If your model number includes SCPH-39000 through SCPH-39004 or SCPH-37000, you have a V7.

■ If your PS2 is from Japan and your model number is SCPH-39000 or SCPH-39006, you might have a V8 PS2. I don't know of any major differences on the mainboard between V7s and V8s.

■ If your model number includes SCPH-50000 through SCPH-50004 and your date code is not 3D, you have a V9 PS2. If your date code is 3D, you have a V10. V9s and V10s are also missing the IEEE1394 port and may have an infrared receiver sandwiched between the Reset and Eject buttons.

Table 9.1 Identifying V1, V2, and V3 PS2s

Version	Serial Number (First Two Digits)	Date Code
V1	U1	0D
V2	U0	0D
V3	U1	1A
V3	U2	0D

Opening the PS2

Our first hack is performed on the bottom of the PS2's mainboard. Opening the PS2 and exposing the mainboard can be tricky if you've never done it before. The following instructions apply to V4 PS2s, so you may have to modify them slightly for PS2s made after the V4. If you own a V3 or earlier, some of the later steps may not apply at all.

WARNING: HARDWARE HARM

The PS2 mainboard and connected assemblies contain many electrostatic-sensitive components. You must always be grounded before touching the inside of your PS2 or you risk damaging these components. The easiest way to ground yourself is to buy an anti-static wrist
strap and connect it to a grounded source. If you do not have a wrist strap, you can ground
yourself by touching a piece of metal (such as the edge of your desk) before touching the
inside of your PS2.

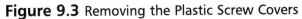

1. Turn the PS2 over so the bottom is facing up. You should notice either eight or 10 square
   indentations; these are covers for the case screws. Using either your fingernail or a small flat-
   head screwdriver, pry up each of these covers to expose the screws (Figure 9.3).

Figure 9.3 Removing the Plastic Screw Covers

2. Using a Phillips screwdriver, remove the case screws. You may meet some resistance because
   the screws could be glued shut. Just turn them counter-clockwise until you hear a snap and
   the screw should easily turn the rest of the way.

3. If you have a warranty sticker (usually found next to the A/V connector on the back),
   remove it.

4. Flip the PS2 back over and face the front of the PS2 away from you. The expansion bay
   should be to your left and the A/V connector to your right. Slowly lift the top half of the
   case. You will have to move it slightly forward to remove it from the joypad assembly and
   the DVD drive. Be careful not to lift the case too fast, since it is still connected to the
   Reset/Eject button assembly. See Figure 9.4 for details.

Figure 9.4 Removing the Top Case Cover

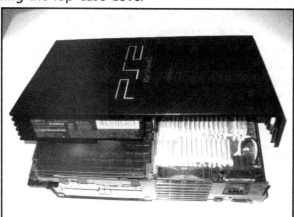

5. Remove the Reset/Eject button assembly from the top half of the case by pulling the assembly down from its corner until it snaps off. Pull back on the assembly and it should slide out of the notch in the front of the case. Set the assembly down next to the PS2, keeping the ribbon cable intact.

6. Remove the two brass screws that hold the joypad assembly in place.

7. Remove the brass screw on the far right side of the rear Fan/Power assembly. Do not remove the screw in the assembly that is closer to the DVD drive.

8. Carefully lift up the Fan/Power assembly and you should notice another brass screw between the optical connector and the A/V connector. The fan is connected to the main-board, so if you lift up the assembly too fast you could damage the connector. Remove the screw there.

9. While holding the joypad assembly and the Fan/Power assembly, turn the PS2 over. Make sure the front of the PS2 is facing away from you. You should now be able to lift up the bottom of the PS2's case. Set it aside.

10. Your unit should now resemble Figure 9.5. The green PCB on the left is the power supply unit (PSU). Remove the four brass screws that secure the PSU in place.

Figure 9.5 The Bottom of PS2 and PSU

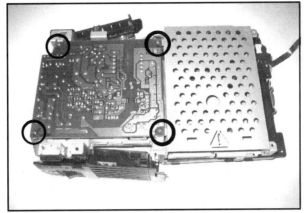

11. The PSU is also connected to the PS2 mainboard with a four-pronged connector. Carefully lift the PSU to disconnect it. You should notice a small two-wire connector going from the fan to the mainboard. Pull straight up on this connector, grabbing the wires that are the closest to the mainboard connector. Set the PSU and Fan/Power assembly aside.

12. Remove the plastic sheet on top of the metal casing. Also remove the metal housing for the internal hard drive. See Figure 9.6.

Figure 9.6 Bottom Metal Casing

13. Remove the eight tiny brass screws. There are four of these screws underneath the plastic sheet. Two more screws secure the expansion bay connector, and two more are along the right side of the metal casing, above the DVD drive. Remove the tiny black screw located underneath the DVD drive.

14. The large metal casing is attached to the DVD drive with two tabs closest to you and one tab in the front. Pry these tabs and carefully lift up the metal casing.

You might want to prop up the mainboard on the left side near the A/V connector. I used the expansion bay cover as a prop (see Figure 9.7).

Figure 9.7 Bottom of PS2 Mainboard Exposed

Your PS2 is now completely disassembled and we can begin the hacks!

Installing a Serial Port

In embedded systems, the serial port is often the lifeline of the system. It can be used to load programs, receive status messages, and for debugging software running on that system. Like most SoC designs, the Emotion Engine EE includes an on-chip Serial Input/Output Ports (SIO) port used internally by the EE's kernel to output debugging and status messages and to start the kernel debugger. For additional information regarding the PS2 EE please refer to the section "PS2 System Overview" towards the conclusion of the chapter.

In your own homebrew software, SIOs can be used to output debugging messages, or it could be used to support a full remote debugger such as GDB (http://sources.redhat.com/gdb). The PlayStation 2 Linux operating system also supports a serial console over SIO. The main benefit of using SIO over a USB link cable or the official PS2 Network Adapter is that SIO is a direct connection to the EE, whereas the other methods are arbitrated by the IOP. If something goes wrong and the IOP crashes, you have little to no means of recovering your program on the EE. Also, the SIO cable we're going to build supports up to 115.2kbps, which is a fairly high-speed connection.

The cable that we'll be building for this hack requires only five wires soldered onto the PS2's mainboard and a simple interface circuit that needs only 15 connection points.

Preparing for the Hack

Table 9.2 lists the parts required to build the SIO cable and interface board and Figure 9.8 shows a picture of the components. You can order samples of Maxim's MAX3323EEPE from the company's Web site (www.maxim-ic.com). Be sure to order the DIP version of the chip. The rest of the parts can be found locally at Radio Shack or online at many electronics distributors.

Table 9.3 shows the wire colors I chose for the connections.

Table 9.2 Parts List

Quantity	Part	Comments
1	MAX3323EEPE	Maxim, www.maxim-ic.com
5	0.1μF monolythic capacitors	Radio Shack part# 272-109
1	Female DB9 connector	
1	Plastic DB9 hood	
1	Sixteen-pin IC socket	Radio Shack part# 276-1998
1	PC board	Radio Shack part# 276-148
5	30AWG wire	Approximately 12" in length
1	DB9 serial cable	Optional
1	Five-pin plastic male and female connectors	Optional

Figure 9.8 Required Parts for SIO Cable

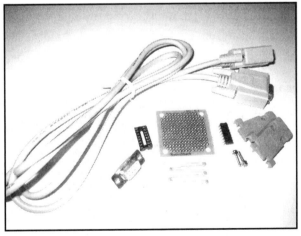

Table 9.3 Serial Cable Wire Colors

Color	Signal
Red	+3.3V (Vcc)
Black	Ground (GND)
White	EE core voltage (VCORE)
Blue	EE_TXD and PC_TXD
Green	EE_RXD and PC_RXD

Performing the Hack

WARNING: HARDWARE HARM

The PS2 mainboard contains many heat-sensitive surface-mount components. Never use a soldering iron that is higher than 15 watts. If you have a variable-watt iron, make sure that it's set to 15 watts before you begin soldering.

The bottom side of your PS2's mainboard should be exposed, with the A/V connector closest to you and the memory card connector facing away from you. See the preceding "Getting Inside Your PS2" section for details on how to get to your mainboard. If you have a V4 or higher mainboard, you should be looking at something similar to Figure 9.7. We'll start with the wires that connect the PS2 side of the serial cable:

1. Locate the +3.3V pad. Figure 9.9 shows the location on a V4 mainboard. Most modchip installation Web sites (such as www.dms3.com) show the +3.3V location for your specific mainboard version. Solder one end of the red wire to this point.

Figure 9.9 Location of the +3.3V (Vcc) Pad

2. On the left side of the mainboard, you should see printed text including "GH-" followed by a three-digit number. Somewhere in this area is a silver rectangle we'll use for ground. Figure 9.14 shows this location. You may see oxidation (small brown spots) on the rectangle. Solder one end of the black wire to this point.

3. The area to the right of the text is directly beneath the EE (which is mounted on the other side). You should see many small capacitors surrounding the area and several large ones positioned in the center. Look at the upper-right corner of the EE and you should notice four small silver square-shaped pads positioned in a vertical line. There will be a gap in between the top pad and the bottom three. This is the EE's SIO port as denoted in Figure 9.10.

Figure 9.10 Location of Ground (GND) and EE SIO

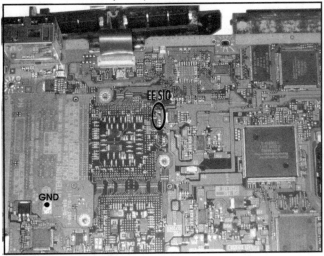

4. The first point that we'll connect from the EE SIO will be our most difficult one: the EE_RXD pin. The top square pad is EE_TXD. If you follow the EE_TXD pad back to its via, you'll find EE_RXD sitting on a via directly above it. Figure 9.11 shows a close-up of the EE_RXD via, EE_TXD pad, and VCORE capacitor. Be careful not to connect the incorrect via in the area which is attached to a small resistor; the EE_RXD via isn't connected to anything else on this side of the board. Carefully solder one end of the green wire to the EE_RXD via.

WARNING: HARDWARE HARM

A *via* is a small circle-shaped hole found on the mainboard. It usually connects one layer or side of the curcuit board to the opposite side. In this hack, one of our points (EE_RXD) is connected to a small via. Note that vias are different from *pads*, which are small square- or circle-shaped solder points.

Because vias connect the different layers of the mainboard, if they are damaged they can "sink" into the mainboard layer and the mainboard can be destroyed. This happens if you apply too much heat to the via. To avoid damaging your mainboard when connecting EE_RXD, do the following:

1. Using a jeweler's screwdriver, gently scratch the surface of the via to remove the soldermask that covers it.
2. Apply paste flux to the exposed via.
3. Apply a small amount of solder to your soldering iron and quickly touch it to the via so that the solder moves from the iron onto the via.
4. Tin the wire used for connecting EE_RXD.
5. Apply a small amount of flux to the tinned wire.
6. With the tinned wire on top of the via, momentarily touch the iron to the glob of solder on the via so it attaches to the tinned wire. The key here is being as brief as possible when heating the via, but still ensure that there is a good solder connection between the wire and the via.

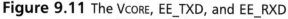

5. Next, solder one end of the blue wire to the square EE_TXD pad, also denoted in Figure 9.11.

6. The last point we need to solder to on the mainboard is +1.7V, also known as VCORE. This is usually found on one end of the large black or beige capacitors underneath the EE. Usually there is one right next to the second square pad as shown in Figure 9.11. Solder one end of the white wire to the end of the capacitor where you see a small beige dot on the mainboard.

Figure 9.11 The VCORE, EE_TXD, and EE_RXD

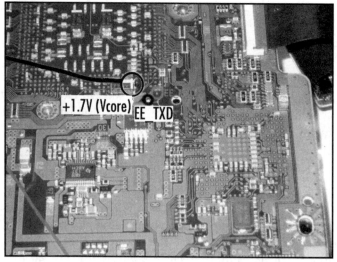

7. With all five points connected (Figure 9.12), use either masking tape or epoxy to secure them to the mainboard to act as a stress relief. If you have V4 or higher, there should be a notch on the left side where the cables for the power button assembly fit. Route your wires through this notch so that they stick out of the left side of the PS2 (Figure 9.13).

Figure 9.12 Installed SIO Wiring

Figure 9.13 Mainboard Ready for Reassembly

8. Now it's time to reassemble your PS2. As you replace the metal casing that fits over the bottom, you should notice a small screw hole between the A/V connector and the optical connector. This hole is normally used to secure the PS2 to a store display. If you plan on mounting the interface circuit board on the outside of the PS2, you can feed your wires through here and through the fan and power button assembly. The wires can be seen coming out of this hole in Figure 9.14. To finish the PS2 reassembly, follow the previous "Getting Inside the PS2" section in reverse.

If you decide to use a five-pin plastic header, you should connect the wires to the female end at this time. If you're using a header, tape the wires together after fitting them or encase them in heat-shrink tubing. Figure 9.14 shows a 5-pin connection attached to the wires.

Figure 9.14 The Completed Five-Wire SIO Connector

With all of the internal wiring completed, it's time to build the external interface board. The schematic is shown in Figure 9.15. On the DB9 connector of the PC serial cable, PC_RXD will connect to pin 2, PC_TXD will connect to pin 3, and GND will connect to pin 5.

Figure 9.15 SIO Interface Schematic

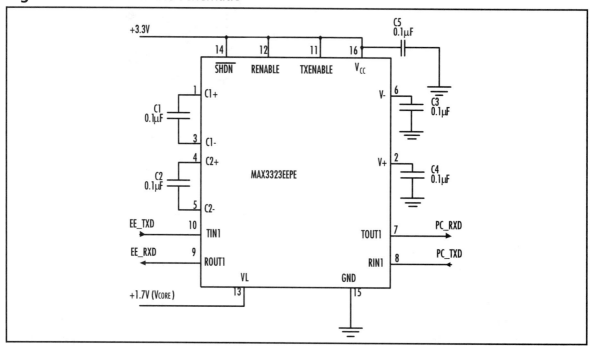

Because I used a five-pin plastic plug, I mounted the male end on one end of the board and the wires for the PC serial cable on the opposite end. For the serial cable itself, I took an unused DB9 serial cable and cut off both ends. Next, I exposed enough of the wires to solder to the interface board, and at the opposite end I attached PC_TXD, PC_RXD, and GND to a female DB9 connector enclosed in a plastic hood. Figures 9.16 and 9.17 show the top and bottom of the completed board.

Figure 9.16 Top View of External SIO Cable

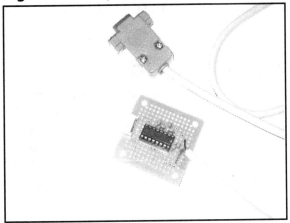

Figure 9.17 Bottom View of External SIO Cable

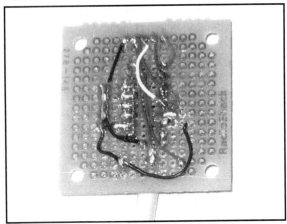

Testing

To test your interface board, connect the interface to the PC and connect the other end to the PS2. Using a terminal program (such as HyperTerminal which comes with Windows) set your serial port to 38400 baud, 8 data bits, no parity, 1 stop bit, and no hardware flow control. Power on your PS2. If the cable is working properly, you should see messages similar to the ones in Figure 9.18.

Figure 9.18 EE Boot Messages

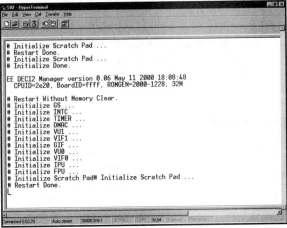

Under the Hood: How the Hack Works

This hack works by taking advantage of the undocumented SIO port of the PS2's Emotion Engine (EE). Details of the SIO can be found in the "PS2 System Overview" section. A standard RS232 serial port in desktop PC's generally use +/-12V to define a logic 0 (space) and logic 1 (mark). The EE is powered using a +1.7V source, so if the SIO pins were connected directly to a PC serial port without any voltage conversion, the signals that the PC sent to the EE could possibly destroy the device. The MAX3323 device is a "level shifter" which converts the voltage levels output by the EE to the levels the PC requires and vice versa. The +3.3V power source supplied by the PS2 is required to power the MAX3323.

Booting Code from the Memory Card

On August 15, 2003, I released the "Independence exploit" for the PS2 which enables the PS2 to boot any software stored on a standard PS2 memory card simply by launching a PS1 game. Any PS1 game can be used as long as the game's unique *title ID* has been written to the file on the memory card that contains the exploit. When you power on the PS2 with a PS1 game already inserted into the DVD drive, the exploit takes over as soon as the PS2 displays the Sony Computer Entertainment banner. The exploit can also be triggered by inserting a PS1 disc and launching the disc manually from the PS2's browser.

NEED TO KNOW... PS2 INDEPENDENCE WEB SITE

The official Web site for the Independence exploit is www.0xd6.org/ps2-independence.html. Here you can find the latest version of the exploit and tutorial information about memory card save files and setting up the exploit using Windows. Since the exploit's release, numerous guides and tutorials have popped up on the Web detailing the steps to get various pieces of homebrew software to run from the memory card. Some of this software includes the Naplink USB boot loader (http://naplink.napalm-x.com), the Pukklink and ps2link Network Adapter loaders (www.ps2dev.org, in the Loaders section), and the PS2Reality group's MediaPlayer (www.ps2reality.net). Many more types of software are currently being developed, and using the exploit to load a boot loader has proven to be the easiest way to load custom software. Though the term "exploit" may sound nefarious, this discovery has opened the doors to an entire community of homebrew programmers for the PS2.

Preparing for the Hack

The most difficult part of this hack is finding a way to get the files onto a memory card. If your PS2 is already modded or you use the "swap trick" to boot CDRs, you can use a disc image called Exploit Installer written by Nicholas Van Veen. A tutorial for this installation is available http://ps2.consolevision.com/ps2homebrew3.shtml.

NEED TO KNOW... THE RIGHT MEMORY CARD

The Independence exploit will only work with a Sony PS2 memory card or any third-party memory card that supports MagicGate. It will not work with a PS1 memory card or with non-MagicGate PS2 cards.

If you have no other method of loading a program on the PS2, you can buy one of several memory card adapters that connect to the PC via a USB cable. Doing a Web search for "USB memory adapter" or "PS2 memory card adapter" will give you a bunch of places to buy one, or you could visit www.lik-sang.com.

Performing the Hack: Preparing Title.DB

In order for the exploit to "trigger" off your PS1 game, you must add that game's unique title ID to the TITLE.DB file that is stored on the memory card. I've written a command-line utility called titleman to make it easier to do this. You can grab a Windows executable version of titleman from the tutorial section of the Independence Web site, or you can choose to compile it from source yourself.

NEED TO KNOW...

I don't know of any graphical utilities to manage the TITLE.DB file. You need to have some basic familiarity with the text-based command line, which is sometimes called Command Prompt in the Windows Start menu. It can be accessed by using **Start | Run** and typing in either **command** or **cmd** and pressing **Enter**. If you are using a UNIX-based system (including Mac OS X), consult your system's manual to find out how to access and use the command-line.

The titleman program options are listed in Table 9.4. The first step in creating a TITLE.DB file is to use the *–c* option. This creates TITLE.DB on disk and stores the exploit payload and a few standard title ID entries.

Table 9.4 The titleman Program Options

Option	Description
-c	Create a new TITLE.DB and initialize it
-a	Add one or more title IDs to TITLE.DB
-d	Delete one or more title IDs from TITLE.DB
-l	List all of the title IDs stored in TITLE.DB
-o	Specify an alternate output file
-v	Be verbose; output status messages

The original titleman tool contains the PS2 executable that launches the BOOT.ELF file from the memory card. BOOT.ELF is stored in the Your System Configuration folder that can be seen in the PS2's browser. The physical name of this folder is:

- BADATA-SYSTEM for PS2s bought in North America
- BEDATA-SYSTEM for PS2s bought in Europe
- BIDATA-SYSTEM for PS2s bought in Japan or other Asian territories

When you are preparing the game save (see the section "Saving TITLE.DB to the Memory Card"), be sure to use the correct name for your PS2's territory.

Next, you must add each title ID for that PS1 game that you want to use to trigger the exploit. The title ID can usually be found underneath the game's ESRB rating icon on the printed side of the game disc. If you got the ID from the front of the disc, you need to convert it to the format that the PS2 expects. For example, on the front of my Street Fighter Alpha disc is the ID SLUS-00197. To convert it, I need to change the dash to an underscore and add a period between the third and fourth digits of the five-digit number following the dash. So, SLUS-00197 becomes SLUS_001.97.

You can also locate the title ID by loading the disc on a PC and opening the SYSTEM.CNF text file stored on the disc. The value after the equals sign (=) for the BOOT option is the title ID. If you found the title ID in the SYSTEM.CNF file, it is already in the required format and does not need to be converted.

Once you have collected the title IDs for all the PS1 games you want to use, you can add them to TITLE.DB individually or by using titleman's *batch mode*. To add them individually, use **titleman –a title_id**. So in my example, I would type **titleman –a SLUS_001.97**.

Batch mode is an easier way to add multiple IDs at once. To use batch mode, place all your title IDs on individual lines in a text file, and use the *–a* option with the batch filename. You must prefix the filename with the "at" symbol (@) in order for it to be recognized as a batch file. You can include comments in the batch file by using a semicolon as the first character of the comment line. Figure 9.19 shows a sample batch file.

Figure 9.19 A Sample titleman Batch File

```
; Xenogears (disc 1)
SLUS_006.64


; Xenogears (disc 2)
SLUS_006.69


; Broken Helix
SLUS_002.89


; Suikoden
```

Continued

Figure 9.19 A Sample titleman Batch File

```
SLUS_002.92

; Suikoden II
SLUS_009.58

; Sentient
SCUS_941.10

; Blood Omen: Legacy of Kain
SLUS_000.27
```

The full listing of the steps required to add a single title (Street Fighter Alpha) are given in Figure 9.20.

Figure 9.20 All steps to create and add an entry to TITLE.DB

```
$ titleman -c
$ titleman -a SLUS_001.97
```

If you make a mistake while adding a title ID or if you want to remove an ID you've already added, use titleman's −*d* option. You can delete individual IDs the same way you added them, or you can use batch mode.

If you need to check which IDs you've already added to TITLE.DB, use the −*l* option.

Choosing BOOT.ELF

Version 0.1 of the exploit loads the executable file BOOT.ELF from the memory card after the exploit has taken over. BOOT.ELF is stored in the same folder as TITLE.DB. If you want to start developing your own software for the PS2, the best choice for BOOT.ELF is ps2link, an Open Source boot loader for loading programs via the official PS2 Network Adapter. The latest version of ps2link is available at www.thethirdcreation.net/tools, or from www.ps2dev.org (in the Loaders section).

If you are interested in streaming movies, MP3s, and Ogg Vorbis files over the network, you will want to install PS2Reality's MediaPlayer. You'll find tutorials for using the MediaPlayer with the exploit at www.ps2reality.net. (Warning: the site is in Spanish!)

Finally, if you want to fire up some of your old Sega Genesis games, Nicholas Van Veen's PGEN Genesis emulator also works well with the exploit. You can download PGEN from http://pgen.game-base.ca.

To use any of the previous programs with the exploit, they must be setup properly so that they are loaded as soon as the exploit takes over. Some programs contain specific instructions in the README file shipped with the program. Failing that, you can try renaming the programs main .ELF to BOOT.ELF (for example, rename PGEN_11.ELF to BOOT.ELF).

Saving TITLE.DB to the Memory Card

Now that we've created TITLE.DB listing all of the game titles that we want to trigger the exploit with, we need to find a way to get the file onto the memory card. There are several ways of doing this:

- **Using Nicholas Van Veen's Exploit Installer** This method either requires your PS2 to have a modchip installed or you must be willing to perform the swap trick. Although this method is convenient, I don't recommend swapping, since it is potentially damaging to your PS2 (or requires a hardware modification). You can grab the Exploit Installer from www.ps2newz.net/forums/showthread.php?threadid=14803

- **Using a commercial USB memory card adapter** Memory card adapters allow you to transfer "game saves" directly to a memory card inserted into the adapter and connected to your PC. To use this method, you must either create a brand-new game save using the name "Your System Configuration" and the save folder for your PS2's territory, or you can open an existing save and rename it. Once you have created your save, copy TITLE.DB and BOOT.ELF into it. Make sure that both the TITLE.DB and BOOT.ELF filenames are in all capitals or the exploit won't work. Once you have created this save, transfer it to your memory card using the software provided with your adapter.

- **The nPort utility** Napalm, the development team that wrote the Naplink USB boot loader, also developed a utility called nPort for transferring game saves between the PC and PS2 using an existing USB connection (in Naplink) or by using the official network adapter (in Pukklink or ps2link). The PS2 Independence Web site provides an .npo file (the format expected by nPort) that contains all the required export files. The site also features a tutorial that provides details on how to use nPort to save the exploit. You can find nPort at http://wire.napalm-x.com.

Independence!

Once you've saved the exploit to the memory card, insert the card into the PS2 and pop in any one of your PS1 games that you've added to the title ID list. After the disc loads, you should see a brief white flash followed by the initial screen of your BOOT.ELF program. If the game you insert goes into the normal PS1 emulator, recheck your TITLE.DB contents using the −l option and make sure you spelled the title ID correctly. Also verify that you have the correct PS1 game inserted. If you get a red screen while loading the exploit, make sure that you have BOOT.ELF in the same folder as TITLE.DB. Any other errors that you notice will be specific to the application that you chose as BOOT.ELF.

Under the Hood: How the Hack Works

The PS2 is able to emulate PS1 software through a combination of hardware emulation and a software PS1 graphics emulator called PS1DRV. Whenever you boot a PS1 game on your PS2, the system browser first loads and executes PS1DRV from the BIOS. PS1DRV performs a number of configuration steps such as setting the disc speed and reading specific graphic parameters for the selected game. Finally, it initializes the graphics emulator and reboots the IOP into PS1 mode. Now the IOP takes over, and the PS1 game is loaded from disc. Graphics are emulated using a special SIF DMA channel from the IOP to PS1DRV on the EE.

When a PS1 disc is inserted into the PS2, the system browser reads the disc's title ID from a file on disc called SYSTEM.CNF. SYSTEM.CNF also contains other PS1 boot parameters such as the default video mode that the game was written to use. The game's title ID is passed along to PS1DRV so that PS1DRV can select parameters for its graphics emulator tuned to each individual game. If the system browser can't find SYSTEM.CNF on the PS1 disc, the value '???' is passed to PS1DRV instead.

When PS1DRV looks for game-specific parameters for its graphics emulator, it searches three locations: a built-in table, SYSTEM.CNF on disc, and a file on a memory card called TITLE.DB. The TITLE.DB file is stored in a system folder reserved for BIOS programs. If the PS2's region of sale is Japan or Asia, this folder is called BIDATA-SYSTEM; if the region is Europe, it's called BEDATA-SYSTEM; and if the region is North America, it's called BADATA-SYSTEM.

I found the Independence exploit within the routines that parse the title ID out of TITLE.DB. A main TITLE.DB loading routine that I'll call *load_mc_title.db()* is responsible for loading the TITLE.DB from the memory card into RAM. It calls another routine, *find_title_params()*, to locate the title ID within the loaded TITLE.DB and return a string value containing its parameter values. It's interesting to note that the way TITLE.DB is loaded into RAM makes the exploit extremely easy to implement. TITLE.DB is loaded to the fixed RAM address 0x20800000, and the entire contents of the file are loaded. This means that we can include an entire program to take over after the exploit inside TITLE.DB and know exactly where it loads!

The *find_title_params()* routine is passed three parameters: the address where TITLE.DB is loaded (*title_db*), the address of a string variable to receive the parameter values (*params*), and the title ID to search for (*title_name*). It executes a loop to search each line (a line is terminated by an ASCII line feed, carriage return, or both) for the title ID. If it finds the title ID, it scans the rest of the line following the title ID and an equals sign to look for the terminating characters. Once those are found, it copies this string into the *params* string value. This copying is where the exploit occurs.

Ideally the parameter value associated with a title ID would be around 25 bytes, including the terminating line feed. In the *load_mc_title_db()* routine, Sony allocates 256 bytes to store this value, and these bytes are stored in RAM next to a very important EE register, the return address or *$ra* register. On the MIPS architecture, when a routine executes another routine, it saves *$ra* to RAM because the CPU automatically updates *$ra* to point to the last instruction of the calling routine. Once the called routine has finished executing, *$ra* still points to this instruction, so when the caller itself prepares to exit, it must first restore *$ra* from RAM. In the *load_mc_title_db()* routine, the *$ra* that is saved before calling *find_title_params()* is located after the space allocated to store the *params* string value.

When *find_title_params()* copies the parameter string into *params*, it uses the C function *strcpy()*, which copies one string of arbitrary length over another string. The *strcpy()* function has no boundary checking, so it will copy the entire string until it finds the terminating NUL (ASCII 0) character. This means that if we were to construct a string inside TITLE.DB that is longer than the 256 bytes allocated for *params*, we could overwrite the saved *$ra* register (since it is stored in RAM after the *params* value). Whatever value that *$ra* is overwritten with becomes the next address executed after *load_mc_title_db()* exits, and this can be any RAM address that is accessible by the EE.

This type of exploit, called a *buffer overflow*, is commonly found in software for which there is no boundary checking on strings or other values loaded from data files. It is easily preventable, as is the case with the Independence exploit in PS1DRV. Using the standard C function *strncpy()*, you can enforce the maximum length of the copied string. If Sony had originally used *strncpy()* with a maximum length of 256, the exploit would've never been possible.

So once we construct this string inside TITLE.DB, where do we point *$ra*? Remember that *load_mc_title_db()* loads the entire contents of TITLE.DB into RAM, at the fixed address 0x20800000. We can point *$ra* to any address after TITLE.DB's load address. In the Independence exploit, I used the fixed address 0x20810110, to allow enough room for approximately 200 entries in TITLE.DB. When *load_mc_title_db()* exits, *$ra* points to this address, and my code assumes control of the PS2.

Other Hacks: Independent Hard Drives

With the launch of Sony's PlayStation 2 Linux Kit (released in May 2002) and the official Network Adapter (released in August 2002), PS2s have gained an often overlooked addition: hard disk drive (HDD) support. In addition to the official Sony HDD that shipped with the Linux Kit, PS2 owners can also use off-the-shelf HDDs that fit the IDE connectors on the network adapter. While Sony's official HDD for consumers (i.e. those people who didn't buy the Linux Kit) is expected to be released in March 2004, homebrew software is already being written to take advantage of existing HDDs.

In November 2003, Nicholas Van Veen, along with others including myself, developed and released *libHDD*, a set of libraries and drivers for homebrew software to access the HDD. libHDD also includes support for Sony's official file system layout to be used by games that access the HDD. libHDD is available for download at http://ps2dev.org/kb.x?T=967. Using libHDD, programs designed to run from the memory card can access data or even other programs stored on the HDD. This opens up a range of potential projects, from emulators that support loading ROMs from the HDD (PGEN already does) to media players that play audio and video saved to the HDD. Hopefully, as more homebrew developers release HDD-aware programs, the PS2 will gain more recognition as a consumer hardware hacking platform.

PS2 System Overview

The PS2 is built on a parallel architecture—it achieves high performance by splitting program tasks among multiple processors and coprocessors. A typical PS2 game will decide logic and game flow on the main processor, handle user input and audio on an auxiliary (or sub) processor, and transform 3D geometry on one of two high-speed coprocessors. Contrast this to the traditional PC-based architecture, where only a single processor is dedicated to user input, game logic, and graphics output. Of course, modern 3D graphics cards now come equipped with a high-speed programmable graphics processing unit (GPU) that can offload 3D lighting and vertex calculations from the main CPU onto the graphics card.

Understanding the Emotion Engine

The heart of the PS2 is a 64-bit Toshiba MIPS processor dubbed the Emotion Engine, or EE (Figure 9.21). The EE is the predecessor of ArTile Micro's TX79 line of System-on-a-Chip (SoC) processors. A SoC design is one in which all the external peripherals required to manage the system are integrated onto a single chip. For example, a common TX79 chip, the TMPR7901, integrates the MIPS CPU core, an SDRAM memory controller, a PCI bus controller, and an Ethernet controller, among other peripherals. The main benefits of SoC processors are reduced manufacturing costs and better performance between the integrated peripherals. SoC designs usually contain one or more high-speed internal buses that interface with external peripherals using a slower, shared system bus.

The EE includes the following documented on-chip peripherals:

Figure 9.21 The Emotion Engine

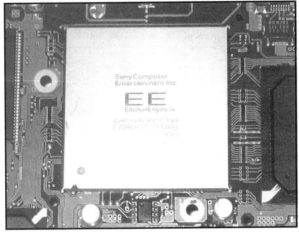

- MIPS R5900 CPU core

- Two vector processing units (VUs or VPUs)

- Floating point unit (FPU)

- DMA controller (DMAC)

- Interrupt controller (INTC)

- Programmable timers

- Sub-CPU interface (SIF)

- Two VU interfaces (VIFs)

- Graphics Synthesizer (GS) interface (GIF)

- Image processing unit (IPU)

It also includes the following undocumented peripherals:

- RDRAM controller [(R)DRAMC]

- Serial I/O port (SIO; UART)

- JTAG (IEEE 1149.1) Boundary-Scan interface

NEED TO KNOW... DIVINING DOCUMENTATION

A detailed examination of all the EE's integrated peripherals would fill several chapters. The hardware manuals shipped on Disc 1 on the PlayStation 2 Linux Kit (www.playstation2-linux.com) provide an invaluable resource to the inner workings of the PS2's Emotion Engine and Graphics Synthesizer. If you do not own the kit, you can find basic information on the Emotion Engine's CPU core in the hardware manuals for the EE's descendant, the TX79 processor, which can be found at www.semicon.toshiba.co.jp/eng/index.html. You can find tutorials on programming the PS2 at www.ps2dev.org and www.oopo.net/consoledev.

The Serial I/O Port

The SIO implements a high-speed UART with an 8-byte transmit first in, first out (FIFO) and 16-byte receive FIFO. It also includes the common CTS and RTS signals for hardware-based flow control. Although the SIO-related pins are unconnected in consumer PS2s, the EE's BIOS and runtime kernel use the SIO to output status messages during the PS2 boot process.

The SIO isn't documented in the EE User's Manual, so I had a look in the PS2's BIOS for the initialization and character output code. I also found a wealth of information on the SIO interrupt and hardware registers in the Toshiba TX79 Core Architecture Manual, the TMPR7901 hardware manual, and the TMPR4925 hardware manual. It turns out that the TX79 Core Architecture Manual is nearly identical to Sony's EE Core User's Manual, except that all SIO-related documentation was removed from the latter.

After studying the BIOS and kernel SIO code, the available documentation, and writing a few test programs, I was able to assemble a reasonably accurate list of registers and definitions. The EE's SIO shares most of its registers with the TX49 implementation, but I couldn't find any indication that DMA was supported. It also shares a few register definitions with the TX7901's UARTs. Table 9.5 shows the SIO register map.

Table 9.5 The SIO Register Map

Address	Name	Description
0x1000f100	SIO_LCR	Line control register
0x1000f110	SIO_LSR	Line status register
0x1000f120	SIO_IER	Interrupt enable register
0x1000f130	SIO_ISR	Interrupt status register
0x1000f140	SIO_FCR	FIFO control register
0x1000f150	SIO_BGR	Baud rate control register
0x1000f180	SIO_TXFIFO	Transmit FIFO register
0x1000f1c0	SIO_RXFIFO	Receive FIFO register

Using the TX79 manual, I found that when the SIO needs to interrupt the CPU, it triggers a Debug exception and sets bit 12 of the COP0 cause register. The CPU then decodes the SIO interrupt status register to determine the cause of the interrupt. The EE kernel uses the SIO exception as a means to start the kernel's built-in debugger.

To initialize the SIO, you first write a value to SIO_LCR indicating the number of data bits and stop bits and whether to enable parity checking. You can also specify where the baud rate generator will get the clock source used to determine the baud rate. The next step is to reset both FIFOs and to optionally enable any interrupts. Finally, you need to calculate the divisor and the clock value used to maintain the baud rate. The code in Figure 9.22 is an example of how to initialize the SIO with the specified baud rate, using the standard transmission parameters of 8N1 (8 data bits, no parity checking, 1 stop bit).

Figure 9.22 SIO Initialization Code Example

```
#define SIO_FCR_FRSTE 0x01    /* FIFO Reset Enable.  */

#define SIO_FCR_RFRST 0x02    /* RX FIFO Reset.  */

#define SIO_FCR_TFRST 0x04    /* TX FIFO Reset.  */


#define CPUCLK  294912000 /* Used to determine the baud divide value. */


void sio_init(u32 baudrate)
{
        u32 brd;                 /* Baud rate divisor.  */
        u8 bclk = 0;             /* Baud rate generator clock.  */

        /* 8 data bits, 1 stop bit, no parity checking, and use the CPU
           clock for determining the baud rate.  */
        _sw((1<<5), SIO_LCR);
```

Continued

Figure 9.22 SIO Initialization Code Example

```
        /* Disable all interrupts.  */
        _sw(0, SIO_IER);

        /* Reset the FIFOs.  */
        _sw(SIO_FCR_FRSTE|SIO_FCR_RFRST|SIO_FCR_TFRST, SIO_FCR);
        /* Enable them.  */
        _sw(0, SIO_FCR);

        brd = CPUCLK / (baudrate * 256);

        while ((brd >= 256) && (++bclk < 4))
                brd /= 4;

        _sw((bclk << 8) | brd, SIO_BGR);
}
```

Character input and output are straightforward: You write to SIO_TXFIFO to output a character and read from SIO_RXFIFO on input. You'll need to check SIO_ISR to make sure that either the TX FIFO has room for another character or that the RX FIFO has at least one character ready to be read. The code in Figure 9.23, modeled after the ANSI Standard C Library *putc()* and *getc()* functions, demonstrates how to do this.

Figure 9.23 SIO Input/Output Code Example

```
int sio_putc(int c)
{
        /* Block until we're ready to transmit.  */
        while ((_lw(SIO_ISR) & 0xf000) == 0x8000);

        _sb(c, SIO_TXFIFO);
        return c;
}


int sio_getc()
{
        /* Do we have something in the RX FIFO?  */
        if (_lw(SIO_ISR) & 0xf00)
                return _lb(SIO_RXFIFO);
```

Figure 9.23 SIO Input/Output Code Example

```
    /* Return EOF.  */
    return -1;
}
```

The I/O Processor

The I/O processor, or IOP, manages most of the on-board and external peripherals including memory cards, the sound processing unit (SPU), controller pads, and the DVD drive. It is a SoC design from LSI Logic based on the original PlayStation (PS1), and it includes all the PS1's main functions on a single chip. The core of the IOP is a MIPS R3000A CPU running at 36.864MHz (native speed). The IOP's native speed is approximately $1/8^{th}$ the speed of the EE, which runs at 294.9Mhz. When emulating PS1 hardware, the IOP runs at the PS1's original speed of 33MHz. The IOP can directly access 2MB of RAM. It communicates with internal devices and external peripherals via the SBUS.

The Sub-CPU Interface

The IOP is also referred to as the sub-CPU, with the EE being the main CPU. The sub-CPU Interface, or SIF, is a high-speed DMA connection between the IOP and EE. Using the SIF, each processor can transfer data directly into the other processor's RAM. The most common use of the SIF is a Remote Procedure Call (RPC) interface that allows the EE to call routines on the IOP. These routines access the low-level hardware driver corresponding to the RPC and return data via the SIF back to the EE. In this way, the EE can request to read from a file on an inserted DVD, continue its processing, and be interrupted by the IOP after the read request is complete. Also, using the SIF, the IOP can schedule controller data to be sent to a buffer on the EE on every Vblank ("vertical blank", $1/60^{th}$ of a second for NTSC machines, or approximately one frame of video). The EE can access this data without having to make an explicit request for it every single frame.

Additional Web Resources

- **Official ps2dev home: www.ps2dev.org** Contains tutorials, code, boot loaders, and many other resources to get you started writing homebrew software for the PS2.

- **The Third Creation: www.thethirdcreation.net** The home of monthly PS2 demo competition. Many amazing demos are hosted here, all written using Open Source software.

I'd highly recommend that you download any demos authored by adresd; these are among the best.

- **PlayStation 2 Linux Kit: www.playstation2-linux.com** Sony's official home of the PlayStation 2 Linux Kit, a hardware and software development kit that allows you to run Linux on the PS2.

- **Dan Peori's Web site: www.oopo.net/consoledev** Code and tutorials ranging from graphics to the SIF.

- **Lukasz Brunn's Mouthshut: www.mouthshut.net** The home of libITO, one of the first graphics libraries written for PS2 homebrew.

Chapter 10

Wireless 802.11 Hacks

Hacks in this Chapter:

- Wireless NIC/PCMCIA Card Modifications: Adding an External Antenna Connector

- Open AP (Instant802): Reprogramming Your Access Point with Linux

- Having Fun with the Dell 1184 Access Point

- Additional Resources and Other Hacks

Introduction

Hacking wireless hardware is an endeavor steeped in a rich history of experimentation and hobbyist culture. The wireless hardware hacker of today pursues his or her craft with a passion not seen since the amateur radio (also known as "ham radio" or "hams") operators of the last generation. Many wireless enthusiasts are, in fact, connected with the ham community. Once solely the domain of a small group of Radio Frequency (RF) engineers, wireless gear has never been so inexpensive and accessible as it is today. With rapidly declining hardware costs, anybody can learn and experiment with 802.11 equipment with only a small investment.

In this chapter, we review several wireless hacks, tricks, and hardware modifications, including:

- **D–Link DWL650** Card modification for adding an external antenna.

- **OpenAP (Instant802)** Reprogramming your Access Point (AP) to run an open-source version of Linux.

- **Dell 1184 Access Point** Exploring the embedded Linux operating system.

WARNING: PERSONAL INJURY

Please use extreme care when performing any kind of experimentation with RF devices. For more information about the dangers of RF exposure, visit the following URLs:

- www.wlana.org/learn/health.htm
- www.arrl.org/tis/info/rfexpose.html

NEED TO KNOW...

802.11 is a protocol created by the Institute of Electrical and Electronics Engineers (IEEE). This protocol defines a method for transmitting and receiving data communications wirelessly. The original specification was ratified in 1997. This protocol supported 3 physical methods: Frequency Hopping Spread Spectrum (FHSS) and Direct Sequence Spread Spectrum (DSSS) in the 2.4GHz frequency range, as well as Infrared (IR). (Note that IR was never successfully deployed as a commercial option). Speeds of 1Mbps and 2Mbps were supported. In 1999, the IEEE approved 2 new higher speed additions to the protocol: 802.11a and 802.11b. 802.11a defined (up to) 54Mbps Orthogonal Frequency Division Multiplexing (OFDM) at 5GHz and 802.11b defined 5.5Mbps and 11Mbps using DSSS in the 2.4GHz spectrum. In 2003, 802.11g was established to provide (up to) 54Mbps OFDM in the 2.4GHz spectrum. For more information about the 802.11 protocol, please visit http://grouper.ieee.org/groups/802/11/.

Wireless NIC/PCMCIA Card Modifications: Adding an External Antenna Connector

Wireless Network Interface Cards (NICs) typically have a PC Card (also referred to as PCMCIA) form-factor for use in laptops. These cards come in two basic varieties:

- Those with external antenna adapters
- Those without external antenna adapters

For example, Cisco AIR-PCM35x cards have integrated diversity dipole antennas, while the Cisco AIR-LMC35x cards have dual MMCX connectors (no antenna is supplied with the device). Figure 10.1 shows a Cisco card with an integrated antenna, while Figure 10.2 shows a Cisco card with dual MMCX connectors.

Figure 10.1 A Cisco Card with an Integrated Antenna

Figure 10.2 A Cisco Card with Dual MMCX Connectors

For typical indoor applications, an integrated antenna should work just fine. However, these antennas are often low on gain (2.2dBi) and lack the range needed for long distance applications. Having an external antenna connector is desirable because it gives you flexibility. This is particularly important for hobbyist applications (such as connecting Pringles can antennas). When it comes to setting up networks and experimenting with wireless LANs, having flexibility is a key benefit.

Historically speaking, cards with external antenna adapters were sold at a premium compared to cards with integrated antennas. This meant that hobbyists had to either cough up additional cash for a more expensive card or hack their own solution using off-the-shelf parts. Can you guess which path we're going to take?

Preparing for the Hack

In this hack, we will be modifying a D-Link DWL-650. Note that a number of variations exist for the D-Link 650 card so ensure you obtain a standard 16-bit PCMCIA PC Card by comparing your card to the one in Figure 10.3. This is important because D-Link sold 32-bit CardBus NICs for a short time and called them D-Link 650! So really, the only way to be absolutely certain that the card you have on hand is the correct one for this hack is to look at the card...

The items you will need for this hack are:

Figure 10.3 An Unmodified D-Link DWL-650 Card

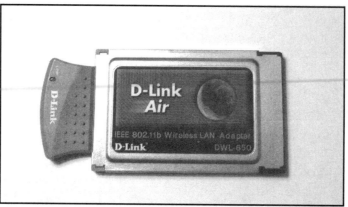

- **D-Link DWL-650 Wireless NIC** An inexpensive PCMCIA card that lacks an external antenna.

- **BNC cable** A small length of Thinnet cable connected to a BNC connector.

- **Soldering iron** To solder the connector wires to the leads on the Printed Circuit Board (PCB).

- **X-ACTO knife** To create a hole in the plastic casing for the wiring.

- **Tweezers or a toothpick** To open the casing and gain access to the PCB.

WARNING: HARDWARE HARM

This hardware modification will void your warranty and potentially violate FCC regulations. This hack should be used for test purposes only and not in a production environment.

You can choose from a variety of cable connectors for attaching your card to an external antenna. Some vendors have proprietary connectors, such as the Cisco MMCX connector. Other connectors are industry standard, such as BNC and N. In our hack, we will use a BNC connector. Don't worry if your antenna uses something other than BNC, because adapters to convert BNC to pretty much any kind of connector are easily available and inexpensive. For more information about RF Connectors, the following Web sites are useful:

- www.rfconnector.com
- www.therfc.com

Furthermore, it's fairly uncomplicated to find a BNC plug with a short length of cable, since you can simply take any old BNC Thinnet cable and snip off the connector (saving a few inches of cable). Figure 10.4 shows an unmodified Thinnet cable.

Figure 10.4 An Unmodified Thinnet Cable

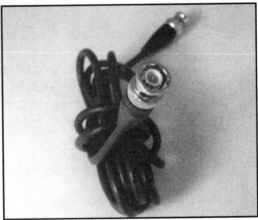

Performing the Hack

Hacking the DWL-650 to add external antenna functionality is performed in three basic steps:

1. Removing the cover.
2. Desoldering a capacitor and soldering it to an adjacent spot on the PCB.
3. Soldering the BNC connector's leads to the PCB.

Removing the Cover

The first step is to open the top cover of the D-Link DWL-650 card and expose the internal antennas. To do this, turn the card upside down (with the MAC address label facing you) and get your tweezers handy. On the short gray tab (protruding from the silver PCMCIA card), you will see four small clasps that hold the plastic cover in place as denoted in Figure 10.5. Each clasp contains two semicircular plastic posts. Use your tweezers to squeeze the semicircular plastic posts together. You might also use a small flat-head screwdriver to wedge the gray plastic pieces apart as you advance to each plastic post. If you don't have tweezers, a toothpick can be wedged into the outer circle and used to leverage the semicircle posts toward each other.

Figure 10.5 The Semicircular Posts Holding the Card Together

Once the posts are sufficiently squeezed together, you can then slowly and gently pry the gray cover off. Note that the cover is held in place by two gray tabs tucked neatly into the silver PCMCIA card edges. You may need to use a small flat-head screwdriver to carefully pry the silver chassis open just wide enough to slide out one end of the gray tabs. Be particularly careful here, since it's nearly impossible to fix the edges of the silver chassis once they are bent by mistake. Figure 10.6 shows the cover once it's been removed.

Figure 10.6 The Gray Cover

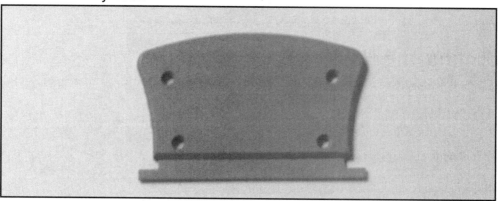

After exposing the antenna compartment (Figure 10.7), you should see some silk-screened labels next to two surface-mount capacitors (C144 and C145). These capacitors are connected to the card's dual internal antennas. You will also notice a silk-screened label for ANT3. That's right—it seems as if

the D-Link card was actually designed to have a third, external antenna. However, it was never implemented and this connector lays dormant—until now!

Figure 10.7 Inside the Antenna Compartment

Moving back to your gray casing and the gray cover you just removed, you will need to bore out a small hole to make room for the BNC cable to pass through. Take your X-ACTO knife and carefully scrape out a small hole in both the top and bottom portions of the gray casing as shown in Figure 10.8. Note that this task is best performed by first removing the gray cover (as described in the previous step) and then separately boring out a semicircle in each half of the gray casing.

Figure 10.8 Making a Hole in the Gray Casing

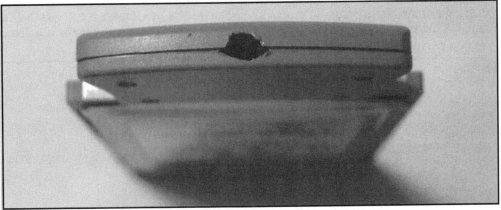

Moving the Capacitor

The second step of the hack is to desolder one of the surface-mount capacitors, either C144 or C145. It doesn't really matter which one you choose to remove. Once the capacitor has been removed, you need to resolder it to the lead labeled ANT3. You can do this by rotating the capacitor 90 degrees. If you chose C145, you will need to rotate the capacitor 90 degrees clockwise. If you chose C144, you will need to rotate the capacitor 90 degrees counterclockwise. In effect, all you are doing is disconnecting one of the surface-mount antennas (the thin diamond-looking leads on the PCB) and electrically connecting it to the ANT3 leads. Figure 10.9 shows a close-up of the antenna compartment before the hack.

Figure 10.9 Antenna Compartment: Close-Up Before the Hack

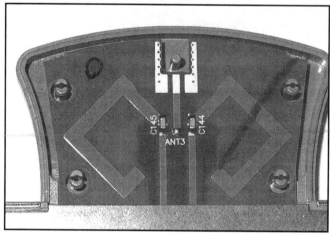

WARNING: HARDWARE HARM

Be very careful when applying heat to the circuit board with your soldering iron. Too much heat may damage the capacitors or the board and may cause the pads and traces to lift up, causing irreparable damage. In practice, it helps to use the tweezers to hold the capacitor in place in the new location while you carefully apply the solder. Sometimes it helps to have a second person involved to lend a hand with the tricky procedure.

Attaching the New Connector

The final step in the D-Link hack is to connect your BNC adapter to the PCB. Prepare your connector by removing the plastic covering and shielding to expose the center conductor and the surrounding copper strands. Figure 10.10 shows a prepared BNC connector.

Figure 10.10 A Prepared BNC Connector Ready for the Hack

The BNC connector should be soldered to the PCB at the gold-colored leads near the top of the antenna compartment. The center conductor of the BNC connector needs to be soldered to the center lead of ANT3, while the outer strands should be soldered to the adjacent pads on the PCB.

Once the soldering is complete, you can reattach the gray plastic cover by sliding in one of the little tabs and wedging the rest of the cover back in place. You should be able to snap it back together with ease. If there is too much resistance, go back and get your X-ACTO knife to widen the hole for your BNC cable a little more. Your completed hack should resemble the image in Figure 10.11.

Remember to be very gentle with your new external BNC cable, because the force of inserting and removing antennas may cause the solder connections to come loose from the internal PCB. Many hobbyists have resorted to applying electrical tape or other reinforcing methods to keep the cable in place and protect the connections from getting damaged. One popular method is to use a hot-glue gun to apply glue to the cable and the surrounding gray casing.

Figure 10.11 The Finished Hack: D-Link DWL-650 with External Antenna Connector

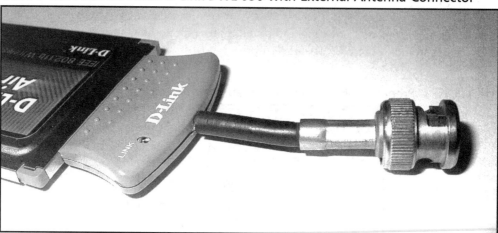

Under the Hood: How the Hack Works

This D-Link hack is a simple example of how you can gain additional functionality from a product that has been intentionally unused by its vendor. It is clear from the PCB design that this NIC was originally intended to support an external antenna (as seen by the ANT-3 pads on the PCB), but it was never implemented. Moving the capacitor simply disables part of the internal antenna circuitry and makes the signal available to an external connection. Note that your card will still work even if you don't attach an external antenna, because diversity mode will allow the still-connected second antenna (on the PCB) to transmit and receive a useable signal.

Diversity mode works by monitoring each antenna and automatically switching to the antenna with the stronger signal. This mode helps reduce errors caused by multipath problems. Multipath errors occur when signals bounce off objects in the transmission path and the same signal arrives at the receiver two times.

OpenAP (Instant802): Reprogramming Your Access Point with Linux

Wireless Internet access using standard off-the-shelf APs is lots of fun. However, traditional consumer-grade APs can be quite feature limited. Sure, it's possible to take an old PC, run Linux, and build your own AP, but the hardware form factors for old PCs tend to be large, clunky, and noisy. With a small form factor, you can install your AP in hard-to-reach places, weatherproof boxes, or tucked away in a corner. Wouldn't it be cool if we could take an off-the-shelf AP and reprogram it with a Linux operating system? That's what you can do with OpenAP, a free software package from Instant802 (http://opensource.instant802.com).

NOTE

If you are unfamiliar with Linux, we suggest you refer to Chapter 14, "Operating Systems Overview," and Chapter 15, "Coding 101," to brush up on your skills before moving on to this hack.

Preparing for the Hack

OpenAP is a completely free and open-source software package. However, it works only with certain hardware devices. Specifically, you need an AP that is based on an Eumitcom WL11000SA-N chipset. The good news is that these can be found in a number of consumer-grade APs, including:

- U.S. Robotics USR 2450 (Figure 10.12)

- SMC EZConnect 2652W

- Addtron AWS-100

- Netcomm NP2000AP

Figure 10.12 The U.S. Robotics USR 2450

These devices can often be found at aftermarket resellers and on eBay and other online sources. Along with the appropriate AP, you also need the following items:

- **Linearly-mapped external memory card** This card needs to be 2MB (minimum) and operate at 3.3 volts. The OpenAP Web site (http://opensource.instant802.com) recommends a MagicRAM Industrial SRAM Memory Card. Another option for the memory card is the Pretec FA2002.

- **Null modem cable** This is the cable you will need to connect your AP to your computer. Using the console port and a terminal emulation program (such as the Windows-based "HyperTerm"), you can communicate directly with your AP.

This hack does not require any special tools, however be sure to have the following items on hand when performing this hack:

- **Screwdriver** To remove the screws of the AP box.

- **9/16" Wrench or Pair of Pliers** To remove the antenna connection from the external box.

- **Needle Nose Pliers** To remove the metal bracket holding down the PCMCIA card.

Performing the Hack

The first step in performing the hack is to obtain the source code for OpenAP which can be downloaded from http://opensource.instant802.com/sources.php. As of this printing, the most current version of OpenAP is 0.1.1. You also need to get the Linux kernel source and untar it into the OpenAP directory. The application source code and kernel source code URLs are provided in the following command-lines.

You can follow these commands to compile the Flash image:

```
wget http://opensource.instant802.com/downloads/openap-0.1.1.tar.gz
tar -xzvf openap-0.1.1.tar.gz
cd openap-0.1.1/
wget http://ftp.kernel.org/pub/linux/kernel/v2.4/linux-2.4.17.tar.gz
tar -xzvf linux-2.4.17.tar.gz
patch -p0 < ./misc/openap-linux-2.4.17.patch
```

By typing **make** and pressing **Enter**, you will be presented with the *makefile* options, as follows:

```
[root@Stephanie openap-0.1.1]# make


Makefile for OpenAP tools, kernel and flash image.


targets -
  tools     : build uclibc and assorted tools
  install   : install uclibc toolchain (must be root)
  bootstrap : configure and build kernel, then flash
  sram      : make sram image


Please see Makefile for details.
[root@Stephanie openap-0.1.1]#
```

In the openap-0.1.1 directory, take a look at the README file for more configuration details. Alternatively, if you prefer to download the prebuilt image from OpenAP rather than compiling your own, you can download it from http://opensource.instant802.com/downloads/sram.img.

Keep in mind that the image file size is 2MB. In order for OpenAP to work, the size of the image file must be equal to the maximum capacity of your SRAM card. This means that a 4MB card must have a 4MB image file. Once you've created the .IMG file (or downloaded it from the OpenAP Web site), you must adjust the file size to the matching size of your card. In a DOS environment (for a 4MB card), you would type the following command: **copy /B sram.img+sram.img sram2.img**.

After your .IMG file is ready, you need to copy it to your SRAM card. In a Windows environment, you can use a program called Memory Card Explorer to transfer the file. You can download a 30-day evaluation version of the Memory Card Explorer software application from www.synchrotech.com/products/software_02.html.

In a Linux environment, you can do both steps (doubling the file size to 4MB and copying the file to the SRAM card) with the following command (assuming that Linux identified your device as /dev/mem0c0c):

```
cat sram sram > /dev/mem0c0c
```

If you had a 2MB card, the command would simply be:

```
cat sram > /dev/mem0c0c
```

Now that your SRAM card is ready, the next step is to install the card into the AP. The idea behind using the SRAM card is that you will boot off of the card only one time in order to program the AP's Flash memory with Linux. After that, all future upgrades can be performed remotely, without reinserting the SRAM card.

Installing the SRAM Card

To install the SRAM card, start by opening your AP case. In our example, we will be using the U.S. Robotics USR 2450. Figure 10.13 shows the AP before modification.

Figure 10.13 The USR 2450 Access Point before Modification

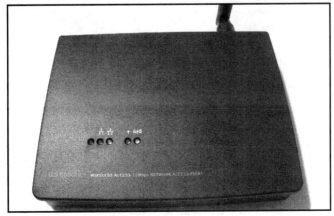

Before you can remove the screws, you need to remove the antenna. This is a simple RP-TNC connector which can be unscrewed in a counterclockwise direction. The RP-TNC connector is held in place by a large nut at its base. Remove this nut with a 9/16" wrench or a pair of pliers. Once the antenna has been removed, you can remove the four screws on the bottom of the AP. Next, gently slide the cover off. Figure 10.14 shows the AP with the cover removed.

Figure 10.14 The AP with the Cover Removed

With the plastic cover out of the way, you will see the wireless NIC in the PCMCIA slot. The card is protected and held in place by a metal brace (Figure 10.15).

Figure 10.15 Before Removing the Card ... See the Metal Brace?

The metal brace can be removed by squeezing one of the plastic posts with a pair of pliers. These plastic posts are similar to the "old school" motherboard spacers that are used to mount computer motherboards to a chassis. Be careful removing these posts, because they can break easily. We recommend removing the post located near the edge of the PCB, as you can use a small string (running between the PCB hole and the hole in the metal bracket) to replace to post in the unlikely event of accidental post damage.

With the metal bracket dislodged, you can now remove the wireless card and set it aside. You'll reinstall it later, so keep it handy.

Next, install the SRAM card in the PCMCIA slot previously occupied by the wireless card.

Before you do anything else, you need to locate the JP2 jumper (two pads surrounded by a white box and "JP2" printed on the board). With the PCMCIA edge connector facing away from you, the JP2 jumper is located below the group of three LEDs, directly to the right of the Flash chip and to the left of the CPU, as denoted in Figure 10.16. When JP2 is shorted (connected) on power-up, the device will boot from the SRAM memory card in the PCMCIA slot instead of booting from the on-board Flash memory. Using a paper clip or short piece of wire, connect the two pads of JP2 together as shown in Figure 10.16.

Figure 10.16 Close-up of the JP2 jumper, with a paperclip inserted

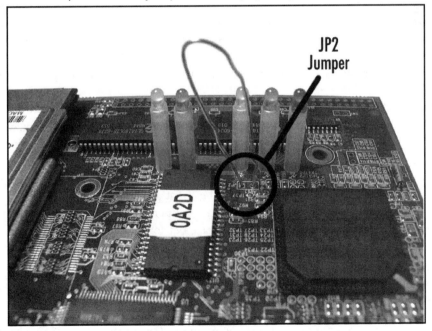

The Flash image you built and installed on the SRAM card contains code to cause the Access Point to write the OpenAP firmware into the AP's Flash memory, so you won't need to reperform this step. Future upgrades can be performed via the OpenAP software.

Power Me Up, Scotty!

The final step of the hack is to power up the device with JP2 shorted and the SRAM card installed. You should observe a green LED and a yellow LED flashing alternately. Once you see this flashing, release the JP2 jumper by removing your paper clip or wire while keeping the device powered up. Be careful not to touch any other components with the paperclip or wire. When the install from SRAM is complete, the device will reboot itself and (assuming the JP2 short is removed), will boot directly from its on-board Flash. You can observe this process by noting that the green and yellow LEDs will now flash back and forth more quickly. This process can take several minutes, so be patient.

Once the process is complete and the device has rebooted, you can remove power and reassemble the AP by reinserting the Wireless NIC, fastening the metal brace, screwing on the top plastic housing, and reconnecting the antenna connector to the outside of the case. With the AP reassembled, you can now fire up a laptop with your favorite AP discovery tool (such as NetStumbler, dStumbler, or Kismet) and look for an AP called instant802_debug (a list of popular AP sniffer tools and their URLs can be found at the conclusion of this chapter). If you see this SSID, your upgrade is successful and you now have a fully functional OpenAP device running Linux!

Under the Hood: How the Hack Works

Under the hood, the U.S. Robotics USR 2450 Access Point is basically a low-powered, single-board computer. It has an AMD ELAN SC400 CPU (based on the Intel 486 core) with 1MB of Flash ROM, 4MB of DRAM, and an RTL8019 NE2000-compatible Ethernet Interface IC. Connected via the PCMCIA interface is a Prism2-chipset Wireless NIC. OpenAP is an elegant hack that essentially takes advantage of this known hardware configuration and replaces the operating system on the AP with its own firmware.

One of OpenAP's most exciting features is the fact that it supports 802.11d bridging. This means that you can expand your wireless network and repeat your wireless signals across several "hops." Most APs connect to the Internet using a wired cable into a digital subscriber line (DSL) or cable modem, but OpenAP can get a connection to the Internet via an adjacent OpenAP (or another 802.11d compliant device) and then extend the coverage of the cloud to anybody within range of its own signal. In essence, your OpenAP can serve as both an 802.11 client and an 802.11 access point at the same time! A group in Palo Alto, California, has developed a cooperative community wireless network built around the OpenAP platform. Visit www.collegeterrace.net for more information about this exciting grassroots movement.

Having Fun with the Dell 1184 Access Point

Following the initial release of the Dell 1184 Access Point, rumors swirled about the possibility that Dell had used an embedded form of the Linux operating system in the device. An exhaustive port scan of the entire port range reveals the following open ports: 80, 333, 1863, 1864, 4443, 5190, and 5566. (A port scan is a search for open ports on a particular host.) Port 80 is for the standard built-in

This will result in the following output:

```
# set default host name
#hostname Wireless_Broadband_Router
# expand /dev/ram0 to ext2 file system
echo "Expand RAM file system image"
/etc/expand /etc/ramfs2048.img /dev/ram0
/etc/expand /etc/ramfs.img /dev/ram1
# mount filesystem and make system directory
echo "Mount filesystem and make system director
mount -n -t proc /proc /proc
mount -n -t ext2 /dev/ram0 /var
mount -n -t ext2 /dev/ram1 /etc/config
chmod 666 /var
chmod 755 /etc
mkdir /var/run
#must be execute before sysconf
checkisp &
reset &
# setup system network
#sysconf config
#sh /etc/bridge
#johnny add
rserver &
reaim &
#server&
#johnny end
#added by tom for start up thttpd
#/bin/thttpd -r -d / &
#/cgi-bin/sysconf.cgi &
```

Did you notice the *#johnny add, #johnny end,* and *#added by tom for start up thttpd* lines? Who are Johnny and Tom? Most likely, they are engineers or developers who helped design the Dell AP or the vLinux distribution. Next, type **ps** to see the list of running processes, which will show something like:

```
PID PORT STAT SIZE SHARED %CPU COMMAND
 1       S    0K      0K   0.0 init
 2       S    0K      0K   0.0 kflushd
```

```
    3       S       OK      OK    0.0  kupdate
    4       S       OK      OK    0.0  kswapd
   16       S       OK      OK    0.0  checkisp
   17       S       OK      OK    0.0  reset
   18       S       OK      OK    0.0  rserver
   19       R       OK      OK    0.2  reaim
   21   S0  S       OK      OK    0.0  /bin/login
   22       S       OK      OK    0.0  /bin/inetd
   23       S       OK      OK    0.0  /bin/thttpd
   24       S       OK      OK    0.0  /cgi-bin/sysconf.cgi
   61      .S       OK      OK    0.0  dproxy
  .69       S       OK      OK    0.0  dhcpd
   79       S       OK      OK    0.0  dhclient
 4446       S       OK      OK    0.7  /bin/telnetd
 4447   p0  S       OK      OK    0.0  sh
 4476       S       OK      OK    0.0  /bin/dporxy
 4499   p0  R       OK      OK    0.0  ps
```

Here, you can see the Web server (/bin/thttpd running as process ID 23) and our Telnet daemon (/bin/telnetd running as process ID 4446).

Want to learn more about the operating system version? Type the following:

```
cat /proc/version
```

This will show something similar to:

```
Linux version 2.2.14-v1.9 (root@localhost.localdomain) (gcc version 2.9-vLinux-armtool-
0523) #5357 Sat Jan 25 17:39:42 CST 2003
```

As you can see, the system once again identifies itself as a Linux distribution. What kind of CPU, you wonder? Type this:

```
cat /proc/cpuinfo
```

You will see something like the following:

```
Processor       : S3C4510/SEC arm7tdmi rev 0
BogoMips        : 44.24
Hardware        : <NULL>
```

Now, would you like to play around with the HTML files that are used in the browser interface? Take a look at the files in /home/httpd. Need to see statistics on frequently used objects in the kernel? Try *cat /proc/slabinfo*. How about current memory usage details? Try *cat /proc/meminfo*. You can even play around with IPChains, ping, gzip, ifconfig, reboot, and other utilities. Have fun and explore! The possibilities are endless for experimenting with your Linux-based Dell 1184 Access Point.

Under the Hood: How the Hack Works

Similar to the USR 2450 Access Point, the Dell 1184 hardware is a single-board computer. The Dell Access Point was designed to run an embedded version of the Linux operating system and all that was needed was to Telnet right into its open arms through port 333. It doesn't require any special tools or reprogramming —it's ready to go, straight out of the box, giving you an easy path into the exciting world of hardware hacking!

Summary

In this chapter, we showed three hardware hacks for wireless networking products. In our first hack, we modified a D-Link DWL-650 wireless NIC to add an external antenna. Most consumer-grade cards do not provide an external antenna connection. Those that do are generally more expensive. However, the D-Link card can be modified to give it support for an external antenna with relative ease. In our hack, we snipped off the end of a Thinnet cable and soldered its BNC connector to the available leads on the D-Link card's PCB. By looking at the PCB, it appears as if the D-Link card has support for an external antenna, but it was never implemented.

In our next hack, we explored OpenAP, an open-source Linux distribution from Instant802. The OpenAP software allows you to reprogram certain brands of off-the-shelf access points with a fully functioning Linux operating system. In our hack, we used a U.S. Robotics USR 2450 AP. The USR 2450 has a special jumper on the motherboard that, when shorted, will cause the AP to boot from an SRAM card if one is inserted into the PCMCIA slot. By removing the wireless NIC from the PCMCIA slot and replacing it with a preprogrammed SRAM card containing a OpenAP image file, we can "reflash" the AP's on-board Flash memory. Then we can remove the SRAM card, replace the wireless NIC, and reboot. Voilá! We now have a Linux machine running on an access point.

In our final hack, we explored the inner workings of the Dell 1184 Access Point. The Dell 1184 contains an embedded Linux distribution. No special tools or reprogramming is necessary and we can simply Telnet to the device on port 333 and gain complete access.

Additional Resources and Other Hacks

This section lists a number of interesting Web sites and other wireless-related hardware hacks. If you're interested in learning more about the wireless hacking community or just wireless technologies in general, follow these links.

User Groups

- **San Diego Wireless Users Group** www.sdwug.org
- **Bay Area Wireless Users** Group www.bawug.org

- **Southern California Wireless Users** Group www.socalwug.org/
- **Orange County Wireless Users Group** www.occalwug.org/
- **NYC Wireless** www.nycwireless.net
- **Seattle Wireless** www.seattlewireless.net
- **Personal Telco** www.personaltelco.net
- **Free Networks** www.freenetworks.org
- **Airshare** www.airshare.org
- **Other User Groups** www.wirelessanarchy.com/#Community%20Groups

Research and Articles

- William Arbaugh, Wireless Research Web Page, www.cs.umd.edu/~waa/wireless.html
- Tim Newsham, 802.11 Wireless LAN Web Page, www.lava.net/~newsham/wlan
- N. Borisov, I. Goldberg, D. Wagner, (In)Security of the WEP Algorithm Web Page, www.isaac.cs.berkeley.edu/isaac/wep-faq.html
- P. Shipley, "Open WLANs: The Early Results of War Driving," 2001, www.dis.org/filez/openlans.pdf
- S. Fluhrer, I. Mantin, A. Shamir, "Weaknesses in the Key Scheduling Algorithm of RC4," Aug 2001, www.wisdom.weizmann.ac.il/~itsik/RC4/Papers/Rc4_ksa.ps
- **IEEE Standards Wireless Zone Web Page** standards.ieee.org/wireless
- **IEEE 802.11 Working Group Web Page** grouper.ieee.org/groups/802/11
- **WarDriving.com Web Page** www.wardriving.com

Products and Tools

- **Airsnort**, 64/128-bit WEP key cracker based on flaws in RC4 Key Scheduling Algorithm, airsnort.sourceforge.net
- **Network Stumbler** www.stumbler.net
- **MacStumbler (OS X)** www.macstumbler.com
- **bsd-airtools (*BSD)** www.dachb0den.com/projects/bsd-airtools.html
- **NetChaser (Palm OS)** www.bitsnbolts.com/netchaser.html
- **KisMAC (OS X)** www.binaervarianz.de/projekte/programmieren/kismac

into a small form factor, iPod sales immediately took off. Since the iPod's introduction more than two years ago, Apple has sold over 2 million iPods and has captured the majority of the MP3 player market. Along the way, the iPod has seen several updates, which are described later in this chapter.

The iPod is only half of the equation, though. Apple also released a free piece of software called iTunes (see Figure 11.2) that works seamlessly with the iPod. iTunes allows you to organize and enjoy your music collection using a slick, powerful interface, and it connects effortlessly to your iPod. In April 2003, Apple introduced the iTunes Music Store (iTMS, as shown in Figure 11.3), which integrates a full-fledged online music store into iTunes, allowing quick and painless purchase of music online. As of this writing, Apple has over 400,000 songs available in the iTMS library. Individual songs can be purchased for 99 cents, with most albums going for $9.99. Over 30 million songs were purchased through iTunes as of January 2004.

Figure 11.2 iTunes for OS X

Figure 11.3 The iTunes Music Store

Hoping to capture an even larger share of the MP3 player market and understanding that the Macintosh market is dwarfed by computers installed with Windows, Apple has started selling Windows-compatible versions of the iPod, formatted with the FAT32 file system instead of Mac HFS+ (which is the standard Macintosh file system that Windows computers do not understand). Third-generation iPods, unveiled in April 2003, no longer distinguish between Macs and PCs; the included Windows software will properly initialize the iPod to work with Windows. In early 2004, Apple introduced a smaller, less expensive version of the iPod called the iPod mini, targeting the high-end Flash ROM-based player market. Apple has also released a version of iTunes for Windows, which is virtually identical to the Macintosh offering, giving Windows users access to the same, high-quality software that Mac users have been enjoying with their iPods.

Since the iPod's introduction over two years ago, Apple has updated the device several times. Some of these revisions have simply involved adding larger-capacity hard drives, but others have been more significant. Three generations of iPods, known simply as first-, second-, and third-generation iPods, as well as the recently unveiled iPod mini, are now on the market. Differences are minor between the first- and second-generation iPods, and those models are very similar in physical appearance. However, in 2003, Apple released the third-generation iPod, which is a new design over previous models and can quickly be distinguished from those earlier models. Figure 11.1 shows a pair of iPods side by side—a first-generation iPod on the left and a third-generation on the right. The differences between the various iPod iterations are detailed here:

- **First generation** Introduced in October 2001 and available initially with a 5GB drive. A 10GB model was added later. These first-generation iPods feature a mechanical scroll wheel that physically rotates about a center Action button. All the buttons on the front face are mechanical. The top of the iPod features a white, plastic plate around the FireWire port, headphone jack, and Hold switch.

- **Second generation** Available in 10GB and 20GB versions, the second-generation iPods replaced the moving scroll wheel with a touch-sensitive, solid-state touch wheel. The buttons on the front face remain the same, but the top plate is stainless steel as opposed to the white plastic of the first generation, and the FireWire port includes a built-in cover. Second-generation iPods are available in Macintosh and Windows-specific versions, although they can easily be reformatted to work with either operating system. A remote control and an iPod case came standard with the unit.

- **Third generation** Third-generation iPods were introduced with a completely new form factor, although one that is still immediately recognizable as an iPod. Gone are the buttons around the touch wheel, replaced by a row of four touch-sensitive, backlit buttons immediately above the wheel. Third-generation iPods are noticeably thinner than previous iPods, thanks to a much smaller and lower-capacity internal battery. A new docking port is located at the bottom of the unit, and the wired remote and headphone plugs have been separated into two distinct jacks at the top. Higher-capacity models come standard with a dock, a wired remote, and a case. These accessories can also be purchased separately. Third-generation iPods work with both Macintosh and Windows computers—the included Windows installation software reformats the hard drive appropriately. As of this writing, Apple is offering third-generation iPods in 15GB, 20GB, and 40GB configurations.

- **iPod mini** In January 2004, Apple introduced a new line of iPods dubbed the iPod mini. Designed to compete with the high-end Flash ROM-based (solid-state memory) player market, the iPod mini features a 4GB hard drive in a form factor the width and height of a business card and only 1/2" thick. Encased in anodized aluminum and available in five colors, the iPod mini features the same user interface as its full-sized siblings and supports FireWire and USB 2. In order to save space on the front face, Apple made the four buttons found on the third-generation iPod part of the touch wheel, which now doubles as a four-function button (each compass direction on the wheel can be pressed to activate the button). Because the iPod mini was introduced as this book was being completed, we discuss only the full-size iPods in this chapter.

Figure 11.4 The Backside of a 20GB Third-Generation iPod

Due to their popularity, iPods have become a target for hardware hackers and other curious people wanting to open them up and poke around inside. However, there are very practical reasons to open an iPod—mainly to replace the internal battery. The Li-Ion battery chemistry the iPod uses is generally better than previous battery technologies (such as nickel cadmium or nickel metal hydride, neither of which were used in any iPods), but people tend to use their iPods quite a bit, and even Li-Ion batteries do not last forever. The most common concern regarding the iPod is the fact that Apple designed it so the battery cannot be replaced by end users. Only recently has Apple made available a battery replacement program, which requires you to send your iPod to Apple and pay $99 plus return shipping charges for them to install a new battery in your iPod. And there is no guarantee that you will even receive the same iPod in return! If you're willing to dive into opening your iPod yourself (something that requires a bit of patience), you can replace the internal battery for about half the cost of sending your iPod to Apple, and you won't be without an iPod while you wait. We'll show you how in this chapter.

In addition, we'll describe how to upgrade the hard drive in a 5GB iPod as well as reformatting an iPod so it can be used with either a Macintosh or Windows system. Finally, we'll discuss the iPod's built-in (but undocumented) diagnostic mode. At the end of the chapter, we'll touch briefly on some other hacks you can perform, such as installing Linux on your iPod, and present a list of additional iPod resources so you can further explore the device on your own.

Opening Your iPod

One thing that iPod owners will quickly notice is there is no obvious way to open the case. There are no visible screws, tabs, or anything of that nature—just a sleek, metal plate somehow affixed to the back of the iPod. The two halves of the iPod are held together by a series of plastic tabs that run along both sides of the case, holding the metal half of the device securely in place. Unfortunately, this ensures that taking apart the iPod, which was never intended for end users, is a tricky proposition.

However, there are compelling reasons to open the iPod, especially if your battery has died (or is nearing depletion) and you want to save some money by replacing it yourself. Be warned, however, that you must be patient when opening the iPod or you can easily damage the case.

Preparing for the Hack

We will separately describe how to open a first-generation iPod and a second- or third-generation iPod. The best tool to open your iPod with is some type of stiff plastic, such as the wedges we'll use below. If you can avoid it, do not use a metal screwdriver to pry your iPod open, as the risk of damaging the case is much greater. The metal case can be permanently bent and the plastic of the case will scratch easily, so care and patience must be applied when opening the iPod. One of the battery kits we purchased came from PDASmart (www.pdasmart.com) and include two plastic sticks with tapered, wedge ends (not unlike a flathead screwdriver) which are ideal for opening iPods (see Figure 11.5). We also purchased batteries from Laptops For Less (www.laptopsforless.com), and they include a single jeweler's screwdriver for opening the iPod.

WARNING: HARDWARE HARM

Apple never intended end users to open the iPod and thus made it rather difficult to do so. The iPod is held together by a series of plastic tabs that clip onto the metal part of the case. To open the case, you must exert force between the plastic half of the case and the metal half to flex the case enough so the tabs become detached from the metal. In doing this, you can permanently bend the metal half of the case, as well as cause cosmetic damage to the plastic half along the seam where the two halves come together.

Therefore, extreme patience and care are required when you're attempting to open an iPod. Using a tool to pry into the case can very easily bend the metal, so you must be diligent and work slowly. If you use a small screwdriver you'll want to be especially careful not to slip when exerting force while prying, as you can easily put a nice gouge in the case exterior.

Figure 11.5 Plastic Wedges for Opening an iPod

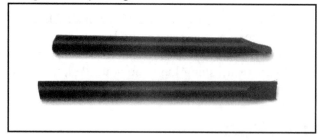

First-generation iPods are easier to open as you can begin prying at the top of the case near the FireWire port. Second and third-generation iPods do not have this advantage, so you must start along one of the sides.

First Generation iPods

Let's begin:

1. Using one of the wedges, start by prying between the stainless steel cover and the plastic of the case at the top of the iPod (see Figure 11.6). Prying at the top will allow you to open a small gap on the side of the case where you can then use one of the other wedges to start undoing the plastic tabs. To see what you're aiming for, look ahead to Figure 11.9, which shows what the tabs look like when the case is open.

Figure 11.6 Start Prying at the Top of the Case

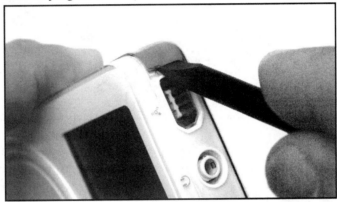

2. With one wedge firmly in place at the top of the iPod, use a second wedge to start working along the side, as shown in Figure 11.7.

Figure 11.7 Working Along the Edge

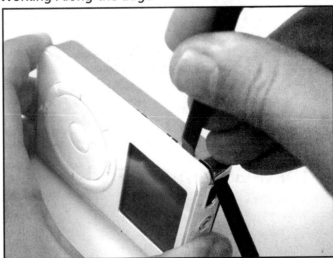

3. Continue working your way along the edge of the iPod until you have all the clips on one side undone (see Figure 11.8).

Figure 11.8 Continue Working Down the Edge

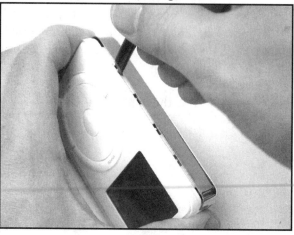

4. Once you reach the corner opposite from where you started and have all the clips undone on one side of the iPod, you are past the most difficult stage and can separate the two halves (see Figure 11.9). You may now proceed with other hacks, such as replacing the iPod battery or swapping out the hard drive, which are described later in this chapter.

Figure 11.9 Lifting Apart the Two Halves of the iPod

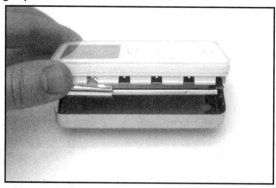

Second and Third-Generation iPods

Apple changed the design of the second-generation iPods so you can't start prying at the top of the unit near the FireWire port. Third-generation iPods constitute a completely new design over the first two iPod generations and suffer a similar problem. Unfortunately, this makes them a bit trickier to open. While we depict a third-generation iPod in the pictures, the procedure is similar for second-generation iPods.

1. Work one of the plastic wedges along the seam on the side of the iPod until you are able to insert it between the metal back and the case (see Figure 11.10).

Figure 11.10 Prying into the Case

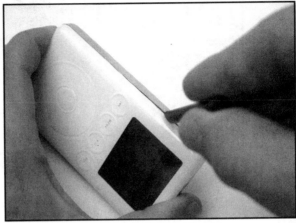

2. With one of the wedges inserted in the case, insert a second wedge into the gap you've created and work it along the edge to pop out the tabs holding the case together. Your goal is to push each of the tabs inward until they release from the metal half of the case.

Figure 11.11 Continue Prying Along One Side

3. Continue working along the one side until you have all the tabs unclipped (see Figure 11.12).

Figure 11.12 Unclip all the Tabs

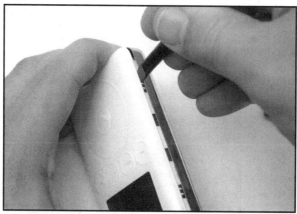

4. With one side unclipped, you should be able to separate the back of the iPod from the front half (see Figure 11.13).

Figure 11.13 Opening the Case

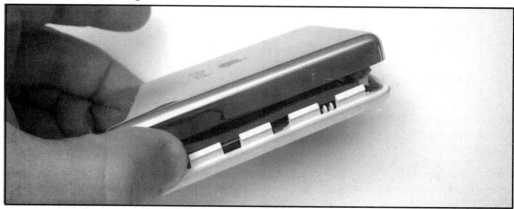

If you're opening a third-generation iPod, the metal half of the case is connected to the bottom half by a thin ribbon cable. Do not try separating the two halves completely without first disconnecting the cable or you may do permanent harm to your iPod. Figure 11.14 shows where the cable is connected to the top half of the case. You can choose to either disconnect the cable or leave it connected and flip the metal half of the case over so it is resting next to the top half of the case.

WARNING: HARDWARE HARM

Unlike first- and second-generation iPods, the third-generation iPods' metal cover is connected to the top half of the unit with a thin ribbon cable. Do not be hasty in separating the two halves, because you can easily damage this cable. You can choose to disconnect the cable (the connector is shown in Figure 11.14) or carefully place the two halves of the case close to each other on a flat surface while working on the iPod internals.

Figure 11.14 Connector Holding Two Halves Together

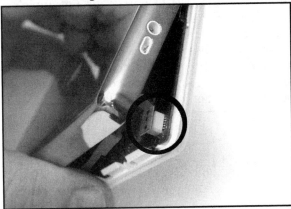

With your iPod open, you may now proceed with the hack of your choice, including replacing the iPod battery or swapping out the hard drive, both of which are described in this chapter.

Replacing the iPod Battery

Sooner or later, it will come time to replace your iPod's battery. Li-Ion power cells are a big improvement over older battery chemistries, but they are not infallible. Eventually your iPod's battery will no longer hold a charge or it will be sufficiently weak where you're not getting nearly as much time out of your iPod as you did when it was new. When that time comes, you have three choices:

1. **Throw out your iPod and buy a new one** Apple would love you to choose this option, but most people do not consider the iPod a "disposable" item, given its high price tag. Thus, this is not an option for the majority of people.

2. **Send your iPod to Apple and pay them to replace the battery** Apple recently began a program whereby you can send them your iPod and, for $99 (plus shipping and sales tax if applicable), they will replace its battery. Besides being relatively expensive, this choice deprives you of your iPod while you're waiting for Apple to return it. Also, Apple makes no guarantee that you'll receive your original iPod back.

3. **Open your iPod and replace the battery yourself** Several companies sell iPod batteries for around $50 and often include a tool (a screwdriver or plastic implement) that you

can use to open your iPod. Once you have the device open, swapping the old battery for a new one is relatively trivial. Opening the iPod is the hardest part.

Since you're reading a book on hardware hacking, we'll assume that you're opting to replace the battery yourself.

NEED TO KNOW... iPOD BATTERY LAWSUIT?

Just before this book went to press, the law firm of Girard Gibbs & De Bartolomeo LLP posted a page on its Web site called "Investigation of Apple's iPod." The firm indicated that it is "investigating a potential class action against Apple Computer, Inc., on behalf of iPod owners whose batteries have died or lost their ability to hold their charge." The Web page has since been taken down, but while it was up the firm was asking iPod users who experienced problems with their battery to submit information via a form on the page.

After the page was posted, Apple began offering a battery replacement program, but it's unclear if this potential litigation had any influence on Apple's decision to set up the program.

Preparing for the Hack

For this hack, all you need is a tool to open the iPod (a plastic wedge or two, a firm piece of thin plastic, a small screwdriver, or something similar) and a replacement battery.

To demonstrate this hack, we ordered new batteries from Laptops for Less (www.laptopsforless.com) and PDASmart (www.pdasmart.com). At the time of this writing, the batteries cost $50 to $60 each, plus shipping. PDASmart also offers a mail-in service that is less expensive than Apple's battery replacement program. You can also find iPod batteries for sale on eBay, but if you go this route you need to be careful not to end up purchasing a used battery that might be in worse condition than the battery you intend to replace.

NEED TO KNOW...

Apple made many changes to the iPod when it designed the third-generation models, the battery being one of them. Third-generation iPods have a much smaller battery than earlier models, presumably to reduce the thickness of the iPod. Although Apple certainly succeeded in making the newer iPods thinner, the third-generation iPods have a noticeably shorter battery life as a result. Figure 11.15 shows the difference in size between the two batteries.

When ordering a new battery for your iPod, you want to make sure you specify the correct battery type. You'll be pretty disappointed if you open your iPod up only to discover that you ordered the wrong battery.

Figure 11.15 iPod Batteries: First- and Second-Generation (Top) and Third-Generation (Bottom)

Since the battery and internals are unique between the first- and second-generation iPods and the third-generation iPods, we will describe battery replacement separately.

Battery Replacement: First- and Second-Generation iPods

Follow these steps:

1. The first thing you'll want to do is open your iPod, as described in the first section of this chapter. Once you have the iPod open, put aside the metal half of the case and place your iPod face down on a flat surface, as shown in Figure 11.16. The battery is sitting on top.

Figure 11.16 The First-Generation iPod Opened and Ready for the Hack

2. The battery is connected to the iPod motherboard by a power connector visible at the lower-left corner of Figure 11.16. Holding the battery in place are two thin rubber strips at both ends of the iPod, sandwiched between the battery and the hard drive (which is directly under-

neath the battery). Figure 11.17 shows one of these strips at the top of the iPod. In this picture, you can also more clearly see the battery power cable plugged into the motherboard.

Figure 11.17 Rubber Strips

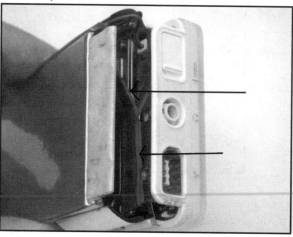

3. Using a screwdriver, carefully pry between the hard drive and the battery, undoing the glue on the rubber pieces, as shown in Figure 11.18.

Figure 11.18 Prying the Battery from the Rubber Strips

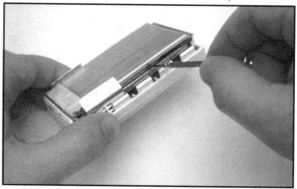

4. Once you have separated the battery from the rubber strips, you can unplug it from the iPod motherboard and properly dispose of it (see Figure 11.19).

Figure 11.19 Removing the Old Battery

5. With the old battery removed, you can now swap in the new battery that you purchased (see Figure 11.20). Orient the new battery in the same direction as the old battery. Plug the power connector into the iPod motherboard, taking care as you insert the connector. The connector will fit in only one orientation; so do not force it into place. For easier access to the connector on the motherboard, you can temporarily move aside the rubber strip that partially covers it.

Figure 11.20 Connecting the New Battery

6. With the new battery connected, move the rubber strip back into place (if you moved it out of the way) and firmly attach the battery atop the hard drive, as shown in Figure 11.21.

Figure 11.21 Affixing the Battery to the Hard Drive

7. Take care that the power cable is tucked away at the top of the iPod (see Figure 11.22).

Figure 11.22 Power Cable Safely Tucked Away

8. Once you have the battery securely attached into place, you can reattach the cover (see Figure 11.23). The metal cover should snap easily into place. If it does not, make sure there are no obstructions before you attempt to close the cover.

Figure 11.23 Reattaching the Metal Half of the Case

9. Once you have your iPod back together, you'll want to charge the battery for a minimum of three hours before using the device (see Figure 11.24).

Figure 11.24 Charging the New Battery

Battery Replacement: Third-Generation iPods

Follow these steps:

1. Carefully open your third-generation iPod as described in the first section of this chapter. Once you have your iPod opened, it should resemble the image in Figure 11.25.

Figure 11.25 The Third-Generation iPod Opened and Ready for the Hack

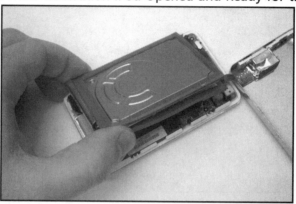

2. First, you'll need to remove the hard drive (see Figure 11.26). The hard drive is sitting on top of the other iPod circuitry, buffered by a piece of blue rubber. The hard drive is connected to the iPod via a small ribbon cable that connects directly to the motherboard. Slowly lift up the hard drive to disconnect this cable, and set the hard drive aside.

Figure 11.26 Removing the Hard Drive

3. Now that the hard drive has been removed, we have easy access to the battery. The battery is the large black component highlighted in Figure 11.27. The battery connector is immediately to the left of the battery (see Figure 11.28).

Figure 11.27 The iPod Battery

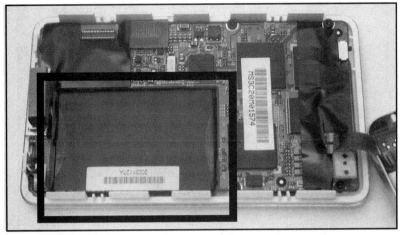

4. Carefully use a small screwdriver to pry the battery from its compartment. Be careful not to make contact with the circuit board below the battery, because you could damage it. Before the battery can be completely removed, you will need to disconnect the power cord. However, the cord is wrapped around a part of the circuit board, as shown in Figure 11.28. You can use a screwdriver to help remove the wires from underneath the board.

Figure 11.28 The iPod Battery Connector

5. With the wires out of the way, you can remove the battery from its compartment in the iPod, as shown in Figure 11.29.

Figure 11.29 The iPod Battery Removed

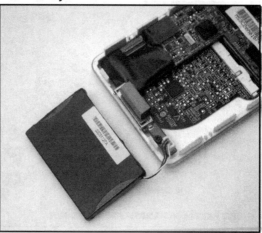

6. Disconnect the battery from the motherboard by gently pulling the power connector straight up. With the old battery removed, you can now plug the new battery in, taking care as you insert the connector (see Figure 11.30). The connector will only fit in one orientation, so do not force it into place.

Figure 11.30 Inserting the New iPod Battery

7. Before you can place the battery back into its compartment, you must first wrap the battery power cord around the tip of the circuit board. You can use a small screwdriver to assist you, as shown in Figure 11.31.

Figure 11.31 Tucking In the Power Cable

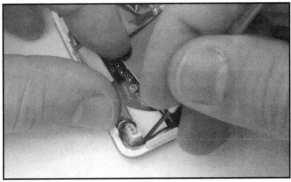

8. Once you have reattached and properly routed the power cable, you can place the new battery inside the case. Your iPod should now resemble the image in Figure 11.32.

Figure 11.32 New Battery Installed in Place

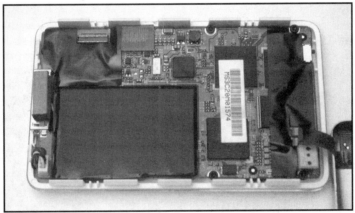

9. Now you can reassemble your iPod. Reattach the connector on the hard drive to the connector on the motherboard. The connectors are highlighted in Figure 11.33.

Figure 11.33 Reattaching the Hard Drive

10. After you've plugged the hard drive back in, you can then place it back on top of the board (see Figure 11.34).

Figure 11.34 Hard Drive Back in Place

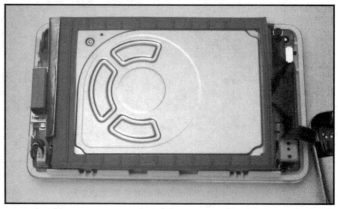

11. Finally, place the metal half of the case back on top of the iPod and snap it into place (see Figure 11.35). Take care not to pinch or put too much stress on the thin ribbon connector on the iPod motherboard while you are manipulating the two halves of the case.

Figure 11.35 Snapping the Case Back Together

12. Once you have your iPod back together, you'll want to charge the battery for a minimum of three hours before using the device (see Figure 11.36).

Figure 11.36 Charging the new Battery

Upgrading a 5GB iPod's Hard Drive

The first iPod Apple released contained a 5GB hard drive, which was an impressive amount of storage at the time. However, it has since been eclipsed by iPods with much larger disk space. The largest iPod available as this book goes to press is a 40GB version, allowing for up to eight times the storage of the early 5GB iPods. Unfortunately, the iPod uses a PCMCIA form-factor 1.8-inch hard drive made by Toshiba, and replacement drives are not easy to obtain. However, used iPod drives come up frequently for auction on eBay, giving you an opportunity to either upgrade your 5GB iPod to a higher capacity or replace a nonworking drive with a good one to get your iPod back in working order.

Keep in mind that there is a fairly limited upgrade path for the 5GB iPod. Drives from third-generation iPods will not work in the first-generation iPod, and drives larger in capacity than 10GB (such as the 20GB drive used in the second-generation iPod) will not fit in the first-generation case due to the increase in thickness.

Preparing for the Hack

For this hack you'll need the following:

- A 5GB iPod that you want to upgrade

- A replacement hard drive (an example is shown in Figure 11.37)

- A tool for opening the iPod (such as one or two plastic wedges, a thin, firm piece of plastic, or a flat-head screwdriver)

eBay is a good source for used iPod drives, and they can often be found for much less than you'd pay to buy a new (or used) iPod. If you're unsure of the drive's capacity, you can find it printed in the lower-left corner of the sticker on the top of the drive (highlighted in Figure 11.38).

Figure 11.37 A 10GB iPod Hard Drive

Figure 11.38 Drive Capacity Printed on the Hard Drive Sticker

Performing the Hack

The first thing you'll want to do is open your iPod as described in the first section in this chapter. When you have the case off, your iPod should resemble the image in Figure 11.39.

Figure 11.39 iPod Opened and Ready for the Hack

1. To get to the hard drive, we first have to remove the battery that sits on top of it. The battery is held into place by sticky rubber pads sandwiched between the battery and the hard drive. The battery is also connected to the motherboard with a power cable. The easiest way to remove the battery is to use a small screwdriver as a lever (see Figure 11.40). Take care not to exert force with the tip of the screwdriver on either the battery or the hard drive, because you may puncture them; instead, use the shaft of the screwdriver to pry between the battery and the hard drive.

Figure 11.40 Pulling the Battery and Hard Drive Apart

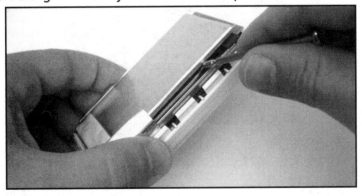

2. Once you have peeled the battery off the top of the hard drive, it will still be connected to the motherboard. Before disconnecting the battery, let's first remove the rubber pads from the top of the hard drive (see Figure 11.41), because one of them may be obscuring access to the battery connector and we need to remove the pads anyway to apply them to the new drive. Note that the rubber pads in your iPod may not look exactly the same as those pictured.

Figure 11.41 Rubber Pads on Top of the Hard Drive

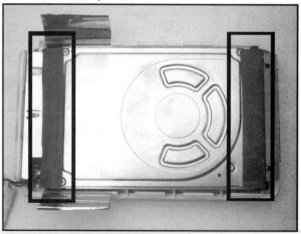

3. Carefully peel the rubber pads from the top of the drive (see Figure 11.42). **Put them aside** for now; we will be attaching them to the new drive once we've installed it **into the iPod.**

Figure 11.42 Removing the Rubber Pads

4. With the rubber pads removed, we can now easily unplug the battery. Although it's **not** imperative that we disconnect the battery, it does make removing and installing **the new** hard drive easier. Carefully unplug the battery connector by pulling it straight **up off the** motherboard (see Figure 11.43). Once the battery has been disconnected, **set it aside.**

Figure 11.43 Disconnecting the Battery

5. With the battery out of the way, we can now remove the hard drive. The hard drive is resting on four small rubber pads and is plugged into the motherboard with a connector on one edge of the hard drive. Carefully pry the bottom of the hard drive from each rubber pad (see Figure 11.44).

WARNING: HARDWARE HARM

Be extremely careful in performing this procedure. Do not use the motherboard as direct leverage for prying up the hard drive, because you can easily damage the motherboard and render your iPod inoperable. Instead, wedge the screwdriver between the rubber pads and the hard drive, as shown in Figure 11.44.

Figure 11.44 Prying the Hard Drive from the Rubber Pads

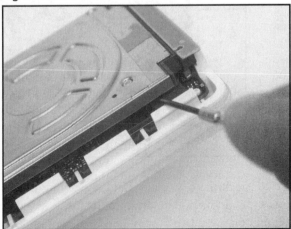

6. Once you have separated the drive from the rubber pads, you can disconnect the drive from the connector on the motherboard. This connector is very fragile, so take care when unplugging it from the drive. The easiest way to do so is to wedge a flat-head jeweler's screwdriver between the drive and connector to work it loose (see Figure 11.45). After you disconnect the drive, you can set it aside.

Figure 11.45 Disconnecting the Hard Drive

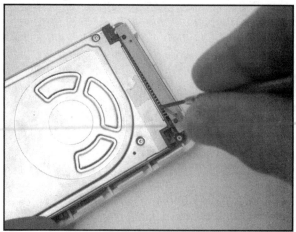

7. If any of the rubber pads are still attached to the hard drive, remove them and place them in the appropriate corner of the motherboard, where they were originally resting. Your iPod should now resemble the image in Figure 11.46.

Figure 11.46 Exposed iPod Motherboard

8. Now it's time to attach the new drive. Before you plug the drive in, make sure it is oriented the same way as the old drive. The drive connector is keyed and can be plugged into the motherboard only one way (see Figure 11.47).

Figure 11.47 The Hard Drive Connector

Taking care that the drive is oriented properly (the label side of the drive should be facing the iPod motherboard), plug the hard drive in as shown in Figure 11.48. Do not exert too much force when plugging in the drive—if it doesn't slide in easily, make sure the drive is not upside down.

Figure 11.48 Plugging In the New Hard Drive

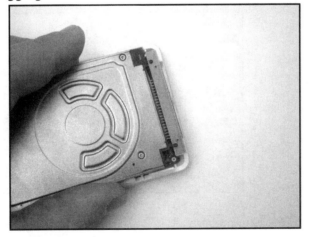

9. After plugging the drive into the connector, place it back on the motherboard's rubber pads, taking care that the drive is properly centered in the case. With the drive placed in the case, it should resemble Figure 11.49.

Figure 11.49 The New Hard Drive Resting in the Case

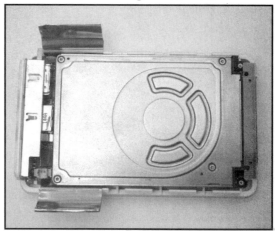

10. Now it's time to plug the battery back into the motherboard. Carefully plug the connector into the board, taking care that the plug is oriented in the right direction. The plug is keyed and will fit into the connector only one way, so do not try to force it (see Figure 11.50).

Figure 11.50 Reattaching the Battery

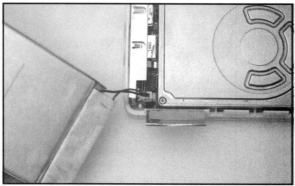

11. Now replace the long rubber pads that you removed earlier by attaching them to the replacement drive in the same locations as they were on the old drive (see Figure 11.51). Note that the rubber pads in your iPod might not exactly resemble those in the picture.

Figure 11.51 Replacing the Rubber Pads

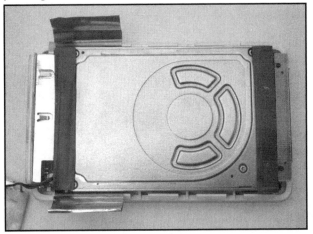

12.   After replacing the rubber pads, place the battery on top of the hard drive. Take care to properly align the battery on top of the hard drive, or you may have problems getting the case back together. Also, tuck the battery power cable underneath the metal housing at the top of the iPod to move it out of the way (see Figure 11.52). Apply enough pressure to the battery to ensure that it is firmly attached to the rubber pads.

Figure 11.52 Battery Back in Place

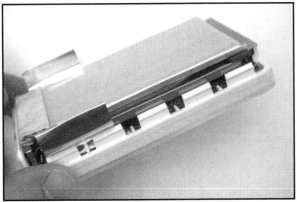

13.   Fold the two pieces of metal foil back over the battery. Finally, snap the stainless steel cover back over the case (see Figure 11.53). If the cover does not slide easily over the case, make sure there are no obstructions before continuing. The cover should snap into place easily.

Figure 11.53 Replace the Cover

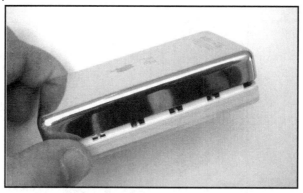

14. After you've got the iPod back together, turn it on. If the upgrade was successful, you should be able to use your new iPod immediately (see Figure 11.54).

Figure 11.54 Ahhh, Music!

Of course, you'll probably want to plug your iPod into your computer and copy your music onto it. If you upgraded your iPod with a larger hard drive (going from 5GB to 10GB, as we did in this chapter), you now have twice as much storage space. If the drive was formatted for use with a Macintosh and you need to use your iPod with a Windows machine, or vice versa, read the next section, which explains how you can perform this magic.

From Mac to Windows and Back Again

First-generation iPods were intended for use solely with Macintosh computers. As demand for the iPod grew, Apple released the second-generation iPods, which included support for Windows computers. To this end, Apple sold two different versions of the second-generation iPod—models for Windows computers and models for Macs. Third-generation iPods do away with this duplicity in packaging and simply come with an install disk that will properly format the iPod's hard drive for Windows (new iPods come pre-formatted with the Macintosh HFS+ file system). Fortunately, all iPods can be formatted to work with Windows or the Macintosh using software available from Apple.

Preparing for the Hack

All you need for this hack are the following:

- An iPod you'd like to "switch"

- A Windows or Macintosh computer with a FireWire port (or a USB port if you have a third-generation iPod)

- An Internet connection so you can download the appropriate software from Apple's Web site

WARNING

Performing this procedure will cause the iPod Updater software to reformat your iPod's hard drive with a new file system, thus deleting anything stored on the drive. If you have music or other files stored on your iPod and you don't want to lose them, make sure you first back up the files onto your computer!

Going from Windows to Macintosh

If you're using a first- or second-generation iPod, you will need to download the iPod Software Updater 1.3.1. If you're using a third-generation iPod, you will need to download the iPod Software Updater 2.0.1 (or later) instead. The updaters can be found at www.info.apple.com/usen/ipod.

1. After downloading the correct version of the software for your iPod, run the updater, as shown in Figure 11.55. This example demonstrates using the iPod Software Updater 1.3.1, but the procedure is similar for later Updater versions.

Figure 11.55 The Macintosh iPod Software Updater Installer

2. Go through the install process, which will install the updater on your computer. When installation is complete, plug your iPod into your Macintosh. Locate the iPod Software Updater on your computer, which should be located in your **Applications | Utilities** folder.

3. With your iPod plugged into your Macintosh, start the iPod Software Updater by double-clicking the **iPod Software Updater** icon (see Figure 11.56). Click the **lock** icon in the lower-left corner of the dialog box, type in your password, and click the **Restore** button (see Figure 11.57).

Figure 11.56 The iPod Software Updater Icon

Figure 11.57 The iPod Software Updater

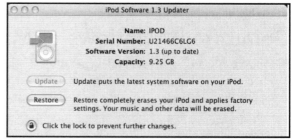

4. After you click **Restore**, you will be prompted with a confirmation dialog box. Confirm that you want to restore your iPod to its factory settings. After the updater has completed, unplug the iPod and then plug it back into your computer. That's it! Now you can copy music and other files onto your iPod.

Going from Macintosh to Windows

If you're using a first- or second-generation iPod, you will need to download the Windows 1.3 iPod Updater. If you're using a third-generation iPod, you will need to download the Windows 2.1 (or later) iPod Updater instead. The updaters can be found at www.info.apple.com/usen/ipodwin.

1. After downloading the appropriate software, locate and run the installer, as shown in Figure 11.58. Go through the install process, which will install the updater on your computer. This example demonstrates restoring an iPod using the iPod Software Updater 1.3, but the procedure is similar for later Updater versions.

Figure 11.58 The Windows iPod Software Updater Installer

2. If your iPod is connected to your Windows computer, eject it and unplug it from the computer. Locate the iPod Updater that you just installed (see Figure 11.59). It should be located under **Start | Programs | iPod | System Software 1.3** (or 2.1 if you're installing that version instead).

Figure 11.59 Locate and Run the iPod Updater

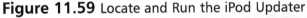

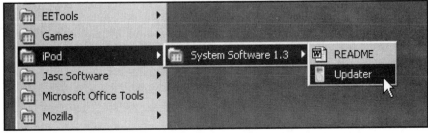

3. After you start the Updater, plug your iPod into the computer. The iPod installer screen should acknowledge that the iPod has been plugged in and resemble the image shown in Figure 11.60.

Figure 11.60 The Windows iPod Updater

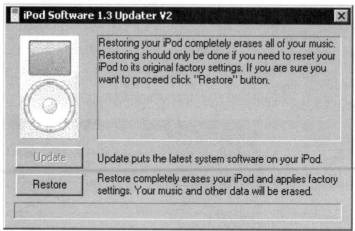

4. Now click the **Restore** button. After the updater has completed, unplug the iPod and then plug it back into your computer. That's it! Now you can copy music and other files onto your iPod.

iPod Diagnostic Mode

The iPod has several built-in diagnostic features that can help you troubleshoot problems with your iPod. Most diagnostic features are accessed through a hidden, undocumented menu, but there is also a disc scan mode that you can access separately. Each version of the iPod firmware contains a diagnostic mode, though some of the commands differ.

The Diagnostic Menu

To enter the diagnostic menu:

1. Reset your iPod by pressing and holding the **Menu** and **Play** buttons for 5 to 10 seconds. When the iPod resets and the Apple logo appears, press and hold **Previous**, **Next**, and **Action** (the center button). If you do this properly, you'll briefly see a reversed Apple logo, and a menu will then appear. The menu may differ based on the firmware version installed in your iPod. Figure 11.61 shows the diagnostic menus for first-generation and third-generation iPods.

Figure 11.61 The iPod Diagnostic Menu

First-Generation iPod 1.3.1 Firmware
Installed

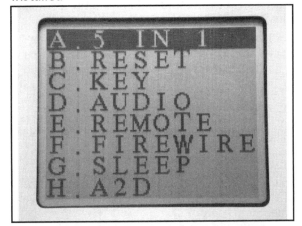

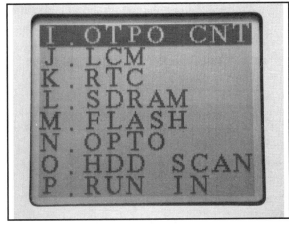

Third-Generation iPod 2.1.0 Firmware
Installed

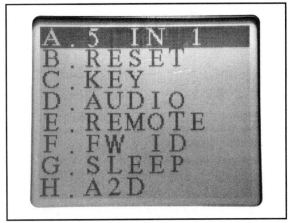

2. The menu is two screen pages long, and you can scroll through the items by pressing the **Previous** and **Next** buttons. Pressing the **Action** button will start the test of the highlighted selection. Press the **Play** button after a test has completed to return to the menu. To exit the diagnostic mode, reset your iPod by holding down the **Menu** and **Play** buttons for 5 or more seconds.

Some of the menu items are fairly obvious, but the function of others can only be guessed at. Table 11.1 describes what we know about each test.

Table 11.1 iPod Diagnostic Menu Functions

Item	Name	Description
A	5 IN 1	Runs tests J through N in succession.
B	RESET	Resets the iPod (equivalent to pressing and holding **Menu** and **Play** for more than 5 seconds).
C	KEY	Gives you several seconds to press all the buttons. If all buttons aren't pressed within the allotted time, you see a "KEY FAIL" message.
D	AUDIO	Presumably tests the audio hardware.
E	REMOTE	If a remote control is not found, displays "RMT FAIL."
F	FIREWIRE (or FW ID)	Displays "FW PASS" if successful. Most likely tests the FireWire bus.
G	SLEEP	Puts the iPod to sleep, requiring a reset to wake it up.
H	A2D (or CHG STUS)	Appears to test the power subsystem, displays a hex value and the text "CHG OK FW 1 BAT 1." Text displayed differs based on firmware version and whether the iPod is charging.
I	OTPO CNT	Tests the scroll wheel.
J	LCM	Tests the display. Press the **Action** button to view each of the four test screens (the first being a blank screen).
K (1.3.1)	RTC	It's not clear what this test checks, although RTC most likely refers to the on-board Real-Time Clock.
K (2.1.0)	CHG STUS	Appears to test the power subsystem, displays a hex value and the text "CHG OK FW 1 BAT 1." Text displayed differs based on firmware version and whether the iPod is charging.
L (1.3.1)	SDRAM	Memory test. Displays "SDRAM PASS" upon success.
L (2.1.0)	USB DISK	Doesn't do anything noticeable, but presumably it tests the USB subsystem on third-generation iPods.
M	FLASH (or CHK SUM)	It's unclear what this test is for, but it's possible it may calculate a checksum of the Flash ROM.
N (1.3.1)	OPTO	This test cannot be activated on first-generation iPods featuring a mechanical scroll wheel. iPods with a touch wheel list the test as "WHEEL A2D." When activated, a screen appears with the text "WHEEL A2D" and a bar, requiring a reset to exit. Presumably tests the optoelectronic circuitry of the touch wheel.
N (2.1.0)	CONTRAST	Allows you to test the contrast control using the touch wheel to adjust the contrast.
O	HDD SCAN	Performs a scan of the hard disk. This test will take several minutes to complete.
P	RUN IN	Runs through a repeating series of tests of various aspects of the iPod's hardware.

Disk Check

The disk check mode scans your iPod's hard drive for problems while displaying a progress bar.

1. To enter disk scan mode, first reset your iPod by pressing and holding the **Menu** and **Play** buttons for 5 to 10 seconds. When the iPod resets and the Apple logo appears, press and hold the **Previous**, **Next**, **Menu**, and **Action** buttons. If done properly, the disk scan will start and you'll see a graphical display with a scrollbar at the bottom (see Figure 11.62).

Figure 11.62 iPod Disk Check Mode

2. The disk check will take several minutes to complete, so be patient. If the disk check completes without problems, your screen will resemble the image in Figure 11.63.

Figure 11.63 iPod Disk Check Mode Complete

Additional iPod Hacks

Given the iPod's popularity, users have developed many iPod-related hacks. The following are a few interesting hacks that we don't have space to explore here in detail but that you should be aware of in case you're looking for additional ways to void your warranty. Further information about each hack can be found at the provided links.

Installing Linux on an iPod

If you're a Linux fan, you've probably heard the phrase, "But can it run Linux?" Most of the time the answer is a resounding, "Yes!" This answer rings true for the iPod as well. A version of uClinux (www.uclinux.org and www.ucdot.org) has been ported to run on the iPod. uClinux is a derivative of Linux intended for constrained embedded systems and devices without Memory Management Units (MMUs). Although the iPod does have an MMU, its features are not sufficient to support the standard Linux kernel.

To install Linux on the iPod, you must overwrite the existing software on the iPod to allow the iPod to boot into Linux. Therefore, you should back up your iPod hard drive before attempting to install Linux. Instructions on how to do this are provided at the *Linux on iPod* site listed at the end of this paragraph. If you're a Linux fan and want to experiment with Linux on the iPod, you can have some fun with this, but you probably will want to continue using the software that came with your iPod to play music—at least until Linux-based iPod software further evolves. You can learn more about installing Linux on the iPod at http://ipodlinux.sourceforge.net.

Repairing the FireWire Port

On first- and second-generation iPods, the act of inserting and removing the FireWire cable on your iPod causes a good amount of stress on the iPod's internal FireWire port (see Figure 11.64). Because there is no strain relief on the port, over time the solder joints connecting the FireWire port to the iPod's motherboard can break. Signs of this problem include a loose or wiggling connector, not being able to charge your iPod, or your computer not recognizing the iPod when you plug it in.

Figure 11.64 An iPod FireWire Port

If you suspect your FireWire port might be damaged and you're comfortable with soldering small devices, you can open your iPod and resolder the connections to the FireWire port yourself. You can also apply some hot glue to the FireWire port to help provide some stress relief so this problem (hopefully) does not reoccur. If you'd prefer not to do this repair yourself, PDASmart (http://pdasmart.com/ipodpartscenter.htm) offers a mail-in service whereby they will fix the FireWire port for significantly less than Apple would charge for the same repair.

Scroll Wheel Fix

First-generation iPods feature a mechanical scroll wheel that spins around a center point, as opposed to later iPod models that use a solid-state touch wheel. The scroll wheel tends to become loose or "sloppy" with time, allowing it to spin more freely. Unfortunately, this can result in frequent and undesirable volume changes when you're using your iPod, especially if you're in motion. However, this problem can be solved with a small amount of effort.

1. This hack involves removing the scroll wheel and center button, preferably by using a piece of masking (or similar) tape to lift up the wheel and button. (Do not use a knife to pry up the wheel!) Under the scroll wheel is a small metal bearing that the wheel snaps onto, which allows it to spin in place (see Figure 11.65).

Figure 11.65 iPod Scroll Wheel Internals

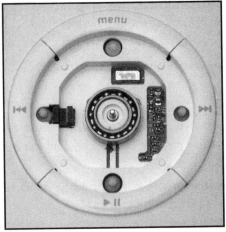

2. Once you have the device open, you can clean away any grease or debris from the bearing and then apply new grease. Be careful of petroleum-based products, however, since they can degrade plastics.

You can find more information on this hack at www.ipoding.com/modules.php?op=modload&name=News&file=article&sid=486.

iPod Resources on the Web

A large number of Web sites have sprung up on which you can learn more about the iPod, buy various iPod accessories and products, and discuss the iPod with other fans. The following is a short list of such sites; a quick search on Google will reveal many more:

- **iPod Home Page: www.apple.com/ipod** This should be your first stop when you're looking for iPod information. From here you can download the latest iPod software and browse through a wealth of information about the iPod and, of course, links to the Apple Store, where you can buy iPods and iPod accessories.

- **iTunes Home Page: www.apple.com/itunes** No iPod is complete without iTunes, Apple's free digital jukebox that is custom-tailored for the iPod. Versions for Macintosh and Windows computers are available. iTunes also provides you access to Apple's iTunes Music Store, allowing you to browse a large library of music that can be purchased and downloaded to your computer online.

- **iPodLounge: www.ipodlounge.com** If you'd like to keep up on the latest iPod news, the iPodLounge is a great place to start. Updated frequently with iPod-related news, iPodLounge also features original editorial content, reviews of iPod products, an informative FAQ, active iPod forums, and much more.

- **iPod Hacks: www.ipodhacks.com** iPod Hacks contains a variety of information about the iPod, including hacks and mods as well as iPod-related software you can download. There's also a forum where you can discuss the iPod with other iPod fans.

- **Everything iPod: www.everythingipod.com** If you're looking for iPod accessories, this site has quite a bit to offer. Product categories include accessories, cables, cases, headphones, speakers, and more.

- **Laptops for Less: www.ipodbattery.com** If you need a replacement battery for your iPod and don't want to pay $99 for Apple's iPod Battery Replacement Program, you can order iPod batteries here.

- **PDASmart: www.pdasmart.com** Another source for replacement iPod batteries, PDASmart also offers a mail-in service that is less expensive than Apple's iPod Battery Replacement Program.

Chapter 12

Can You Hear Me Now? Nokia 6210 Mobile Phone Modifications

Hacks in this Chapter:

- Nokia 6210 LED Modification
- Data Cabling Hacks
- Other Hacks and Resources

Introduction

The mobile phone is one of the most widespread, complex pieces of hardware around these days. On one hand, mobile phones are advanced radios. On the other hand, they are miniature computers. The functionality of the mobile phone is controlled by both the device hardware and its internal firmware/software. Therefore, aside from real hardware hacks, we will also discuss some ways to modify the software through the use of hardware aids.

For the description of the hacks in this chapter, we use the Nokia 6210 GSM mobile phone (see Figure 12.1). This phone, introduced in 2001, was one of the first to support Internet browsing through Wireless Access Protocol (WAP).

Nokia is one of the best-known mobile phone manufacturers in the world. The Finnish company originally started as a paper manufacturing company that moved from rubber products to power and telecommunications to the company that now has between 40 and 50 percent of the mobile phone market. Since about 1984, Nokia has produced portable phones in many different models.

Figure 12.1 The Nokia 6210

The first hack in this chapter is the modification of the backlight color of the mobile phone. Replacing the light-emitting diodes (LEDs) is within the realm of the hobbyist using a small soldering iron and a steady hand.

Next we will look at interfacing to your mobile phone through different types of data cables connected to your PC. The data cables open up a number of possibilities to interact with and modify your phone's software. The type of cable used for Nokia phones depends on several things, such as the model of the phone and what you want to use it for (downloading contacts, using the phone as a modem, or the like). A data cable can also be used to enable a diagnostic mode that gives you insight into the phone's internal workings and its radio protocols. For the Nokia 6210, two cables can be used: the DAU-9P and DLR-3P. Another type of cable is the *flashing cable*, which allows you to reprogram the phone's Flash ROM.

Nokia 6210 LED Modification

The main point of this hack is to change the default color of the LEDs in your mobile phone. Although the model used in this example is the Nokia 6210, you can perform the hack with a wide variety of other mobile phone brands and models.

 ## Preparing for the Hack

To prepare for the hack, we first need to choose and order the LEDs we will use to replace the phone's original LEDs.

Choosing the desired color of LED to use in your phone is based on personal preference. Take care to ensure that the size of the LED will fit in your particular model of phone, because different models need different size LEDs. The LED sizes (and other discrete surface-mount components such as resistors and capacitors) are defined by an industry standard code (see Table 12.1). Table 12.2 shows a listing of required LED sizes for well-known Nokia models.

Table 12.1 LED Type Codes and Their Respective Sizes

Type Indication	Size (L x W)
0402	1.0mm x 0.5mm
0603	1.6mm x 0.8mm
0802	2.1mm x 0.7mm
0805	2.0mm x 1.25mm
1104	3.0mm x 1.0mm
1106	3.0mm x 1.5mm
1206	3.2mm x 1.6mm
1208	3.2mm x 2.0mm

Table 12.2 Required Number and Size of LEDs for Various Nokia Phones

Model	No.	Type
Nokia 3210	10	0603 or 0805
Nokia 33xx	8	1206 or 0805
Nokia 51xx	12	0603 or 0805

Continued

Table 12.2 Required Number and Size of LEDs for Various Nokia Phones

Model	No.	Type
Nokia 5210	11	0603
Nokia 5510	8	1206 or 0805
Nokia 61xx	12	0603 or 0805
Nokia 62xx/63xx	10	1206 or 0805
Nokia 71xx	4	1206
	6	0603 or 0805
Nokia 82xx	12	0603
Nokia 83xx	10	0603
Nokia 8810	12	0603
Nokia 8850/90	14 or 16	0603

Figure 12.2 shows a drawing of a surface-mount LED. On the backside of the components, a symbol, dot, or other marking is used to help distinguish between the anode and cathode of the diode. In the same figure you can see the schematic symbol for an LED.

Figure 12.2 Schematic Symbol and Physical Outline of an LED

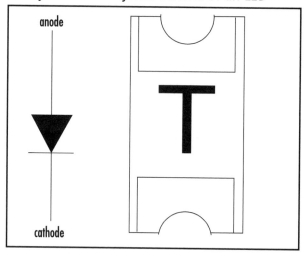

As shown in Table 12.2, the Nokia 6210 requires 10 LEDs of the type 0805 or 1206. In this case, we purchased ultra-bright blue 0805 LEDs (see Figure 12.3) from a local electronics store. This hack is simple in nature but serves as great practice for your soldering skills.

Figure 12.3 A Strip of Blue 0805 LEDs Used in Our Hack

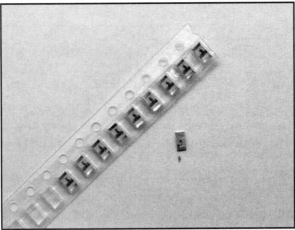

Before opening your phone, be sure to safely back up any data that is stored on the device. Depending on the brand and model, you can use vendor-supplied software and data cable. Other times you can store your contact information by copying it from phone memory onto a SIM card. Do not forget to copy down any settings that may not get copied over with a backup, such as WAP or GPRS connection information, voicemail number, and so forth.

The Nokia phone is held together with four Torx-type screws, so a size T-6 screwdriver is required.

Performing the Hack

The procedure for replacing the LEDs is broken down into a number of steps:

1. Open the phone.
2. Remove the old LEDs.
3. Insert the new LEDs.
4. Increase the LED power.
5. Put the phone back together.

Opening the Nokia 6210

Here are the steps involved in opening the phone:

1. To open the phone, you must remove the battery to give you access to the four Torx screws (see Figure 12.4). Simply remove the battery by releasing the battery latch and sliding the battery away from the phone.

Figure 12.4 The Back of the Nokia 6210 with Battery Removed; the Four Torx Screws Are Visible

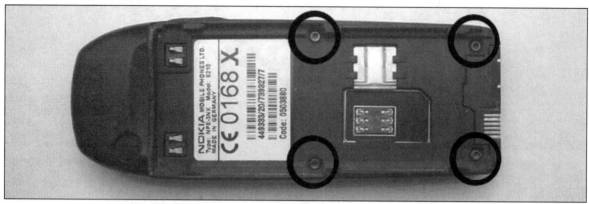

2. After removing the screws, the front and back halves of the phone are still held tightly to each other. This is due to five clips that are part of the plastic housing. By inserting a small screwdriver at the correct positions, you can create enough room to slowly open the phone further (see Figure 12.5 and 12.6).

Figure 12.5 Step 1: Releasing the Plastic Housing Clips from One Side of the Phone

Figure 12.6 Step 2: Releasing the Plastic Housing Clips from the Other Side of the Phone

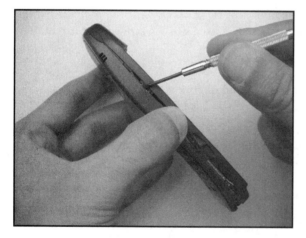

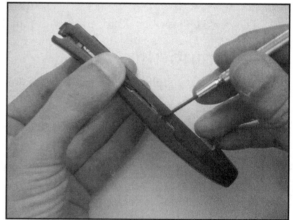

3. Although the phone is almost open, one more step is required. Slowly move the front and back parts of the housing sideways while feeling for the release of the clips at the top (see Figure 12.7). The three top clips are connected to the front case and can take a bit of work to release. Never force this process or you may damage the clips.

Figure 12.7 Releasing the Top Clips

4. With the phone finally open, you will be left with two pieces: a plastic back housing and the front housing containing the PCB (see Figure 12.8). As you can see, most of the phone's circuitry is covered by metal shielding plates. With radio equipment, these shielding plates are important to reduce electrical interference.

Figure 12.8 The Opened Nokia 6210

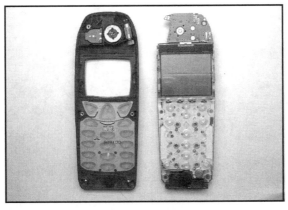

5. The PCB is attached to the front side of the phone with a single Torx screw, which also attaches to the antenna. This part should be removed as shown in Figure 12.9.

Figure 12.9 Removing the Antenna

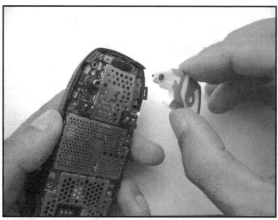

6. You are now left with a PCB and a plastic keypad connected to it. The keypad is connected with four clips to the PCB, as shown in Figure 12.10. You can remove the keypad by first releasing the two plastic clips at the bottom, as shown in Figure 12.11. The two metal top clips then give way easily.

Figure 12.10 The PCB Showing Keypad Clips

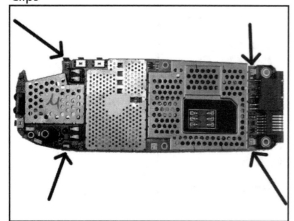

Figure 12.11 Lifting the Clips of the Keypad

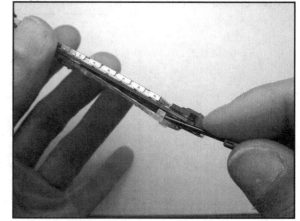

Before proceeding with actually getting at the LEDs, we also need to remove the shielding plates. These are just clamped to the edges, which are soldered to the PCB. The plates have bent sides with small notches that fall into the edges. With a small screwdriver you can simply release one notch at a time until at some point the whole plate just comes off the edges. The LEDs are all under the shielding plate with the SIM contacts, but for easier handling, all plates were removed in this case.

7. Unfortunately, several of the LEDs (six out of 10) are located directly under the edges of one of the metal shielding covers. This shielding must be removed or it will be nearly

impossible to remove the old LEDs and solder in the new ones. Luckily, the shielding can be removed fairly easily. In Figure 12.12, you can see how to remove the edges with two simple cuts at each of the corners. Repeat this process for the bottom edge that covers another two LEDs. Next, slowly move the edge back and forth with a pair of pliers until the solder joint gives way, allowing you to easily pull the edge loose (see Figure 12.13).

Figure 12.12 Removing the Edges of the Metal Shielding

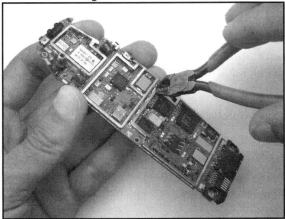

Figure 12.13 Successful Removal of the Metal Shield Edges

9. The metal shield needs to be modified slightly to allow it to be safely reconnected to the phone after the hack. Because the edges of the shield have been clipped off as described, there is a risk that the shield will short-circuit with other components on the PCB. Therefore, simply use the pliers to cut away the small clips around the perimeter of the metal shield (see Figure 12.14). This will ensure that the shield will not come into contact with any components.

Figure 12.14 Removing the Clips from the Perimeter of the Metal Shield

Removing the Old LEDs

Before continuing with the hack, take care to note the orientation of the original LEDs. The new LEDs should be arranged in the exact same configuration or else they will not work. Take a picture of your circuit board or sketch out the LED configuration of your particular phone. Figure 12.15 shows a detailed picture of the LED locations and orientation of the Nokia 6210. Also note that the LEDs are shining to the other side of the PCB through a hole. Figure 12.15 shows the side where the LEDs are attached, but they shine through the other side.

Figure 12.15 Nokia 6210 LEDs; Note the Orientation Marks

1. Now it is time to tackle the desoldering of the LEDs. This requires a soldering iron with a very small tip. Using a small screwdriver or toothpick, gently push on the backside of the PCB while applying heat to the edges of the LED (see Figure 12.16).

WARNING: HARDWARE HARM

Use a small amount of pressure when removing the LEDs. Pushing a little too hard with the soldering iron can rip the whole LED from the board, possibly causing irreparable damage to the PCB. Also, be sure not to bend the circuit board, since doing so can cause cracks in the traces and will render your phone useless.

Figure 12.16 Desoldering the Existing LEDs by Gently Pushing from Behind While Soldering

Inserting the New LEDs

When you have successfully removed all the old LEDs, the next step is to prepare for inserting the new ones.

1. Make sure you remove the excess solder from the pads from which the LEDs were just removed. Next, use some alcohol or flux remover to clean away any residue.

2. When you are satisfied that the board is properly cleaned, it is time to fit in the new LEDs. It is important to realize that the LEDs are actually shining through the PCB to the other side from where they are attached. To see if they fit properly into the circuit board, place one of them over the hole (where the light shines through) with a pair of tweezers. In the case of our hack, it appeared that despite the right size of the LED solder pads, the middle part of the LED was too big for the holes. To solve this problem, we used a file to widen the holes drilled into the circuit board (see Figure 12.17).

Figure 12.17 Widening the Holes of the PCB to Allow the LEDs to Fit

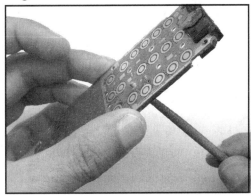

3.   Once the PCB has been modified to fit the new LEDs, it is time to solder them into place. To do this, first retrieve your notes on the orientation of the original LEDs. Position the PCB horizontally so the LEDs will stay put as you are soldering them in. When soldering the LEDs, apply just enough heat to provide a good solder joint. Too much heat may damage the LED. As shown in Figure 12.18, a pair of tweezers can help hold the LED in place while you solder it.

Figure 12.18 Soldering the New LEDs into Place

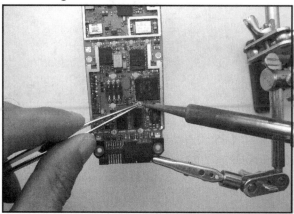

Increasing the LED Power

Depending on the type of phone and the type of LED used, the intensity of the replacement LED may be too bright or too dim. This is due to the forward voltage, current, and efficiency of the LED. To control the current going to the LEDs, current-limiting resistors are added in series. (You can find more information on electronic theory in Chapter 2, "Electrical Engineering Basics.") In the case of the Nokia 6210, the schematic of how the LEDs are connected is shown in Figure 12.22. In the schematic, two groups of LEDs can be distinguished. On the left is a group of six LEDs for the keypad; on the right is a group of four LEDs for the display.

To increase the voltage drop over the LEDs, we need to change the total resistor value (combined value of two parallel resistors) at the top of the schematic to a value of 2.2 ohms for the keypad LEDs and 3.3 ohms for the display LEDs. However, because of the low values of these resistors, the room in tolerances in general and the fact that it is much more convenient, we decided to use jumpers directly to the 3.6 volts instead. To achieve this, we only need to short one resistor for both the display and keypad LEDs. When we examine the PCB for the phone, we can find the resistors on the side in the same area as the LEDs. The exact location of the resistors is shown in Figure 12.19. We can do this by soldering a little piece of wire over the two ends of the resistor. Due to the size, often a single drop of solder or a single strand of a wire will do the job as well. Be careful not to heat the resistor too much or else it might come off the board completely.

Figure 12.19 Location of the LED Current-Limiting Resistors

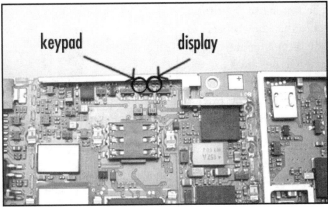

Putting the Phone Back Together

When all the LEDs have been soldered into place, you should power on the device to make sure all the new LEDs illuminate before putting the phone back together. To do so, simply place the battery onto the metal battery contacts on the main PCB. Be careful to align the battery and the PCB in the proper position. With the battery in place, press the tiny power button located at the top of the circuit board. A successful hack will resemble the image of 10 bright shining LEDs shown in Figure 12.20.

Figure 12.20 A Successful Hack: New LEDs Shining Through the Circuit Board

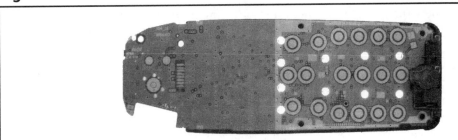

The process of putting the phone back together is the exact opposite of opening the phone (described at the beginning of this chapter):

1. Put all the shielding plates back in place. Make sure the clips of the shielding plate do not short-circuit with any components on the PCB. Next, attach the keypad back onto the PCB. Be sure that the contacts at the top of the keypad make good contact with the copper areas on the PCB. Replace the keypad cover and fit the PCB back into the front side of the phone's plastic housing.

2. On the opposite side, connect the antenna back to the PCB and secure with the Torx screw. Finally, connect the bottom side of the phone's plastic housing and push together. Make sure you hear an audible click as the clasps connect between the top and bottom pieces of the housing. Screw in the four Torx screws and replace the battery.

Figure 12.21 A Successful Hack: The Finished Phone with New Lighting

If everything went well, when you turn the phone on, you should have a new backlight color for your display, as shown in Figure 12.21!

Under the Hood: How the Hack Works

A schematic diagram of how the LEDs are connected into the phone is shown in Figure 12.22. The LEDs are designated as D1 through D10, the current-limiting resistors are R1 through R4, and the transistors are Q1 and Q2. The transistors are used as switches to allow current to flow into the diodes, thus illuminating the lights. The hack is very simple, due to the fact that all we are doing is replacing the LEDs on the circuit board.

The current flow into the LEDs needs to be adjusted accordingly to meet your desired brightness. This is done by changing the value of the current-limiting resistors, which can be calculated using Ohm's Law. For the Nokia 6210, the VCC supply voltage is 3.6V. Each group of LEDs is in parallel (one group of six and the other group of four), so the current flowing through the limiting resistors will be evenly distributed through the LEDs. So, assuming a typical forward current of 7mA through each LED (which will usually produce a not-too-bright illumination) and a forward voltage of 3.5V for a blue LED (a red LED typically has a forward voltage of 2V and a green LED has a forward voltage of 2.2V—different-colored LEDs have different voltage drops, so it is not often that you can just replace one color LED with another and assume you will have the same brightness and not damage the part), the resistance is calculated as follows:

$$R = V / I$$

where:

- R = resistance (ohm)
- V = voltage (V)
- I = current (A)

Group 1: R = Effective resistance of R1 and R2 = $(V_{CC} - V_F) / I_F = (3.6 - 3.5) / (0.007 \times 6) = 2.38$ ohms

The closest standard resistor value is 2.2 ohms, 5% tolerance.

Group 2: R = Effective resistance of R3 and R4 = $(V_{CC} - V_F) / I_F = (3.6 - 3.5) / (0.007 \times 4) = 3.57$ ohms

The closest standard resistor value is 3.3 ohms, 5% tolerance.

As you can see from these calculations, the resulting resistor values are very small. For this reason and because manufacturing tolerances generally allow for some additional load, we decided to replace the resistors with jumpers (see Figure 12.22). This will result in slightly brighter LEDs.

Figure 12.22 The Schematic for the Lighting in a Nokia Phone, Including the Jumpers

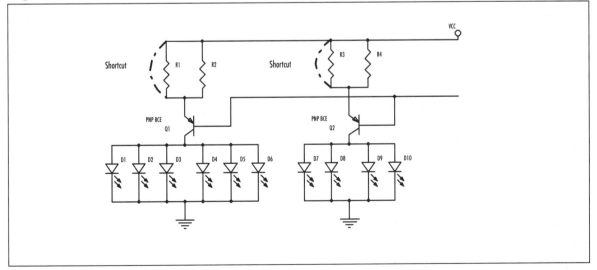

Data Cabling Hacks

As was mentioned at the start of this chapter, most hacks on mobile phones involve software hacks instead of hardware hacks. The very specific hardware combined with the surface-mount technologies makes it difficult to perform many hardware-based hacks. This section aims to give some insight in the hacks involved on the software level. Again we use the Nokia phone as an example, but many other brands of phone present similar possibilities.

Data cables are used to interface a PC with special features of the cell phone. The cables are either standard cables produced by the manufacturer (for data synchronization, backups, loading new ring tones, and so on) or a homebrew cable made by a hardware hacker. The data cables open up a number of possibilities to interact with and modify the software of your phone. A data cable can also be used to enable a diagnostic mode that gives you insight into the phone's internal workings and its radio protocols. As mentioned earlier, another type of cable is the flashing cable, which allows you to reprogram the phone's Flash ROM.

Before we take a closer look at cables, we need to clarify something about the phone models by Nokia. Over time Nokia has produced a wide range of phones, each with a variety of features and options. However, many of the phones also have features in common, such as the way the underlying software operates.

The Nokia 6210 belongs to the DCT-3 generation of Nokia phone. Newer models of Nokia phones manufactured in and after 2002 belong to the DCT-4 generation. Table 12.3 shows many of the Nokia DCT-3 generation phones. The cable information that we discuss in this chapter is relevant for the DCT-3 series. DCT-4 has some improvements in the security mechanisms surrounding software access and hacking and will not be discussed here, though much information is available on the Web.

Table 12.3 Listing of the Most Common Nokia DCT-3 Models

Model	Nokia Type
2100	NAM-2
3210	NSE-8
3310	NHM-5
3315	NHM-5
3330	NHM-6
3350	NHM-9
3410	NHM-2
3610	NAM-1
3810	NHE-9
5110	NSE-1
5110i	NSE-2
5210	NSM-5
5510	NPM-5

Continued

Table 12.3 Listing of the Most Common Nokia DCT-3 Models

Model	Nokia Type
6090	NME-3
6110	NSE-3
6110i	NSE-3i
6150	NSM-1
6210	NPE-3
6250	NHM-3
7110	NSE-5
8210	NSM-3
8250	NSM-2
8810	NSE-6
8850	NSM-2
8855	NSM-4
9000	RAE-1N
9000i	RAE-4
9110	RAE-2
9110i	RAE-2i

Data Cables

Data cables are logically divided into two parts:

- The physical cable
- The protocol transmitted over the cable

Nokia phones use and understand two separate protocols:

- MBUS
- FBUS

MBUS is an older and slower protocol. It uses a single pin to transmit and receive serial data and one pin for ground. It is a half–duplex protocol at 9600bps. The FBUS protocol is newer and faster and uses two pins to transmit full–duplex serial data at 115.2kbps and one pin for ground. The protocol format between MBUS and FBUS varies. FBUS has been reverse-engineered by several groups and people over time. The most well known open-source implementations of these protocols are Gnokii (www.gnokii.org) and Gammu (www.mwiacek.com/gsm/gammu/gammu.html).

The physical cable that is used to connect the phone to the serial port of the PC contains active parts that usually serve level-conversion purposes but sometimes contain more complex logic. For the

Nokia 6210, two types of cable are available: One is the DAU-9P cable that provides both MBUS and FBUS protocol interfacing, and the other is the DLR-3P cable that provides an AT command interface just like a normal Hayes modem. This way you can use the 6210 to act as a modem without using any additional drivers. However, to achieve this goal, the DLR-3P cable contains more advanced logic, including a microprocessor. The unofficial Nokia Data Cable Web site, www.atrox.at/datacable/index.html, is run by Adrian Dabrowski and contains intimate details of the various cables and protocols.

To look a bit deeper at how the cables work, we first have to examine the connector on the bottom of the cellular phone (see Figure 12.23), where the data cable connects. Table 12.4 lists the pinouts of the connector (provided by www.nobbi.com/steck-nok.htm). This connector provides nine multipurpose pins for MBUS and FBUS communication, accessory connections, and power/charging.

Figure 12.23 The Pinout for the Connector on the Nokia 6210

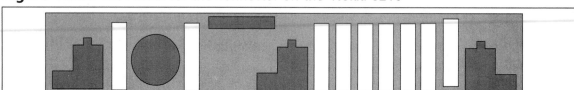

Table 12.4 Nokia 6210 Conductor Functions

Pin	Name	Function	In/Out
1	CHARGE	Charging voltage	In
2	CCONTROL	Charging control	Out
3	MIC / XMIC	Analog audio in	In
		Accessory mute	Out
		Headset detect	In
4	AGND	Analog ground	
		Power source for DLR-3P-cable	Out
5	EAR / XEAR	Analog audio out	Out
		Accessory detect	In
6	MBUS	Bidirectional serial bus	In/out
7	FBUS RX	Serial data in	In
8	FBUS TX	Serial data out	Out
9	SGND	Signal ground/charging ground	

When we look at the cables, the simpler of the two is the DAU-9P cable (schematic shown in Figure 12.24). The cable is essentially just used for level conversion between the RS232 signals from the PC and the signals for the Nokia phone. The Maxim MAX3232 device is a standard RS232 "level shifter" to bring the RS232 levels to voltages that the Nokia can handle. The circuitry in the cable is also powered through the RS232 port, passing voltages from the port into a 78L02 voltage regulator to create a 2.6V VCC.

Figure 12.24 Schematic for a DAU-9P Cable by Adrian Dabrowski, www.atrox.at/datacable

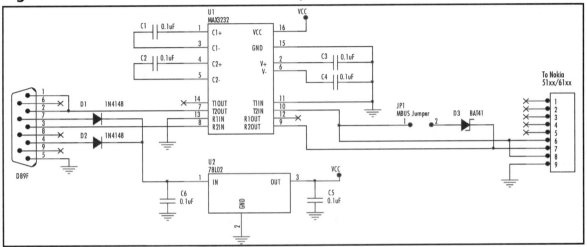

The main difference between the DLR-3P and DAU-9P cables is that the DLR-3P actively performs part of the FBUS protocol handshake within the cable (schematic shown in Figure 12.25). By pulling pin 3 of the phone to a logic LOW level, it signals the phone to apply power to pin 4. This power is then used to power the circuitry in the cable. Next, the phone begins communicating using the MBUS protocol, and the Microchip PIC16F84 processor receives the commands and responds with an acknowledgment. When the phone receives the acknowledgments from the PIC, it switches to a mode in which it accepts normal Hayes-style AT commands from a PC on the FBUS lines.

Figure 12.25 Schematic for a DLR-3P Cable by Adrian Dabrowski, www.atrox.at/datacable

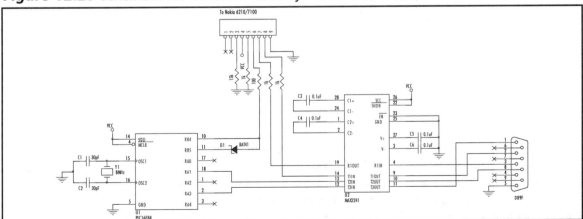

Flashing Cables

Flashing cables are used for reprogramming the Flash ROM device inside the phone. The cables are primarily used by the manufacturer or service personnel to update the phone's software/firmware. The flash cable can also provide you with calibration data and other debugging information. Although Nokia does not endorse using a flash cable on your phone, knowledge about how this process works is now public.

The flash cables we discuss in this chapter are meant for the DCT-3 generation of phones. The DCT-4 generation incorporates new encryption methods and code signing to make modifications to the Flash ROM more challenging; they aren't discussed here.

The flash cable uses the same connector interface as shown in Figure 12.23. However, the pins are used in a different way compared to the "regular" DAU-9P and DLR-3P cables. The protocol used to communicate between the phone and the PC is similar to the I2C serial protocol. Because timing is critical with this protocol, the serial port cannot be used. Instead, these cables are controlled from the PC's parallel port, which is more suitable for timing-sensitive applications. The schematic for a DCT-3 flash cable is shown in Figure 12.26. Software can be found on Dejan Kaljevic's Web site at http://users.net.yu/~dejan.

Figure 12.26 Schematic for a DCT-3 Flash Cable by Dejan Kaljevic, http://users.net.yu/~dejan

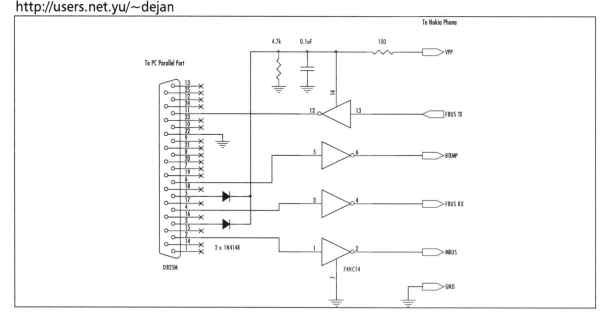

On power up, the Nokia phone performs a check of the MBUS line. When MBUS is pulled to a logic LOW level instead of following the normal path to your phone, the phone enters a bootstrap mode in which it accepts code transmitted from the PC. The flashing code sent to the phone is essentially a miniature operating system that can report the status of the phone, read contents of the Flash memory, and erase or write Flash memory blocks.

Net Monitor

One of the interesting features built into Nokia DCT-3 phones is the Net Monitor mode. This is a diagnostic facility that allows you to test and monitor several aspects of the phone. The Net Monitor functionality has been removed from DCT-4 version phones.

The Net Monitor menu allows you to examine the internal functionality of your phone and the GSM network is it connected to. You can even modify the way it operates on the GSM network.

To enable the Net Monitor, a data cable and special software are used. Several tools have been created for this purpose, and most can be found on the Internet by searching for terms like "N-Monitor" and "Net Monitor Activator." One of the best-known tools is Logo Manager (a demo version is available at www.logomanager.co.uk).

The software sends a special FBUS security command to the phone, which enables a new menu item on the phone. Once you do this, when cycling through the menus on your phone, you should come across a display like the one shown in Figure 12.27. From this menu we can now start to explore the different options.

Figure 12.27 The Net Monitor Menu

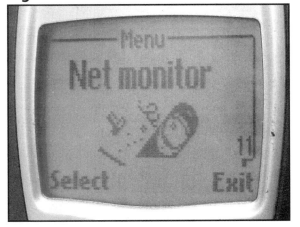

Figure 12.28 Entering the Desired Test Number

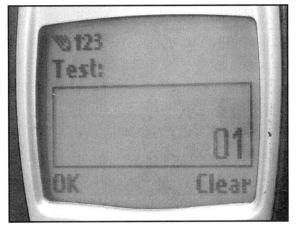

The options in the Net Monitor are called Tests and are each identified by a number. When we press **Select** in the menu, we are presented a screen in which to enter a test number (see Figure 12.28).

Enter test number **01** and press **OK**. We are now presented with a screen showing blocks of letters and numbers (see Figure 12.29).

WARNING: HARDWARE HARM

Do not enter arbitrary test numbers in the test entry menu unless you know exactly what the test is for. Some functionality within the tests may alter the behavior of your phone, preventing it from working properly. Two of the most extensive resources of Net Monitor tests can be found at www.mwiacek.com/gsm/netmon/faq_net0.htm and www.nobbi.com/download/nmmanual.pdf.

Figure 12.29 Test 01: Showing the Phone's GSM Parameters

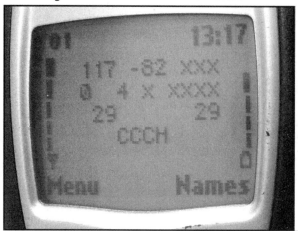

At the top left of the display, the test number is shown. The other numbers on the display give information related to the current link with the GSM network. This link is established with a base station, and the display informs us that it is currently on the Common Control Channel, or CCCH. Other information is identified as follows (from http://home.tiscali.cz:8080/ca517880/netmon_0.8.doc):

```
+++++++++++++         #############
+abbb ccc ddd+        #CH RxL TxPwr #
+ e ff g mmmm+        #TS TA RQ RLT #
+ nnn     ppp+        # C1      C2  #
+    oooo     +       #    CHT      #
+++++++++++++         #############
```

```
a     H, if carrier numbers are scrolled when hopping is on. Otherwise ' '.
bbb   When mobile is on TCH:
              DCH carrier number in decimal.
      When mobile is NOT on TCH:
              CH means carrier number in decimal.
              If hopping is on, used channels are scrolled
              when display is updated.
ccc   rx level in dBm, minus sign not shown if <=-100
ddd   tx power level. If transmitter is on, symbol *
       is shown in front of the power level value.
e     Time Slot, range is 0 - 7
```

```
ff      Timing advance, range is 0 - 63
g       rx quality (sub), range is 0 - 7
mmmm    Radio Link Timeout value. If value is negative, 0 is shown.
        Maximum value is 64. When mobile is NOT on TCH then xx is shown.
nnn     value of the path loss criterium (C1). Range is -99 - 999.
oooo    type of current channel:
        THR0 : TCH HR subchannel 0
        THR1 : TCH HR subchannel 1
        TFR  : TCH FR
        TEFR : TCH EFR
        F144 : TCH FR data channel, speed 14.4 kbps
        F96  : TCH FR data channel, speed 9.6 kbps
        F72  : TCH FR data channel, speed 7.2 kbps
        F48  : TCH FR data channel, speed 4.8 kbps
        F24  : TCH FR data channel, speed 2.4 kbps
        H480 : TCH HR data channel, speed 4.8 kbps, subch 0
        H481 : TCH HR data channel, speed 4.8 kbps, subch 1
        H240 : TCH HR data channel, speed 2.4 kbps, subch 0
        H241 : TCH HR data channel, speed 2.4 kbps, subch 1
        FA   : TCH FR signalling only (FACCH) channel
        FAH0 : TCH HR signalling only (FACCH) channel, subch 0
        FAH1 : TCH HR signalling only (FACCH) channel, subch 1
        SDCC : SDCCH
        AGCH : AGCH
        CCCH : CCCH
        CBCH : CCCH and cell broadcast receiving on
        BCCH : BCCH
        SEAR : SEARCH
        NSPS : MS is in No Serv Power Save state
ppp     value of the cell reselection criterium (C2).
        Range is -99 - 999. If phone is phase 1 then C1 value is shown.
```

To show that this is actual information being displayed, Figure 12.30 shows the same test but actually engaged to another mobile phone. The transmitter power level is now shown, timing information is given, and a different type of channel is shown.

Figure 12.30 Test 01: Information Displayed When the Phone Is Engaged in a Call

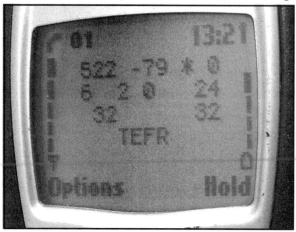

One of the cool tricks with the Net Monitor is that you can also modify the phone's behavior through the tests. For example, it is possible to have the phone only use so-called "barred base stations." These are base stations that the operator (the cell phone carrier) does not want the phone to use. This could be for all kinds of reasons such as maintenance or testing. The base station is flagged by a barring flag that the mobile phone can check and normally honors. By using test **19** on the phone, we can change the phone's behavior to reverse the effect of the flag and only use barred base stations (CELL BARR REVERSE) or to ignore the flag and use both normal and barred base stations (CELL BARR DISCARD). When we enter test **19** in the entry menu twice in a row, we see the display in Figure 12.31.

Figure 12.31 Test 19: Ignoring Barred Base Stations

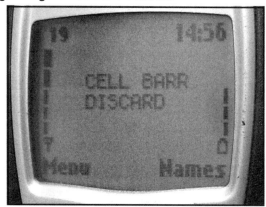

To inspect if any barred base stations are nearby, we can use tests **03**, **04**, and **05**, which list information on other base stations within the phone's vicinity. A mobile phone continuously monitors for more cells than the one it is currently connected to in order to switch to a new cell when reception falls below a certain level. In Figure 12.32, you can see neighboring cells, of which one is a barred cell identified by a *B* instead of *N*, for normal base stations.

Figure 12.32 Test 03: Base Stations Within the Phone's Vicinity

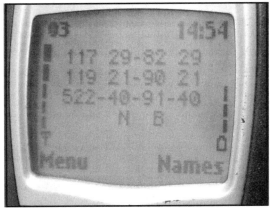

There are many other interesting test modes within the Net Monitor:

- **Test 11** Display network parameters.

- **Test 20** Display the phone's charging state.

- **Test 23** Display battery information.

- **Test 88** Display current MCU and DSP software/firmware versions.

- **Test 241** Disable the Net Monitor menu. (You will need the special enabling software to turn it on again.)

- **Test 242** Only allow tests 01 through 19.

Other Hacks and Resources

This chapter only showed a small portion of the possible hacks and experiments you can perform with your mobile phone. Visit the resources below for more ideas and hacks:

- **NUUKIAWORLD, www.panuworld.net/nuukiaworld/index.htm** One of the best Nokia-related hardware-hacking sites.

- **Embedtronics, www.embedtronics.com/nokia/fbus.html** Another hardware-hacking site with details of the FBUS and SMS protocols.

- **JBPhonetech, www.burrillj.fsnet.co.uk** LED backlight changing supply and fitting service. Also provides details of do-it-yourself LED modifications.

- **Nobbi's GSM Site, www.nobbi.com/monitor/index_en.htm** Provides detailed information and software to enable Net Monitor mode.

- **Project Blacksphere, www.blacksphere.tk** Information database and community of diehard mobile phone hardware hackers and reverse engineers; lots of software tools and detailed information.

- **MADos, http://gsmfreeboard.eu.org, www.nokiaport.de/RE, http://nokiafree.org/forums** A completely new operating system created for the Nokia phone. Information can be found in the listed forums.

Chapter 13

Upgrading Memory on Palm Devices

Hacks in this Chapter:

- Hacking the Pilot 1000 and Pilot 5000
- Hacking the PalmPilot Professional and PalmPilot Personal
- Hacking the Palm m505
- Technical Information
- Palm Links on the Web

Introduction

Whether you are walking down a busy city street or eating at restaurant in a small town, it is impossible to look around without seeing someone using a personal digital assistant, or PDA. But it wasn't always like this. At one time, a PDA user would get stares and hear chuckles from nosey outsiders wondering what this thing was, this high-tech gadget like something out of *Star Trek,* that they were using.

Palm OS-based PDAs are arguably the catalyst for the entire PDA and mobile device consumer market. Though other devices, such as the Apple Newton and the Tandy Zoomer, existed before the Palm, many handheld PDAs failed quickly due to a number of factors, including high prices, bulky design, and an unreceptive market. However; nothing came close to the reaction generated by the release of the Palm device.

Palm Computing, Inc., was formed in 1992 to produce software for existing PDA manufacturers. The company began development on its own handheld electronic organizer in 1994. In March 1996, when the Pilot 1000 and Pilot 5000 devices were released, Palm was in the right place at the right time. The devices were designed with user simplicity in mind, featuring a date book, address book, to-do list, and memo pad. This simplicity was a staple of the Palm "economy" that led to a small and efficient PDA, a tight-knit community of third-party application developers, and unit sales soaring quickly into the millions. Figures 13.1 and 13.2 show product shots of the original Pilot PDA hardware.

As the first PDA to make waves in the mainstream market, the Palm became the favorite device for gadget freaks worldwide and an instant target for hardware hacking. Since the first releases in 1996, many different flavors of Palm device have been created. The product line continues to expand today, though millions of the earlier Palms are still in use and serve as great entry-level devices.

Through a number of changes over the years, Palm, Inc. (with a recent name change to PalmOne), develops and controls the hardware solutions. PalmSource, Inc., develops and controls the operating system. The Palm OS is now licensed to a number of major vendors in the mobile device and cellular phone markets, including Handspring, Sony, IBM, Kyocera, Samsung, Qualcomm, Franklin Covey, TRG, Symbol, Fossil, and Garmin.

For a detailed look into the history of Palm from a business perspective, we suggest picking up a copy of *Piloting Palm: The Inside Story of Palm, Handspring, and the Birth of the Billion-Dollar Handheld Industry,* written by Andrea Butter and David Pogue.

Figure 13.1 The Original Pilot/PalmPilot with Clear Engineering Case, Front

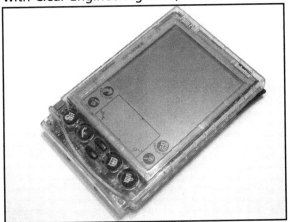

Figure 13.2 The Original Pilot/PalmPilot, Back

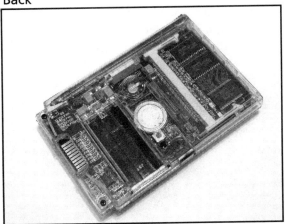

Model Variations

This chapter details the hacking of three different Palm devices to increase the available RAM on each: the Pilot 1000, the PalmPilot Professional, and the Palm m505. The Pilot 5000 and PalmPilot Personal versions can also be hacked with only a few additional steps. User applications and data are stored in RAM, so the more memory available, the more information that can be stored on the device. Table 13.1 lists the device hacks detailed in this chapter, showing memory amounts that are available to the user before and after the upgrades.

Table 13.1 Device Hacks in This Chapter, Showing Available Memory Before and After

Device	Memory Before Upgrade	Memory After Upgrade
Pilot 1000	128kB	1MB
Pilot 5000	512kB	1MB
PalmPilot Personal	512kB	2MB
PalmPilot Professional	1MB	2MB
Palm m505	8MB	16MB

The hardware designs for the earliest Palm models—the Pilot 1000 (OS 1.0, 128kB RAM), Pilot 5000 (OS 1.0, 512kB RAM), PalmPilot Personal (OS 2.0, 512kB RAM), and PalmPilot Professional (OS 2.0, 1MB RAM)—are all the same. The only difference among them is the configuration of the removable memory module located on the back of the device. This memory card allows easy user upgrades from a Pilot 1000/5000 to the newer PalmPilot Personal or Professional with a simple swap of a card. From a hardware hacker's point of view, this removable memory card is a dream come true. The process of modifying the card to increase the available RAM size is simple and straightforward because the Palm engineers left unpopulated memory chip footprints available on the board.

The memory cards used in the Pilot 1000 and Pilot 5000 devices were the same, though the Pilot 5000 had a 512kB RAM chip on board instead of a 128kB RAM chip.

The memory cards used in the PalmPilot Personal and PalmPilot Professional devices were the same, though a different design than the earlier Pilot version. The PalmPilot Professional contained an additional 512kB RAM chip than the PalmPilot Personal (for a total of 1MB).

The Palm m505, released in March 2001, has a drastically different design than the older models described here. It no longer has an external, removable memory card, and no components are accessible to the user without opening the entire case. However, the class of hack is still the same: adding more RAM to the device and giving the user more memory space to work with.

Many other memory upgrade hacks exist for other Palm devices, all based on the same class of hack as the one we discuss here. Furthermore, other companies are providing upgrade services for around $100 (such as from www.palmpilotupgrade.com or www.pdatechcenter.nl/home_english.html), but a do-it-yourself modification is much more fulfilling. See the "Palm Links on the Web" section at the end of this chapter for more information.

Hacking the Pilot 1000 and Pilot 5000

The goal of this hack is to upgrade the available RAM of the Pilot 1000 from 128kB to 1MB. With a few additional steps, the Pilot 5000 device can be upgraded from 512kB to 1MB.

Preparing for the Hack

To prepare for hacking your Pilot, be sure to:

1. HotSync the device to your desktop to back up all data.

2. Remove the two AAA batteries from the back of the device, accessible by sliding open the battery cover. When the batteries are removed, all applications and data stored in RAM will be erased. Once the batteries are replaced at the end of the hack, the system will be completely reinitialized.

No special tools are required for this hack—just a soldering iron and a flat-tip jeweler's screwdriver. The following is a list of the necessary components for the hack. Figure 13.3 shows a picture of those components.

- Two U1, U2 Toshiba TC518512AFT-80V 512K x 8 Low-Power, Low-Voltage Static RAM (32-pin TSOP package)

- One U5 Toshiba TC7S08FTE85L Single two-input AND gate (SOT23-5 package)

- One 1/2" piece of jumper wire (22-26AWG)

NOTE

Toshiba has discontinued the TC518512AFT device. If you cannot obtain this exact component, the Toshiba TC554001AFT-70V or Samsung KM68V4000BLT or KM68V4000BLTI with a -7L, -8L, or -10L suffix can be used as a drop-in replacement, both of which have lower power consumption (leading to a longer battery life for the Palm device). Other second-source parts may exist that could also be used. The required components may be difficult to obtain in small quantities. The parts are common on many of the early Pilot and PalmPilot memory boards, so you could purchase a pre-owned board (on eBay, for example) specifically to use the components on it.

Figure 13.3 Required Parts for the Pilot 1000/5000 Hack

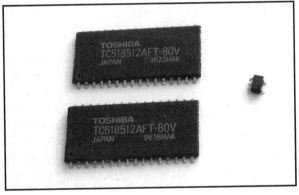

Removing the Memory Card

The Pilot 1000, Pilot 5000, PalmPilot Personal, and PalmPilot Professional all use a removable memory card located on the back of the device.

1. To access the memory card, you must remove the plastic cover from the case by sliding it away from the device (see Figures 13.4 and 13.5).

Figure 13.4 Removing the Plastic Cover: Grasping the Device

Figure 13.5 Removing the Plastic Cover: Sliding the Cover Off

2. The memory card is held into place by two tabs on the left and right side of the memory card connector. Once the cover has been removed, the memory card can be extracted by pushing the tabs toward the edge of the device and gently lifting the card up and out (see Figures 13.6 and 13.7). You should be able to remove the card using little force.

Figure 13.6 Removing the External Memory Card: Pushing the Tabs

Figure 13.7 Removing the External Memory Card: Lifting the Card

The removed memory card should resemble the images shown in Figures 13.8 and 13.9.

Figure 13.8 Pilot 1000 128kB Memory Card Front (160-0086 REV B)

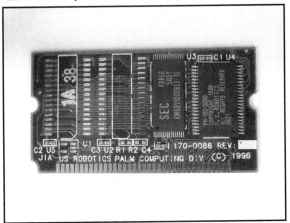

Figure 13.9 Pilot 1000 128kB Memory Card Back (160-0086 REV B)

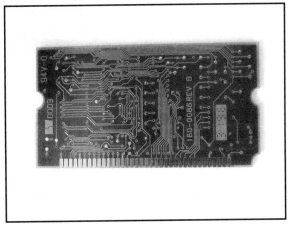

NOTE

Two versions of the Pilot 1000/5000 PCB layout exist. The part number and revision can be found printed on the back of the PCB. The version used in this chapter is 160-0086 REV B. An earlier version, 160-0086 REV P1, requires an additional cut and jumper to complete the hack, as discussed later in the chapter. Both memory cards have "170-0086" silk-screened on the front.

Adding New Memory

1. Before adding new memory to the card, we need to first remove U3, which is the Samsung KM68V1000BLT-7L 128kB Static RAM component. We won't need this part anymore.

WARNING: HARDWARE HARM

Be careful when removing the part not to scratch or damage any of the surrounding components or pull up any PCB traces. The easiest ways to remove a surface-mount part are with an SMD rework station, a flat-blade solder tip (as shown in Figure 13.10), or the ChipQuik SMD Removal Kit (www.chipquik.com), which reduces the overall melting temperature of the solder on the SMD pads and enables you to lift the part right off the board. (See Chapter 2, "Electrical Engineering Basics," for a step-by-step example.)

Figure 13.10 Removing U3 from the Memory Card

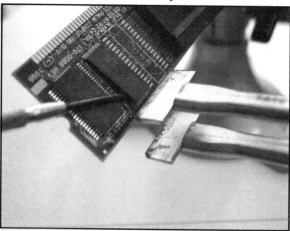

2. After removing U3 (see Figure 13.11), inspect the footprint area to make sure there are no stray solder pieces or solder bridges between pins. If there are, simply move the soldering iron between the pads to free the connections.

Figure 13.11 Memory Card With U3 Removed

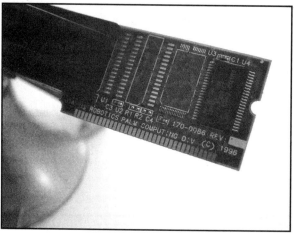

3. Next, solder the two Toshiba TC518512AFT-80V (or suitable replacement) Static RAM devices to the unpopulated footprints U1 and U2 on the front of the PCB (see Figure 13.12). Be sure to properly align pin 1 of the device (denoted by a small dot next to the pin on the top of the package) with the angled silk-screen mark on the PCB.

Figure 13.12 Memory Card With New SRAM Devices Soldered into Place

4. Next, solder the Toshiba TC7S08FTE85L AND gate to the unpopulated footprint U5 on the front of the PCB. This device can fit properly on the pads in only one orientation.

5. Add a jumper wire to the R1 location on the front of the PCB (the two pads are above and between the "R1" and "R2" silkscreen markings).

If you have the 160-0086 REV B memory card, the modification is complete. Your newly hacked board should resemble Figure 13.13.

Figure 13.13 Hacked Pilot 1000 Memory Card With 1MB RAM

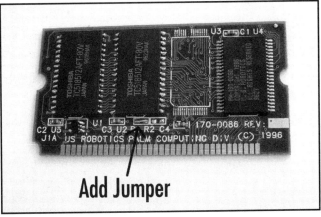

To restore your data previously stored in RAM, simply HotSync the device to your computer.

If you have a 160-0086 REV P1 memory card, two additional steps are necessary:

1. First, you need to cut the thick trace between U5 pin 1 and the via (the hole immediately to the left of U5).

2. Next, solder a jumper wire from U5 pin 1 to U2 pin 22. Both steps are denoted in Figure 13.14.

Figure 13.14 Modifying the 160-0086 REV P1 Memory Card: Two Additional Steps

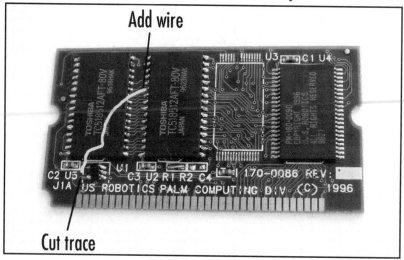

The Pilot 5000 512kB memory card uses the same PCB and a similar parts placement as the Pilot 1000 128kB card shown in this chapter. It will also be denoted with either "160-0086 REV B" or "160-0086 REV P1" on the back and "170-0086" silk-screened on the front. If you have a Pilot 5000 512kB memory card that you want to upgrade to 1MB, only two additional steps are required:

1. Solder the Toshiba TC518512AFT-80V (or suitable replacement) Static RAM device to the unpopulated footprint U1.

2. Move the resistor from R2 to R1 (the set of two pads directly to the left).

Under the Hood: How the Hack Works

Figure 13.15 shows the original Pilot 1000 with 128kB RAM before the hack. Figure 13.16 shows the after-hack Pilot 1000 with 1MB RAM.

Figure 13.15 Before Hack: Pilot 1000 With 128kB RAM

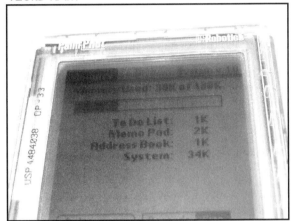

Figure 13.16 After Hack: Pilot 1000 With 1MB RAM

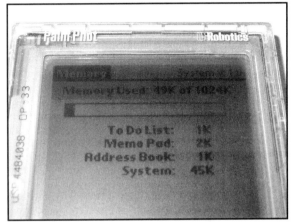

The support for additional memory already exists on the removable memory card, as shown by the unpopulated footprints on the PCB. Figure 13.17 shows a schematic of the Pilot 1000/5000 memory card.

NOTE

Unused connections from the Pilot are not shown.

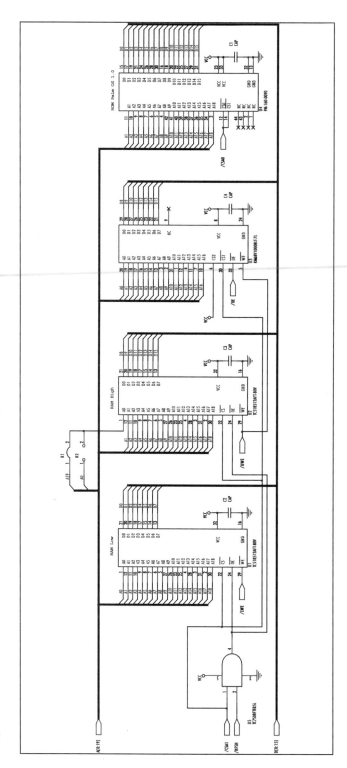

Figure 13.17 Schematic of Pilot 1000/5000 Memory Card (160-0086 REV B)

Both Toshiba TC518512AFT-80V 512kB SRAM devices (U1 and U2) are selected with the chip select A1 (/CSA1) line from the Pilot. The lower write enable (/LWE) and upper write enable (/UWE) lines are used to select which 512kB SRAM will be written to at that point in time, either the low segment (U1) or the high segment (U2), respectively.

The Toshiba TC7S08FTE85L AND gate (U5) is used to combine the refresh (/RFSH) and /CSA1 lines from the Pilot into a single output enable (/OE) line for the SRAM. The /OE line, which is active low, is pulled low by the DragonBall processor when it wants to read data from the SRAM.

The /RFSH line is a holdover from the Dynamic RAM (DRAM) support by the DragonBall processor. All the required DRAM lines are brought out to the external memory card of the early Palm devices. DRAM requires a refresh to ensure that the contents stored in memory remain valid. On each refresh, which happens hundreds of times a second (dependent on the specifications of the DRAM), the contents of each memory cell are read. Due to the way in which the memory cells are constructed within the DRAM, the reading action "refreshes" the contents of memory. We have not encountered any Palm memory card that uses DRAM, though the support is there.

The two 0 ohm resistor pads, R1 and R2, are used to select the high or low address bit for the 512kB SRAM (U2). The other 512kB SRAM (U1), which is installed only in the 1MB configuration, is the low segment, and address line A0 is always connected. For example, if only U2 were in place (the original card, for a total of 512kB), the R2 pads would be shorted, which would connect A0 from the Pilot to A0 of the RAM. When both 512kB RAMs are installed on the card (the hacked card, for a total of 1MB), the R1 pads would be shorted instead, which would connect A19 from the Pilot to A0 of the RAM. This makes U2 the high segment of RAM while U1 remains the low segment. R1 and R2 should never be shorted at the same time.

The common components on all memory cards are the 512kB ROM (marked PM-160-0090 for OS 1.0) containing the Palm operating system and the bypass/decoupling capacitors (denoted as C1-C4), which help reduce electrical noise on the power supply line.

Hacking the PalmPilot Professional and PalmPilot Personal

The goal of this hack is to upgrade the available RAM of the PalmPilot Professional from 1MB to 2MB. With a few additional steps, the PalmPilot Personal can be upgraded from 512kB to 2MB.

Preparing for the Hack

The preparation and required parts for this hack are the same as for the previous Pilot 1000/5000 memory upgrade hack.

Removing the Memory Card

The Pilot 1000, Pilot 5000, PalmPilot Personal, and PalmPilot Professional all use a removable memory card located on the back of the device. The first step of this hack is described in detail in the "Removing the Memory Card" section of the Pilot 1000/5000 hack.

Once the memory card is removed, it should resemble the images shown in Figures 13.18 and 13.19.

Figure 13.18 PalmPilot Professional 1MB Memory Card Front (160-0222 REV A)

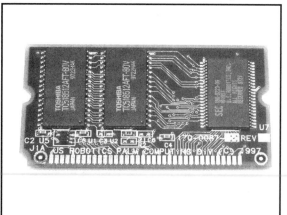

Figure 13.19 PalmPilot Professional 1MB Memory Card Back (160-0222 REV A)

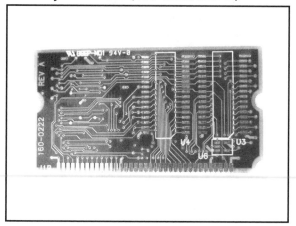

Need to Know...

Two versions of the PalmPilot Personal/Professional PCB layout exist. The part number and revision can be found printed on the back of the PCB. The version used in this chapter is 160-0222 REV A. An earlier version, 160-0184 REV B, requires an additional cut to complete the hack, as discussed later in the chapter. The REV A board has "170-0087" silk-screened on the front, while the REV B board has "170-00."

Adding New Memory

For this hack, you need to solder components to the three unpopulated footprints on the back of the memory card.

1. First, solder the two Toshiba TC518512AFT-80V (or suitable replacement) Static RAM devices to the unpopulated footprints U3 and U4 on the back of the PCB (denoted by U502 and U504 for the 160-0184 REV B memory card), as shown in Figure 13.20. Be sure to properly align pin 1 of the device (denoted by a small dot next to the pin on the top of the package) with the angled silk-screen mark on the PCB.

Figure 13.20 Memory Card With New SRAM Devices Soldered into Place, Back

2. Next, solder the Toshiba TC7S08FTE85L AND gate to the unpopulated footprint U6 on the back of the PCB (denoted by U3 for the 160-0184 REV B memory card). This device can fit properly on the pads in only one orientation.

If you have the 160-0086 REV B memory card, the modification is complete. Your newly hacked board should resemble Figure 13.21.

Figure 13.21 Hacked PalmPilot Professional Memory Card With 2MB RAM, Back

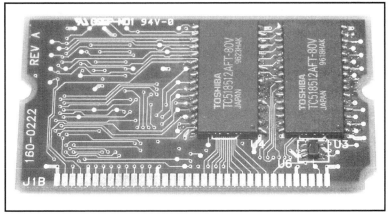

If you have a 160-0184 REV B memory card, add a wire jumper to the R4 location on the front of the PCB. The pads of R1, R2, R3, and R4 are located in a block on the upper-right corner of the board. The pads for R4 are the two lower-right pads of the block.

To restore your data previously stored in RAM, simply HotSync the device to your computer.

The PalmPilot Personal 512kB memory card uses the same PCB and a similar parts placement as the PalmPilot Professional 1MB card shown in this chapter. It is also denoted with "160-0222 REV A" on the back and "170-0087" silk-screened on the front. If you have a PalmPilot Personal 512kB memory card that you want to upgrade to a PalmPilot Professional 1MB card, only three additional steps are required (denoted in Figure 13.22):

1. Solder the Toshiba TC518512AFT-80V (or suitable replacement) Static RAM device to the unpopulated footprint U1.

2. Move the resistor from R2 to R1 (the two pads directly above).

3. To expand the 1MB board to 2MB, follow the upgrade details in this chapter.

Figure 13.22 Modifying the PalmPilot Personal 512kB to a PalmPilot Professional 1MB: Two Additional Steps

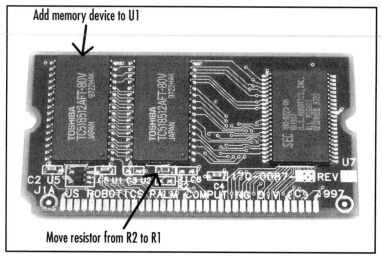

Under the Hood: How the Hack Works

Figure 13.23 shows the original PalmPilot Professional with 1MB RAM before the hack. Figure 13.24 shows the after-hack PalmPilot Professional with 2MB RAM.

Figure 13.23 Before Hack: PalmPilot

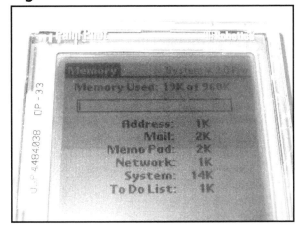

Figure 13.24 After Hack: PalmPilot

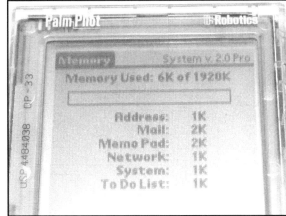

NOTE

Not all the RAM on the memory card is actually available to the user. For example, the original PalmPilot Professional 1MB card only shows an available memory of 960K and the hacked 2MB card only shows an available memory of 1920K. The Palm OS uses a portion of the available RAM for system purposes.

The support for additional memory already exists on the removable memory card, as shown by the unpopulated footprints on the PCB. Figure 13.25 shows a schematic of the PalmPilot Personal/Professional memory card.

NOTE

Unused connections from the PalmPilot are not shown.

Figure 13.25 Schematic of PalmPilot Personal/Professional Memory Card 160-0222 REV A

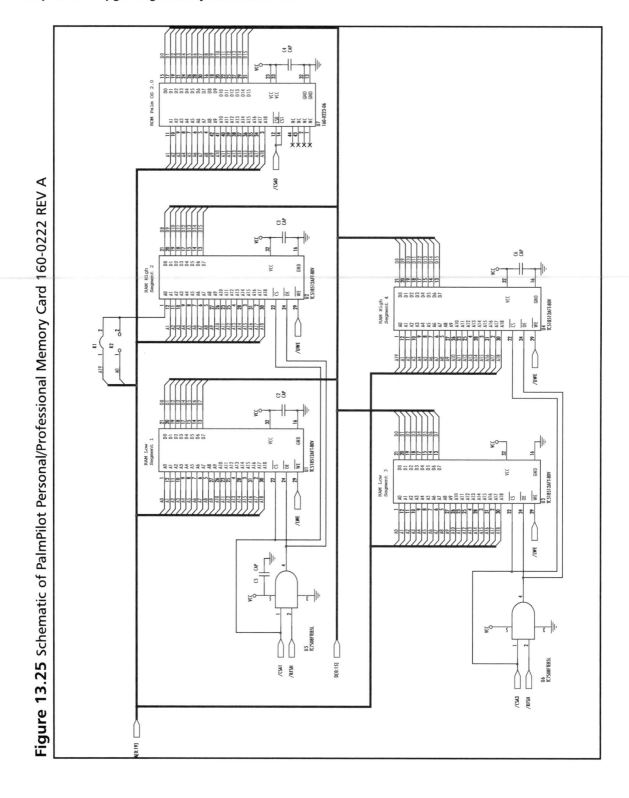

After the hack is completed, there will be four Toshiba TC518512AFT-80V 512kB SRAM devices on board, comprising a total of 2MB. The total available RAM is separated into two 1MB segments, each containing two 512kB devices. The first 1MB segment, containing the two original SRAM parts U1 and U2, is selected with the /CSA1 chip select from the PalmPilot. The lower write enable (/LWE) and upper write enable (/UWE) lines are used to select which 512kB SRAM device will be written to at that point in time, either the low segment (U1) or the high segment (U2), respectively.

The second 1MB segment, containing the newly added SRAM parts U3 and U4, is selected with the /CSA3 chip select from the PalmPilot. The lower write enable (/LWE) and upper write enable (/UWE) lines are used to select which 512kB SRAM device will be written to at that point in time, either the low segment (U3) or the high segment (U4), respectively.

The two Toshiba TC7S08FTE85L AND gates (the original U5 and the added U6) are used to combine the refresh (/RFSH) and chip select lines (/CSA1 for the first 1MB segment, and /CSA3 for the second 1MB segment) from the PalmPilot into output enable (/OE) lines for the SRAM devices. The /OE line, which is active low, is pulled low by the DragonBall processor when it wants to read data from the SRAM.

The /RFSH line is a holdover from the DRAM support by the DragonBall processor. All the required DRAM lines are brought out to the external memory card of the early Palm devices. DRAM requires a refresh to ensure that the contents stored in memory remain valid. On each refresh, which happens hundreds of times a second (dependent on the specifications of the DRAM), the contents of each memory cell are read. Due to the way in which the memory cells are constructed within the DRAM, the reading action "refreshes" the contents of memory. We have not encountered any Palm memory card that actually uses DRAM, even though the support is there.

After adding three more components to the back of the memory card, the extra 1MB RAM segment is automatically handled by the Palm operating system.

The common components on all memory cards are the 512kB ROM (marked "160-0223-06" for OS 2.0) containing the Palm operating system and the bypass/decoupling capacitors (denoted as C2–C6), which help reduce electrical noise on the power supply line.

Hacking the Palm m505

The goal of this hack is to upgrade the available RAM of the Palm m505 from 8MB to 16MB. Figures 13.26 and 13.27 show product shots of the Palm m505 hardware.

Figure 13.26 The Palm m505, Front

Figure 13.27 The Palm m505, Back

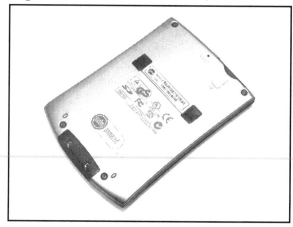

 Preparing for the Hack

To prepare for hacking your Palm m505, be sure to:

1. HotSync the device to your desktop to back up all data. When you open up the device and disconnect the system power, all applications and data stored in RAM will be erased. Once the power is replaced at the end of the hack, the system will be completely reinitialized (with the exception of data stored in Flash ROM).

2. If your device has a screen protector flap, remove it by simply sliding it out of its holder. This will make it easier to remove the back cover of the Palm while it is lying on its face.

3. Remove any external SecureDigital memory cards.

The only component needed for this hack is the following:

■ 1 Samsung KM416S8030BT-GL (or –FL, –F8, –G8) 16MB Low-Voltage Synchronous Dynamic RAM (54-pin TSOP II package)

A Torx driver (size T5 or T6) is required to remove the screws from the back of the device, and a soldering iron is needed to remove the old memory component and add the new one. Figure 13.28 shows a picture of those components.

NOTE

Samsung has discontinued the KM416S8030 part number scheme. If you cannot obtain this exact component, any Toshiba TC59SM716AFT, Hynix Semiconductor HY57V281620, or Vanguard International VG36128161BT family (low-power versions only) can be used as drop-in replacements. Other second-source parts could also be used. The 8Mbit x 16 SDRAM configuration that is needed is common on many PC100 DIMM memory cards used in laptops. A 128MB card containing eight 16MB chips would be ideal for this hack, leaving you with a few extra pieces in case of a mistake. You could purchase a pre-owned board (on eBay or from a computer parts store, for example) for $10 to $25 specifically to use the components on it.

Figure 13.28 Required Components for the Palm m505 Hack

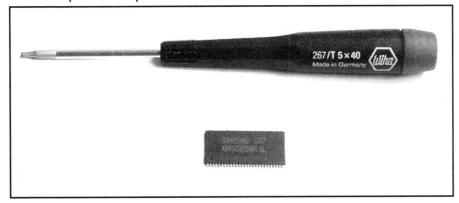

Opening the Palm

The Palm m505 casing is held together by four Torx screws. Usually, size T6 is used if the device was manufactured in the United States, and size T5 is used if the device was manufactured in Hungary. However, this does not always hold true; the model used in this chapter was manufactured in the United States and is held together with a T5 size.

1. Using the suitably sized Torx driver, simply unscrew the four screws. Two screws are located in the upper-left and -right corners of the back of the unit, and two screws are located on the bottom-left and -right of the unit on both sides of the HotSync connector (see Figure 13.29).

Figure 13.29 Unscrewing the Palm m505

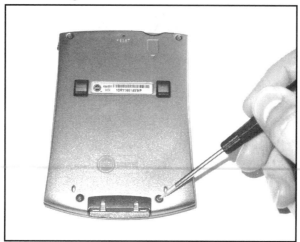

2. After the four Torx screws are removed, carefully pry the metal backing from the back of the device. This can be done by running your fingernail or a flat-head screwdriver around the edge where the backing connects to the Palm (see Figure 13.30). The metal backing is held on with a few tabs situated around the inside of the device that need to be released. Once the tabs are released, the metal backing can be easily removed.

Figure 13.30 Removing the Metal Backing

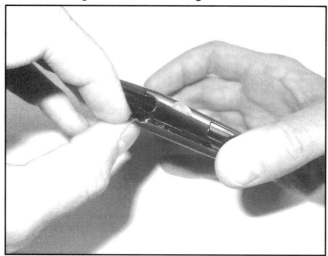

With the metal backing removed from the Palm m505, we now have complete access to the internal circuitry. Your unit should resemble the image in Figure 13.31.

Figure 13.31 Opened Palm m505 Showing Back Side of Circuitry

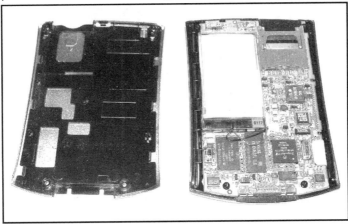

Removing the Main Circuit Board

1. We now need to gain access to the main circuit board so we can remove the old RAM device and solder on the new one. First, take away both sides of the Palm housing from the circuitry. The circuit board is simply press-fit into the case, so it should come out fairly easily if you turn the entire unit upside down. If that doesn't work, lightly press on the LCD display on the front of the Palm. The circuitry should just pop out the other side.

WARNING: HARDWARE HARM

Be sure to take extreme care when handling the exposed Palm circuit board. Take proper antistatic precautions, and be gentle with all connectors.

2. With the circuit board removed from the housing, first disconnect the internal rechargeable battery by disconnecting the small two-conductor plug (see Figure 13.32).

Figure 13.32 Disconnecting the Internal Battery

3. Next, the LCD panel needs to be removed in order to give us unobstructed access to the Palm circuit board. Removing the display is a two-step process, as shown in Figures 13.33 and 13.34. First, with the back of the device facing you, use your right hand to reach underneath the circuitry and flip the LCD panel up and to the right. Your unit should resemble the image in Figure 13.33.

Figure 13.33 Removing the Display: The LCD Panel Flipped Up and Right

4. Next, remove the flex connector that connects the display to the rest of the Palm circuitry (see Figure 13.34). Be very careful to not bend or tear the flex cable and connector, because the assembly is very fragile.

Figure 13.34 Removing the Display: Remove the Flex Connector

Removing the Memory

Now that we have unobstructed access to the Palm circuit board, we can remove the original Samsung K4S641632D Synchronous DRAM memory device from the Palm circuit board (denoted with an arrow in Figure 13.35). This component provides 8MB of RAM in a 4-bank × 1MB × 16-bit configuration. We will be replacing this chip with the Samsung KM416S8030BT-GL device, which provides 16MB of RAM in a 4-bank × 2MB × 16-bit configuration.

Figure 13.35 Palm m505 Circuit Board Showing 8MB RAM Device to Remove

WARNING: HARDWARE HARM

When removing the RAM device, be careful to not scratch or damage any of the surrounding components or pull up any PCB traces. Using the ChipQuik SMD rework kit makes it easy to remove the fine-pitch memory device.

After following the instructions on the package (which consist of simply applying a standard no-clean flux to the SMD pins and then applying a low-melting-point solder), you can easily remove the surface-mount part from the board. Use rubbing alcohol to remove any residue from the solder pads. Verify that the solder pads are clean and free from cuts or solder jumps before proceeding to the next step. Your circuit board should resemble the image in Figure 13.36.

Figure 13.36 Palm m505 Circuit Board with Old RAM Removed

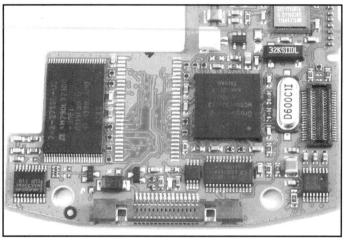

Adding New Memory

With the old 8MB RAM device removed, it is time to add the new 16MB RAM in its place. Simply solder the Samsung KM416S8030BT-GL (or suitable replacement) SDRAM to the now empty footprint. Be sure to properly align pin 1 of the device (denoted by a small dot next to the pin on the top of the package) with the black triangle mark on the PCB. When the new memory is successfully soldered into place, your circuit board should resemble the image in Figure 13.37.

Figure 13.37 Palm m505 Circuit Board with New 16MB Device Soldered into Place

To complete the hack, a final step is required. A 0-ohm, four-resistor array (also called a *jumper* or *resistor network*) located on the front of the circuit board needs to be moved. Moving the jumper will redirect the high-order address and bank-switch lines going to the SDRAM device from the DragonBall microprocessor. This configures the Palm m505 to use 16MB of RAM instead of the factory-default 8MB. Figure 13.38 shows the resistor network (denoted with an arrow) that needs to be desoldered and moved to its new location.

Figure 13.38 Palm m505 Circuit Board Showing Jumper to Move

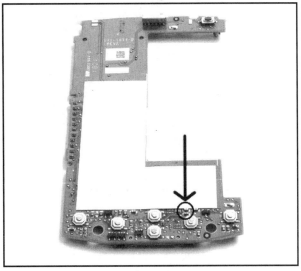

This step is extremely tricky because the jumper is very small and you need to have a steady hand to unsolder it from the original location and resolder it to the new location (the set of pads to the

immediate left of the original). Figure 13.39 shows the original location of the memory configuration jumper. Figure 13.40 shows the jumper moved into its new location. If you lose or damage the original resistor array, a replacement part can be installed in its place (Panasonic EXB-38VR000V, Digi-Key Part #Y9000CT-ND).

Figure 13.39 Memory Configuration Jumper, Original Location for 8MB

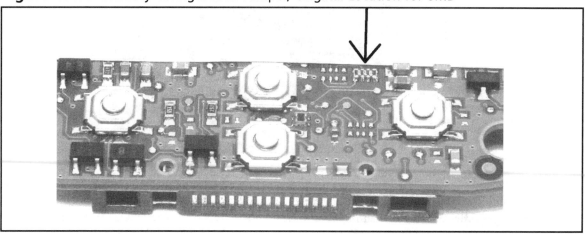

Figure 13.40 Memory Configuration Jumper, New Location for 16MB

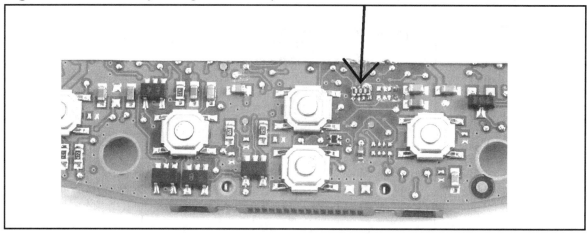

On the new footprint, the rightmost pad is unused and unconnected, so if you accidentally create a solder bridge on the right side of the device (which is easy to do, as you can see in Figure 13.40), the memory hack will still function as intended.

When you are changing the location of the jumper, it may help to peel back a bit of the white protective sticker on the circuit board to give you more room to maneuver the soldering iron. This protective sticker exists to prevent the traces from the main circuit board from coming into contact with the metal backing of the LCD module. If you peel the sticker back, be sure to replace it when you are done with the relocation process.

Now that the jumper has been moved, the memory upgrade modification is complete. After replacing the circuit board into the Palm housing, reconnect the LCD and battery and reassemble the case. The device should simply power up in its factory reset condition and show 16MB of available RAM. If the unit does not immediately power up, press a paper clip into the small Reset hole on the back of the device to reset the Palm.

To restore your data previously stored in RAM, simply HotSync the device to your computer.

Under the Hood: How the Hack Works

Figure 13.41 shows the original Palm m505 with 8MB RAM before the hack. Figure 13.42 shows the after-hack Palm m505 with 16MB RAM.

Figure 13.41 Before Hack: Palm m505 With 8MB RAM

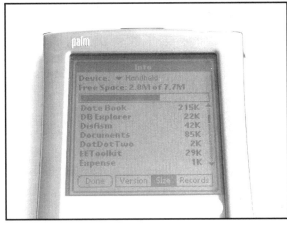

Figure 13.42 After Hack: Palm m505 With 16MB RAM

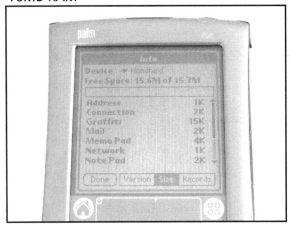

The support for additional memory already exists in the Palm m505, as shown by the simple memory replacement and the additional footprint location for the jumper.

The original Samsung K4S641632D Synchronous DRAM memory device installed in the Palm m505 provides 8MB of RAM in a 4-bank × 1MB × 16-bit configuration. The 16MB device, Samsung KM416S8030BT-GL or equivalent, provides 16MB of RAM in a 4-bank × 2MB × 16-bit configuration. The pinouts for both devices are exactly the same, and the only difference is the size of each of the four banks (which are increased from 1MB to 2MB each). Rumor has it that the device could also be upgraded to a 32MB RAM capacity using a 4-bank × 4MB ×16-bit configuration device, though the Palm OS will not support the entire memory size without software modification to the OS.

The critical part of the hack is moving the 0-ohm, four-resistor array. If the jumper was not moved, the Palm would still only recognize 8MB of RAM, even if the 16MB device was installed. Moving the jumper will redirect the high-order address and bank-switch lines going to the SDRAM device from the DragonBall 68VZ328 microprocessor. This configures the Palm m505 to use 16MB of RAM instead of the factory-default 8MB.

There are two groups of eight jumper pads on the Palm M505 circuit board. They are all located between the cursor keys and the To Do key on the front of the circuit board. The connections to the pads are denoted in Figure 13.43, showing the original 8MB configuration on the right and 16MB configuration on the left. Only six of the eight pads are actually used. The remaining pads (the far right pair of each group) are unused and unconnected. With the 0-ohm resistor array in place, the four sets of top and bottom pads will be connected.

Figure 13.43 Jumper Pad Connections: Right, Original 8MB Configuration; Left, 16MB Configuration

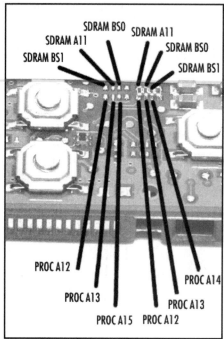

With the resistor array in its original 8MB configuration, the lines between the processor and SDRAM are connected as follows:

- Processor address line A12 to SDRAM address line A11

- Processor address line A13 to SDRAM bank select line BS0

- Processor address line A14 to SDRAM bank select line BS1

With the resistor array moved to the 16MB configuration, the lines between the processor and SDRAM are connected as follows:

- Processor address line A12 to SDRAM bank select line BS1

- Processor address line A13 to SDRAM address line A11

- Processor address line A15 to SDRAM bank select line BS0

By rearranging the lines between the SDRAM and the processor, the additional address line A15 is used as a high-order bank-select switch. Since the size of each bank in the SDRAM is now 2MB instead of 1MB, A14 is not used for memory configuration purposes.

Technical Information

This portion of the chapter discusses some additional technical details of the Palm OS and Palm PDA hardware.

Hardware

Hardware devices running the Palm OS currently use either the Motorola DragonBall MC68328 microprocessor family (based on the Motorola MC68EC000 core) or the Texas Instruments OMAP processor family (based on the ARM core). The original DragonBall processor, released in 1995, has been joined by two subsequent updates, the DragonBall EZ and the DragonBall VZ. Each release has become more streamlined for use in PDAs and other portable devices. Table 13.2 shows a selection of Palm OS devices and their core processors.

Table 13.2 A Selection of Palm OS Devices and Their Core Processors

Device	Processor Type
U.S. Robotics PalmPilot Personal/Professional	DragonBall (16MHz)
3Com Palm III	DragonBall EZ (16MHz)
IBM WorkPad c3 (Palm V)	DragonBall EZ (16MHz)
Kyocera QCP 6035 smartphone	DragonBall EZ (16MHz)
Palm Computing m105	DragonBall EZ (16MHz)
Palm Computing m500/m505	DragonBall VZ (33MHz)
Handspring Treo 300	DragonBall VZ (33MHz)
Palm Zire 71	OMAP310 (144MHz)
Palm Tungsten T2	OMAP1510 (144MHz)

Early and low-end Palm devices are powered by two standard alkaline AAA batteries, which are removable and replaceable. High-end and newer models contain a nonremovable, internal lithium-ion (Li-Ion) battery (rechargeable through the HotSync cradle or external charging device). Alkaline batteries typically last longer than their rechargeable counterparts and add a level of convenience in emergency situations, since they are available in almost any retail store. The disadvantage to using non-rechargeable batteries is that they must be properly discarded after use.

Palm devices use battery-backed RAM to store application and user data. The operating system and other nontransient components are often stored in Flash-based ROM devices. The memory for each Palm OS device resides on a module known as a *card*. Each card is a logical definition and does not necessarily correspond to a physical card (although it does on the original Pilot and PalmPilot hardware). The Palm OS is designed to be modular in that multiple cards (each containing RAM, ROM, or both) can be functional in a given device. This allows for future expansion in which a Palm device might contain an internal card (e.g., RAM and ROM for the operating system) and an external card (e.g., user application and data storage). For example, many Palm devices contain an expansion slot for SecureDigital/MultiMediaCard (SD/MMC) memory cards. The Sony CLIÉ family of Palm devices supports the Sony Memory Stick.

File System

Memory requirements are typically less for the Palm OS than for other embedded operating systems such as Windows CE/Pocket PC. The RAM in a Palm device is used for volatile storage and is logically divided into dynamic memory and storage memory.

Dynamic memory, analogous to RAM installed in a typical desktop system, is used as working space for the program stack and short-term data (e.g., pen strokes, key presses, system events, video memory, global variables, and user interface structures). The size of the dynamic memory region depends on the OS version and on the total memory on the Palm device and changes constantly during device use.

The remainder of RAM is used as *storage memory*, analogous to a disk drive. RAM sizes of current Palm devices range from 1MB to 32MB. Though the size might seem small, a standard Palm OS application ranges in size from 2kB to 100kB.

Memory Map

The base starting addresses for the RAM and ROM areas of Palm devices vary depending on the processor type, as does the memory range allocated to each memory card. The DragonBall family of processor supports up to 4GB of address space. Figure 13.44 shows the memory maps and relevant regions for typical Palm OS devices using DragonBall, DragonBall EZ, or DragonBall VZ processors.

Figure 13.44 Base Addresses of Relevant Memory Regions by Processor Type

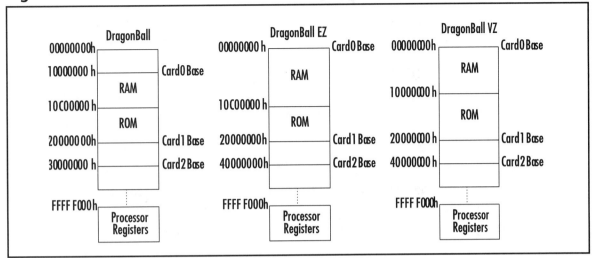

The Palm uses chip select /CSA0 to access the ROM. Early versions of Palm devices had 256kB or 512kB of ROM. Current versions contain up to 8MB of Flash ROM and typically have over 2MB of unused space available for user (non-system) storage. The contents of Flash ROM are nonvolatile and remain intact even with loss of battery power to the device. HandEra's JackFlash tool (www.han-dera.com/Products/JackFlash.aspx) takes advantage of the unused memory areas of Flash memory to back up user applications and databases.

Chip selects /CSA1 and /CSA3 are used to access the RAM. For earlier Palm devices with 1MB of RAM, only /CSA1 is used. For devices with larger RAM areas, such as the Palm III (which has 2MB of RAM), /CSA3 is used to access the second segment of RAM.

Database Structure

The Palm File Format Specification provides a detailed view into the file formats supported by Palm OS. In general, all data conforms to one of the three defined file types:

- **Palm Database (PDB)** Record database used to store application or user data.

- **Palm Resource (PRC)** Resource database (similar structure to a Palm database). Applications running on Palm OS (also referred to as *programs*, *executables*, or *binaries*) are simply resource databases containing code and user interface resource elements.

- **Palm Query Application (PQA)** Palm database containing Web content for use with Palm OS wireless devices.

Databases are similar to files on a disk drive; the difference is that they are stored in a sequence of memory chunks called *records* or *resources* instead of in one contiguous area. The database file in device memory contains header information and a sequential list of pointers to records or resources. The records within a database are similarly structured with record header information and record data.

Palm Links on the Web

The Web has a great number of resources for fans of Palm devices. This section provides just a small sampling of the hundreds (if not thousands) of Palm-related Web sites to whet your appetite.

Technical Information

If you are interested in learning more about the intricate details of the Palm OS and its underlying hardware, the following sites serve as good starting points:

- **Palm Developer Resources** www.palmone.com/us/developers
- **PalmOS.com Developer Documentation** www.palmos.com/dev/support/docs
- **Motorola MC68328 DragonBall Integrated Processor User's Manual** http://e-www.motorola.com
- **ARM Processor Documentation** www.arm.com/documentation

Palm Hacks

This chapter hits only the tip of the iceberg when it comes to hacking your Palm. Hardware hacking and Palm devices go hand in hand, as can be seen by the variety of hacks available for the devices:

- **Palm de COOL! www.fureai.or.jp/%7Emori-t/e_whatsnew.html** Eclectic collection of Japanese Palm hacks, mostly visual effects.
- **Stephanie's Handspring Visor Modification Page www.felesmagus.com/visor**
- **Peter Strobel's Pilot Pages: www.pspilot.de** Technical information and do-it-yourself modifications.
- **Pilot Hardware Main Page www.massena.com/darrin/pilot/luiz/hardware.htm** Technical information and do-it-yourself modifications.

More Memory Upgrades

- **Palm III (2MB to 4MB)** www.harbaum.org/till/palm/memory/index.html
- **Palm III (2MB to 8MB)** www.interlog.com/~tcharron/Palm8M/III8M.html
- **Palm IIIe (2MB to 4MB/8MB)** www.interlog.com/~tcharron/Palm8M/IIIex.html
- **Palm IIIx (4MB to 8MB)** www.interlog.com/~tcharron/Palm8M/IIIex.html
- **Palm V (2MB to 8MB)** www.interlog.com/~tcharron/Palm8M/V8/V8.html
- **Palm m100 (2MB to 8MB)** www-2.cs.cmu.edu/~tew/m100hack

Memory

Memory, or *random access memory* (*RAM*), is a special part of your computer that is designed to hold temporary information. It's very fast, but it's also volatile—it goes away when you turn off the computer or when battery power is removed. Whatever a program is doing at any given moment needs to be tracked in memory. Managing memory is one of the OS's most important jobs.

Sometimes it seems like we shouldn't have to worry about memory anymore. I remember how proud I was when I upgraded the first computer I ever personally owned to 640KB of memory, and right now I'm typing on a computer with 512MB of memory. That's 1,000 times as much memory as my first computer, but my current computer is certainly not 1,000 times faster or more efficient or useful than that first one. (Heck, with my constant Internet connection, this computer probably makes me much *less* efficient.) But the more memory we have accessible to us, the more developers are going to write programs that use a lot of memory. No matter how much space you have, your programs may end up using it all. So it's very important for the operating system to manage memory as quickly and as efficiently as it possibly can.

Physical Memory

Physical memory is a type of hardware that the computer can retrieve information from very quickly. Information stored at any address on the hardware can be directly accessed with an address that refers to a specific location on the hardware. Because this direct access allows information to be retrieved from any random point in memory, this sort of memory is known as *random access memory*.

As Figure 14.1 illustrates, a program can request the information that is stored in physical memory at any location. Here the program requests the data stored in physical memory at the location addressed *0K*. The information in that memory location—in this illustration, the letter *A*—is returned to the program.

Figure 14.1 Memory Management: Direct Access to Physical Memory

Physical Memory

Address block starts at 0K   A

1K

2K

3K

4K

5K

6K

7K

8K

Program requests
information in memory
block that begins at
0K.

NEED TO KNOW... ALPHABET SOUP

The basic unit of measurement computers use is a *bit*. A bit represents a 0 or a 1, and you can think of it as a kind of on or off switch. When the switch is on and electricity is running, that's a 1. When the switch is off and the electricity stops flowing, that's a 0. In a nutshell, all a computer does is manage these pulses of electrical energy, these ones and zeros.

We don't usually talk in bits. The smallest reasonable size that we deal with on a computer is a *byte*. A byte is 8 bits, and as you can see, that is still pretty small. It takes about a byte to store a single character such as, say, this one: A. Or this one: B. Writing "hack" requires four bytes, or 32 bits.

- *K*, *kB*, and *KB* are abbreviations for *kilobyte*, which means approximately 1,000 bytes (but, to be exact, is 1,024 bytes).
- *M* and *MB* are abbreviations for *megabyte*, which means approximately 1,000,000 bytes or 1,000KB (but, to be exact, is 1,048,576 bytes).
- *G* and *GB* are abbreviations for *gigabyte*, which means approximately 1,000,000,000 bytes, 1,000,000KB, or 1000MB (but to be exact, is 1,073,741,824 bytes).

You can find more details about this terminology in Chapter 2, "Electrical Engineering Basics."

The OS manages memory in the appropriately named *memory manager*. The memory manager keeps track of what memory is being used, allocates unused memory to processes that request it, and takes care of which memory is stored in your memory chips and which is temporarily stashed on your hard drive.

Wait, why are we storing memory on the hard drive? After we went to all the trouble to explain the difference between memory and disk, now we're confusing it again. See, even though memory gets cheaper all the time, disks get cheaper all the time, too. And a disk is much, much cheaper than memory. So you're always going to have more disk space than you have memory. Why not take advantage of the cheaper resource? Moreover, some computers have hardware limitations on the amount of memory that can possibly be available to a single program, but you as the developer might want your program to use more memory than that limit allows. This is where virtual memory comes in.

Virtual Memory

Virtual memory maps logical memory addresses to physical memory addresses. The hard disk can be used as if it were cheap—and slow—memory. The memory manager takes care of remembering which information lives on the physical memory and which information is stored on the hard disk. A program doesn't have to worry about where the memory is stored, because that information is hidden from it. The memory manager creates simpler artificial memory addresses, presents them to the program, and takes care of the translation itself.

Figure 14.2 illustrates this translation. The program requests the information stored in the location at the address *0K*. The memory manager looks at its memory map and sees that the virtual address *0K* corresponds to the physical address *5K*. The memory manager retrieves the data from physical memory—in Figure 14.2, the letter *A*—and returns it to the calling program. The program never learns that the information was actually stored in a different location in physical memory, because the memory manager takes care of the translation behind the scenes.

Figure 14.2 Memory Management with Virtual Memory

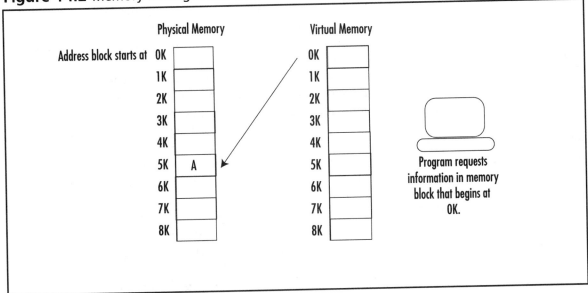

Hard disks, though cheap, are much slower than physical memory, so we hope that we are only storing rarely used sections of the code on the disk. Figuring out which sections of code can easily be parceled out to RAM rather than to the hard disk can be a job either for the OS designer or for the conscientious application designer who wants her program to run very quickly.

NEED TO KNOW...A NOTE ON TERMINOLOGY

Strictly speaking, you can have a virtual memory system without using your hard disk for memory at all. All a virtual memory system does is map real memory addresses to artificial memory addresses that are presented to the application. In practice, any virtual memory manager you use will almost certainly use a hard disk as secondary memory hardware.

As you can see, the term virtual memory refers to all memory that is accessed through the virtual memory manager, whether it is RAM, hard disk, or other storage medium. And both RAM and the hard disk are forms of physical memory. In general usage, though, you'll often see the term physical memory used to refer to RAM, and virtual memory used to refer to that portion of your memory that is being stored on your hard disk.

File Systems

Let's face it, it doesn't matter how good your computer is as a glorified calculator if there isn't a place to store your files. Your documents, your Web browser, your word processor, the program that plays media files, and your games all have to live somewhere on the disk, and you need to be able to access them quickly and easily.

Your storage needs to be long-term. We don't need to get into the electrical engineering of how long-term information is physically stored, but let's think about the logical structure for moment. There's a lot of bytes of information on your hard disk. If you have to go rifling through all those bytes every time you need to find your Web browser, you're going to spend a lot of the day looking for programs and files. So your storage needs to not only last but to be *accessible*. It also needs to be accessible to multiple programs at once. Even though your average home user doesn't need concurrent access to very large numbers of files, he's still playing music files that he can also view in a folder listing, or he's editing the alarms on his PDA while the clock program keeps track of which alarms are coming up.

Managing all this is the job of the *file system*. The most important thing from your perspective is what the files are named and whether or not you can access them. Filenames and file paths are just logical ways of looking at a collection of bytes that might be spread out all over a physical disk. When you tell your computer "I'd like the file C:\My Documents\Invitations\garden-party.doc" (see Figure 14.3), it doesn't have some special drawer to find that information in. Instead, your computer might have an index to the top level of the C: drive. It will look in that file to figure out where to find information about the directory My Documents. This will send it to some other portion of the disk, where it might find another index file that has information about all files in that directory. The computer will look in this index file, which represents the My Documents directory, and find a pointer to an index file that represents the Invitations directory. At last, in the index file of the Invitations directory, the computer will find a pointer to the location of the file named garden-party.doc. This is a pretty simplified view of the process, but it covers the basics.

Figure 14.3 A Hierarchical File System

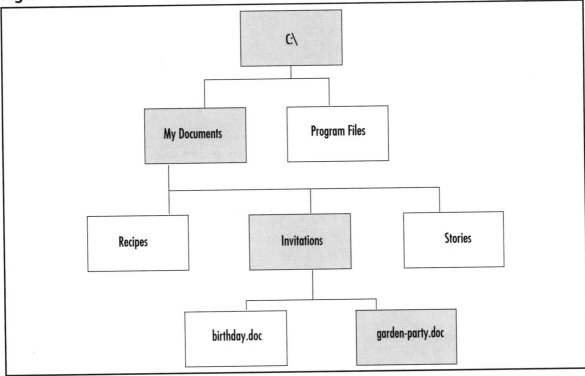

The file system also keeps track of whether or not you have permission to read, write, or execute the file in question. These are the *attributes* of the file. The file system is what lets you read, write, create, and delete files. It keeps track of the free space and can let you know if you need to free some space by erasing files. If areas of the physical disk are in bad condition and no longer able to store data, the file system can keep track of that information so it doesn't attempt to write to those blocks of the disk. (Some disks can also keep track of that information themselves, using on-board firmware.)

Cache

Remember how we mentioned that disks are much slower to access than memory? Operating system designers have different ways to speed up access to hard disks. *Cache* can be thought of as the opposite of virtual memory. Where the virtual memory manager is used to store information that logically belongs in memory on the physical hard disks, cache is used to store information that logically belongs on the disk in—you guessed it—memory.

Reading from memory and writing to memory are much faster than reading from disk and writing to disk, so for frequent read/write operations, cache will make the computer much faster. Of course, information in memory is dynamic and gets lost in the event of a power failure, unlike information in a hard disk. Operating system designers have come up with various strategies to prevent data loss from the cache in the event of a computer crash. The balance is always between efficiency and safety. The most efficient method is to synchronize data between the cache and hard disks on a regular basis—say, every 30 seconds. Less efficient but far less likely to lose data in the event of a crash is a *write-through cache*, which writes data to the disk every time some chunk of data, maybe 1KB, is written to the cache.

Input/Output

Often, when we're talking about our computers and we point to them, we don't point to the CPU, the central processing unit that does all the important computing work. Instead, we bang on the monitor or the keyboard. Input and output are how we think about our computers. We use keyboards, mice, trackballs, CD-ROMs, and network connections to get information into the computer. We use monitors, speakers, discs, and network connections to get information out. A computer without input/output capabilities could be the most powerful system in the world and still be useless.

An OS is responsible for controlling all these physical input and output devices. It needs to be able to send commands to each of the devices—hopefully in a reasonably generalized way, so we don't need to write too much specialized code. The OS needs to be able to handle when things go wrong and "listen" to interrupt messages from the various hardware devices.

Processes

Your computer at home can play music while you browse the Web and have a word processor open in the background with a term paper you have to finish. Your TiVo can play back a program and record a program at the same time. Even your tiny PDA can display your address book while keeping track of the alarms you have set. All modern computers can do multiple things simultaneously.

Once you have multiple processes, you need a way to manage them. For one thing, they're all competing for the same resources. Your Web browser needs your hard disk (to check your bookmarks and to record cache information), your memory (to save information about the parts of Windows that aren't currently visible on your screen), and your sound card (when you get to that annoying Web page that plays a little tune when you load it). But your music program also needs your hard disk (where your music files are stored), your memory (where it has saved the play list you requested), and your sound card (to play the music)! How do these two programs decide which program gets the resource, if they request access to the hard disk at the same time?

It gets even more complicated when you're looking at something that must be computed in real time. If your TiVo is going to record *Survivor* at 8:00 P.M., it can't be busy thinking about how to play back an old episode of *The Simpsons* at the same time. You'll get very cranky if you tell your TiVo to play back that episode where Homer sells his soul for a doughnut, and it tells you "Please be patient. I'm trying to record *Survivor*." How does your TiVo manage to start recording *Survivor* on time without making you notice any unacceptable delays?

Elegant solutions to these problems are an essential part of designing an operating system.

NEED TO KNOW... DINING PHILOSOPHERS

If you decide to devote further study to OS concepts, be sure to check out the *dining philosophers problem*. Posed by computer scientist Edsger W. Dijkstra in 1965, the dining philosophers problem is one of the classic resource allocation problems of the field, dealing with deadlocks and the problems systems can get into if multiple processes are waiting for each other to finish. How dry can a topic be if one of its classic problems involves five philosophers eating spaghetti around a circular table, without enough forks to go around? One of the goals of any operating system designer is to make sure that none of the philosophers starves.

System Calls

When a developer writes an application, she needs to communicate with the operating system to access files and other resources. She does this by using *system calls*—library functions that other programs can run to give them access to OS functionality, such as file creation. As a general rule, developers writing in high-level languages often won't directly use system calls. Instead, they'll use some higher-level library function, and the high-level function will take care of making the low-level system call, which in turn takes care of issuing instructions to the operating system.

Shells, User Interfaces, and GUIs

All these memory managers, system calls, and input/output device drivers don't make up the thing on your screen you actually type and mouse at. That's the *shell*, the *command-line interface (CLI)*, the *user interface (UI)*, or the *graphical user interface (GUI)*.

NEED TO KNOW... A NOTE ON TERMINOLOGY

- A *GUI* is always graphical. Microsoft Windows, MacOS X, and X Windows are examples of GUIs.
- A *CLI is* a screen in which you type commands without windows or menus (strictly speaking, anyway, although menu-based programs can be written for text-only terminals). MS-DOS and the UNIX command line are examples of CLIs.
- A *UI* is either textual or graphical; it's a generic term.
- A *shell* is usually a CLI, though some people use *shell* synonymously with *UI*, to mean any generic user interface.

The UI is the layer between you and the rest of the OS. When you run Windows Explorer on a Windows machine, use the Dock on a MacOS X system, or type **date** on a UNIX system, you're using the UI.

NOTE

If you are in interested in more detailed information on the topic of OSs, a good place to start is the book *Modern Operating Systems*, by Andrew Tannenbaum (Pearson, 2001).

Device Drivers

What would we do if there weren't *device drivers*? Say you wanted a program to read a file from a hard disk. Without a device driver, you would need to know how many sectors and cylinders the disk had, what kind of motor it used, what commands were used to control the read/write arm, and all sorts of detailed mechanics.

Figure 14.4 illustrates a very simplified program talking to devices without device drivers to help with the mechanics. This program that operates without device drivers needs to be able to communicate with every possible keyboard, hard disk, and similar component that we might use while running the program. It doesn't just need to know how to move a disk arm to a cylinder—it needs to know how to move the disk arm on every possible model of hard drive to a cylinder. (This description is something of an oversimplification: Some of the work is done by the hard disk's on-board firmware. But, there's still an enormous amount that the OS needs to know before it can talk to a disk.)

Figure 14.4 A Program Interacting Directly With Diverse Devices

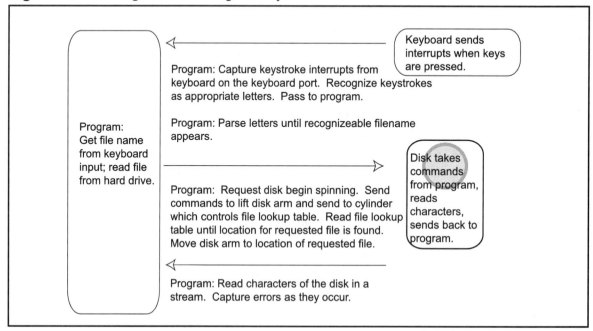

WARNING: HARDWARE HARM

People who know the limitations of the hardware generally write device drivers. Usually your hardware manufacturer or OS manufacturer will provide the necessary device drivers, but sometimes you'll need to write your own. For example, a device driver might be unavailable for your hardware, or the available device driver might be unnecessarily conservative or restrictive. If you aren't sure of the physical limitations of the device—maximum safe clock speed of your processor, for example, or maximum safe refresh rate of your monitor—you can do irreparable harm to your equipment. When writing your own device driver, be sure you know the physical limitations of the hardware! Exciting as the smell of melted processor can be (and yes, this really does happen), it's probably not what you want to wake up to.

The job of the device driver is to know all this information about the hardware for you. All your application needs to do is tell the device driver, "Read this information from this disk." The device driver translates your request into a detailed sequence of commands that instruct the physical disk how to find and read your information, as we can see in Figure 14.5.

Figure 14.5 A Program Interacting With Device Drivers Between It and the Hardware

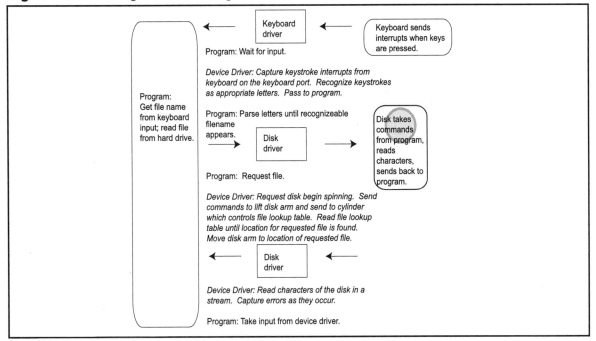

Ideally, you don't want to care how the device works when you're writing a program. You don't want to know if you're talking to network input, hard disk input, or keyboard input if you write a program that says, "Capitalize all words from my input stream." And you certainly don't want to know details like "To get data from my Fujitsu hard drive, spin the middle platter, then move the seek head over to the fourth cylinder," or "To get data from my Microsoft Natural Keyboard, listen for the interrupts coming in on interrupt line 4." Anything hardware-specific that the OS needs to know goes into the device drivers. A simple device driver might be able to handle an entire class of devices—all serial mice, for example. A more complex and device-specific device driver might be needed to make best use of some piece of hardware's special features, such as a mouse with a scroll wheel.

Block and Character Devices

There are two main kinds of input/output devices: character devices and block devices. A *character device* doesn't have fixed-size *blocks* (chunks of data that the device sends through to be processed one at a time) and can only be accessed in order: the first piece of data, followed by the second, followed by the third, and so on. Character devices deal with streams of characters that just keep coming or that you deliver. A network connection is a character device, as is a keyboard connection. A roll of sticky tape can be thought of as a sort of character device. You can take any amount of sticky tape you want, but you can't get to the tape in the middle until you've dealt with the tape at the end of the roll (see Figure 14.6).

Figure 14.6 Sticky Tape Seen as a Character Device

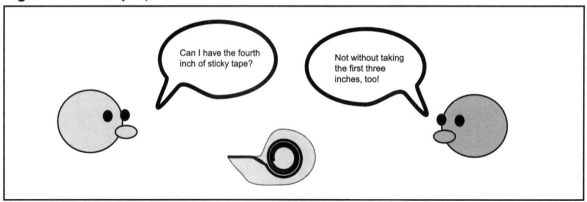

Just like a roll of sticky tape, the magnetic tape drive illustrated in Figure 14.7 works as a character device, giving you each unit of data in the order it appears on the tape, without letting you skip directly to the part you want.

Figure 14.7 A Magnetic Tape Drive

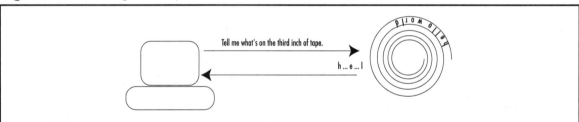

Block devices, such as CD-ROMs and hard disks, store information in addressable blocks of a fixed size. Any block on a block device can be accessed directly; the blocks don't need to be accessed in order, as they do with a character device. A bookshelf, illustrated in Figure 14.8, can be thought of as a sort of block device. Each book on a bookshelf is a block of information, and you can pick up any book directly without going through any other book.

Figure 14.8 A Bookshelf as Block Device

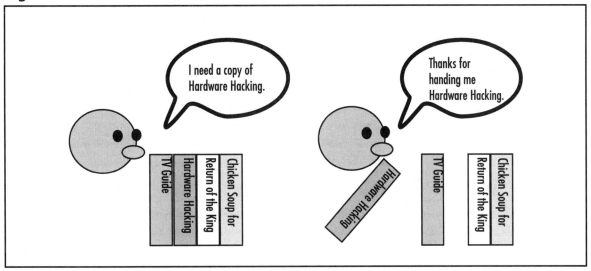

A standard hard disk is one of the most common block devices. In Figure 14.9, a program requests the data that is stored on sector 2 of a hard disk and receives that data directly, without having to first read through sector 1.

Figure 14.9 A Block Device With Direct Access

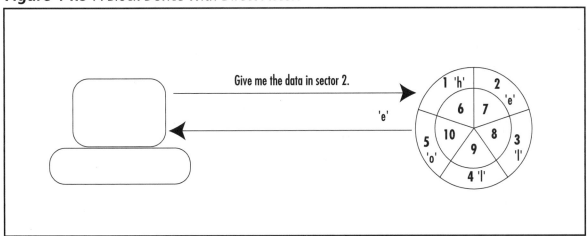

NOTE

If you are in interested in more detailed information on the topic of device drivers, check out books for device drivers specific to the operating system you're working with:

- For Linux, you can start with the book *Linux Device Drivers*, by Alessandro Rubini and Jonathan Corbet (O'Reilly, 2001). Available online at www.xml.com/ldd/chapter/book/.
- For Windows, try *Getting Started with Windows Drivers*. MSDN Web site, available online at http://msdn.microsoft.com/library/default.asp?url=/library/en-us/gstart/hh/gstart/z_gstart_hdr_5pwn.asp.
- You can also try the Windows Embedded Device Driver site, at www.microsoft.com/windows/Embedded/ce.NET/techinfo/devdd.asp.
- For VxWorks, you can use *VxWorks: Device Drivers in a Nutshell*, by Prasad Ayyalasomayajula and Allen Tully. Available online at www.ayyalasoft.com/VxWorks-device-drivers.htm.

Properties of Embedded Operating Systems

In its most simple form, *embedded system* is a special-purpose computer built into a special device. Embedded systems are often designed to run on specialized hardware such as cellular phones, PDAs, and *set-top boxes* (which connect to your television, such as TiVos or computer game systems). Embedded systems have special constraints. Since they are usually included in the category of consumer electronics (although they run the entire spectrum of use—embedded systems are also used in industrial robots and on space missions), embedded systems need to be able to run on cheap, mass-produced hardware often with limited power. Therefore, they must be:

- Inexpensive
- Small (to run on cheap hardware)
- Conservative in power use

A *real-time operating system* (*RTOS*) needs to run in a predictable and deterministic fashion, no matter what is running on the system at any given time. An RTOS is likely to have the following characteristics:

- It will be small, using very little memory, which is likely to be limited on embedded systems.
- It will be likely be portable to other types of processors.
- Most processes will be preemptable by hardware events of a higher priority.
- The system should have predictable and deterministic response rates for any given operation.

This isn't to say it should be fast—the extra load necessary to keep all events controlled and to give priority where it is needed might make the system relatively slow. But it will be predictable, which is what is necessary. Think about the computer that controls the antilock brakes in your car. Would you rather have your brakes work very fast sometimes and very slowly sometimes, or would you rather know exactly how long it will take your brakes to respond?

Memory management is a particularly difficult problem in embedded operating systems. On one hand, embedded operating systems usually run on very minimal hardware, which has little or no hardware support for complex memory management. On the other hand, the "predictable" and "deterministic" requirements for real-time operating systems actually increase the need for complex memory management. Two simultaneous processes running in shared memory space can corrupt one another and crash both processes, and even the entire system. Solving this problem—that is, how to have protected memory on minimal hardware—is one of the difficulties of RTOS design.

Linux

The term *Linux* is often used as an umbrella term to mean "Linux and a whole lot of other things." Linux itself is simply the operating system *kernel*, the core parts of the software necessary to manipulate the hardware, control processes, and create a very simple and basic user interface. In general, when somebody talks about Linux, they usually mean a Linux kernel and a collection of tools. Since many of these tools were created by the GNU, some people call a standard Linux installation GNU/Linux, but this terminology is rare.

Linux contains many powerful OS features, including multitasking (the ability to do multiple tasks at once), threads, virtual memory, loadable device driver modules, and networking.

Open Source

Open source might be a movement, an ideology, or a business plan, but in its simplest formation, open source is about licensing. An open-source product is one that is distributed under a license that allows the right to read, redistribute and sell, modify, and freely use the source code and software.

NEED TO KNOW... OPEN-SOURCE RATIONALES

There are many different theories about why open source is good. The GNU Project (gnu.org) calls its software "free software" and not "open source," using open-source innovator Richard Stallman's formulation: "free as in 'free speech,' not as in 'free beer.'" This group's philosophy is ideological: They believe that information deserves liberty and that it is morally wrong to have restrictive licenses. The Open Source Initiative, or OSI (opensource.org), has a much more pragmatic philosophy: They believe that the most reliable and high-quality code will be produced by the independent peer review that is fostered by open licenses. Although the two organizations have fundamentally different motivations for their support of free software and open source, the results are very similar. The Open Source Initiative's qualifications for certifying a software license as "OSI Certified" result in licenses that, for the most part, the more ideological GNU Project approves of.

Linux is by far the most successful open-source operating system in use. It isn't the only one by a long shot, however. FreeBSD, OpenBSD, and NetBSD are other successful open-source platforms, and Darwin, the BSD-based operating system that lies underneath MacOS X, is open source as well! Just because Linux is open source doesn't mean that nobody can make a profit off it. Companies and organizations such as Debian, Red Hat, and Yellow Dog all sell or give away their own *distributions* of Linux: a base Linux kernel bundled with usability tools, documentation, software to make installation easier, and technical support.

Software designed for one Linux distribution will probably work on another—as long as both distributions are using the same tools, libraries, and compilers. For this reason, building software on a Linux system can occasionally be very frustrating. Because Linux systems are so powerfully modular— that is, because each system can be running different versions of the various software components as needed—the Linux system in front of you might look very different from the Linux system in front of me. This is where the various distributions really show their strengths. If the user can say, "I'm using Debian 3.0. Does your product work on that?", compatibility tests are made far simpler.

History

In the late 1960s, some developers at Bell Labs started working on a project they called UNIX®, an outgrowth of an earlier Bell Labs project called Multics. UNIX was a powerful operating system with very useful features, and other development teams—primarily at the University of California at Berkeley—began work on their own versions, fiddling with and improving AT&T's code. The Berkeley operating system was powerful and robust and quickly became popular, but users still needed to purchase a license for the base code from AT&T (owners of Bell Labs after the breakup of Bell). The licenses from AT&T became more and more expensive, and in 1989, the developers at Berkeley separated out most of the code that they had written themselves and that was therefore not subject to the AT&T license. They released that code separately in what became the first of the freely redis-tributable software licenses. They quickly followed this release with a complete rewrite of what became known as *BSD*, which was a UNIX derivative written entirely from scratch and therefore no longer bound by the AT&T license.

NEED TO KNOW...

In this day and age of concern over intellectual property, people buy and sell, and ownership shifts around. The source code to the original AT&T UNIX® is now owned by SCO, but the trademark to the word *UNIX* is owned by The Open Group. The many UNIX derivatives that exist need to avoid trademark violation. They tend to call themselves things like "UNIX-like," "*NIX," "UN*X," or "UNIX-variant." In everyday speech, users tend to refer to them all as "UNIX," but the trademark does exist.

Meanwhile, back on the East Coast, Richard Stallman at MIT had spent the 1980s developing GNU (the recursive acronym stands for *GNUs not Unix*), a collection of programs and development tools that run on UNIX systems and UNIX variants. Licensed under the *GNU Public License (GPL)*, all the GNU Project's tools are freely modifiable and redistributable. Hackers went to work improving and fine-tuning those original programs, and before long, the GNU variants of most tools available for UNIX derivatives were more powerful than commercially released variants. By the late 1980s, the GNU Project had produced enough tools that they had almost an entire operating system. The only thing that they were missing was a kernel of their own.

Enter Linus Torvalds. In 1991, he was a student at the University of Helsinki in Finland. Inspired by the operating system Minix, a simple kernel that had been designed by Andrew Tannenbaum to teach operating system concepts to students, Linus began work on his own kernel. He released his new kernel, which he called Linux, under the GPL, and posted it on the Internet for suggestions and code tweaking. Linux was designed to run with the existing GNU utilities. Thanks to Torvalds' willingness to ask for help and take suggestions, his kernel quickly grew into the relatively robust system that is widely used today. You could argue that with all the effort widespread developers have put into the Linux kernel, the GNU utilities, and the accompanying device drivers, tweaks, tools, and other bits of code, your typical Linux distribution is the product of the collective brainpower of the Internet working together for a common goal. And you would be right.

Embedded Linux (uCLinux)

Linux's appeal for designers of embedded systems rests in two of its core features: its open licensing and its modularity. Because it is an open-source product, companies that are trying to keep costs down find Linux attractive, especially compared with the ever-increasing licensing restrictions on some proprietary products. Additionally, a Linux installation can be very small. A basic installation of Linux can contain just the kernel and a few necessary device drivers. Because Linux is so modular, it is a trivial matter to strip away those parts of the OS that the embedded system designer doesn't need, leaving the final running system small and fast. Linux also runs on nearly every processor in existence, which makes it extremely attractive for developers who want some flexibility in their hardware choices. On the downside, standard Linux is not designed as a real-time operating system and is lacking the level of process interrupts that allow the operating system to behave deterministically. Some effort has gone into improving the process management for real-time versions of Linux to allow true interruptibility.

Right now, the real upside for using Linux on an embedded system is its price and extensibility. The downside is that it's not a system designed specifically for the purpose, so it takes some stretching to make it work like an RTOS.

Because it is so easy and inexpensive to hack Linux, programmers have made Linux run on diverse hardware platforms, from traditional computers such as Macintosh and Sparc to consumer electronic devices such as the iPod, Xbox, PlayStation2, and Palm Pilot. For one example, see the Linux Xbox project (http://xbox-linux.sourceforge.net) More information on the uCLinux development community is available online at www.uclinux.org and www.ucdot.org.

Product Examples: Linux on Embedded Systems

Here are some products that use embedded versions of Linux :

- TiVo (Digital Video Recorder—but you knew this one)

- Sharp Zaurus (line of PDAs)

- G.Mate Yopy (PDA with games and music ability)

- Motorola A760 Linux/Java handset/PDA (PDA, cell and speaker phone, digital camera, video player, MP3 player)

- Panasonic broadband terminal/IP phone (Internet phone with Voice over IP)

- Dream-Multimedia-TV's Dreambox (digital radio, cable and satellite receiver, digital video recorder)

- Philips iPronto (home entertainment system control, home electronic control)

- empeg car audio player (car MP3 stereo)

- Mercedes-Benz UMTS test car (a navigation, Internet access, and game center module that has not yet been released—but when it is, *do not* try to hack the software on your car.

VxWorks

VxWorks is a commercial product made by Wind River Systems (www.windriver.com) that is used in many consumer electronic devices. VxWorks has a multitasking kernel with pre-emptive scheduling, as is appropriate for an RTOS. Its interprocess communications are swift, and its memory management is relatively efficient. It can support multiple processors and has a simple debugger. Because it is designed strictly for embedded systems, VxWorks programs are written on a standard platform, compiled into VxWorks programs, and ported over to the VxWorks systems.

Wind River provides a commercial development toolkit with integrated compilers, debuggers, and other tools. A developer can also choose to use a standard C or C++ compiler rather than the VxWorks Developer's Toolkit.

Product Examples: VxWorks on Embedded Systems

Here are some products that use VxWorks on embedded systems:

- Mars Pathfinder mission (Remember the Pathfinder? Went to Mars, sent us pictures? Some of its software was VxWorks.

- Apple AirPort Wireless Gateway (network gateway)

- Honda ASIMO Humanoid Robot (toy or experiment, depending on who you ask)

- Siemens Mobile Network GGSN @dvantage CPG-3000 (high-end corporate networking hardware)

Windows CE

Microsoft Windows 1.0 was introduced in 1985, but it wasn't until the release of Windows 3.1 in 1992 and Windows 3.11 (Windows for Workgroups) in 1993 that the windowing system built on top of MS-DOS started to become widely used. In 1993, Microsoft also started releasing its Windows NT line and began to pave its way into the corporate market by providing a set of graphically administered tools that eased security, control, and file sharing for corporate users.

In 1996, Microsoft entered the embedded operating systems market with the first release of Windows CE. The current release of Windows CE, Windows CE .NET, has now been joined by Windows XP Embedded, a modularized version of the popular desktop version of Windows. Both are now developed in .NET, Microsoft's framework for development. A developer can use VisualStudio.NET as the programming environment and can write code in:

- Microsoft Visual Basic.NET

- Visual C++.NET

- Visual C#.NET

- Visual J#.NET

- JScript.NET

- A selection of approved third-party tools

Windows XP is the member of the Windows Embedded family intended for larger systems with more complexity, such as automated teller machines (ATMs). Windows CE .NET is intended for smaller, less complex RTOS applications.

Any handheld computer that runs both a variant of Windows CE and Microsoft's suite of handheld applications can be called a *Pocket PC*. A Pocket PC (www.pocketpc.com) can be made by one of a variety of hardware manufacturers, as long as it conforms to Microsoft's software guidelines.

Concepts

Windows CE is attractive to developers because of the familiar Windows-style interface it gives users. It also allows developers who are comfortable with Windows development and .NET to work in the familiar platform. More importantly, because Windows CE includes a subset of the Win32 API, porting limited versions of existing Windows programs becomes possible.

Windows CE is a preemptive multitasking operating system. Multiple processes can be running at one time, with each process running in a protected section of memory. A process consists of one or more threads, each with a different scheduling priority. Because Windows CE is real time, it needs to guarantee that events are noticed quickly. To do this, there is a high-priority *interrupt thread* running at all times, to catch events and schedule responses appropriately.

Windows CE has a hierarchical architecture, with its various components layered on top of one another. The lowest layers hold the parts of the OS responsible for talking directly to hardware: the *OEM Abstraction Layer (OAL)*, which is responsible for handling the most basic components of the computer, such as the power and the clock, and the *device driver layer*, which manages all the other physical devices. Then come the layers that handle graphics and windowing, communication, and other basic kernel functionality. On the very top comes the file system and the user interface.

Windows CE makes extensive networking and communications capabilities available to the programmer, giving you access to standard wired and wireless communication. It has support for USB, which—assuming you're prepared to write the device driver if there isn't a generic one available—gives you flexibility about the hardware which may attach to your Windows CE system.

NEED TO KNOW...

Windows CE supports an extensive range of communication protocols that allow your Windows CE device to communicate with other systems:

- **Networking features** Protected Extensible Authentication Protocol (PEAP), firewall, Network Driver Interface Specification (NDIS) 5.1, utilities, Universal Plug and Play (UPnP), VoIP, TCP/IP, TCP/IPv6.
- **Local Area Network (LAN)** 802.11, 802.1x, 802.3, 802.5, Wireless Protected Access (WAP).
- **Personal Area Network (PAN)** Bluetooth, Infrared Data Association (IrDA).
- **Wide Area Network (WAN)** Dial-up networking, point-to-point, telephony API, virtual private networking (VPN).
- **Servers** File Transfer Protocol (FTP), file and print, Simple Network Time Protocol (SNTP), Telnet, Web server.

Windows CE also gives access to basic security protocols and to user interface design. Smaller versions of some of the core Windows programs (from Internet Explorer to Freecell) are already written for Windows CE.

If you do programming in Windows CE but you want a more full-featured operating system to test in, you can write programs using the .NET development tools on a standard Windows machine and test them in Windows CE—based software emulators.

Product Examples: Windows CE on Embedded Systems

- Alva MPO 5500 mobile phone/PDA (PDA aimed at the visually impaired)
- BSquare Power Handheld (PDA)
- Gotive H41 mobile communicator (PDA, cell phone, GPS, and barcode reader)
- iPAQ Pocket PC h5550 (PDA)

- Neonode N1 "limitless" mobile device (PDA, cell phone, digital camera, came device, jukebox, and remote control)

- Bernina artista 200E (sewing machine—yes, we're serious. The sewing machine industry is extremely high-tech these days.

- Hitachi Wearable Internet Appliance, or WIA (Head-mounted wearable computer with a tiny screen that flips over your eye.

Summary

Understanding the operating software of a computer or electronic device is much more difficult than it seems at first glance. Yet it's also very rewarding. Think about how much fun you'll have when you connect some strange old legacy bit of hardware to your PDA, or when you manage to make your TiVo do strange and glorious tricks. There's too much variation on types of hardware to give you more than the roughest overview in this chapter, but we hope we've given you a good introduction to what you can do.

This chapter has provided a basic introduction to the concepts of operating systems as well as to a few specific OSs that should be useful in your hacking adventures. In electronic devices and computer systems, operating systems are a key function that provides a layer of abstraction between user program and the actual hardware, and a good understanding of the systems will make your future programming projects much more successful. With the resources of an OS at your fingertips, you can manage hardware devices, computing resources, and software processes like a pro.

Additional References and Further Reading

- *Modern Operating Systems,* **by Andrew Tannenbaum (Pearson, 2001)** A good place to start if you are interested in more detailed information on the topic of OSs.

- **Embedded.com: www.embedded.com** This site has general Internet resources and links about embedded systems.

- **HowStuffWorks: http://computer.howstuffworks.com/operating-system.htm** Offers a good introductory tutorial to operating systems.

- **The Memory Management Reference: www.memorymanagement.org** Has a great glossary and some good articles.

- **Linux Devices: www.linuxdevices.com** Provides great links, articles, and forums about Embedded Linux.

- **Linux Devices: www.linuxdevices.com/articles/AT2352793488.html** An interesting article about Embedded Linux in real-world applications.

- *Embedded Linux Journal:* **www.eljonline.com** Linux Devices' online magazine.

- **Windows Devices: www.windowsdevices.com** Just like Linux Devices, but for Embedded Windows.

NEED TO KNOW... A NOTE ABOUT STORAGE STRUCTURES, C, AND ASSEMBLY LANGUAGE

Hash tables and linked lists are high-level data structures and are not built in to any standard implementations of C or assembly language. Many C programs include homegrown implementations of linked lists and hash tables (which are fairly easy to write) because they are so very useful. We can't teach you the details of every implementation, but we can teach you enough about the basics to recognize them and to know how to use them when you see them.

Structures

Before we go into details about the various storage structures, let's start with the miscellaneous storage structure: the appropriately named *structure* (see Figure 15.2). Structures (sometimes called *records*) are conglomerations of different types of data. For example, a pizza recipe structure might hold:

- An array (illustrated in Table 15.1) of ingredients to make the crust
- A linked list (as illustrated in Table 15.4) of ingredients to make the toppings
- One bowl
- One oven

Figure 15.2 A Pizza Recipe Structure, With Elements We'll Explore in More Detail Shortly

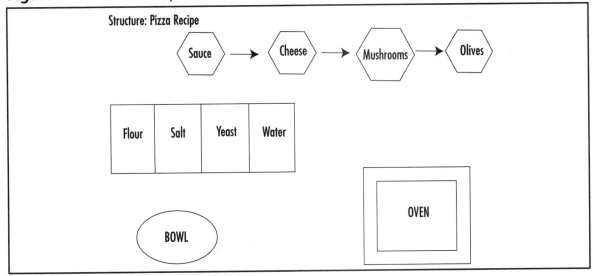

Structures are handy mostly as a logical organization aid. In a large and complex program, you might use a structure to make it easier for you to remember what data should be treated as part of one logical unit.

Arrays

One way of storing data is in an *array*. An array is like a long row of post-office boxes. Each post-office box has a unique number on its door and contains mail for one person or family. When a post-office customer wants to check her mail, she looks in the box with her number on the door. Her mail is always stored in that box.

In an array, the computer cordons off an area of memory that holds the information being stored, just like the post-office wall is filled with post-office boxes. Each virtual post-office box is called an *array element*. Each element stored in the array is indexed by a number. If you want to retrieve the information stored in the fourth chunk of the array, for example, you would request the information telling the computer the array's name and the chunk you want to retrieve. For example, your array might be called *greetings* and contain all the different ways to say hello. An example of array *greetings* is shown in Table 15.1.

Table 15.1 The Sample Array *greetings*

The Array greetings	
element 1	hello
element 2	bonjour
element 3	zdravstvuite
element 4	hola

Now *greetings(4)* contains the string *hola*. Your pseudocode program might say:

```
print to screen greetings(4) + " world!"
```

which would produce the output:

hola world!

NEED TO KNOW... A NOTE ABOUT NUMBERING

In most programming languages, numbering actually starts at 0, not at 1. A list with four elements will have those elements numbered 0, 1, 2, and 3. So the array in Table 15.1 will actually look more like the array shown in Table 15.2.

Figure 15.5 Code With Confusing Variable Names

```
while i exists          /* if the next bowl isn't empty */
    fetch k             /* take the ingredient from the current bowl */
    i                    /* move to the next bowl */
    delete m            /* put the previous, empty bowl in the sink */


when i doesn't exist    /* when you're done, */
    delete j             /* put the last bowl in the sink */
    bake n               /* and put the pizza in the oven! */
```

This piece of pseudocode means the same thing as far as the computer is concerned, but it doesn't really make any sense to you or me. Whenever possible, use variable and function names that have meaning to you in the context of your program. Doing so might involve a little bit more typing now, but it will make your life much, much easier later, when you have to fix a bug in your code.

Code Readability: Pretty Printing

In most modern programming languages, an excess of white space is ignored by the computer. This means that you can use as many—or as few!—tabs and space characters as you need. Your program will be easier to read later if you format it so that it is clear how the program flows. When it comes to the nitty-gritty details of formatting, there are as many preferences as there are programmers. However, a couple of broad conventions have been agreed on as generally useful:

- Use a new line to indicate a new command. Figure 15.4 could have been written in just two lines, but it would have been much harder to read:

  ```
  while nextBowl exists; fetch Ingredient; nextBowl; delete prevBowl.
  when nextBowl doesn't exist; delete Bowl; bake pizza.
  ```

- If a block of text is part of a loop, function, or conditional structure, use leading white space to show the lines of code that are being evaluated similarly. Here is the code from Figure 15.4 without leading white space in the loop and conditional and without white space separating the two blocks of code. This is much harder to read than the sample with white space:

  ```
  while nextBowl exists
  fetch Ingredient
  nextBowl
  delete prevBowl
  when nextBowl doesn't exist
  delete Bowl
  bake pizza
  ```

Introduction to C

C is a runtime environment that exists on nearly every platform. For historical reasons, almost every system in existence can run compiled C programs. C is a platform-independent compiled language, but it has a large library of hardware-specific, low-level system calls available to help us access the hardware. On its own, C is a very small language; it doesn't even know how to display text to the screen! But every C installation comes with the C *standard libraries*, which provide the programmer with a host of handy functions.

C is a *compiled* language. This means that we write the program in the English-like language that you're learning here and then use another program (a *compiler*) to convert it into commands the computer can understand and execute.

NEED TO KNOW... YOUR COMPILER

 Many different C compilers are available. You might be using a command-line compiler, for which you write your program in a text editor such as Notepad, Emacs, or vi and then compile your program with a command such as *cc myprogram.c -o myprogram.exe*. You might be using a graphical programming environment, where you write and compile your program in an easy-to-understand window, with compilation just another menu item or button to press. We can't teach you the ins and outs of the compiler you'll be using, because they're all different. Refer to your compiler manual for instructions on how to compile your C program.

History and Basics of C

C was invented by Dennis Ritchie (based on work done by Kenneth Thompson) in the early 1970s as a language intended for programming on Thompson's brand-new UNIX operating system. C was standardized into what we now know as *ANSI C* in the mid-1980s. For many years, C was primarily used for programming on UNIX and its variants, but it is now a widespread standard. C and its descendents (including Visual C and C++) are among the most widely used programming languages.

Printing to the Screen

A C program is just a sequence of commands. Let's start with our first program, the ubiquitous "hello, world," which is the first program you will learn to write in almost any programming language (see Figure 15.6).

Figure 15.6 The Hello, World Program

```
#include <stdio.h>

main()
{
        printf("hello, world\n");
}
```

Let's break down this program. The meat of any C program, the part that runs when you execute the program, is in the *main* block. This main block is a special-purpose *function* that tells your program to begin its work here. You can see the declaration of the main block on line 3 of Figure 15.6. Those parentheses after the word *main* are required after any function and are used to pass arguments to the function if you need any (we'll get to some details of function calls and argument passing soon). In this program, we aren't passing any arguments to the main function, so the parentheses are present but empty.

After a function's initial line, all statements that belong to that function are grouped together with curly braces {}. In this program, those curly braces are on lines 4 and 6. Anything between those curly braces (in this case, line 5) is part of the function. So in this program, the heart of the main block is the command on line 5:

```
printf("hello, world\n");
```

The command *printf*, like *main*, is a function. Notice that it begins with the function name (*printf*) followed by zero or more arguments in closing parentheses (in this case, one argument, which is equal to the string *"hello, world\n"*). *printf* is the formatted print command. Here it is printing to the screen the contents of its argument: the characters *hello world* followed by \n. In a C character string, a single character preceded by the backslash character (\) has a special meaning. \n is the C notation for printing a new line to the screen. You can't put a new line directly in a quoted string, for example:

```
"here is my first line
here is my second"
```

This is not valid C. To write those lines to the screen, your command would have to be:

```
printf("here is my first line\nhere is my second\n")
```

or a variant:

```
printf("here is my first line\n");
printf("here is my second\n");
```

or:

```
printf("here is ");
printf("my first line\nhere is my second\n");
```

The separate *printf* commands don't change where the new-line characters are printed on the screen. Only the *n* characters create new lines.

NEED TO KNOW... SOME INTERESTING CHARACTER STRING ESCAPE SEQUENCES

Several similar sequences cause *printf* to display something special to the screen. Some are very special types of characters, such as the audible alert bell that *printf* sounds when given the character sequence *a*. Most are designed simply to escape the meaning of some other character (hence the name *escape sequences*), to allow *printf* to print the literal character instead of trying to interpret the meaning. For example, if we need to display a double quote mark (") on the screen, we need to prevent *printf* from parsing the special meaning of the double quote mark as "here is the beginning or end of a character string." Some of the more interesting escape sequences include:

- \\n newline
- \\t horizontal tab
- \\? question mark
- \\' single quote
- \\" double quote
- \\a alert bell

Earlier we mentioned that C doesn't really have much complex functionality of its own and doesn't even know how to output characters to the screen in any simple way. Well, that's where line 1 of Figure 15.6 comes in. C has standard libraries that provide that basic functionality that is not built into the language. To make your final program as small as possible, you include only the standard libraries you need into your program. Line 1 includes the standard library *stdio.h,* which is responsible for standard input and output functionality. The included library provides us with the *printf* function.

One last character we haven't covered: that semicolon (;) at the end of line 5. C commands are separated by semicolons, not by white space, so the following commands are legal:

```
printf("here is");
printf("my first line\nhere is my second\n");
```

But this next example isn't:

```
printf("here is")
printf("my first line\nhere is my second\n")
```

Data Types in C

C is a *strongly typed* language. This means that the language distinguishes among the different types of data it can process. It's important to recognize data types for many reasons. For one thing, your programming language needs to allocate storage for any information you intend to store. To store the integer 8 is relatively simple; you need as much space is the computer will take to store that integer. But what if you want to store the real number 8? (To program efficiently, you're going to use things you learned in math class! Remember that integers are only the numbers $-\infty,...,-3,-2,-1,0,1,2,3,...,\infty$, but that real numbers also include numbers like 3.759.) If you want to store the real number 8 to, say, three points of precision (that is, so you can distinguish between 8.000 and 8.003), you'll need a lot more storage space in the computer. And if you want to be able to distinguish between 8.000 and –8.000, you'll need even more space. So it's important to use the right data type for your variable, or you can rapidly run out of memory for your program.

C has only a few data types:

- **Int** An integer.

- **Float** A single precision floating-point number (basically, a real number).

- **Double** A double precision floating-point number (basically, a real number with extra precision).

- **Char** One character.

You can qualify these data types with *short* (if you aren't using very large numbers and want the program to allocate space effectively) and *long* (if you are using very large numbers). You can also qualify the data types with *signed* (if it matters to you whether the numbers are positive or negative) and *unsigned* (if you're not going to be using negative numbers and you want the program to allocate space effectively). For entry-level programming, you won't use any of these qualifiers, but you'll want to be able to recognize them if you see them in somebody else's code.

If you've done some programming before, you might notice two types that are missing here: Booleans and character strings. Booleans (the values *true* and *false*) are usually represented in C as a special case of integers. Character strings are arrays of characters. We'll talk more about how to implement character strings later.

Mathematical Functions

You know what's really great about computers? They know how to do arithmetic, so we don't have to. Many basic mathematical functions are included in the language C, and to use them, you don't need to include any standard libraries. A standard library called *math.h* provides more complex mathematical functions such as sines, cosines, logarithms, powers, and the like, but you don't need to use it for simple mathematics. Figure 15.7 displays a program that calculates the number of minutes in a day.

Figure 15.7 Mathematical Example

```
#include <stdio.h>


main()
{
      /* variable declarations */
      int seconds, minutes, hours;
      int total;
      seconds = 60;        /* number of seconds in one minute */
      minutes = 60;        /* number of minutes in one hour */
      hours = 24;        /* number of hours in one day */


      total = seconds * minutes * hours;        /* calculate total */
      printf("there are %d seconds in one day.\n", total);
}
```

When you run this program, your computer should print out the line:

there are 86400 seconds in one day.

Let's step through this program to see what we did. You recognize line 1—it includes the standard input and output library. We're using this library to get the *printf* command, which will print the results of our mathematical equation. Line 3 begins the main function, and line 4 provides the curly brace that tells the program "the lines between here and the matching curly brace belong in the main function."

The first new line we've seen in this program is on line 5: /* *variable declarations* */. This is a C comment: a line of the program that is there for your benefit only but is ignored by the compiler. Anything between the initial /* and the closing */ is a *comment* and not part of the program. The comment on line 5 lets us know that we are about to *declare variables*.

Variables in C are declared before use. A declaration, which consists of a data type and some number of variable names, tells the program the sort of information that is going to be stored in that variable. In Figure 15.7, the variables are defined in two lines:

```
int seconds, minutes, hours;
int total;
```

Because they're all of the same type (*int*—that is, integers), we could have declared them all in one line:

```
int seconds, minutes, hours, total;
```

or on four separate lines as follows:

```
int seconds;

int minutes;

int hours;

int total;
```

C doesn't care how you lay it out, so you should use whichever method makes your code most readable for you. You might split conceptually—variables that all refer to one function on one line and to another function on a second line—or by any other method you like.

After you've declared your variables, you can assign them. *Assignment* gives a value of the appropriate type to the variable you have even a declaration. In this case, the appropriate type is integer, so we assign each variable name its initial value as follows:

```
seconds = 60;

minutes = 60;

hours = 24;
```

So before we begin the computation, the variables contain meaningful values.

On line 13, the actual calculation occurs:

```
total = seconds * minutes * hours;
```

Most of these characters should be fairly familiar:

- Equals sign (=) is the *assignment operator*, which places the results of the calculation to the right of the equals sign into the variable on the left.

- The asterisk (*) says to multiply, just like you would use × in a written calculation: seconds × minutes × hours.

- To add and subtract you would, predictably, use the plus sign (+) and the minus sign (-), respectively, and to divide, you would use the slash (/).

The statement on line 14 is another *printf* statement, but this one looks a little different. For one thing, it has two arguments separated by a comma: a quoted character string and a variable name.

```
printf("there are %d seconds in one day.\n", total);
```

The *printf* function does more than just output simple character strings to the screen. It can do complex output formatting. The first argument to the *printf* function is always a character string. That character string can contain some number of substitution characters, each one in the format % followed by a letter. For each substitution character, the *printf* function takes an argument explaining which variable will have its contents substituted into the character string.

In this example, the substitution character is *%d*. This is C for "take the value of the variable for the corresponding argument and display it as a decimal integer." The argument that corresponds to *%d* is *total*. In the preceding calculation, the value of *total* was set to 60 * 60 * 24, or 86,400. So for this example, the function's output will be:

there are 86400 seconds in one day.

NOTE

This nonintuitive removal of the variable from the printing string isn't present in some higher-level languages. In Java, for example, the preceding statement would be:

```
System.out.println("there are " + total + " seconds in one day.");
```

You might ask why we set the number of seconds in a minute, the number of minutes in an hour, and the number of hours in a day as variable values. After all, aren't variables supposed to be, well, variable? But there are always 60 seconds in one minute, always 60 minutes in one hour, and always 24 hours in one day. And in fact, there is a way to create a *symbolic constant* to hold this kind of information that will never change. Instead of declaring and assigning the following variable:

```
int seconds;
seconds = 60;
```

you can define a symbolic constant:

```
#define SECONDS_IN_HOUR 60
```

Every occurrence of *SECONDS_IN_HOUR* will be replaced at compilation time with your replacement text, *60*. Note that there is no semicolon completing a *#define* line. By convention, symbolic constants are written in all capital letters to distinguish them from variable names, which are conventionally some combination of upper- and lowercase letters.

Control Structures

Remember all those control structures we learned about the beginning of the chapter? Well, C can do all of those. We'll look at two forms of looping (*for* loops and *while* loops) and two forms of conditional branching (*if/then/else* statements and *switch* statements). Unconditional branching in C is implemented with function calls, which we'll deal with in the next section.

For Loops

The *for* statement is a loop that operates until a certain condition has been met. This concept is shown in Figure 15.8.

Figure 15.8 A Sample *for* Loop

```
int i;


for ( i = 1; i <= 10; i++)
{
    ...

}
```

There are three components to the loop's control mechanism, all stored within the parentheses. Look at the three parts of the statement in Figure 15.8, separated by semicolons. First:

```
i = 1
```

This part of the loop initializes any variables that will be used during the loop's control. Here we are taking a variable *i* (which has been declared beforehand as an integer—*int i;*) and initializing it to 1. The second part of the *for* loop's control gives a test condition:

```
i <= 10
```

This test is evaluated. In this case it is asking whether or not the variable stored in *i* is less than or equal to 10. If it isn't, a program exits this *for* loop and continues on with whenever it was doing before the loop was entered. If it is, the body of the loop is executed. Before we re-enter the loop and perform all this once more, we do the third step of the *for* loop:

```
i++
```

This step increments the counter variable we are using in the loop. This command tells C to add 1 to the variable stored in *i*.

The first time this program runs, the variable *i* will be initialized to 1, the program will test to see if 1 is less than or equal to 10, and it will discover that it is. The body of the loop will be executed, the variable *i* will be incremented by the statement *i++* to 2, and the process will begin again. After the tenth time this program runs, the variable *i* will be incremented to 11, and the loop will stop.

Comparison Operators and Increment/Decrement Operators

In this section you were introduced to two new operators: $<=$, a comparison operator, and $++$, an increment operator.

Comparison operators test some relation between the value on the left and the value on the right:

- $<$ Is less than.
- $<=$ Is less than or equal to.
- $>$ Is greater than.
- $>=$ Is greater than or equal to.
- $==$ Is equal to.
- $!=$ Is not equal to.

NOTE

To test if two values are equal, the comparison operator has two equals signs (= =). To assign a value to a variable, the assignment operator has one equals sign (=). Don't get them confused! If you accidentally write a comparison statement like $i = 10$, your statement won't test to see if the variable *i* is equivalent to 10; that will assign the value 10 to your variable.

Increment and *decrement operators* provide shorthand for adding or subtracting one to a variable:

- $i++$, $++i$, and $i = i + 1$ all add 1 to the value of *i*.
- $i--$, $--i$, and $i = i - 1$ all subtract 1 from the value of *i*.

WARNING

Actually, the three forms do have subtly different meanings having to do with timing and precedence. These distinctions shouldn't matter at this level of programming, but be aware that they exist as you move on to more advanced programming tasks.

While Loops

A *while* loop is very similar to a *for* loop, but rather than having the variable initialization and incrementation controlled by the loop itself, they happen elsewhere. We *initialize* the variable before we ever enter the *while* loop, *test* the variable value in the loop control, and take care of any *variable modification* inside the body of the loop. A version of the loop we created earlier implemented with a *while* loop might look similar to the code in Figure 15.9.

Figure 15.9 A Sample *while* Loop

```
int i;
i = 1;

while ( i <= 10 )
{
        ...
        i++;
}
```

The counter variable is set before we begin the loop. When we enter the loop, we perform the test: Is the variable less than or equal to 10? If it is, we enter the loop, perform some code in the block, and finish incrementing the counter variable as part of the block.

If/Else

An *if* statement performs conditional branching. In an *if* statement, we test to see if the condition is true, do something if it is, and possibly do something else if it isn't. We've done tests as part of the *while* loops and *for* loops, but there is no looping built into *if* statements. An *if* statement might look similar to that shown in Figure 15.10.

Figure 15.10 A Sample *if/else* Statement

```
int i;
...
if ( i == 1)
{
        [A: some lines of code here]
}
else if ( i == 2 )
        [B: only one statement can go here]
else
{
        [C: some lines of code here]
}          /* end if statement */
```

First, our *if* statement tests to see if the variable is equivalent to 1. If it is, it executes the lines of code enclosed in the braces and terminates the statement (that is, no code in the *else* clauses of this statement will be executed). If it isn't, it looks to see if there is an *else* clause, and there is. The first *else* condition says to run another test: Is the variable equivalent to 2? If it is, we enter that block of code (notice that there are no braces around that next section of code; this is permissible as long as there is only one semicolon-terminated statement in the block) and don't execute any other *else* clauses in this *if* statement. If the variable isn't equivalent to 2, we move on to the final clauses. Because there is no *if* after this final *else*, all other cases execute this block of code:

- If we enter this *if* statement when the variable *i* is equal to 1, we will execute only the line of code labeled *A*.

- If we enter this *if* statement when the variable *i* is equal to 2, we will execute only the line of code labeled *B*.

- If we enter this *if* statement when the variable *i* is equal to any number other than 1 or 2, we will execute only the line of code labeled *C*.

Switch

A *switch* statement is like a special case of a multileveled *if/else* statement. In each test of an *if* statement, you can test for something different. For example, you could write a program similar to Figure 15.11.

Figure 15.11 A Too Complex *if/else* Statement

```
if ( foo == 1 )
{
        . . .
}
else if ( bar <= 39 )
{
        . . .
}
else if ( baz == 's' )
{
        . . .
}
```

But often your tests are much simpler than this and you just want to test for assorted values of a single variable (which is, in fact, what we did in the example we used to learn *if* statements). *Switch* statements deal with this special case of testing simply to see if one expression matches one of a number of values (see Figure 15.12).

Figure 15.12 A Sample *switch* Statement

```
switch (foo)
{
        case 1:
                [A: some lines of code]
        case 2: case 5:
                [B: some lines of code]
            break;
        default:
                [C: some lines of code]
            break;
}
```

This code is running a test on the variable named *foo*. If the variable *foo* is equivalent to 2 or to 5 (the line *case 2: case 5:*), it will execute the lines of code we've marked *B* and then break out of the *switch* statement. If the variable *foo* is equivalent to 1 (the line *case 1:*), it will execute the lines of code we've marked *A*, but because there is no *break;* statement, *it will also execute the lines of code labeled* B. Be careful of this; remember to use *break*! If the variable *foo* is equivalent to any number other than 1, 2, or 5, it will execute the code labeled *default*, the code we've marked *C*.

NOTE

The lines of code after a "case" in a *switch* statement do not need curly braces around them. The switch statement itself does need curly braces.

Storage Structures

Arrays, Pointers, and Character Strings

A *pointer* is a special kind of variable. Its job is to contain the address of another variable. The address is the location in the computer's memory where the second variable lives. Your house address is a pointer to where on your street, in your town, you live. Knowing your address, we can come find you. Similarly, the variable's address tells the computer program how to find that variable in memory.

Pointers and their cousins *address operators* and *arrays* can be extremely powerful, but they can also be very confusing. Understanding pointers and dereferencing are the biggest hurdle in learning C. They won't make sense all at once; don't worry, it will sink in over time! Once you master this concept, you'll be well on your way to becoming a great programmer.

To begin, let's imagine that we have an integer variable called *my_variable*. If we want a pointer to it, we can declare one using the ampersand (&) operator to find the address of *my_variable*. We begin by declaring the two variables, one integer and one pointer to integer:

```
int my_variable;
int *my_pointer;
```

The asterisk (★) in front of *my_pointer* defines *my_pointer* as a pointer to some other value. In this case, since the declaration begins *int ★*, we know it's a pointer to a value of type *integer*. The point refers to some as-yet unnamed spot in memory, with no value yet assigned (see Figure 15.13).

Figure 15.13 Declaring a Pointer

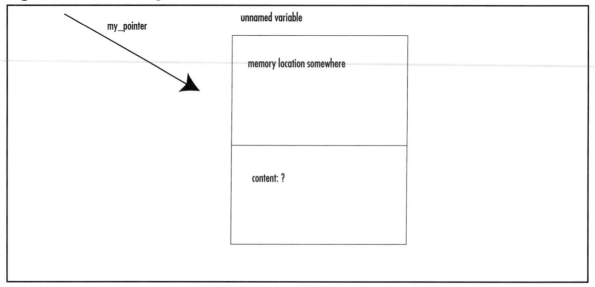

Now we follow the declaration with an assignment:

```
my_pointer = &my_variable;
```

Figure 15.14 illustrates this assignment. Though the integer named *my_variable* has no value yet, it does have an assigned memory location that's large enough to hold an integer value. The variable *my_pointer* points to *my_variable*. The ampersand (&) character in front of *my_variable* sends out the address of the memory location that has been set aside to store the variable's contents. The assignment of this value to *my_pointer* means that *my_pointer* always knows the memory location of the variable held in that location. That is, *my_pointer points to my_variable*.

Figure 15.14 Assigning a Pointer to an Address of Another Variable

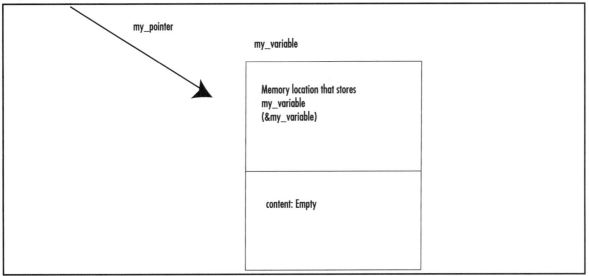

The integer stored in *my_variable* (and pointed to by *my_pointer*) can then be assigned into the location pointed at by *my_pointer*. Figure 15.15 illustrates the pointer once the value has been assigned with the command:

```
*my_pointer = 10;
```

Figure 15.15 Pointer Assignment

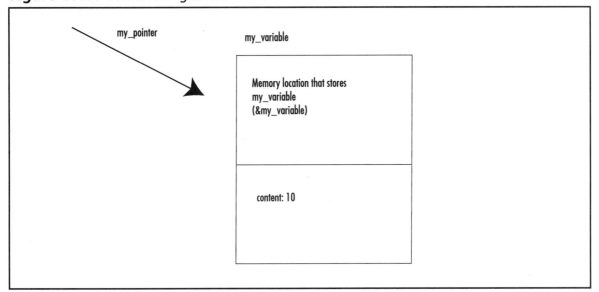

Note that when we are giving the address of the integer to *my_pointer* (*my_pointer* = *&my_variable*), we don't need to use the asterisk (★); we are assigning an address (obtained through the ampersand [&] operator) to a pointer variable, which takes an address without transformation. But when we give an actual integer value to *my_pointer* in with the command ★*my_pointer* = *10*, we don't want to change the address of the thing that is being pointed to, but the thing itself, its content—so we need to use the asterisk (★) to show that extra level of indirection. The ★ character is called the *dereferencing* operator because it tells our code not to look at the address reference but at the object it points to, or references.

Arrays in C can be thought of as a special case of pointers. When you declare an array that contains 10 units in C, you're creating your array (like a row of post-office boxes) in 10 consecutive chunks of memory.

As you can see in Table 15.6, the elements are referenced by the array name and their locations in the array: *my_array[0], my_array[1],…, my_array[9]*.

Table 15.6 An Array as Pointers

Array my_array						
my_array[0]	my_array[1]	my_array[2]	my_array[3]	my_array[4]	my_array[5]	my_array[6]
my_array[7]	my_array[8]	my_array[9]				

This is the most straightforward way to deal with arrays. But when you're looking at code other people have written, you might notice that they have declared arrays with pointers. See, there's a tricky little side effect in the direct memory addressing that pointers give you. We set up a pointer to the new array:

```
my_array_pointer = &my_array[0];
```

(which, in C shorthand, can also be written as *my_array_pointer* = *my_array;*—the name of the array is synonymous with the address of the first element). *my_array_pointer* is an address in memory. That address in memory points to the first element in 10 consecutive chunks of memory that comprise my array. So in a nifty and incredibly confusing operation called *pointer arithmetic*, you can access the second element of the array by saying:

```
*(my_array_pointer+1)
```

Confusing? As though that weren't bad enough, here's a new wrinkle: Declaring a pointer doesn't actually allocate enough memory for the entire array. If you decide to declare your arrays by using pointers instead of array notation, you'll have to learn how to allocate memory using the library function *malloc*. For entry-level C programming, we recommend sticking to array notation. It's bulkier but much less error prone.

Strings

Strings are any quoted series of characters such as:

```
"Hello, World!"
```

Character strings are a special case of array. Specifically, a string is an array of characters (terminated with an invisible null character, which is notated \0).

The string in Table 15.7, *my_string*, is an array with 14 elements. The 14th element, which we access from *my_string[13]*, is the null character. It's an important part of the string we must not forget, even though we never see it!

Table 15.7 Character Strings as Arrays

String my_string

0	1	2	3	4	5	6	7	8	9	10	11	12	13
H	e	l	l	o	,	*space*	W	o	r	l	d	!	\0

As with any other array, a character string can be declared either with a pointer or with array notation.

```
char *pointer_to_string;
/* declares a pointer to unallocated space of a string of unknown length */
char array_of_string[10];
/* creates an array for a string of 10 characters and allocates the space */
```

The correct amount of space is allocated if you assign a value to the string at the same time that you declare it:

```
char *pointer_to_string = "Hello, World!";
char array_of_string[] = "Hello, World!";
```

Both of these declarations allocate enough space for 14 character strings and populate the strings with the assigned value. As with any other array, we strongly recommend using array notation rather than pointer notation to deal with strings. It is very bulky to guess ahead of time how many characters you would like to allocate, and when you become more comfortable with pointer notation you will probably switch to that style because it is more space efficient. But for now, you will find your code much easier to debug if you stick with array notation.

NEED TO KNOW... WARNING ABOUT UNALLOCATED MEMORY

C will not stop you from accessing data you have not allocated. For example, you allocate an array large enough to hold five integers:

```
int my_array[5];
```

There is nothing in the language preventing you from later trying to grab the 23rd element of your array.

```
int my_number;

my_number = my_array[23];
```

But since you haven't reserved that memory for the array, you have no control over what information might be present in it. It might be empty, or it might be filled with garbage. Or, if that memory doesn't belong to your program, it might crash.

Attempting to read or write unallocated memory might well be the number-one cause of debugging frustration, cursing at computers, and banging heads into walls for a beginning C programmer. A program that looks perfectly valid will suddenly crash, presenting the message:

Segmentation violation, core dumped.

This happens so frequently that way back in 1980, Greg Boyd at Digital Computer Corporation wrote a song about it: "The segmentation violation core dumped blues" (see the lyrics at www.netspace.org/~dmacks/internet-songbook/core-dump-blues.html). It still happens. Just make sure that you allocate unassigned memory before you read it!

Structures

After all that complexity, structures are mercifully simple. A *struct* contains some number of other data types, all conveniently grouped together. In fact, a *struct* can contain other *structs*:

```
/* struct to hold some important info about a tv show */
struct tv_show {
        int channel;         /* what channel's it on? */
        char show_name[50];
        char favorite_actor[50];
};


struct show_to_record {
        struct tv_show show_I_like;
        long time;
};
```

Now we can declare and assign a variable of type *show_to_record*:

```
struct show_to_record IronChef;
struct show_to_record Friends;


IronChef.time = 14;
```

NEED TO KNOW... LIMITATIONS OF THIS CHAPTER

As you can probably guess from the previous paragraphs, which assembler you use will vary based on your hardware and operating system platform. But even on any given platform, there are many different assembly language implementations you can use. On Intel, for example, you can use such assembly languages as A386, GNU *as*, HLA, SpAsm, and MASM. Some of these are relatively high level, offering features that we think of as belonging to high-level programming languages, such as *if/else* statements and *while* loops. Others are very simple, offering not much above the level of the hardware. We don't know which assembler is best for you; we don't know your platform or where you fall on the complexity versus power seesaw. For this chapter, we focus on simple features and give examples using the low-level GNU assembler, *as*, for the Intel 80386 processor. GNU *as* has a simple little-level instruction set, is open source, and is freely available with all Linux distributions. Keep in mind that any code you write will have to be ported to the assembly language you choose.

Components of an Assembly Language Statement

An assembly language statement has four components:

- The label
- The operation
- The operands
- The comments

We examine all these concepts in detail in the subsequent sections.

Labels

Have you ever done any BASIC programming with *GOTOs*? If you have, did somebody give you a supercilious sneer and say, "*Real* programmers don't use *GOTOs*"? Well, now you can sneer right back—because anybody who can program in assembly language *is* a real programmer, and in assembly language, you use *GOTOs*. Oh, we call them *labels*, but don't let that fool you.

If you haven't used labels or *GOTO* statements before, don't worry. The concept is very simple. A label records the memory address of the line of code that contains the label. At any point in the code, your program can *jump* to the memory address of the label:

```
/*
 * Some assembly language code goes here.
 *
 * Do you recognize these lines?  They're comments. In GNU as,
 * any text between "/*" and the next "*/" is a comment,
 * even if it appears in the middle of a line. The comment character
```

```
* may differ (sometimes it is a semicolon (;) or a pound sign (#),
* for example), but the general format is the same.  These lines
* will not be translated into machine language.
*/


my_label:              /* The label is the word and colon at line's start */
    movl $1, %eax      /* Don't worry about what this assembly language */
                       /* command means for now. */


/* More random assembly language code goes here. */


jmp my_label           /* now the program will loop back to that label, so */
                       /* the next line of code it executes will be */
                       /* "movl $1, %eax" */
```

If all you can do is loop under any conditions back to the label, this program will just make endless circles back and forth between *my_label* and the command *jmp my_label*. But even low-level assembly languages provide simple conditionals. In GNU *as*, you can base the decision whether to make the jump on the output of a comparison, as you can see in Table 15.8.

Table 15.8 GNU *as* Jump Commands

GNU as Command	Function
cmpl value_1 value_2	This as statement compares two values and stores a comparison based on the result. It can be followed by a *jump* command, which will make a decision based on the results of the comparison.
je label	Jump to label if *value_1* equals *value_2*.
jg label	Jump to label if *value_2* is greater than *value_1*.
jge label	Jump to label if *value_2* is greater than or equal to *value_1*.
jl label	Jump to label if *value_2* is less than *value_1*.
jle label	Jump to label if *value_2* is less than or equal to *value_1*.
jmp label	Jump to label no matter what. This statement does not need to be preceded by the comparison.

Operations

Two sorts of operations are possible in assembly language. The first sort maps directly to machine language instructions (*opcodes*) and is translated directly into machine language by the assembler. The second sort of operation is a meta-command, a command that tells the assembler to do something, instead of telling the computer to do something. In GNU *as*, the second sort of operation is always preceded by a dot (.) character. This is good shorthand to remember. Even though we haven't introduced either command to you, you know that *.int* is a command directly to the assembler and *popl* translates to a machine instruction. (Just so you know, *.int* reserves storage for some number of integers, and *popl* pops the top value of the stack.)

Operands

First, a bit of terminology: An *operand* is the object of an operation. In the following equation the numbers 3 and 5 are both operands (and the + is the *operator*):

```
3 + 5 = ?
```

The C variables often act as special cases of operands. In the C statement, the number 4.0 and the variable *my_number* are both operands:

```
my_answer = my_number / 4.0;
```

When you read about operands with assembly languages, for all practical purposes you're reading about variable assignment. It's good to know this bit of terminology, though, because your documentation authors might be avoiding the term *variable*; in low-level assembly languages, the use of stored information is different enough from storage in high-level languages that some people prefer not to use the term.

We learned in the C section of this chapter that different kinds of data take up different amounts of space. In GNU *as*, we declare the data by type in order to guarantee enough space.

The possible data types are:

- **byte** For a single byte of computer memory.
- **int** For an integer between 0 and 65535.
- **long** For an integer between 0 and 4294967295.
- **ascii** For one or more characters.

The data storage is declared in the special section of the assembly language program, which is initiated with a statement to the assembler:

```
.section .data
```

Next then the storage itself is declared, with another command to the assembler:

```
.ascii "Hello, world\0"
```

In C, character strings were automatically terminated with the null character (\0). In assembly language, you'll need to add that terminating character by hand.

Sample Program

The best way to understand assembly language is to see a little bit of it. Here's a simple program that does a little bit of addition:

```
/* addition.exe */
/*
 * sample assembly language program in GNU as
 *
 * adds together the numbers "3" and "17"
 */


/* Data section.  We're not using any variables here -- just holding
 * the arguments from the command line in registers, so this
 * section is blank. */


.section .data


/* Text section.  This is the commands of the program. */


.section .text


/* .globl defines a label which has to exist even from outside the program.
 * "_start" is a special-purpose label which tells the program that this is
 * the beginning, similar to "main()" in C. */


.globl _start
_start:


pushl $17          /* push the number 17 onto the top of the stack */
                   /* the stack is the part of memory which is currently */
                   /* being used, like a stack of index cards space are*/
pushl $3           /* push the number 3 onto the top of the stack. */
                   /* now 3 is on top, with 17 beneath it. */
```

```
popl %eax                /* pop the top of value on the stack (3) -- that is, */

                         /* remove it from the stack, and put it in the */

                         /* temporary  register "%eax" */


popl %ebx                /* pop the top of value on the stack (17) -- that is, */

                         /* remove it from the stack, and put it in the */

                         /* temporary  register "%ebx" */


addl %eax, %ebx          /* add together the two numbers, and store the result */

                         /* in the second temporary register, %ebx */


movl $1, %eax            /* in Linux, this is the kernel's system call */

                         /* to exit the program.  When the program exits, */

                         /* whatever value is stored in register %ebx */

                         /* will be the return value of the program. */

                         /* because of our addl command, the value stored */

                         /* in %ebx is the sum of 3+17 */


int $0x80                /* this runs the software interrupt responsible */

                         /* for telling the kernel to exit */
```

After we run this program, we can test the return value of the program to find out the sum of the two numbers. As you might guess from looking at the program, we made this somewhat more complex than it needed to be. We didn't need to push 3 and 17 onto the stack, then pop them both off again in order to add them together. We could have just stored the two numbers directly into the temporary registers. But the purpose of the example was to give you a taste of assembly language.

NEED TO KNOW... STACK TRICKINESS

The top of the stack is in reality the bottom of the stack. Yes, we know, that makes no sense. After all, both "top" and "bottom" are just fake names—what do they really mean in a computer's memory? It's not like there is gravity in the computer defining what is "top" and what is "bottom." What these terms mean is that if you think of memory addresses as having higher numbers at the top and lower numbers at the bottom, the stack grows downward, as illustrated in Table 15.9.

Table 15.9 Stack Direction

Memory That Holds the Stack	Stack Sitting in Memory
Address 22	First entry placed into stack
Address 18	Second entry placed into stack
Address 16	Third entry placed into stack
Address 12	Current top of stack
Address 8	X
Address 4	X
Address 0	X

If we now choose to place another entry in the stack, it will go to address 8. So if we need to manually manipulate the *stack pointer* (stored in register *%esp*), adding a new entry to the stack means *subtracting* from the value of the stack pointer.

Summary

The basis of assembly language is simple to learn. However, learning how to do something with it—that is a whole new kettle of fish. It's very easy to manipulate registers, but how do you know which memory address on your computer will pop up a dialog box on Windows?

In general, we don't use assembly language unless we need to manipulate hardware we can't access with high-level languages or to accelerate a particularly slow section of code.

Additional Reading

If you are interested in learning more about any of the topics in this chapter, we recommend the following books:

- *Structured Computer Organization,* **fourth edition, by Andrew S. Tannenbaum (Prentice-Hall, 1998)** Concepts of computer internals—very important if you'll be doing lots of assembly programming.

- *A Book on C,* **by Al Kelley and Ira Pohl (The Benjamin/Cummings Publishing Company, 1995)**

- *C Programming Language,* **second edition, by Brian W. Kernighan and Dennis Ritchie (Prentice Hall, 1988)**

- *The Art of Assembly Language,* **by Randall Hyde (No Starch Press, 2003)** Focuses on the high-level HDL.

- *Programming from the Ground Up,* **by Jonathan Bartlett (www.nongnu.org/pgubook)** Focuses on the GNU assembly language.

- LinuxAssembly.org: http://linuxassembly.org/ Links to online tutorials and resources.

Index

Numerals and Symbols

A

X

Z

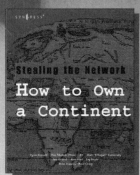

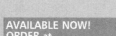